7/03

Shakespeare's Tribe

Shakespeare's Tribe

CHURCH, NATION, AND THEATER
IN RENAISSANCE ENGLAND

Jeffrey Knapp

THE UNIVERSITY OF CHICAGO PRESS
CHICAGO AND LONDON

JEFFREY KNAPP is associate professor of English at the University of California, Berkeley. He is the author of *An Empire Nowhere: England, America, and Literature from Utopia to* The Tempest (1992).

The University of Chicago Press, Chicago 60637
The University of Chicago Press, Ltd., London
©2002 by The University of Chicago
All rights reserved. Published 2002
Printed in the United States of America
11 10 09 08 07 06 05 04 03 02   1 2 3 4 5

ISBN: 0-226-44569-0 (cloth)

The University of Chicago Press gratefully acknowledges the generous support of the John Simon Guggenheim Memorial Foundation toward the publication of this book.

Frontispiece: Elizabethan Maundy (attributed to Levina Teerlinc), miniature belonging to Lady Beauchamp's Will Trustees. Photograph: Norman Mays Studio, Worcestershire. Elizabeth, in the left foreground, is about to wash the feet of the poor women seated behind her. The boys in the center background are choristers. Since children's companies used choristers as actors in their plays at court and (from the 1570s) on commercial stages, these boys were probably also players.

In April 1565 the Spanish ambassador reported to King Philip II that some English Protestants had been offended by the recent Royal Maundy, which they regarded as superstitious. Elizabeth detested such sectarian scruples: according to the ambassador, "she deliberately traced a very large and well-defined cross" at the ceremony "and kissed it to the sorrow of many persons who witnessed it and of others who would not attend the ceremony, but to the joy of others." As Elizabeth later explained to the ambassador, "Many people think we are Turks or Moors here, whereas we only differ from other Catholics in things of small importance."

Library of Congress Cataloging-in-Publication Data

Knapp, Jeffrey.
    Shakespeare's tribe : church, nation, and theater in Renaissance England / Jeffrey Knapp.
        p.   cm.
    Includes bibliographical references and index.
    ISBN 0-226-44569-0 (alk. paper)
    1. English drama—Early modern and Elizabethan, 1500–1600—History and criticism. 2. Church and state—England—History—16th century. 3. Church and state—England—History—17th century. 4. English drama—17th century—History and criticism. 5. Nationalism and literature—England—History. 6. Shakespeare, William, 1564–1616—Religion. 7. Theater—England—History—16th century. 8. Theater—England—History—17th century. 9. Theater—Religious aspects—Christianity. 10. Church and state in literature. 11. Nationalism in literature. I. Title.

PR658.R43 K58 2002
820.9'358—dc21

                                                                2001008308

⊚ The paper used in this publication meets the minimum requirements of the American National Standard for Information Sciences—Permanence of Paper for Printed Library Materials, ANSI Z39.48-1992.

For Dori and Maddie

I should desire them . . . to give over *Ben*, and
Shakespeare, and fall upon *Moses* and the *Prophets*.

FROM THOMAS TRESCOT'S SERMON
The Zealous Magistrate
(1642)

CONTENTS

Preface xi
Acknowledgments xv

INTRODUCTION   1
1. GOOD FELLOWS   23

Part One. England and Christendom

2. ROGUE NATIONALISM   61
3. THIS BLESSED PLOT   80

Part Two. Church and Theater

4. PREACHERS AND PLAYERS   115
5. PSEUDO-CHRISTIANITY   141
    EPILOGUE   169

APPENDIX 1. ROGUE FREQUENCIES   179
APPENDIX 2. AUTOLYCUS   181
APPENDIX 3. POETRY AS COZENAGE   183

Notes 187
Works Cited 241
Index 267

Thanks to a chapter on tobacco in my first book, *An Empire Nowhere*, I've often been asked whether I smoke. But no one who has heard or read a portion of *Shakespeare's Tribe* has ever asked me whether I go to church. The reason, I've learned, is not so much a loss of interest in my possible vices as a painful sense of certainty about them: who else but a devout Christian would want to claim that Shakespeare was religious?

I'd like to begin this book by briefly considering why the thought of a religious Shakespeare makes academics so uncomfortable. In part, the apprehensiveness can be blamed on a now exploded school of Shakespeare criticism. According to the "neo-Christians," as William Empson termed these scholars, passages such as the following speech from *Measure for Measure* counted as proof that Shakespeare's plays should be understood as religious allegories:

> O my dread lord,
> I should be guiltier than my guiltiness,
> To think I can be undiscernible,
> When I perceive your Grace, like pow'r divine,
> Hath look'd upon my passes.

To G. Wilson Knight (1930), these lines made clear that their speaker, Angelo, represented Fallen Man, while their addressee, Duke Vincentio, represented Almighty God. Other critics rightly took the dramatic context of the speech more seriously. They pointed out that, among other things, it is a particular character in a particular situation who sees the Duke as "like pow'r divine"; no other character in *Measure for Measure* praises the Duke so abjectly; while from the start of the play the Duke engages in morally dubious intrigues for the purpose of astounding his subjects and humiliating Angelo. More generally, the critics of Knight and his followers decried the sheer reductiveness of Christian allegorizing when applied to Shakespeare: for Knight's contemporary D. H. Lawrence (c. 1925), the interpretive possibilities in Shakespeare's plays seemed so inexhaustible that Lawrence could characterize Shakespeare as "all things to all men."[1]

Ironically enough, Lawrence borrowed this expression for Shakespeare's infinite variety from the Bible, where the apostle Paul declares in his first letter to the Corinthians that he became "all things to all men, that I might by all means save some." What's more, Lawrence found the protean indeterminacy of Shakespeare's plays in two other "supreme old novels," as he called them, one of which was the Bible. This double association of Shakespeare with Scripture might suggest that Lawrence too was a neo-Christian, if Lawrence did not present the Bible itself as more literature than Scripture (the third "novelist" in his pantheon is Homer). Yet Lawrence's reverence for Shakespeare remains quasi-mystical nonetheless, an instance of what T. E. Hulme (c. 1913) had called "spilt religion," the modern or more precisely Romantic attempt to fashion literature and above all Shakespeare into a kind of secular sublime. It is the continuing authority of this Romantic view, far more than the distant memory of G. Wilson Knight, that makes a religious Shakespeare still seem a contradiction in terms. Thus Harold Bloom's recent best-sellers echo Keats, Hazlitt, and Coleridge, as well as Lawrence, in venerating Shakespeare's plays as a "secular Scripture" and Shakespeare himself as all things to all men, "at once no one and everyone, nothing and everything." According to Bloom, Shakespeare has become so pervasive and influential throughout the modern world that he now "challenges the scriptures of West and East alike in the modification of human character and personality." And a crucial determinant of Shakespeare's "universal" appeal, in Bloom's scheme, is his having "no theology" at all.[2]

This simultaneously worldly and occult vision of Shakespeare as "like power divine" is the critical perspective against which Stephen Greenblatt has set much of his work on Shakespeare's plays and Renaissance culture generally. Skeptically appraising the Romantic characterization of Shakespeare as "the supreme purveyor of 'empathy,'" Greenblatt has aligned the protean adaptability of a playwright who is all things to all men not with "imaginative generosity" but with "the improvisation of power." The final chapter of *Renaissance Self-Fashioning* (1980), for instance, associates the "ability to insert oneself into the consciousness of another" with the grasping imperialist rather than the selfless altruist; empathy, in Greenblatt's account of *Othello*, means "the ruthless displacement and absorption of the other." To substantiate such demystification and prove that Shakespeare had passions and interests like anyone else, Greenblatt has striven, with brilliant success, to return Shakespeare's plays to their original cultural context. Yet his polemical entanglement with the neo-Romantics has made it difficult for him to question what I regard as the fundamental ahistoricism in their account of Shakespeare: their belief that Shakespeare was a purely secular dramatist. According to Greenblatt, Shakespeare's special "psychic mobility" became possible only when the Renaissance "separated" such adaptiveness from the "imitation" of Christ and Paul (who in William Tyndale's sixteenth-century translation "fashioned" himself "in all things . . . to all men"). Over the course of *Shakespeare's Tribe* I will demonstrate how Renaissance theorists no less than Romantic ones believed that actors and playwrights should indeed accommodate themselves to "diverse capacities," as the editors of Shakespeare's First Folio put it.[3] But I will also argue that, for many writers of the period, including Shakespeare, the rationale for such self-fashioning remained essentially Christian, even when commercial motives were acknowledged. Determining what "Christian" meant to Shakespeare and his fellow practitioners will be the burden of this book.

One further source of uneasiness about the notion of a religious Shakespeare is the widely shared belief that we can never know Shakespeare's actual intentions. In its general form, this objection is an empty one: we infer intention whenever we interpret any speech act, and yet our inferences always remain speculative, even when events seem to bear them out. A more specific as well as more credible form of the objection is that Shakespeare tended to keep his opinions to himself. In what follows, I will try to show how this practical barrier to interpretation is less insuperable than critics have generally claimed. By placing Shakespeare in a diverse company of Renaissance theater lovers, theater haters, and theologians, I hope to cast light not only on his religious convictions but also on his reasons for making those convictions so hard to decipher.

My goal, in short, is to help explain Shakespeare, not to endorse the religion he had or the religion he became. But we cannot fully grasp Shakespeare's own aims, I argue, until we come to terms with those religions too.

ACKNOWLEDGMENTS

S everal portions of the book have been previously published and appear here by permission of the publishers. A version of chapter 2 appeared in *Centuries' Ends, Narrative Means*, ed. Robert Newman (Stanford: Stanford University Press, 1996), 138–50, (c) 1996 by The Board of Trustees of the Leland Stanford Jr. University, reprinted by permission of Stanford University Press. A version of chapter 4 appeared in *Representations* 44 (1993): 29–59, (c) 1993 by the Regents of the University of California, reprinted by permission of the University of California Press. Parts of the introduction and chapter 1 appeared in *Shakespeare Survey* 54 (2001): 57–70, reprinted by permission of Cambridge University Press

My thanks go first to the colleagues who helped me write this book and the friends who helped me survive it: Oliver Arnold, James Carson, Deirdre D'Albertis, Michael Danby, Margreta de Grazia, Richard Halpern, Lorna Hutson, Sharon Marcus, Katharine Maus, Samuel Otter, Nancy Ruttenburg, Phillip Schwyzer, George Starr, Ramie Targoff, Wendy Wall, and Lynn Wardley. Paul Alpers, Joel Altman, Richard Helgerson, and Stephen Orgel have been inexhaustible sources of guidance and encouragement. I could not have asked for a better reader of the entire manuscript than Debora Shuger. My two press readers were also wonderfully helpful, and I am grateful for the advice I received from audiences at the University of Virginia, the University of Maryland at College Park, Johns Hopkins University, Princeton University, Northwestern University, University of California—Santa Barbara, University of California—Los Angeles, Texas A&M, CalTech, Kenyon College, Bard College, various Modern Language Association conventions, the Center for Hermeneutical Studies, and the Bay Area Pre- and Early Modern Studies Group.

I also want to thank the staff at the Folger Shakespeare Library and at the Huntington Library, as well as Sonja Albrecht, Sara Austin, Genevieve Guenther, Douglas O'Hara, and Travis Williams. As chair of the Harvard English department, Lawrence Buell generously hosted a semester of research at Harvard. My editor Alan Thomas supported this project from the outset of our discussions about it; my thanks also to his assistant Randolph Petilos and my copy editor Lys Ann Shore. I am profoundly indebted to the Humanities Division at Berkeley, the Doreen Townsend Center for the Humanities at Berkeley, the Folger Shakespeare Library, the National Endowment for the Humanities, and the John Simon Guggenheim Memorial Foundation for their financial support.

This book arose from conversation, real and imagined, with Stephen Greenblatt, Dorothy Hale, and Steven Knapp; I wish I had written something that better reflected all I have learned from them. To Dorothy and to Madeline Hale, I dedicate more than I could ever put in words.

Shakespeare's Tribe

A preliminary sketch by Inigo Jones for the first scene of William Davenant's masque *Britannia Triumphans*, performed at Whitehall before King Charles I on Twelfth Night, 1638. According to the theater hater George Ridpath (1698), *Britannia Triumphans* epitomized the sort of profane "Religion" that was practiced by Charles and Archbishop Laud. Davenant described this first scene as "a prospect of the City of London and the River of Thames, which, being a principal part, might be taken for all Great Britain." At the center of the perspective are old St. Paul's Cathedral and, facing it across the river, the Swan or Globe Theater (just to the left of St. Paul's steeple). Devonshire Collection, Chatsworth. Reproduced by permission of the Duke of Devonshire and the Chatsworth Settlement Trustees. Photograph: Photographic Survey, Courtauld Institute of Art.

But to have divinity preach'd there!
did you ever dream of such a thing?
—Shakespeare, *Pericles*

*❝*T*here [is] no Analogy between Preachers and Players, Sermons and Plays,
Theaters and Churches.*"[1] So writes the most notorious theater hater in
Renaissance England, and the bulk of modern criticism on Renaissance
drama has in effect taken William Prynne at his word: scholars have typically
characterized the theater of Shakespearean England as a secular, even a
secularizing, stage.

They have good reasons for doing so. By the time Shakespeare began to
write plays, the biblical drama of medieval England had all but died, from
causes not entirely natural. It had been censored by Protestant officials concerned with its Catholic provenance, and censorship appears to have hampered the depiction of religious material in the new public theaters as well.[2]
Moralists such as Phillip Stubbes (1583) had long warned England that
players allowed to dramatize the word of God would inevitably contaminate
"divinity" with their "bawdy, wanton shows & uncomely gestures."[3] Following a brief period (1588–89) in which church and state had encouraged the
theaters to vilify the radical Protestant "Martin Marprelate," the authorities
did indeed recoil from the spectacle of "divinity" handled, in their view,
"without judgment or decorum"; by a 1606 act of Parliament, moreover,
players were forbidden to "speak or use the holy Name of God or of Christ
Jesus, or of the Holy Ghost or of the Trinity" profanely.[4] Whether or not
these official strictures had any chilling effect, players in Shakespeare's day
showed little interest in replacing the "old Church-plays" with a biblical
drama of their own. "Unchaste and wicked matters," as one exasperated
Lord Mayor of London (1580) put it, seemed their preferred stock in trade:
against the lonely example of Thomas Lodge and Robert Greene's *Looking
Glasse for London and England* (c. 1590), which includes the biblical figures
Hosea and Jonah in its cast of characters, may be set the far more representative depiction of the city in Thomas Middleton's *A Mad World, My Masters*
(c. 1604), the comedy of a London debauchee who repeatedly swindles his
uncle until he accidentally weds his uncle's whore.[5]

Renaissance theater people and theater lovers were not all so literal-minded as their modern commentators, however. They did not automatically equate religious drama with biblical storytelling, nor did they instinctively view libertine speech and action as insurmountable bars to religious expression. My aim in this book is to prove that a surprising number of writers throughout the English Renaissance depicted plays as godly enterprises, and that their views had a major impact on the theater. Ignorance of these views, or dismissal of them, has distorted our understanding of Renaissance drama in several crucial ways. On the level of practical criticism, secularist readings of Renaissance plays have failed to explain some of the most prominent recurring plots, themes, and character types in the plays, or even to notice the existence of such recurrences. In historiographical terms, the secularist bias among modern critics has helped sustain the myth that piety and popular entertainments in Renaissance England were cultural opposites and waged war on one other (even new-historical critics have tended to abandon their usual skepticism to embrace this fantasy). And finally, by insisting that Renaissance plays were exclusively secular in aim and effect, modern scholars have lent credibility to a paradoxically mystical vision of Shakespeare as a writer so miraculously disinterested that religious beliefs—indeed, beliefs of any kind—could have no hold on him.[6]

Prynne himself was not blind to contemporary claims about the religious value of plays, or to the influence that such claims exerted over theatergoers: he intended his assertion of a fundamental contrariety between church and theater to be a prohibition, not a statement of fact. In the same section of his *Histrio-Mastix* (1633), he deplored the flagrant *dependence* of many English preachers on "poetical Play-house phrases" and "Theatrical gestures." Even worse to his mind was a phenomenon that modern scholars have by and large ignored: the direct participation of clergymen, "disorderly histrionical Divines," in plays. Throughout the reigns of Elizabeth, James, and Charles, clergymen often undertook play-acting as part of their clerical training: "in the Colleges," as the puritan Milton complained in 1642, "so many of the young Divines, and those in next aptitude to Divinity have been seen so oft upon the Stage writhing and unboning their Clergy limbs to all the antic and dishonest gestures of Trinculos, Buffoons, and Bawds." Acting was not limited to fledgling churchmen: according to Richard Corbet, a future bishop, the plays performed before King James at Cambridge in 1615 had "a perfect *Diocese* of *Actors* / Upon the stage: for I am sure that / There was both *Bishop, Pastor, Curate.*" Nor was acting the only form of clerical involvement in the drama: responding to an antitheatrical letter from his fellow Oxonian John Rainoldes, the Elizabethan cleric William Gager (1592) wished that

Rainoldes had thought better of casting aspersions on "those reverend, fa-mous, and excellent men, for life, and learning, and their places in the Church of God, both of our house, and otherwise of the *University*," who had been not only "actors" in plays but "writers of such things themselves."[7]

Theater histories that mention the existence of clergymen-dramatists in the Renaissance generally consign them to the age before Shakespeare's, when the early Reformers championed their cause with such straightfor-wardly religious plays as John Foxe's *Christus Triumphans* (1556) or John Bale's *The Chief Promises of God Unto Man* (1538). By Shakespeare's time, this sort of pious drama may have fallen out of fashion, but more clergymen wrote plays during the second half-century of the English Reformation than during the first.[8] Gager himself was a renowned playwright, who published two of his efforts and had one performed before the queen. Other church-men—Robert Gomersall, for example, and Samuel Harding—published closet dramas; still others, such as Thomas Goffe and Henry Killigrew, wrote plays that were first performed privately and then transferred to the public stage. James Shirley left the clergy for the theater; conversely, some commercial dramatists went on to become clergymen: the best known of them is John Marston. Actors too, most notably the choirboys who played for the children's companies, migrated between church and theater, while some theater professionals had strong family ties to the clergy: John Fletcher and Nathan Field, the principal dramatist and principal player for the King's Men in the years immediately following the deaths of Shake-speare and Burbage, were both the sons of prominent Elizabethan church-men.[9] Further kinds of trafficking between the pulpit and the stage have no doubt fallen from the historical record: according to George Buc, later Mas-ter of the Revels, Shakespeare informed him that an unnamed "minister" had written the comic history play *George a Greene, The Pinner of Wakefield* (c. 1590) and "acted the pinner's part in it himself."[10]

Even more astonishing than the number and variety of clerical plays during this period is their almost exclusively secular subject matter.[11] Like the majority of his fellow clergymen-dramatists, Gager devised plays on classical themes, with titles such as *Dido* (1583) and *Ulysses Redux* (1592). Gomersall chose to dramatize a relatively contemporary secular topic in his *Tragedie of Lodovick Sforza Duke of Millan* (published 1628). But the most highly regarded clergymen-dramatists of their day produced comedies that, in G. E. Bentley's formulation, "were not so pious as their [authors'] pro-fession might suggest." The title setting of William Cartwright's *The Ordi-nary* (c. 1635), for instance, is a tavern filled with "cheating Rakehells," while the chief difference between the heirs in Jasper Mayne's *City Match* (c. 1637) and Middleton's *Mad World* is that Mayne's debauchee swindles his uncle by staging the *uncle's* marriage to a *pretended* whore.[12]

How did these divinity students—not to mention the clergymen in their audiences—reconcile such coarse productions with their own high callings? According to Marprelate (1589), many of the established clergy were simply too licentious and ignorant to comprehend the "dignity" of their office. Marprelate reports how one day a minister named Glibbery, "who was sometime (simple as he now stands) a Vice in a play," ascended the pulpit

> with a full resolution to do his business with great commendations. But see the fortune of it. A boy in the church, hearing either the Summer Lord with his May-game, or Robin Hood with his Morris Dance, going by the church—out goes the boy. Good Glibbery, though he were in the pulpit, yet had a mind to his old companions abroad (a company of merry grigs, you must think them to be, as merry as a Vice on the stage), seeing the boy going out, finished his matter presently, . . . saying, Ha, ye faith, boy! Are they there? Then, ha' with thee. And so, came down, and among them he goes.

The Brownist Henry Barrow (1591) asserted that, on the contrary, established churchmen were far too learned, at least in the "vain philosophy" taught at college, which had corrupted them into "making not only an art, but a stage play and an occupation of religion."[13] Dissident Protestants could at least agree on the popishness of clergy who in their view had chosen to feed the people with empty pageantry rather than solid gospel, decking themselves in garments "ridiculous, and stage-like, meeter for fools and comedians, than for ministers."[14] Such profaneness had joined preachers to players in a union cemented by the hatred they both bore toward puritans.[15] According to Henry Parker (1641), even "the greatest of the Clergy" had "taken up in Pulpits . . . almost as vile and scurrilous a license of fiction and detraction, as is usual in Play houses, Taverns, and Bordellos." Lucy Hutchinson (c. 1664–71) recalled how by the early years of the seventeenth century the "children of darkness" had made puritans "the sport" not only of "every stage and every table and every puppet-play" but of the pulpit itself, "which was become but a more solemn stage."[16] Looking back on the decade before the civil wars, George Ridpath (1698) concluded that Archbishop "*Laud* and his Clergy" had found the theater "necessary to Ridicule the Puritans" and for that reason "became its Patrons."[17]

Most of the modern criticism that acknowledges at least some ties between church and theater during the English Renaissance echoes Hutchinson and Ridpath in judging those ties to be a matter of sectarian politics.

The two finest books on the subject—David Bevington's *Tudor Drama and Politics* (1968) and Leah Marcus's *The Politics of Mirth* (1986)—make this stance clear in their titles.[18] It would be hard to deny the pertinence of such analysis to the Renaissance theater: even the sympathetic Restoration commentator John Aubrey reports that King James "made" Ben Jonson "write against the Puritans." Yet a secularist view of religion as little more than politics mystified has led scholars to treat the historical record of dialogue between church and theater more reductively than the presbyterian theater-hater Ridpath does. Like Prynne before him, Ridpath notes with disgust how the Laudian "Clergy became at last so enamor'd of the Stage" that "it was too too frequent to have Sermons in respect of their Divisions, Language, Action, Style and Subject Matter, fitter for the Stage from whence they were borrowed, than for the Pulpit." What began as a bond of mere expediency, according to Ridpath, ended as a world turned upside down. Thanks to Laud and the king, "the Universities became infected with the Contagion of the Stage, and they being the Nurseries of Officers for the Church and State it was no wonder, if the Infection spread from them, all over the Kingdom." Ultimately, the theater "grew *Rampant*, and as if it disdained to have any less Adversary than God himself, did boldly usurp on the Sabbath Afternoons. And thus in the Year 1637 Masques were set up at Court on *Sundays*, by his Majesty's Authority, while at the same time *Laud* and his Faction forbad Preaching any oft'ner than once a day."[19]

By Ridpath's time, this vision of the stage as supplanting the pulpit was a hoary antitheatrical nightmare. "Do they not draw the people from hearing the word of God, from godly Lectures, and sermons?" Stubbes had asked; "for you shall have them flock thither thick & threefold, when the church of God shall be bare & empty."[20] The charge, nearly as old as Christianity itself, was laid at the time against other popular entertainments too: the alehouse, the whorehouse, bear-baiting, card-playing, even piping. But by far the most disturbing of the preacher's rivals, to the godly, were the players.[21] Like many another theater hater in the period, Stubbes was appalled to report that some playgoers thought plays were not only more entertaining than sermons but even "as good as sermons" were; in the words of the clergyman John Northbrooke (1577), people "shame not to say and affirm openly, . . . that they learn as much or more at a Play, than they do at God's word preached." Stubbes concluded that plays were worse than atheistical, having been "sucked out of the Devil's teats, to nourish us in idolatry[,] heathenry, and sin."[22] The author of the *Third Blast of Retrait from Plaies and Theaters* (1580) called theaters "the chapels of Satan"; as the eminent puritan divine Richard Baxter later put it (1673), "the Devil hath apishly made these [theaters] *his Churches*, in competition with the *Churches* of Christ."²³ And Ridpath was not the only writer to suggest that Charles's Sunday masques were the devil's pièce de résistance. By 1643 the puritan propagandist "Mercurius Britanicus" could already claim that "it has been an old fashion at Court, amongst the Protestants there, to shut up the *Sabbath* with some wholesome Piece of *Ben Jonson* or *Davenant*, a kind of *Comical Divinity*"; he predicted that the Cavaliers would soon "go near to put down all *preaching* and *praying*, and have some *religious Masque* or play instead of Morning and Evening Prayer."²⁴ Charging the king with treason six years later, the parliamentary solicitor general expressed the wish that Charles had "but studied Scripture half so much as *Ben Jonson* or *Shakespeare*."²⁵

Naturally, the puritans thought of themselves as holding the line against the theater's encroachments. Only preaching and then more preaching, they insisted, would reclaim the people. And to a certain extent, as the religious historian Patrick Collinson has shown, the strategy worked: with such sermonical "exercises" as prophesyings, combination lectures, fasts, and, for extremists, conventicles, the godly appear to have fashioned puritanism into a kind of popular culture. "Play-haunters" were matched by "sermon-gadders": Paul Whitfield White observes that "in London and throughout the provinces, nonincumbent preachers—or 'lecturers,' as they were more commonly called—were hired by city corporations and churchwardens, and in some instances funds that had previously been designated to pay for plays now went to cover the wages of the town lecturer."²⁶ Such hot gospeling, conservative Protestants charged, was the reason that religion was turning theatrical. "They sweat, they blunder, they bounce & plunge in the Pulpit," Thomas Nashe (1593) wrote of puritan sermonizers, "but all is voice and no substance: they deaf men's ears, but not edify."²⁷ Taking a more sober look at the puritan zeal for preaching, Richard Hooker (1597) argued that since the puritans "utterly deny that the reading either of scriptures or homilies and sermons can ever by the ordinary grace of God save any soul," they cannot believe that the content of sermons is what makes sermons edifying: instead, "it must of necessity follow, that the vigor and vital efficacy of sermons doth grow from certain accidents which are not in them but in their maker; his virtue, his gesture, his countenance, his zeal, the motion of his body, and the inflection of his voice who first uttereth them as his own, is that which giveth them the form, the nature, the very essence of instruments available to eternal life." Hooker's point, in short, was that puritans worshipped the preacher's charisma, not his religion; "good books may be blest," the puritan Thomas Shepard (c. 1640) allowed, "but there is not that spirit in them as in lively dispensations of the Gospel by Ministers themselves."²⁸

This obsession with performance, as conformists judged it, transformed religion into mere entertainment: a character in Jonson's *Epicoene* (1609) wondered whether it was now possible to find a chaste wife "when there are so many masques, plays, puritan preachings, mad-folks, and other strange sights to be seen daily."[29]

Catholic polemicists simplified the controversy between the puritans and their enemies by declaring that all Protestant preachers were, like players, "guided with the wind / Of popular applause." Thanks to the break with Rome, the curtailment of the clergy's intercessory and sacramental power, the many reversals in official church policy during the sixteenth century, and the innovation of clerical marriage, the Protestant clergy had for Catholics lost any claim to sacred authority. As the future Marian bishop Cuthbert Scott lamented in 1545, "the holy order of priesthood, which was wont to be had in great reputation as the worthiness of the thing doth require, is so run into contempt, that it is now nothing else but a laughing stock of the people." According to the Elizabethan Catholic Thomas Dorman (1564), Protestant churchmen were such "lewd losels" that they embraced "interlude players" as "brothers" of their "fraternity" and willingly shared with players "the charge of dispensing the word." Reformers, for their part, prided themselves on having rejected the elitism that led another Marian bishop, Edmund Bonner (1554), to describe the priesthood as "most incomparable and superangelical," in John Foxe's report; Anthony Gilby's *Pleasant Dialogue* (1581) mocked Catholics who insisted that "it was never good world with us Priests, since every soldier and every Servingman could talk so much of the scripture: and these foolish Ministers are the cause thereof, which would make all men as wise as themselves."[30] But Protestants themselves regularly bemoaned the "general contempt" for clergymen in England, which seemed to have leveled the field between preachers and players. "These days," wrote the future bishop Thomas Cooper (1589), "we are become a Stage to the most vile and abject men at all times, and in all places, in the Streets, in Shops, at Tables, at Feasts, at Councils, even to the very playing scaffolds, which I speak with tears, and are scoffed at, even of the vile and contemptible players."[31]

Over the past two decades, such contemporary testimony to the theater's rising influence in comparison to the church has at last begun to be taken seriously, in particular by the anthropological literary critics Stephen Greenblatt and Louis Montrose. Both scholars see the theater as the beneficiary of a spiritual crisis in England sparked by the Reformation. Once "the Elizabethan regime had suppressed most of the ritual practices and popular religious festivities of late medieval Catholic culture," Montrose argues in his *Purpose of Playing* (1996), the English people had to look elsewhere for the "symbolic forms" that might endow "their material existence with greater coherence and value." According to Montrose, they could turn to "the spectacles of royal and civic power" that took the place of Catholic rites, or seek "a substitute for the metaphysical aid of the medieval church in a welter of occult practices," but London's citizens may have found "another alternative" to traditional religion in the "collective and commercial, public and profane" experience of the theater. In *Shakespearean Negotiations* (1988), Stephen Greenblatt similarly portrays the Shakespearean theater as appropriating the "ritual" that "the official religious and secular institutions" of Elizabethan England were in the process of "abjuring." Insofar as ritual thus became associated with the essentially "fraudulent institution" of the theater, this shift, according to Greenblatt, seemed to confirm the official Protestant position that ritual too was fraudulent. But for Greenblatt the theater as fiction-maker "evacuates everything it represents"; when a play such as *King Lear* (c. 1605) mimics the official critique of ritual, therefore, both ritual and the official critique are fictionalized, "emptied out." Freed of any doctrinal claims on it, ritual becomes theater merely, yet as theater it holds greater attractions for its audience, Greenblatt suggests, than a church now hollowed out and bare: "evacuated rituals, drained of their original meaning, are preferable to no rituals at all."[32]

The problem with these otherwise powerful accounts of the theater as symbolically compensating for the loss of Catholicism is that they take contemporary criticism of both pulpit and stage *too* seriously, and end up reproducing its partialities. Neither Greenblatt nor Montrose, in other words, credits the established church with any cultural capital of its own, nor *a fortiori* can either scholar imagine the church as investing the Shakespearean theater with any religious purpose.[33] (Montrose goes so far as to omit the Protestant church from his list of "metaphysical" alternatives to Catholicism.) In his essay on "Theater and Religious Culture" in *A New History of Early English Drama* (1997), Whitfield White counters that Protestantism must have figured significantly in the "composition, performance, and reception" of plays because "Reformation orthodoxy was, by the midpoint of Elizabeth's reign, not merely the official doctrine of the national church but internalized as a major feature of the national consciousness." Debora Shuger (1996) makes a similar point, trying to strike a balance between the secular provenance of Renaissance drama, on the one hand, and the secularist biases of modern criticism on the other: "if it is not plausible to read Shakespeare's plays as Christian allegories, neither is it likely that the popular drama of a religiously saturated culture could, by a secular miracle, have extricated itself from the theocentric orientation informing the discourses of politics, gender, social order, and history" at the time.[34]

Other literary historians—among them Donna Hamilton, Huston Diehl, Bryan Crockett, Claire McEachern, Kristen Poole, and Ramie Targoff—have joined Shuger and White in arguing for the centrality of religion to the study of Renaissance drama.[35] These scholars have provided an indispensable corrective to the historiographical blind spots of political and anthropological critics alike, but the "cultural saturation" theory they share with Shuger and White nonetheless concedes part of the secularist position it means to oppose, insofar as it depicts Renaissance playwrights as "Christian" only cognitively or subliminally, rather than purposively and devotionally.[36] Not even this compelling revisionism, in other words, allows the possibility that Renaissance plays may have been intended and received as contributions to the cause of true religion.

"They shame not to say and affirm openly, . . . that they learn as much or more at a Play, than they do at God's word preached." To grasp how a theater with little apparent religious content might ever have been regarded as spiritually edifying, it is necessary to take the theater's contemporary defenders seriously too. Some modern critics have treated certain Renaissance plays as intentionally religious without resorting to the point-by-point allegorizations that Shuger and most other recent scholars find unpersuasive. Roy Battenhouse (1969), for instance, argued that Shakespearean drama "evokes" Christian values in two negative ways: first, by contrast with the moral and spiritual "deficiencies" of its characters, and second, by the cues of its shadowy Christian "symbolism."[37] Yet Battenhouse's readings of an implied Christianity in Shakespeare never address the contemporary testimony, both for and against the theater, that compared plays to sermons *in general*, as either compatible or competing modes of edification. Neither the christianizing nor the secularizing critics have asked whether Shakespeare and his contemporaries were capable of envisaging their profession itself—their acting and playwrighting—as a kind of ministry.

Throughout this book—which is deeply indebted to the work of Bevington, Marcus, Greenblatt, and Shuger, in particular—I argue that English theology and ecclesiology shaped the drama at a fundamental level, in helping to determine the conceptualization of the player and the playwright as professions, and of the theater as an institution; these self-images in turn disposed theater people toward the enacting of certain confirmatory plots, themes, and characters on the stage; and thus religion had a crucial say in the creation of plays, in their content, and, by extension, in their presumed social effects. This is not to say that theater people passively absorbed the religion saturating their culture and then, as it were, leaked that religion into their plays. In the first place, there was no single religion suffusing Renaissance England as Whitfield White implies, but rather many religions from which to choose: not simply Catholicism or Protestantism, for the Christian believer, but also kinds of Catholicism and kinds of Protestantism. Conversely, the official rhetoric of these various sects was in general so antitheatrical that any contemporaneous attempt to elaborate how the theater promoted true religion would have required both inventiveness and determination rather than mere receptivity. Even as he was prosecuting Prynne for *Histrio-Mastix*, Laud (1634) could bring himself to say only that plays were "things indifferent," once you "take away the scurf and rubbish which they are incident unto."[38] Finally, religion had a more direct role in the production of plays than as the deep structure of dramatized ideology; it provided rationales and even motives for acting and playwrighting.

Rarely did any theater lover say so directly. For the most part, protheatricalists made explicit reference only to the moral power of the stage, "where man may see his virtue or his crime / Laid open, either to their vice's shame, / Or to their virtue's memorable fame."[39] Fear of church and state repression generated caution: when it was reported in 1610 that the theatrical entrepreneur Philip Rosseter had deemed plays to be as good as sermons, he was summoned by the Bishop of London, before whom he recanted his "most vile, spiteful speeches" the next day.[40] Antitheatricalism had such broad cultural authority, moreover, that it colored the thinking of theater people themselves. Petitioning the Earl of Salisbury from the prison to which he and George Chapman had been committed for authoring *Eastward Ho*, Jonson (1605) represented himself as barely able to name the ignominious "cause" of his woes: "a (the word irks me that our Fortune hath necessitated us to so despis'd a course) a Play, my Lord." E. A. J. Honigmann and Susan Brock have shown that even while the standing of those "at the top of the profession had improved by the 1630s, the great majority [of actors] wanted to be known as gentlemen, citizens or yeomen rather than as players when they identified themselves in their wills' opening sentences." After surveying the formal protheatrical literature of the period, Jonas Barish concludes that "the defense of the theater . . . , as distinct from the defense of poesy, gets under way slowly and clumsily" because "the defenders still share too many of the prejudices of their opponents to conduct an effective rebuttal."[41] But a lack of confidence in their ability to grapple outright with critics and censors did not prevent audiences from flocking to plays or informally defending them in terms that antitheatricalists labeled "blasphemy intolerable"; nor did social and legal insecurities stop theater people from producing elaborate defenses of the stage, as Barish notes, "in the fictive domain of the drama itself."[42] Consequently, any history of Renaissance protheatricalism must rely to an unusual extent on indirect evidence: on the implications of plays, and the distorted image of those implications in the antitheatrical literature of the period. Toward the end of the Renaissance, when church and state support emboldened theater lovers to defend the stage more openly, their greater assurance shed light on earlier protheatricalism but in the process subtly transformed it, too.

Some of the plays I offer as evidence, such as *Henry V* and *Bartholomew Fair*, will be familiar to many readers. To make my case about general theatrical trends, I also examine a larger number of plays that do not often receive critical comment. Whether famous or obscure, most of the drama I analyze belongs to one of two genres. The first is the history play, which reflects on England's religious settlement more overtly than any other dramatic genre in the period; the second is the comedy, which is interesting for the opposite reason, its ostensible lack of any serious religious commentary. Across these genres, I focus on three popular scenarios for Renaissance plays: a "rogue" scenario, a "counter-Crusading" scenario, and a "conformist" scenario. All of these scenarios express views of English Christianity that theorize in turn the professional circumstances in which the scenarios were produced.

Some of the antitheatrical texts I discuss will also be familiar to many readers—perhaps too familiar, insofar as the aims of these texts have come to seem obvious and their influence limited. As Bentley pointed out decades ago, however, antitheatrical sentiment was hardly restricted to the very few extremist tracts in the period that were entirely devoted to the denunciation of plays: "the Corporation of the City of London and several of the great City companies which it represented," for instance, "were consistent and vocal opponents of the commercial theater almost throughout the period." What's more, a multitude of Renaissance books and pamphlets on a wide variety of subjects criticized the theater en passant. Bentley cites the incidental antitheatricality in Stow's *Survey of London* (1598), but a more telling case in point is that bible of puritans, Lewis Bayly's *Practise of Pietie* (c. 1611), reissued over forty times before the theaters were shut down in 1642. Far fewer publications at the time championed playing, either systematically or incidentally; the contrast suggests, again, that antitheatricalism was deeply imbedded in the culture, and that theater people were forced for the most part to improvise defenses of their profession from discourses weighted heavily in favor of their opponents.[43]

I emphasize that theater people defended their *profession* (no anachronism for the period) because their apologies for plays crucially invoked not just a practice but also a community of practitioners.[44] By "theater people," I mean the "quality" or "fraternity" of actors, dramatists, entrepreneurs, hired men—the "we" typically invoked in the prologues and epilogues of plays.[45] These various practitioners often worked together under the aegis of a playing company, but to refer to theater people as theater companies would be misleading in several ways. First, the agency of a company is logically distinguishable from the agencies of its individual participants, even when those participants might be thought to have had collective intentions: thus a company and not its participants might have contracted to stage a play at court, but the participants and not the company might have aspired to win greater respect for their profession in their local communities. Second, dramatists were generally paid by companies to write plays, but they were not usually members of the company that paid them; Bentley suspects that only eight playwrights throughout the period "had oral or written contracts with their companies."[46] Many playwrights never wrote for the companies at all, but instead fashioned entertainments for the colleges, the Inns of Court, schools, great houses, and other private venues, including the closet. Yet they often promoted the same conception of acting and playwrighting as their professional counterparts. More commonly, it is true, the amateurs expressed contempt for the professionals, and such divisiveness could surface within the ranks of the professionals too: the dramatists Greene, Nashe, and Dekker, for instance, all spoke disparagingly of players.[47] If the fellowship that I designate as "theater people" was more inclusive than a playing company, it was also to a considerable extent notional (as the lack of a contemporary term for "theater people" would suggest), and thus it represented as much a matter of contestation at the time as the similarly notional fellowships of church and nation. Nonetheless, such indefiniteness made it possible to envision a theatrical community so open-ended that it could include not merely the players and the playwrights but the audience too—and even make claims on church and nation. To designate a fellowship that could thus range in generality from one's friends or fellow workers to one's countrymen or fellow Christians, Jonson used the term "tribe," which carried a mildly ironic charge for him, meant to highlight the loose, unsettled nature of the affiliations it wittily invoked.[48] He had practical reasons for defining his professional community so inexactly: before becoming a dramatist, Jonson had pursued the still lowlier occupations of actor, soldier, and bricklayer. It seems no accident that the theater person whom Greene belittled as a similar "*Johannes factotum*" or jack-of-all-trades—Shakespeare, a part-owner of his company as well as one of its actors and playwrights—should have helped Jonson foster an expansive vision of the tribe they shared.[49]

But fellowship in the theater represented more than a protheatrical ideal: the profession actively shaped the beliefs and pursuits of its members. Antitheatricalists insisted on this point: thus the theater hater Thomas Gainsford (1616) argued that, while "execrable oaths, artificial lies, discoveries of cozenage, scurrilous words, obscene discourses, corrupt courtings, licentious motions, lascivious actions, and lewd gestures" were "incident to other men," in players these vices came "by profession."[50] Gainsford's logic may be applied to professional actors and playwrights more dispassionately. As I hope to show, commercial theater people tended to favor religious beliefs that suited their profession, if they did not first favor professional beliefs that suited their religion. But I do not want to claim that all theater people professed the same religious beliefs or the same notion of how the theater might enact those beliefs. Apologists who ascribed Christian value to the stage imagined and described that value variously: the theater could be envisaged as an aid to preaching, a model of religious conformity, a promoter of antisectarianism, and even a dispenser of teaching and sacraments rivaling the church. Still less is it my intention to maintain that all theater people were religious or shared the same level of conviction in the self-conceptions they professed or even professed one religious position or professional self-conception consistently: Marlowe, for instance, seems to have gloried in double-dealing of all kinds, while "honest" Jonson wavered between recusancy and conformity as well as protheatricality and antitheatricality throughout his life. Although we regularly pretend otherwise, we cannot with any certainty infer the beliefs of an individual based on his or her membership in a group, not even a group as self-conscious about its beliefs as a religious sect (a Brownist, for instance, may have harbored a secret admiration for bishops, or may not have recognized that he admired bishops, or may not have understood that he was not supposed to admire bishops). Yet belonging to a group and experiencing the practical as well as ideological pressures upon it does *incline* an individual to *profess* certain general beliefs, especially about the group itself. I do want to maintain, therefore, that in most cases theater people defended themselves within the logic of their socially stronger and more respectable enemies—which, on the one hand, encouraged a pious bent to protheatrical arguments and, on the other hand, meant that this piety would have to appear paradoxical, if it appeared openly at all. Some theater people, of course, had no interest in legitimating the theater, but the typical indirection of protheatrical arguments meant that even the most libertine dramatists could, if they wished, pretend to a religious purpose their plays nowhere expressed. Thus the dazzlingly profane *Gallathea* (c. 1585) of John Lyly implies that its sexual comedy has somehow reoriented the play-world from a ruined pagan temple onstage at the start of *Gallathea* to an actively functioning church offstage at the end.

As Margot Heinemann and Martin Butler have demonstrated, not all the theater's critics shared the same religious views either. Three of the five best known antitheatricalists in Elizabethan England—Stubbes, Anthony Munday, and Stephen Gosson—do not seem to have sided with puritans in any consistent way.[51] By the same token, puritans are known to have attended plays, bought playbooks, and even patronized dramatists. But Heinemann and Butler do not offer a single definite instance of a puritan who *wrote* in favor of the theater.[52] Relatively few theater lovers of any persuasion published defenses of plays, so the silence of the playgoing puritan is not as anomalous as it seems—which drives home, once again, how any account of Renaissance protheatricality must in large part remain inferential. Yet theater people exploited the lack of protheatrical puritan writing as a boon: it helped them persuade many contemporary and future audiences that all puritans were theater haters and all theater haters were puritan.[53] A central claim of this book is that this simplification of antitheatricalism into a puritan pathology ultimately homogenized, and debased, protheatricalism too.

Chapter 1, "Good Fellows," provides an overview of the assumptions that encouraged and shaped belief in the religious potentiality of the Renaissance theater. In this chapter I show how antitheatrical discourse, along with other contingent pressures on the stage, such as the theater's lowly social status and the censorship rules that barred plays from openly considering doctrinal questions, disposed protheatricalists to align the theater with one reformist Christian tradition in particular. This tradition was Erasmian, and its chief tenet was inclusiveness. To theater haters such as Stubbes, the fact that "so many flock to see plays" instead of sermons proved only "that the number of Christ his elect is but few, and the number of the reprobate is many." Stubbes wanted players to be excluded from communion; Prynne thought that playgoers should be excluded too. Any pretense of "religious teachings" in the theater had *a fortiori* to be regarded "as profane, exploded and shut out" of the church.[54] To combat such strictures, protheatricalists were virtually compelled to emphasize just how open Christ intended his church to be. While theater haters regularly denounced players as disgraceful lowlifes given to consorting with "the very scum" of the people, protheatricalists countered that players had charitably chosen to minister to the supposed reprobate in terms suiting the capacities not of the players but of the vice-ridden and ignorant in their audience.[55] The enforced silence of the stage on doctrinal matters encouraged theater people to associate this ac-commodative teaching, as Erasmus had, with a doctrinal minimalism that further opened the church's doors to the unlearned, while the exposure of theater people to puritan assault led them to bemoan, with Erasmus, the evils of sectarianism. Prynne himself acknowledged the surprising success of theater people in thus correlating playgoing with religious communitar-ianism: "he that speaks against [plays], or comes not at them," Prynne com-plained, "is forthwith branded for a Schismatical, or factious *Puritan*."[56]

Chapters 2 and 3 constitute a section entitled "Christendom and En-gland" that examines the Christian inclusivism of the stage in the broadest terms that theater people themselves applied to the issue. Perhaps the most widely accepted conclusion that modern scholarship draws from its secular-ist vision of Renaissance English drama is the belief that Renaissance plays, particularly Renaissance history plays, were nationalist.[57] But the chief source of Shakespeare's history plays, Holinshed's *Chronicles* (1577), notes that when London heard news of the Catholic victory against the Turkish navy at Lepanto in 1571, "there were bonfires made through the City, with banqueting and great rejoicing, as good cause there was, for a victory of so great importance, to the whole state of the Christian common wealth."[58] In chapters 2 and 3 I argue that English Protestants generally remained un-certain whether their basic collective identity as Christians bound them to a national, parochial, or supranational fellowship; Christendom thus repre-sented not a subsidiary but rather a determinative issue for the understand-ing of "imagined communities" in Renaissance England.[59] And theater people filtered their dramatizations of England's relation to Christendom through the lens of a distinct but analogously complex question of collective identity: their own struggle to portray themselves both as an estimable pro-fessional community and as worthy members of English society generally.

From the start of the Reformation, Catholic polemicists insisted that En-glish Protestants had schismatically broken from the rest of Christendom and thereby shattered the bonds of community within England too. Chap-ter 2, "Rogue Nationalism," shows how even the most vigorous Protestant apologists were forced to admit these charges to a degree. Bad enough in their eyes was an England that seemed increasingly pestered with "rogues," as vagrants came to be called during this period; far worse was the growing tendency of the English people "to rogue abroad from their own Churches up and down in the Country after factions and firebrands, and Schismatical Conventicles."[60] Hoping to rebuild community in England and in Chris-tendom generally, moderate English theologians followed the lead of Eras-mus in maintaining that the major Christian sects agreed in the "Essentials and Fundamentals" of faith.[61] With the partially fortuitous opposition of puritans both to these ecumenicalists and to the stage, the personnel of England's theaters were encouraged to see themselves as moderates in conflict with the sectarians who were tearing England apart.

Antitheatricalists enabled a still closer correlation of the theater's interests with those of Protestant England by branding itinerant players as "rogues" and by exhorting playgoers who believed that they could "learn any good" from plays to "consider in how palpable darkness they wander, while they forsake the truth and cleave to fables." Sir Thomas More (1520) had defended the peripatetic Erasmus from charges of vagrancy by associating his "wandering" with his nonpartisan dedication to the "common good."[62] In the same way, rather than dispute their own persistent relegation to the status of vagrants, whom the eminent puritan William Perkins (d. 1602) described as commonly "of no civil society or corporation, nor of any particular Church," theater people increasingly chose to dramatize communities of rovers who purposely cast off "particular" affiliations.[63] Further encouraged by a censorship that kept doctrinal controversy off the stage, playwrights fashioned comedies that differentiated the bad errancy of factious puritans, "fitter for woods, and the society of beasts than houses, and the congregation of men," from those merry wanderers who had renounced a puritanically "precise" vision of fellowship.[64] According to the later plays in this "rogue" tradition, theater people actually exemplified the broadmindedness that was characteristic of the English people and that had motivated them to undertake only a moderate, Erasmian reform of the Catholic church in the first place.

Yet how was such broadmindedness to help unite Christians across national boundaries? Chapter 3, "This Blessed Plot," shows how the plays that we now regard as the chief exemplars of English nationalism during the period—the Elizabethan history plays—posed this supranational question with particular urgency. While certain characters in the histories may praise England for its self-sufficiency, the plots of the histories typically associate a separate England with the havoc of foreign war, invasion, and civil war. The Reformation magnified all these threats for England: even if God had vanquished the Spanish Armada and thus far preserved the true faith, internal unrest was thought to encourage England's Catholic enemies, and "there is no one thing that sooner engendereth such discord," apprehensive Protestants maintained, "than contention for religion." Although few scholars have noted it, Elizabethan history plays repeatedly reflect on the break with Rome by dramatizing England's earlier abandonment of the Crusades, and the shadow of the Crusades is not dispelled in these plays even after England's Crusaders return home. As they reenact England's separation from the rest of Christendom, in other words, the histories also recurrently uncover a kind of internationality within the "English" isle: the French blood of England's kings, for instance, or Welsh and Scottish rebels, or the outlaw society of the erstwhile crusader Robin Hood. If the histories thus tend to suggest that England could not purge itself of internal estrangements by turning away from Rome, they also ponder whether England's turning inward might paradoxically enable it to resolve the "civil wars of Intestine dissensions" among Christian sects and even renew the Christian commonwealth.[65]

There was an orthodox Protestant framework available for elaborating such a hope in the Erastianism of England's religious settlement. While *The Book of Common Prayer* required an unprecedented liturgical uniformity throughout "all the whole realm," it also emphasized that the English "condemn no other nations, nor prescribe anything, but to our own people only"; according to church apologists, the way to reunite Christendom was to stop worrying about how different Christian nations managed their spiritual affairs and instead allow each country to "use such ceremonies, as they shall think best to the setting forth of god's honor, and glory."[66] Elizabethan history plays assimilated this notion of a simultaneously particular and universal church to the community organized within the roguish theater and then released to the world at large. But for Shakespeare especially, the dramatization of English history by a fellowship of putative vagabonds broadened the limited relativism of *The Book of Common Prayer*, throwing into question the possibility and even desirability of a national church. Not repudiating the Crusades so much as redefining them, the histories of Shakespeare and other playwrights aimed to differentiate the true church from any particular polity while, obscurely, directing English sights westward rather than eastward, toward the conversion of pagans in the New World.

The second two-chapter section of my book, "Church and Theater," considers protheatrical theories in the English Renaissance that imagined plays as directly ministering to audiences. These theories I divide by chapter into sacramental and homiletic views of the theater. In each case I show how the protheatrical mode in question drew on inclusivist tenets of mainstream English Protestant theology. Chapter 4, "Preachers and Players," examines Shakespeare's notion of his plays as enacting a reformed communion; chapter 5, "Pseudo-Christianity," highlights a protheatrical tradition that depicted acting as the key to church conformity, and church conformity as the key to acting. Conservative English Protestant accounts of both communion and conformity tended to depreciate aggressive evangelism; this preference for moderation suited not only the antipuritanism of theater people but also their necessary indirection in treating religious matters. Yet institutional differences between church and theater (by which I mean differences in tradition, organization, practice, and social status) altered the development within each institution of the theological premises they jointly favored. No established clergyman would have publicly sanctioned the sacramental role that Shakespeare assigned to the theater, except perhaps in the fictive domain of the clergyman's own plays; few were prepared to argue as vigorously as theater people did for a greater toleration not only of Catholic dissidence but of flagrant vice.

Antitheatricalists did credit plays with a sacramental function, albeit a satanic one: "*Stage-plays*," wrote Prynne, "*are the cup and table of Devils.*" By the time the first permanent theaters in England opened their doors, Protestant polemicists had long been laboring to turn English communicants from "gazers" into "receivers." Deploring the idolatrous pageantry of the mass, they taught the people that the sacramental elements of bread and wine were "trifling" in themselves, unable to convey Christ materially; in receiving communion, therefore, worshipers were instructed to "stick not in the corporal things, and things which are object to our eyes, hands, taste and feeling, as the papists teach the people," but rather to "arise to the consideration of spiritual things hereby accordingly." Antitheatricalists insisted that the theater was working to reverse these reformist lessons: "what strangers they are at the Lord's Table," exclaimed Bayly of "most who now live," "what assiduous spectators they are at Stage-plays." The spectacle of a play such as Shakespeare's *Henry V*—not to mention its historical setting, Corpus Christi antecedents, and violence—seemed to theater haters to ally the stage with popish superstition, particularly "that sacrificing bloody altar of the blasphemous breaden god, the romish Idol."[67]

Yet the early Protestant clergymen-dramatists maintained that plays could actually help the English people "arise to the consideration of spiritual things." In the prologue to his *Chief Promises* (1538), for instance, Bale assured his audiences that they would see "no trifling sport" or "gaudish gear" in the play to come, "But the things that shall your inward stomach steer / To rejoice in God for your justification, / And alone in Christ to hope for your salvation." In the same spirit, the prologue to Nicholas Grimald's *Christus Redivivus* (c. 1540) asked its audience to view the play "not only with the outward eye, but with the heart, drinking it in deep." This, I argue, is the dramaturgical tradition that *Henry V* invokes when its prologue urges spectators to employ their "thoughts" and "imaginary forces" on the "ciphers" they are about to witness.[68] Although the play lacks the straightforwardly religious content of earlier Reformation drama, the prologue's heavy emphasis on the trifling nature of its performance suggests that Shakespeare regarded the ostensible profaneness of *Henry V* as paradoxically more in keeping with the Protestant injunction to "piece out our imperfections with your thoughts" than the overtly "edifying" matter of Bale's and Grimald's plays had been.[69] Shakespeare seems to have believed (and I use such tentative language throughout this book to emphasize his exceptional reticence) that censorship helped him not merely sustain his sacramental purpose but achieve it in some measure. "The first cause why they were ordained," Bishop Jewel (d. 1571) says of sacraments, "is, that thereby one should acknowledge another, as fellows of one household, and members of one body."[70] Throughout *Henry V* Shakespeare silently contrasts a violent "fellowship" of warriors financed by a corrupt Catholic church to the peaceful communion of an audience in active remembrance of blood spilt. If he refuses to press the analogy to sacramental controversy, it is not because he thinks his play constitutes a secular alternative to religious ritual, as Greenblatt or Montrose might claim, but rather because he believes he can best promote an inclusive as well as inward understanding of the sacrament by muting his own potentially alienating views on religious reform.

The hotter Bayly was as distressed by such moderation as by stage-plays: "whereas heretofore those have been counted most *holy*, who have showed themselves most *zealous* in *their Religion*," he lamented, "they are now reputed most *discreet*, who can make the least *profession* of their *Faith*." In part, Bayly meant to decry the minimally doctrinal religion that theater people found so congenial—a mere moralism of "pious practices and virtuous performances," as the godly saw it. But Bayly also wanted to underscore how fear of religious controversy had spawned a generation of time-servers: as Johann Wigand argued (in a work translated in 1562), "men compt it a light trifling matter, nay marry, they reckon it a singular witty part, that they can craftily cloak and dissemble religion, and handle themselves in all outward affairs after such sort, as if a man were familiarly linked to both parts [i.e., Catholic and Protestant]." Such critics could hardly believe that the English church refused to demand any stricter conformity in religion than to require the people to attend Sunday service, but apologists argued that the church could in charity require nothing more: "religion cannot be driven into men by force," Bishop Sandys (1585) asserted, although "men by force may be driven to those ordinary means whereby they are wont to be brought to the knowledge of the truth."[71] As I show in chapter 5, theater people seized on this official toleration of mere outward conformity in religion as a golden opportunity to extenuate their professional stake in "hypocrisy."[72] And they defended the coerciveness as well as the evasiveness of conformism in turn, portraying even the notorious Catholic dissident Sir Thomas More, for instance, as a godly temporizer, a "most religious politician," who played the part that church and state demanded of him.[73]

According to the antitheatricalists, however, players could not even pretend to have pious aims, because they enacted "far more Vices" than "Virtues" on the stage. Yet here too conformism came to the theater's aid. In its charitable concern for sinners, the church, Hooker argued, could justifiably embrace not only dissemblers but also those "whose apparent wickedness testifieth even in the sight of the whole world that God abhorreth them." For Hooker, as for other conformists, it was impossible to separate the pure from the impure and in any case counter-productive to try, because the basic goal of conformity was to draw unbelievers into the machinery of a necessarily gradual conversion. Theater people took this toleration of outward vice still further. Favorably contrasting their crowd-pleasing deceits to the supposedly self-righteous duplicity of the puritan, play after play suggested that the pretense of vice would better attract sinners to their possible conversion than the "religious outside" of the puritan ever could.[74]

So useful were puritans for defining and defending the religion of the theater that theater people grew addicted to satirizing them, even though this ridicule directly belied the theater's claims to inclusiveness, as Prynne underscored, and enraged a powerful enemy. Other serious complications for protheatricalists, such as censorship, social stigmatization, and the enactment of vice, led theater lovers to take idiosyncratic stands—for instance, on rogues as catalysts of religious reform—that further weakened their efforts to present theater culture as somehow ecumenical in spirit. To modern commentators, perhaps the most obviously exclusionary feature of the Renaissance theater was the absence of female actors from the stage. But the English clergy were equally all-male, and it is interesting to note that the comparison of players to rogues appears to have weakened gender barriers in the theater, although to a minimal degree: the one woman whom we know to have spoken from a commercial stage during this period, Mary Frith, went by the name of "Moll Cutpurse," which is how she figured in Dekker and Middleton's city comedy *The Roaring Girl* (1610).[75]

At the end of the seventeenth century, an anonymous respondent to the theater-hating Ridpath appears to acknowledge that religious defenses of plays had come to seem implausible when he concedes that "the Stage does not presume to stand in Competition with the *Pulpit*, in that peculiar and sacred advantage of teaching the *Mystery* of *Faith*, but only pretends to be subservient to it in the other arm of the *Pulpit*'s duty, the *Improvement and Regulation of our Manners.*" Yet his *Stage Acquitted* (1699) turns out to surrender far less of the theater's earlier spiritual pretensions than it professes to do. While humbly maintaining that "the *Pulpit* gives the *Rule*, the *Stage* the *Example*," the author of *The Stage Acquitted* also insists that "a bare Precept is less touching than *Example*"—which means that he implicitly grants players a more "lively" influence over "the minds of the Auditory" than preachers can exert. Ridpath's puritanical strictures spur his adversary to even grander assertions. Rather than downplay Laud's sponsorship of the theater, *The Stage Acquitted* proclaims "that the *whole body* of the *Clergy* of the *Church* of *England* in the time of the *Martyr* [Charles I], did in an *extraordinary* manner encourage Plays." In similar fashion, *The Stage Acquitted* refuses to treat the king's sabbath masques as a scandal to be extenuated: "King *Charles* cou'd not have thought of a better *entertainment*, for the *Sundays* after *Evening prayer*," *The Stage Acquitted* proudly declares, "than a diversion, which tended to the confirmation of the Doctrine of the day." "Give the Dramatic Poet his due praise," the author demands of Ridpath, "and confess, that while the *Pulpit* took our *serious hours* to inculcate its Doctrines, the Poet made a farther Conquest, and invaded even our hours of pleasure, and turn'd the opportunity of *Vice* to the service of *Virtue.*"[76] Long after the defeat of the puritans, the thought of their antagonism to the theater continued to brighten visions of players taking religion where the preachers could not follow.

CHAPTER 1

Good Fellows

Saint *Paul became all things to all men*, stooping unto them for their good: CHRIST came down from heaven and emptied himself of majesty in tender love to souls: shall not we come down from our high conceits, to do any poor soul good?

—Richard Sibbes, *The Bruised Reed, and Smoaking Flax* (1630)

fearing a lost soul, I then turn'd Devil,
To prove your better Angel.

—Master Changeable in
A New Tricke to Cheat the Divell (c. 1624–39)

W hy, asked William Prynne (1626), were puritans "hated of all sorts, and kinds of men"? Because they were "too frequent in hearing and reading of God's word"; because they would "reprove men for their evil courses" and not "bear them company in their sins"; because they refused to "swear, whore, drink, dice, game inordinately, misspend their time, haunt Plays and Taverns, and play the good fellows as others do."[1] The godly in churches, the good fellows in alehouses and playhouses: these were the rival camps into which "hot" Protestant writers divided Renaissance England, and their coupling of tavern with theater remains hard to refute. The first theaters of London were in fact inns converted to the purpose; thereafter, as Andrew Gurr reminds us, "all the playhouses had arrangements for selling ale on their sites, so that whether they counted as taverns or playhouses was a matter of name rather than function."[2] The tavern, moreover, was a favorite setting for plays, which often represented alehouse vices in loving detail: even Thomas Randolph's university comedy *The Drinking Academy* (c. 1625) opens with a character "spewing." And the personnel of London's theaters were themselves notorious for their dissipations. Calling the playwrights Robert Greene and Thomas Nashe a pair of "notable good fellows," Gabriel Harvey (1592) recounted how a drunken feast of theirs had caused the death of Greene, who took ill "of a surfeit of pickle herrings and rhenish wine." Christopher Marlowe was murdered at a tavern; Randolph reportedly met his own "untimely" end "by indulging himself too much with the liberal conversation of his admirers"; and Shakespeare, it was said, having drunk "too hard" at a "merry meeting" with his fellow playwrights Michael Drayton and Ben Jonson, "died of a fever there contracted."[3]

Naturally, there were theater people who took exception to the label of "good fellow." Like Thomas Heywood, they argued that their entire profession ought not to be censured "for the misdeeds of some": "many amongst us," wrote Heywood (1612), "I know to be of substance, of government, of sober lives, and temperate carriages." But such attempts to dignify the profession were fatally weakened by the theater people who actively courted reputations as good fellows: men such as Nashe (1592), who in replying to Harvey's account of Greene's death, praised his friend Greene for having had no other care in the world than to scratch out enough money "to conjure up a good cup of wine with at all times." Styling himself along with Greene "a scholar and a good-fellow," Nashe made a pledge to Harvey "by this blessed cup of sack which I now hold in my hand and drink to the health of all Christian souls in," to let his readers know that he was wassailing as he was writing. In the epilogue to *A Woman Killed With Kindness* (1603), even Heywood likened his play to wine and his audience to taverngoers—an "honest crew" of taverngoers, he insisted.[4]

Thirty years after Nashe's own death, the passage of time had done so little to alter the received opinion of theater people that the playwright William Heminges (son of Shakespeare's friend and partner John Heminges) could apply the terms of Nashe's self-portrait to nearly all the best known dramatists of the period. Writing an elegy (c. 1632) on the finger Randolph lost "in a fray" with "a Riotous Gentleman," Heminges imagined the finger as conveyed to the underworld by a procession of more than thirty English "Poets," among them Shakespeare, Jonson, Webster, Chapman, Heywood, Dekker, Middleton, Massinger, Shirley, Brome, and Ford. When Heminges has Charon demand his fare from the group, Taylor the Water Poet explains why they should not be expected to pay: "These are all good fellows and a Jovial pack / that hath spent all their means In smoke and sack." Heminges champions these dissolute colleagues by favorably contrasting them, as Nashe had, to a common self-"righteous" enemy. Unmoved by Taylor's plea, Charon pushes the finger-mourners aside for some decidedly unjovial paying customers: "three or four meager fellows thin and raw / with envy not with study, and they came / with Orphants' goods new Gull'd at Amsterdam." These are puritans, who not only refuse to help the poets but, "such was their Charity," wish that Randolph himself "were slain" along with his finger, because his plays "against the Brotherhood" have caused "the reprobate" to laugh puritans "to scorn."[5]

Equally offensive to the puritans in Heminges's poem is their most acclaimed satirist at the time and, not coincidentally, the most brazen tavern-goer among Renaissance theater people—Shakespeare's fellow reveler, Jonson.[6] As John Aubrey (c. 1680s) decorously put it, the creator of Ananias Tribulation and Zeal-of-the-Land Busy "would many times exceed in drink." Jonson's celebrated carousals at the Mermaid, the Devil, the Sun, the Dog, and the Triple Tun were said to have inspired his playwrighting: according to Furor Poeticus in Robert Wilde's *The Benefice* (c. 1641), "every half quarter of an Hour" Jonson required "a glass of Sack" to be "sent of an Errand into his Guts, to tell his Brains they must come up quickly, and help out with a Line." Not even death was thought capable of ending his drinking: in 1691 a wit envisaged Jonson "now Toping above in *Apollo's Whitehall*." Indeed, posthumous tributes regularly hailed Jonson as the "*Genius*" of inebriated poets. "Fetch me *Ben Jonson's* Skull, and fill't with Sack," writes the author of *A Preparative to Study* (1641): "If there be any weakness in the Wine, / There's virtue in the Cup to make 't divine." So firmly had Jonson's place in the mythology of London's tavern culture been established by mid-century that one proprietor thought it worth his while to christen his alehouse "Ben Jonson's Head."[7]

Jonson encouraged this image of himself through his writings as well as daily habits. In the Induction to *Every Man Out of His Humor* (1599), for instance, the drunken Carlo Buffone enters carrying a cup of "*Canary*," called "*Castalian* liquor" by "our *Poet*," Buffone says, "when he comes abroad (now and then) once in a fortnight, and makes a good meal among Players": "an honest pure rogue, he will take you off three, four, five of these, one after another, and look villainously when he has done, like a one-headed CERBERUS (he do' not hear me I hope) and then (when his belly is well ballas't, and his brain rigg'd a little) he sails away withal, as though he would work wonders when he comes home." One of those promised wonders, Buffone adds, is the play at hand, whose title causes Buffone some postprandial apprehension: "'Sblood, and he get me out of the humor he has put me in, I'll trust none of his Tribe again, while I live."[8]

If such passages show Jonson delighting in the charge of good-fellowship, others indicate how fiercely he resented the puritan corollary that he was godless too. True it is, Jonson concedes in the preface to *Volpone* (published 1607), that some playwrights have "embark'd" on a "bold adventure for hell," but he himself has "ever trembled to think toward the least profaneness." Not only are his plays free of irreligion, he insists, they are positively edifying, because the true dramatist is "a teacher of things divine, no less than humane." In 1619 Jonson told William Drummond that he had "a mind to be a churchman," and it was as a churchman that he appeared to a future minister who visited him in 1632:

> His whole Discourse
> Was how Mankind grew daily worse and worse,
> How God was disregarded, how Men went
> Down even to Hell, and never did repent,
> With many such sad Tales; as he would teach
> Us Scholars, how hereafter We should preach.
> Great wearer of the bays, look to thy lines,
> Lest they chance to be challeng'd by Divines:
> Some future Times will, by a gross Mistake,
> *Jonson* a Bishop, not a Poet make.[9]

How are we to square the good fellow in Jonson with the divine? The question looks unanswerable only if we take the puritanical view of a godly life as gospel—which has indeed been the curious position of nearly all modern scholarship on Renaissance drama. Yet Jonson seems to have perceived no more necessary tension between his faith and his good-fellowship than Nashe did when raising his blessed cup to the health of all Christian souls. On the contrary, Jonson told Drummond that at his first communion after renouncing Catholicism, "in token of true Reconciliation, he drank out all the full cup of wine." While the comedy of this anecdote makes it tempting to dismiss Jonson's pretensions to godliness as a mockery or a delusion, one of his boon companions in the alehouse was a future bishop, Richard Corbet, who probably helped arrange the honorary M.A. that Jonson received at Oxford in 1619.[10] And Jonson found considerable favor with others in the clerical elite, some of whom he "adopted" as "Sons of Ben" and members of his "Tribe." In *Jonsonus Virbius* (1638), a collection of memorial verse compiled six months after Jonson's death by another future bishop, Brian Duppa, nearly a third of the thirty-one contributors had taken or would soon take holy orders—and three of these men too went on to become bishops. Far from hiding such clerical connections, one of the volume's poems maintained that "Grave Preachers" had been using the "wit and language" of Jonson's plays as "golden Pills, by which they might infuse / Their Heavenly Physic" into their parishioners.[11] By the time *Jonsonus Virbius* was published, moreover, at least two of its clergymen-contributors, William Cartwright and Jasper Mayne, had written plays themselves; even

Heminges the dramatist and finger-mourner appears to have taken holy orders. If the drama of Jonson and his fellow playwrights was as secular a medium as Renaissance puritans and modern critics make it out to be, why would clergymen have taken such pains to eulogize a dramatist, and why would dramatists have become clergymen?

What most deeply ties the Renaissance theater to the church as well as to the tavern, I will argue, is the robust conception of communion one glimpses in Nashe's and Jonson's self-characterizations. That is to say, Nashe and Jonson saw a spiritual virtue in good-fellowship; so did many of their contemporaries, both in and out of the theater; and this broad consensus hinged on the belief that the church ought to minister to the ignorant and corrupt as well as to the enlightened and virtuous. Radical Protestants regarded the practical consequences of such inclusivism as intolerable: "the whole communion in the Church of England, is so polluted, with profane and scandalous persons," exclaimed the separatist John Robinson (1610), "as that even in this respect alone, were there none other, there were just cause of separation from it."[12] But theater people found aid and comfort in thinking of the church as what the separatist Henry Ainsworth (1608) derisively termed "a misceline multitude of believers and infidels, holy and profane." According to the antitheatricalists, after all, "the common haunters" of the commercial theaters consisted "for the most part" of "the lewdest persons in the land, apt for pilfery, perjury, forgery, or any roguery, the very scum, rascality, and baggage of the people, thieves, cut-purses, shifters, cozeners; briefly, an unclean generation, and spawn of vipers." If the church saw fit to minister to lewd persons, why should the theater not do the same?[13]

This correlation of open theater and open church was further encouraged by the widely held belief that ministers should suit their teachings to the diverse capacities of their congregations. As the moderate puritan Richard Bernard advised his colleagues in *Two Twinnes* (1613), a clergyman "must bring forth of his treasury, both new and old, variety of matter fitting the Auditory." After Christ, who according to another moderate puritan, Richard Sibbes (1630), took upon himself "our familiar manner of speech" as well as "our nature," the perceived exemplar of such adaptiveness was St. Paul: "in all things I fashioned myself to all men, to save at the least way some," Paul asserts; "I please all men in all things, not seeking mine own profit, but the profit of many, that they might be saved." Antitheatricalists condemned theater people for their excessive willingness to please: "players are discredited in the very subject of their profession, which is only scratching the itching humors of scabbed minds with pleasing content and profane jests." But the church's linkage of rhetorical adaptiveness to evangelical inclusiveness encouraged theater people to portray themselves instead as communitarian by profession.[14]

In the comedy *Two Wise Men and All the Rest Fools* (published 1619), for instance, a character notes that lawyers are said to "gain by falling out of neighbors, & friends," whereas ale-sellers "grow rich by meeting of good fellows, and sitting together lovingly"; the play's epilogue associates theater people with the ale-sellers, "for it were against reason and our own ends to drive hence that company, which we wish rather doubled, than out of it one to be spared." Responding to the charges of critics such as Sidney (c. 1581–83) that commercial English plays were "mongrel" in form and matter, the actor-dramatist Heywood (1624) countered that English playwrights made their drama misceline on purpose, to suit their heterogeneous audiences. "Lest the Auditory should be dulled with serious courses," Heywood argued, playwrights "in every Act present some Zany with his Mimic action, to breed in the less capable, mirth and laughter: For they that write to all, must strive to please all." Part of the attraction that Jonson and the theater held for clergymen was the promise to learn, in Heywood's Pauline formulation, how to "fashion themselves to a multitude."[15]

This inclusivist goal may best be described as Erasmian, first, because Erasmus championed it, and second, because the label properly resists sectarian categorization. The communitarian principles I have outlined were espoused by a wide variety of Christian writers during this period; some of these writers, moreover, hoped to transcend what they regarded as false distinctions among religious factions. Erasmus himself strove so mightily to avoid being identified with one faction or another that he was claimed and disclaimed by controversialists on all sides. Opposing the injunction of 1547 that required every English parish to purchase a copy of Erasmus's *Paraphrases*, the Catholic bishop Stephen Gardiner professed to "agree with them that said Erasmus laid the eggs and Luther hatched them"; conversely, the Jesuit pamphleteer Robert Parsons (1603) mocked John Foxe for making Erasmus, no "protestant at all," "the father, & first master of new gospeling in England."[16] Recent historians have demonstrated the breadth as well as the depth of Erasmus's influence on English Protestantism: while A. G. Dickens and Whitney Jones, for instance, "discern in the basis and development of the Elizabethan Settlement a 'cool Erasmianism' to set alongside the 'cool Erastianism' so often described," they also note the importance of Erasmus to English Puritanism. I want to add a further complexity to this picture: at least eight of Erasmus's early English translators had a hand in playwrighting.[17] As widely embraced as Erasmus's inclusivist views may have been, in other words, they seem to have held a special appeal for writers interested in drama.

Erasmus was indeed a favorite author of Jonson's, and Jonson did more than any other dramatist to popularize the good-fellow brand of Erasmianism that became a central feature of Renaissance English theater. In the first section of this chapter I will show how Jonson and his disciples embraced an Erasmian conception of Pauline adaptiveness as a rhetorical ideal, even a paradigm for plot and character. In the second section I will explain how Jonson's characterization of himself as an "honest pure rogue" belonging to an ambiguously defined "Tribe" surprisingly epitomizes both the seriousness and the complexity of his inclusivism. In the third section I will turn from Jonson to Shakespeare and argue that, unlike Jonson, Shakespeare tried to differentiate an Erasmian theater from the antipuritanism that he worried might fracture good Christian fellowship beyond repair.

I

In one comedy by a Son of Ben, Richard Brome's *The Weeding of Covent Garden* (1632), drink proves to be a literal measure of faith. Or of zeal, rather: "I'll undertake one good fellow, that has but just as much religion as will serve an honest man's turn, will bear more wine than ten of these giddy-brain'd Puritans, their heads are so full of whimsies," exclaims the wit Mihil from his alehouse bench. His hypothesis is soon confirmed by his puritan brother Gabriel, who falls drunk beside him: Mihil remarks, "I hope it will work out his superfluous zeal / And render him civil Christian again." Once again Mihil's words bear fruit, for when Gabriel wakes from his drunkenness, he finds himself purged of his "vain imaginations" and proceeds to renounce his puritanism.[18]

Satires such as Brome's make it easier for modern readers to appreciate how deeply the "civil" Christian was loathed by puritan polemicists. Time and again he appears as a figure for scorn in their own writings, espousing some version of the following creed: "I mean well: I hurt no man: nor I think no man any hurt: I love God above all: and put my whole trust in him: what would ye have more? they preach and teach, they can tell us no more but this." The speaker in this case is Atheos, from George Gifford's *The Countrie Divinitie* (1581), a dialogue purporting to elucidate and then confute "certain points of the religion, which is among the common sort of Christians."[19] Atheos's interlocutor, Zelotes, is a traveler who has met Atheos by chance and straightaway inquires whether Atheos's town has "a preacher." "I am persuaded we have the best Priest in this Country," Atheos replies, "we would be loath to forego him for the Learnedest of them all." "He is as gentle a person as ever I see: a very good fellow, he will not stick when good fellows and honest men meet together, to spend his groat at the Alehouse: I cannot tell, they preach and preach, but he doth live as well as the best of them." Zelotes counters that a swineherd can do as much; he wants to discover whether Atheos's minister can "teach" his flock "to know the will of God, and reprove naughtiness among" them. "Yes that he doth," Atheos blithely responds, "for if there be any that do not agree, he will seek for to make them friends: for he will get them to play a game or two at Bowls or Cards, and to drink together at the Alehouse: I think it a Godly way, to make Charity: he is none of these busy Controllers." Zelotes can bear no more of this praise for a mere "pot companion," and he spends the rest of the dialogue denouncing both the minister and Atheos as ignorant carnal men who have blindly turned aside from the true path of salvation, the word of God preached. Yet Atheos continues to insist that his life without preachers and teachers is no less Christian than that of Zelotes: "God forbid that all those should be awry which are not learned: is it not enough for plain country men, plowmen, tailors, and such other, for to have their ten commandments, the Lord's prayer, and the belief? I think these may suffice us, what should we meddle further? I know men which are no Scripture men, which serve God as well as the best of them all, will ye condemn such?"[20]

A religion of sociability rather than learning; beliefs that "may suffice us" in the place of "superfluous zeal": such congruencies between the views of Gifford's bumpkin and of Brome's city sharper are salient enough to indicate that Atheos's so-called "country divinity" had a wider currency at the time than Gifford pretends. Zelotes says as much in responding to Atheos's notion of sufficient knowledge: "many which are otherwise very wise men use much your doltish sayings, and think they speak very wisely."[21] Gifford's portrait of civil irreligion in England unmistakably reflects the mainstream theology of the established church.

This theology was, in many crucial respects, inclusivist. A basic demand of Protestantism, after all, was that Christianity be made more accessible to the laity, most notably through vernacular renderings of the Bible and liturgy. The English church took further steps to broaden its evangelism, steps that can be roughly classified as inclusivist approaches to doctrine, to edification, and to reformation. While each approach shades into the others, heuristic distinctions among them help clarify the purpose of contentious tracts such as Gifford's. Questions of doctrine and teaching have an obvious relevance to *The Countrie Divinitie*, and I will therefore consider them first.

Concern for the spiritual needs of the uneducated led English theologians to elaborate what one might call a two-tier conception of Christian doctrine. "For we may not think that Heaven was prepared for deep Clerks only," Bishop James Ussher observes in his *Briefe Declaration of the Universalitie of the Church of Christ* (1624), "and therefore beside that larger measure of knowledge, whereof all are not capable, there must be *a Rule of faith common to small and great*; which as it must consist but of few propositions, (for simple men cannot bear away many) so is it also requisite, that those articles should be of such weight & moment, that they may be sufficient to make a man wise unto salvation." Ussher echoes a famous passage in Erasmus's *Paraclesis* (1516; translated 1529) in which Erasmus cautions his readers not to identify Christianity with a complex system of beliefs and thus effectively "appropriate unto a few men that thing which Christ would have most common. . . . Only a very few [of us] can be learned, but all can be Christian." In the *Enchiridion* (1504; trans. 1533), Erasmus insists that the essential matter of Christian doctrine can and should be contained "in a few articles" only. English Protestants took up the challenge of simplifying Christianity long before Ussher did: "above all else," as the historian Bernard Verkamp remarks, "the early English reformers were intent upon restoring a proper balance between the fundamentals and non-fundamentals of the Christian religion."[22] Some of the results were codified in the Thirty-nine Articles and the Book of Common Prayer (which notably rehearses the Apostle's Creed at morning prayer, evening prayer, baptism, and communion); but in less formal ways too a spirit of doctrinal minimalism came to pervade the English church, including many of its puritan clergy. In his *Christian Advertisements and Counsels of Peace* (1608), for instance, the puritan Bernard asserts that "there is no part of holy Scripture, which every Christian is not necessarily bound to seek, and desire the knowledge of, so far forth as in him lieth"; and yet, he adds, we cannot deny that "the penitent Thief that was crucified with Christ, and the Eunuch, even then, when he was baptized by *Philip*, were in the state of salvation," no matter how "ignorant" they must have been on many doctrinal points. "The only fundamental truth in religion," Bernard concludes, "is this: *That Jesus Christ the son of God, who took our nature of the Virgin Mary, is our only and all sufficient Savior.*" Just as committed to broadening the church by limiting the number of doctrinal prerequisites for salvation, the conformist Edmund Bunny in his *Treatise Tending to Pacification* (1584) also reduces "the material and essential points of Christian Religion" to a single brief precept: that we "rest in Christ alone, for the whole work of our redemption."[23]

When Atheos gives voice to similar views, he reasonably concludes that the preaching of secondary Christian truths amounts to superfluous zeal.

But Ussher, intent on reconciling his inclusivist stake in fundamentals with his scholarly commitment to higher Christian learning, tries to avoid such minimalism by redescribing fundamentals later in his sermon as the necessary "groundwork" in the edification or building up (*edificatio*) of a Christian rather than the sufficient basis for "unity" and even "equality" among Christians: "For let us preach never so many Sermons unto the people, our labor is but lost; as long as the foundation is unlaid, and the first principles untaught, upon which all other doctrine must be builded." Yet a latent suspicion that teaching anything other than first principles might be elitist leads Ussher to dissociate preaching in general from the work of foundation-building. To his mind, the transmission of fundamental Christian truths requires a practice better suited to "the capacity of the common Auditory" than preaching is—catechism. In his *Two Twinnes*, Bernard similarly argues that those who think to preach without having catechized beforehand "set on a roof, before they lay the foundation"; spiritual "children," he adds (switching scriptural metaphors), must first drink the "Milk" of catechism before they can digest the "strong meat" of sermons.[24]

In theory, catechism too was a broadly accepted entailment of Protestant inclusivism: according to Bernard, even "the Papists confess, that the ground, which we have gotten of them, is by Catechizing."[25] The beauty of catechism (for the Protestants) was its congruity with "the simpler sort" in both message and method: it delivered essential principles to the ignorant in a form they could easily grasp. If mainstream preachers such as Ussher and Bernard stopped short of believing that catechism thus did all the necessary work of Christian instruction, they nevertheless embraced it as an authoritative model for their ministry.[26] Even *The Countrie Divinitie* is catechistical in style as well as in dialogic structure: Gifford explains that the "matter itself is not handled as a disputation between deep divines, but after the manner of ploughmen and carters." A year later Gifford issued a similarly catechistical *Dialogue Betweene a Papist and a Protestant, Applied to the Capacity of the Unlearned*, while in the following year he published an actual catechism. Yet *The Countrie Divinitie* plainly lacks the inclusivist spirit that attracted Ussher and his fellow conformists to catechism in the first place. In part this difference seems to stem from Gifford's anxiety that catechism might encourage the Atheos-like conviction that one need learn only so much and no more. As the historian Ian Green writes, "the idea of an essential core of religious knowledge" was "implicit in the way" catechists "described their works, either on the title-page or in a preface: 'the sum of Christian religion', 'the main and fundamental points' or the 'grounds of divinity', the 'several heads' or the 'first principles' of religion, 'the ABC of Christianity', 'milk for babes', and so on." (Gifford's own *Catechism* professes to "contain" *The Summe of Christian Religion*.) Yet the more obvious source of friction between catechistical theory and practice in *The Countrie Divinitie* is Gifford's outright contempt for "the common sort of Christians"—"all the pack of ye," as Zelotes calls them. Atheos ends the dialogue unconverted, "for all my travail in teaching you," as Zelotes bitterly remarks: "But I looked for no other reward from ye: the black Moor cannot change his hue, nor the Cat of the mountain her spots." How can Zelotes claim any serious commitment to teaching Atheos if he viewed Atheos from the start as incapable of being taught?[27]

Not even catechism, Bernard declares in his preacher's manual *The Faithfull Shepheard* (1607), will edify the people whose catechist remains aloof from them: "if thou beest proud and cannot stoop to their capacity, or impatient to hear an ignorant answer, or disdainful to be familiar; few will come to thee willingly, and none but by force; and these will profit little by thee." For Erasmus, too, clerical outreach to the ignorant requires above all a charitable forbearance. Perhaps no theme is more central to Erasmus's conception of ministry than Christ's patience and humility in continually "tempering" or "accommodating" his message to his audience.[28] As Erasmus puts it in a famous letter to Justus Jonas (1521), Christ "says one thing to the multitudes, who are somewhat thick-witted, and another to his disciples; and even so he has to bear with them for a long time while he gradually brings them to understand the celestial philosophy." A stark contrast for Erasmus is the arrogance of Luther, who has sacrificed Christian fellowship to his own "zeal for the purity of the Gospel." Nothing could be further from the "savage torrent" of Luther's "invective," Erasmus maintains, than the "civility [civilitatem]" and "meekness" of Christ, who "attuned [attemperavit] himself" not merely to the intellectual capacities of his listeners but to their "feelings" also. And Paul imitated the accommodationism of his master, exemplifying the Christian "civility [civilitate]" that Erasmus believes Luther so sorely lacks: "Thus does Paul become all things to all men," Erasmus explains, "that he might gain them all for Christ, training his disciples to teach with all gentleness, without estranging any man by harshness of behavior and language, but by their meekness winning over even those who are stubborn and hard to please."[29]

When Richard Hooker in the preface to his *Lawes of Ecclesiasticall Politie* (1593) chastises puritans for the "high terms of separation" they use in styling themselves "The brethren, The godly, and so forth" while they condemn "the rest of the world" as "worldlings, timeservers, pleasers of men not of God, and such like," he means to criticize not only the sectarianism of puritans but also their related opposition to serving the time and pleasing men.[30] In his letter to Jonas, Erasmus insists that the church needs "time-servers"; his *Paraphrase* of 1 Corinthians extols Paul's "diligence and readiness to please." Hooker repeatedly characterizes the policy of the English church in the same audaciously dubious terms. One revealing example is his treatment of the puritan complaint that the church had incorporated "prayers for earthly things" in its liturgy. In book 5 of the *Lawes* (1597), Hooker admits that the "perfect" in "judgment" know they should pray for heavenly grace alone, "but the tender kindness of the Church of God it very well beseemeth to help the weaker sort which are by so great odds mo in number, although some few of the perfecter and stronger may be therewith for a time displeased." This "weaker" majority find their way, according to Hooker, "by sense" rather than by any "spiritual capacity." Hence the church, "respecting what men are," has chosen to incorporate prayers into its liturgy that would appeal to the sense, in the hopes that such prayers would gradually train carnal worshippers to direct their sights "heavenward." By seeming to indulge worldlings, in other words, "the Church under hand, through a kind of heavenly fraud," actually "taketh therewith the souls of men as with certain baits."[31]

The English preacher John Bury makes the same general point in his sermon *The Moderate Christian* (1631): since "we shall as soon catch fish with a *naked hook*" as convert the profane man "with tart *invectives*," Bury argues, ministers must instead practice what made Paul so "skillful" a "*fisher* of men," his "holy art of *pleasing.*" "Art," like Hooker's "fraud," is no merely decorative metaphor for Paul's civil Christianity: it distinguishes an accommodative stooping to the capacities of the ignorant from an Atheos-like satisfaction with fundamentals only. As the preacher John Trapp (1647) asserts in his own *Commentary* on 1 Corinthians, "ministers must turn themselves into all shapes and fashions both of spirit and speech to gain souls to God." The alehouse minister of *The Countrie Divinitie* might defend himself in similar terms: a "gentle" clergyman, no "busy controller," he might claim that he had made himself a good fellow to the good fellows—not, as Zelotes would say, to "flatter" his parishioners in their "foul and beastly sins," but rather to bear with their ignorance while he gradually converts them. Paul's example proved to Erasmus that it is no blameworthy "deceit [fucus]" to hide one's real feelings for a time and simplify, soften, or even defer the truth in the hopes of gaining souls: it is rather "a sort of holy cunning [sancta quadam vafricie]." "With how much cunning [vafricie] did not Paul play the chameleon, if I may say so," Erasmus observes in his *Ratio verae theologiae* (1519), "so that from all directions he might bring some gain to Christ?"[32]

For Ussher, the successfully accommodative catechist requires a similar combination of humility and craft. In his concern that the church embrace the ignorant as well as the educated Christian without sacrificing higher learning to simple religion, Ussher chides those "great Scholars" who "possibly may think that it standeth not so well with their credit, to stoop thus low, and to spend so much of their time in teaching these rudiments and first principles of the doctrine of Christ. But they should consider, that the laying of the foundation skillfully, as it is the matter of greatest importance in the whole building, so is it the very masterpiece of the wisest builder." The task of adapting one's learning to the ignorant, Ussher continues, will "put us to the trial of our skill, and trouble us a great deal more, than if we were to discuss a controversy, or handle a subtle point of learning in the Schools." Although the puritan Bernard is less eager to associate such artfulness with clergymen, even he praises the catechist in the terms that his first publication, *Terence in English* (1598), had applied to the dramatist Terence: as Terence is "pleasant, and very profitable," so the catechist "greatly pleaseth the people" and "profiteth" them too.[33]

"In all things I fashioned myself to all men, to save at the least way some": after the work of Stephen Greenblatt, it would be hard not to notice the stress that Tyndale's translation (1534) of 1 Corinthians places on the theatricality of Paul's adaptiveness. According to Erasmus in Miles Coverdale's translation of the *Paraphrases* (1549), Paul "tempered" his "appearance" to the "capacities and minds" of his auditors, "altered" himself "into every fashion" for their sake.[34] Calvin too (1551; translated 1577) sees Paul's commitment to edifying all men as transforming him into a kind of actor: "To be made all things, is to change himself into all forms, according as the matter required, or to take upon [him] diverse persons according to the variety of men" (Calvin's Latin, "personas . . . induere," even more strongly signifies a playing of roles).[35] By the same token, a sympathetic account (1626) of an anonymous English Jesuit operating in Worcestershire reports how "this Father kept in store all kinds of dresses which he used to adopt according to circumstances; appearing one while as a clown upon a pack horse, then in splendid attire entering the houses of the nobility, he made himself, like the Apostle, 'all things to all men, that he might gain all.'"[36] These examples from diverse decades and religious persuasions certainly lend support to Greenblatt's claims about the pervasiveness of artful "self-fashioning" as a concept in this period, but they also indicate that Greenblatt is too quick to associate such self-fashioning with the rise of secular individualism. When

Erasmus, Calvin, the anonymous Jesuit, and Trapp praise Paul for turning himself "into all shapes and fashions both of spirit and speech," they all believe that his purpose was "to gain souls to God."

A truly distinctive development in accommodationist self-fashioning during the English Renaissance was its perceived realization on actual stages. While Renaissance theater people were regularly denounced as "*Chameleon*-like" "time-pleasers," they were often praised in such terms, too.[37] The phenomenon comes clearest in the late cases of Stuart clergymen-dramatists, such as Jonson's "son" Cartwright. One of the many eulogies in the posthumous edition of Cartwright's *Comedies, Tragi-Comedies, With Other Poems* (1651) describes his plays as adaptively teaching "Divinity to tread the Stage"; another celebrates Cartwright's ability "To fill the *Stage*, the *Schools*, and *Pulpit* too; / Thy universal Wit / All Things and Men could fit." In a third eulogy, Cartwright's fellow "Tribe" member and clergyman-playwright Mayne first praises Cartwright the dramatist for knowing "when to vary Shapes, and where, and how," then traces the flowing "Spring" of Cartwright's "Wit" from the stage to the pulpit, where "Thou to all Hearers wert all Things, didst fly / Low to the People, to us Scholars high. / Hadst Milk for Children, and strong Meat for those / Whose Minds, like thine, to Men's perfections rose." Mayne sums up this accommodationism, and at the same time emphasizes the continuity between Cartwright's playwrighting and preaching, by extolling Cartwright's *sancta vafricie*, his "holy Craft": "How have I seen Thee cast thy Net, and then / With holy Cozenage catch'd the Souls of Men?" A later plagiarist (1668) of these lines makes them explicitly protheatrical: Cartwright, he says, was able to "cast his net, and catch souls as well in the Pulpit as the Stage."[38]

Cartwright was not the only clergyman-playwright to be extolled as all things to all men. In 1656 a eulogist for Thomas Goffe claimed that Goffe's plays prove him to have been "*Omnium scenarum homo*, to his glory [rather] than disparagement." Especially in the context of his other writings, Mayne's poem for Cartwright suggests that he made sense of his own career as a preacher-playwright through a notion of civil religion derived from Erasmus. The truest Christians, Mayne asserts in his *Sermon Concerning Unity & Agreement* (1646), are the accommodationists—those who commit themselves, "where our salvation, or the salvation of our neighbors is not concerned, charitably to comply, and sort with their infirmities; neither crossing them by our practice, though perhaps the better, nor perplexing them with our disputes, though perhaps the more rational." To cast such sociability as a means of edification, Mayne expatiates on "the Apostle's (Art shall I say? or) holy commission, to be *all things to all men*":

by complying with the affections of those to whom he wrote, [Paul] first transformed himself into their shapes, and became all things to all men, that he might the better transform them into his, and make all men become like himself. Thus to the Jews he became as a Jew; and put himself a while with them under the Law, that by insensible degrees he might take their yoke from them, and might beget their liking, and entertainment of the Gospel.[39]

Mayne's published poetry consistently credits dramatists with such *sancta vafricie* even if they never left the stage for the pulpit. Spectators who came to Beaumont and Fletcher "to learn obsceneness," Mayne writes, "return'd innocent, / And thankt you for this coz'nage"; in *Jonsonus Virbius*, Mayne recalls how Jonson "ev'n sin didst in such words array, / That some who came *bad parts*, went out *good play*." Just as he praises Cartwright for undertaking "as many ways to save, as They / Who are worst Sinners use to err and stray," so Mayne casts the apparent profaneness of the commercial dramatists he admires as the accommodationist gambit they take to edify their audiences.[40]

Without overt reference to the theater, this artful conception of the ministry or ministerial conception of art was even more plainly expressed by the playwright Nashe in his pamphlet *Christs Tears Over Jerusalem* (1593). The *Tears* blames a perceived resurgence of atheism in England on puritanical churchmen, "ridiculous dull Preachers" who fail to recognize that an atheist will never be persuaded by anything but "humane reasons": "Vaunt you ye speak from the holy Ghost never so, if you speak not in compass of his five senses, he will despise you, and flout you." Like Bury in *The Moderate Christian*, Nashe reminds his readers that "Men are men, and with those things must be moved, that men wont to be moved. They must have a little Sugar mixt with their sour Pills of reproof; the hooks must be pleasantly baited that they bite at. Those that hang forth their hooks and no bait, may well enough entangle them in the weeds, (enwrap themselves in contentions,) but never win one soul." This is just the rhetorical advice that *Jonsonus Virbius* imagines preachers to be taking when they conceal their heavenly physic in Jonson's golden pills; it also helps explain why the clerical contributors to *Jonsonus Virbius* ever chose to fraternize with Jonson and then broadcast that fact in the first place. For rhetoric is only half the accommodationist program, as Nashe and Bury see it; the other half is ecclesiological—making oneself all things *to all men*. When the puritanical exclaim that they would rather "*defy*" the "lewd and profane man" than "*please*" him, Bury argues, they effectively side with the "*Scribes* and *Pharisees*" who "censured" Christ for "eating and drinking with Publicans and Sinners." Yet even "the profanest worldling, the Turk, the Pagan have in them a *nature capable* of that communion and fellowship" the saints enjoy in heaven. Nashe puts the idea more drolly: he exhorts puritan preachers to "love men of wit, and not hate them so as you do, for they have what you want. By loving them and accompanying with them, you shall both do them good and yourselves good; they of you shall learn sobriety and good life, you of them shall learn to utter your learning, and speak movingly." From this perspective, the profane matter of a clerical play such as Mayne's *City Match* would indicate that the author not only studied men of wit in order to improve his preaching but charitably consorted with the wits in order to improve them.[41]

Jonson's repeated insistence that playwrights are able to "steer the souls of men" suggests that he too may have regarded his ostensibly profane art as a kind of holy cozenage.[42] The case is emphatically made in a play Jonson co-wrote early in his career, *Eastward Ho* (1605). As the play begins, the prodigal apprentice Quicksilver urges the virtuous apprentice Golding to "turn good fellow, turn swaggering gallant, and let the welkin roar, and Erebus also"; since these last words constitute a patchwork quotation of Shakespeare's Pistol, Quicksilver's debauchery is immediately associated with his playgoing. Condemning Quicksilver as "a drunken, whore-hunting rakehell," Golding predicts that "nothing" will "recover" him "but that which reclaims atheists, and makes great persons sometimes religious—calamity." The prophecy proves true, in part. Released from his indentures, Quicksilver attempts a gold-hunting voyage to Virginia but is shipwrecked within a matter of minutes and then imprisoned as a vagrant felon. Pleading for mercy from his former master Touchstone also gets Quicksilver nowhere: "Thou hast learnt to whine at the play yonder," Touchstone asserts, and turns his back on Quicksilver's presumed dissembling. But Golding, like a good accommodationist, comes to believe that Quicksilver has a nature capable of repentance.[43] Finding Touchstone intractable toward Quicksilver, Golding hits upon the "device" of pretending to be imprisoned himself in order to make Touchstone a "spectator" of Quicksilver's "miseries." And the plot succeeds: Touchstone both forgives Quicksilver and assures Golding, "whose charitable soul in this hath shown a high point of wisdom and honesty," that his "deceit is welcome."[44] Far from discrediting playgoing, in other words, *Eastward Ho* redefines it, exchanging a virtuous conception of the theater for a debauched one. By analogy to Golding, the charitable player only pretends to be one of the company of good fellows, in order to trick playgoers into witnessing the true course of a prodigal life. This honest "deceit," the play implies, will have a doubly godly effect on the audience. As Quicksilver's fall and conversion will help persuade them to become "religious" (and without their having to experience actual "calamity"), so it will also encourage their own charity toward the "lewd and profane man."

II

Antitheatricalists were unmoved by such accommodationist defenses of plays for several reasons. First, they believed that the commercial objectives of theater people would always override any supposedly godly purpose for staging plays. The dramatist "who writeth for reward," declared Munday in the *Blast*, "neither regardeth virtue, nor truth; but runs unto falsehood, because he flattereth for commodity." In a series of *Adagia* on the subject of adaptiveness, even Erasmus equated the "guile [vafricie]" of actual players with self-aggrandizement, not piety. For instance, Erasmus defined the first adage in the series, "Servire scenae," "To be a slave to the scene," as "a metaphor taken from the actors in plays, who do not behave according to their own judgment but think of only one thing—pleasing the eyes of the public somehow or other, otherwise they will be slow-clapped and hissed off the stage."[45] Antitheatricalists further maintained that theater people could not stoop to the level of rakehells without becoming rakehells themselves. Players "transform themselves so far to the condition of every man," wrote William Rankins in his *Mirrour of Monsters* (1587), "that there is no vice but they are well seen in the same." And playgoers, in the antitheatricalist view, would inevitably suffer the same degradation. "Admit some few good Christians resort sometimes to Stage-plays," Prynne argues in his *Histrio-Mastix* (1633), "yet since they always meet with far more, far greater troops of lewd, deboist companions there, who (without God's preventing grace, which Play-haunters cannot challenge) will certainly *corrupt them in a moment*: it must needs be sinful, be dangerous to resort unto them."[46]

Finally, just as any good Christian would be contaminated by plays, so, the antitheatricalists argued, would any good Christianity. Not even direct sermonizing in the theater could mollify theater haters who were more appalled by the presence of religion on the public stage than by its absence. Condemning biblical plays, the preacher John Northbrooke (1577) declared that "it is better that spiritual things be utterly omitted, than unworthily and unreverently handled and touched." "What fellowship hath righteousness with unrighteousness?" he demanded, "what communion hath light with darkness?" In part, antitheatricalists such as Northbrooke objected to the juxtaposition of Christianity with the "Paganism" that plays regularly invoked, but more intolerable was the very staging of religion, which subjected it to the base players. (Thus some theater haters, such as Stephen Gosson, allowed biblical drama that was intended to be read, not enacted.) North-brooke asserted that players always "mingle scurrility with Divinity" and "exhibit under laughing that which ought to be taught and received reverendly." As the future archbishop Edmund Grindal wrote in 1564, "God's word by their impure mouths is profaned, and turned into scoffs."[47]

To Prynne's mind, playing desecrated the gospel even when the players involved were actual "*Ministers, preaching and praying*" on the stage. *Histrio-Mastix* cites the example of "one *Atkinson* a minister in Bedford the last Christtide, in the Commissary's House there," who "acted a private Interlude, where he made a prayer on the Stage, and chose a Text. *viz.* Acts 10.14. on which he most profanely preached and jested, to the very shame and grief of most that heard him." Since Prynne regarded any recitation of scripture on the stage as the "*highest blasphemy*," his report of Atkinson's profaneness cannot be taken at face value.[48] Yet it would have been entirely traditional for Atkinson "to mingle scurrility with Divinity," as Prynne and his fellow antitheatricalists complained. Before the rise of the public theaters, biblical plays such as the clergyman Lewis Wager's *Life and Repentaunce of Marie Magdalene* (c. 1550–62, published 1566) were often advertised on their title pages as "not only godly, learned and fruitful, but also well furnished with pleasant mirth and pastime."[49] According to the prologue of Thomas Garter's biblical play *Susanna* (c. 1565, published 1578), "nought delights the heart of man on earth, / So much as matters grave and sad, if they be mixt with mirth." Consequently, *Susanna* opens with the Devil bellowing for his "crooked knave" of a son Ill Report, who retaliates by calling his father a "shitten slave." *Marie Magdalene* has even coarser moments: Infidelity invites Mary to play on his "goodly pipe," "so big that your hand can it not gripe," while he later denounces Christ as both a "foolish ass" and a "dog."[50]

For Wager, such crudeness counted as "godly mirth." His view, it seems, was that occasional profaneness kept the audience (particularly the less capable, as Heywood would say) from becoming dulled with serious courses; it baited the clergyman's hook. Although he claimed to be a "learned clerk" whose plays taught religion and virtue "learnedly," Wager nonetheless considered himself to be writing for the uneducated too: "In this matter which we are about to recite, / The ignorant may learn what is true belief, / Whereof the Apostles of Christ do largely write."[51] Framing the play as in part a humble précis of scripture was itself a traditional act. The clergyman John Bale's earlier Protestant *Comedy Concernynge Thre Lawes, of Nature, Moses, and Christ* (1538; revised c. 1547 and 1562), for example, ends with the Ten Commandments rendered "briefly" in verse. Still earlier, an anecdote in the pre-Reformation *Hundred Mery Talys* (c. 1526) tells of a parish priest, "no great clerk nor graduate of the university," who concluded a sermon on "the twelve articles of the Creed" by informing his parishioners, "And if you believe not me, then for a more surety & sufficient authority, go your way to coventry, and there you shall see them all played in corpus christi play." (The moral of the tale is sympathetic to the priest and to the uneducated generally: "they that understand no latin may learn to know the twelve articles of the faith.")[52] Prynne never tells us exactly what Atkinson preached and jested, but if Atkinson's mirth suggests that he thought of himself as stooping to the capacities of his audience, his choice of text suggests that he also thought of himself as teaching fundamental Christian doctrine. Acts 10 ends with Peter's sermon at Joppa; according to Archbishop Edwin Sandys (1585), "all matter needful to salvation is comprised in it. He that hath taken out this lesson, needeth not to learn another."[53]

An even more inclusivist topic in Acts 10 than the matter of Peter's sermon is its audience: Thomas Taylor (1612) referred to the sermon as "the First General calling of the Gentiles," and the specific verse that Atkinson chose to expound represents a key moment in Peter's conversion to the idea that he ought to broaden his evangelism this way.[54] At Joppa, Peter has a vision in which "heaven opened, and a certain vessel descending unto him, as it had been a great sheet knit at the four corners, and let down to the earth: [12] Wherein were all manner of fourfooted beasts of the earth, and wild beasts, and creeping things, and fowls of the air. [13] And there came a voice to him, Rise, Peter; kill, and eat. [14] *But Peter said, Not so, Lord; for I have never eaten any thing that is common or unclean*" (emphasis added). The voice rebukes him: "What God hath cleansed, that call not thou common." When the vision has passed, Peter is invited to the house of the Roman centurion Cornelius, "a just man, and one that feareth God," and here Peter realizes what the vision and voice had been trying to teach him: "Ye know how that it is an unlawful thing for a man that is a Jew to keep company, or come unto one of another nation; but God hath showed me that I should not call any man common or unclean." Peter begins his sermon on this inclusivist note: "Of a truth I perceive that God is no respecter of persons: But in every nation he that feareth him, and worketh righteousness, is accepted with him." As Taylor remarks, Peter thus comes to embrace the truth expressed by Paul in his letter to the Ephesians: that Christ "brake down all partition walls."[55]

For Prynne and his fellow antitheatricalists, plays broke down walls the way rot does: they blighted "the whole body and soul with pollutions." Playgoers were consequently reprehended as "an unclean generation"; "come out from among them," Northbrooke exhorted his readers, "touch no unclean thing."[56] In *Marie Magdalene*, Wager associates such fears of contamination with Christ's enemies. Condemning from the start the "proud arrogancy," "envy," and "evil will" of spectators who have been "offended" by the mixture of "virtues with vice" on the stage, Wager anticipates his dramatization of Infidelity, Malicious Judge, and Simon the Pharisee, who are all appalled that Christ would allow Mary to wash his feet: "for persons defiled, / Ought not among the just to intromit, / But from their company should be exiled." Mary understands that Christ has abolished such scruples: "Let no sinner be he never in so great despair. / Though he were sinful and abominable, / Let him come, and he will make him fair." In his prologue Wager emphasizes that Mary never ceased "to show her self a sinner" even after Christ had exorcised the "unclean" spirits from her, because only pharisees pretend that they are entirely "just, holy, and pure," and it is just such "hypocrites," Wager believes, who attack the stage for enacting vice: "Fain would they have their wickedness still concealed / Therefore maliciously against us they be set." "Against *us*": perhaps Wager's most powerful defense of unclean mixtures on the stage was to join the "faculty" of players without abandoning holy orders or renouncing his "profession" of faith.[57]

Atkinson staged a private interlude, so it is unclear how far he would have carried his own identification with commercial actors—"these uncircumcised Philistines," as Stephen Gosson calls them.[58] But Acts 10 would have enabled Atkinson to thematize more than the mingling of the learned with the ignorant, or of preaching with jesting, or of the outwardly holy with the outwardly profane. Peter's extension of the gospel to Gentile as well as Jew would have suited another conventional topic for Renaissance English plays, the most controversial form of inclusivism defended by the established church: a moderate reformation.

Of all Protestant countries, wrote Edwin Sandys (son of the archbishop) in his *Europae Speculum* (1599), England was "the only Nation that took the right way of justifial Reformation," insofar as it was motivated by "no humor of affecting contrariety, but a charitable endeavor rather of conformity with the Church of Rome, in whatsoever they thought not gainsaying to the express Law of God." Puritans demanded instead that the church be purged of "popish superstitions"; as Anthony Gilby (1581) put it, "Let us not mix the Jews with the Gentiles."[59] But apologists maintained that a reformed church should open its doors to any potential converts, however uneducated, sinful, or even popish they might currently be; if Paul had made himself all things to all men, so should the church strive to accommodate Catholics in all matters of secondary concern—*adiaphora*, "things indifferent"—while gradually weaning them from the old ways. For instance, when faced with the resistance of certain conservative worshippers to taking "common bread" in communion rather than the "wafer" that Catholics had always used, Burghley and Walsingham (1580) advised the bishop in charge "to teach them, that are weak in conscience, in esteeming of the wafer bread; not to make difference. But if their weakness continue, it were not amiss, in our opinions, charitably to tolerate them, as children, with milk."[60]

Gilby and his fellows condemned such accommodationist indulgence as "politic" in the worst sense: "all this," Gilby told the authorities, "is to provide for your own quietness, your own safeties, & your own bellies." According to the puritan Robert Bolton (1625), the "moderation" of "civil" Christians amounted to no religion at all.[61] Yet conformist churchmen countered that a stricter reformation would violate not only charity but also the deep consensus among Christians of all sects on the doctrine that mattered. "Sith we all agree that by the sacrament Christ doth really and truly in us perform his promise," Hooker argued in the *Lawes*, "why do we vainly trouble ourselves with so fierce contentions whether by consubstantiation or else by transubstantiation the sacrament itself be first possessed with Christ or no? a thing which no way can either further or hinder us howsoever it stand." In terms radical enough for Atheos to appreciate, Hooker concluded: "Take therefore that wherein all agree and then consider by itself what cause why the rest in question should not rather be left as superfluous than urged as necessary."[62] Likewise, Ussher's *Briefe Declaration* maintains that if we should compare all "the several professions of Christianity" in the world and "put by the points wherein they did differ one from another, and gather into one body the rest of the articles wherein they all did generally agree: we should find, that in those propositions which without all controversy are universally received in the whole Christian world, so much truth is contained as, being joined with holy obedience, may be sufficient to bring a man unto everlasting salvation." Paradoxically, it was Rome's failure to appreciate this consensus on fundamentals, church apologists claimed, that had sparked the Reformation in the first place; as Laud (1639) put it, "if the Church of Rome, since she grew to her greatness, had not been so . . . particular in determining too many things, and making them matters of necessary belief, which had gone for many hundreds of years before, only for things of pious opinion, Christendom, I persuade my self, had been in happier peace at this day, than, I doubt, we shall ever live to see it."[63] Laud echoes a passage from Erasmus's *Epistles* (1515) in which Erasmus urges Rome to insist only on those articles of faith that "are clearly laid down in Holy Writ or without which the system of our salvation cannot stand. For this a few truths are enough [pauca sufficiunt], and the multitude are more easily persuaded of their truth if they are few." Undergirding such doctrinal minimalism for Erasmus was an irenicism that he regarded as the fundamental Christian truth: as he declared in a later letter (1523), "the sum and substance of our religion is peace and concord," but this "can hardly remain the case unless we define as few matters as possible and leave each individual's judgment free on many questions."[64]

When ecumenical clergymen such as John Donne (c. 1615) defended not only the church's liturgical accommodations of papists but also "that sound true opinion, that in all Christian professions there is a way to salvation," they roused the fury of Protestant and Catholic sectarians alike. He "is not fit for the Kingdom of God," exclaimed the former Jesuit Richard Sheldon in his Paul's Cross sermon (1625), "who like some *Godless Adiaphorizer,* may either say in his heart or speak with his mouth, that any man (so he profess *Christ,* believe on *Christ*) may be saved in such his faith and profession, be it *Popish,* be it *Muscovish;* be it *Pelagian,* be it *Donatian,* be it of any other, *falsely named, form of Faith whatsoever."* In his *Short Treatise* (1605), the future Jesuit John Radford denounced "Adiaphorists, Neuters, and such as say they may be saved in any Sect or Religion" for making of the church "as it were a linsey woolsey medley garment for themselves awhile to mask in, till they might if it were possible rob & spoil her of all virtues, and heavenly treasures."[65] Radford here refers to the Mosaic injunction against "a garment mingled of linen and woolen"; he was far from the only polemicist to link ecumenicalism with unclean mixtures, as of Gentile and Jew. Sheldon claimed that to believe *"Rome* and the Reformed *Churches* agree in the substance of Religion" was "to dream of the uniting of *Sion* and *Babylon;* of *Egypt,* and *Hierusalem,"* or as the puritan Thomas Sutton (1616) put it, "to speak, half in the language of *Canaan,* and half in the language of *Ashdod."*[66]

Like opposition to the misceline congregations and liturgy of the English church, this hatred of English ecumenicalism drew the special attention of theater people, who, as we have seen, were also denounced for yoking light to darkness—often by the very writers criticizing the church. (The same year that Sutton condemned those *"Laodiceans"* who "would make an atonement between the religion of Protestant & Papist *sacra prophanis,"* he did not scruple to single out the actor-playwright Nathan Field "and some other of my quality" from the pulpit, Field claimed, "and directly to our faces in the public assembly to pronounce us damned.")[67] In his *Timber: Or, Discoveries* (published 1641), Jonson condemned religious disputatiousness in terms borrowed from Erasmus's response to Luther, *De libero arbitrio* (1524); Jonson's "Execration Upon *Vulcan"* (published 1640) praised "those wiser Guides" in divinity "whom Faction had not drawn to study sides."[68] Drummond famously decided that Jonson was "for any religion as being versed in both." But Jonson's impeccably anglican "son" Cartwright denounced religious controversy and factionalism just as the tergiversating Jonson did. Cartwright's translation (c. 1640) of Grotius's elegy on Arminius extols the Christian "Whose pure refined Moderation / Condemn'd of all, it self condemneth none; / Who keeping Modest Limits now doth please / To speak for truth, now holds his Tongue for Peace." Such holy time-servers, Cartwright concludes, are the ones who fervently pray that the church will be freed "of mixt dissensions, that *Christ's* City be / Link'd and united in one amity."[69]

Jonson's own desire to break down sectarian walls is registered in the very notion of his "sons" or "Tribe." This is hard to fathom for the obvious reason that tribes are clannish by definition: thus, in Jonson's *Catiline* (1611) Cicero contrasts them to a "universal concourse." Moreover, Jonson's other uses of *tribe* are invariably derisive, as in his references to the satanic "tribe of Brokers" in *The Devil Is an Ass* or the "sooty Tribe" of Alchemists in *Mercury Vindicated:* a tribe in these instances is a faceless band, a kind of select herd. That is how Jonson's admirer, the clergyman-playwright Peter Hausted (1632), envisions puritans: "my tribe with the short hair and long ears."[70] For such satirists, the idea of a tribe perfectly captured the vile elitism that had supposedly led puritans to "contemn and despise all those that be not of their faction as polluted, and not worthy to be saluted or kept company with." In *The Weeding of Covent Garden*, Jonson's "son" Brome presents the puritanical "tribe" as a contradiction in terms, "the brethren of the separation." Why of all things, then, would Jonson choose to think of his own circle as a tribe? Commenting on Jonson's "Epistle answering to one that asked to be Sealed of the Tribe of Ben" (1623), Robert Smuts remarks that the Tribe "looks curiously like a courtly counterpart to the puritan concept of the community of saints."[71]

The puzzle is made even stranger by the pointed biblical resonances of Jonson's terminology. The phrase "sealed of the Tribe of Ben" echoes the seventh chapter of Revelation, which relates that an angel "sealed a hundred and forty and four thousand of all the tribes of the children of Israel," the last of which were the twelve thousand "sealed" of "the tribe of Benjamin." This styling of Jonson's circle as Jews further assimilates them to the conformist caricature of puritans. In his "Exhortation" (c. 1618), Jonson's friend Corbet imagines puritans to be railing in their "Synagogue" against "the *Vanities of Gentiles*"; a character in Robert Davenport's *A New Trick to Cheat the Divell* (c. 1624–39) calls the puritan "a Jewish Christian, and a Christian Jew." Both critics mean to stigmatize the scripturalism and scrupulousness of puritans as well as their tribalism. Bishop Sanderson in 1624 draws on Peter's vision at Joppa to censure the "Judaism" of puritans who spurn the cap and surplice as "rags and relics of idolatry": "In that large sheet of the creatures, which reacheth from Heaven to the earth, whatsoever we find, we may freely kill and eat, and use every other way to our comforts without scruple. God having cleansed all, we are not to call or esteem any thing common or unclean: God having created all good, we are to refuse nothing."[72] In *The Vow Breaker* (c. 1625), the "puritan" Marmaduke Joshua takes his scruples so far as to attempt to hang his cat for her "unclean" killing of a mouse on the sabbath.[73] It is with similar lampoons in mind that "Rabbi" Busy in Jonson's *Bartholomew Fair* (1614) decides to attend the fair and eat pig, "to profess our hate, and loathing of *Judaism*, whereof the brethren stand taxed."[74] The Jewishness of the Tribe aside, Jonson's talk of "sealing" also ties his circle to puritans. According to Hooker, puritans believe the Spirit "doth seal them to be God's children"; in Jonson's *Alchemist*, Ananias distinguishes between the "profane" and "the brethren" who "have the seal."[75] Since Gifford's *Sermons* (1596) identify the seal of Revelation 7 as "the spirit of adoption, . . . wherewith all the elect are sealed," even Jonson's "adoption" of "sons" seems to align his Tribe with puritanical exclusiveness.[76]

Of course, the self-deprecating mirth of these connections is meant to signal a saving difference between the Tribe and their "sober, scurvy, precise" counterparts. In the "Tribe" poem itself, the acid "Test" for entry turns out to be good fellowship, nothing more: "First, give me faith, who know / My self a little. I will take you so, / As you have writ your self. Now stand, and then, / Sir, you are Sealed of the Tribe of *Ben*." As earlier lines make clear, however, this is good fellowship of a particular kind, separated from the boors who either "live in the wild Anarchy of Drink" or else refuse to speak well "of any Company but that they are in."[77] In other words, the Tribe as Jonson sees it falls somewhere between pot-companions and sectarians, although it bears no marks that would strongly distinguish it from either group, whether in the final lines of the "Tribe" poem or in the "Leges Convivales" (c. 1624) that Jonson prescribed for the meetings of his circle in the Apollo Room of The Devil and St. Dunstan's tavern.[78] The "Leges" begins as Michael Drayton's comparable "Sacrifice to Apollo" (1619) had, by dictating who may and may not enter the fellowship of the alehouse, yet Jonson softens Drayton's terms considerably. Whereas Drayton admitted the "Priests of Apollo" and "debarr'd" the "profane Vulgar," Jonson (in Alexander Brome's translation of 1664) discourages "Dunces, Fools, sad, sordid men," while inviting the "learned, civil, merry" ("choice *Ladies*" are welcome, too). In both poems, wine is the sacrament that unites Apollo's celebrants, yet where Drayton had required his priests to drink "in Draughts profound,"

Jonson insists on a "moderate" cup: "On serious things or sacred let's not touch / With sated heads or bellies." Jonson, in short, wants his circle to be both jolly and highminded, select and inclusive, to mingle the sober man and the good fellow as the "Leges" conjoins "sacris" and "poti," or as the Tribe's tavern juxtaposes the Devil with St. Dunstan.[79] Fittingly, the "Leges" was first published (1636) from a copy made at the Devil by a clergyman.[80]

While Prynne would have reviled Jonson's talk of "adopting" and "sealing" as the most profane jesting, the "Leges" suggests that Jonson used such biblical language not merely to mock puritans but also to cross their efforts to divorce the sacred from the profane. The Tribe, the fellowship invoked by this godly mirth, represents Jonson's countervision of a brotherhood broadly rather than precisely drawn, whose ties are no less binding for their looseness. In Revelation 7 the tribe of Benjamin similarly stands as it were on the hinge between particularist and universalist accounts of salvation. It caps the list of the twelve times twelve thousand sealed "of the children of Israel," but it also immediately precedes John's sight of "a great multitude, which no man could number, of all nations, and kindreds, and people, and tongues," before the throne of Christ. In his *Image of Both Churches* (c. 1545), Bale views this sequence of verses as teaching that salvation was meant "not for one country, but for the whole world. First were the Israelites named, forasmuch as they were the peculiar nation whom God first chose for his own people. Israel is mine eldest son, saith the Lord. After them followed in course the Gentiles as the younger son, that we should thereby know"—and here Bale quotes Peter's sermon—"that all people, which fear God and work righteousness, are accepted unto him."[81] As a biblical allusion, Jonson's adoption of sons also points in universalist as well as particularist directions. Paul (a Benjaminite) uses the term "adoption" to signal both the election of the Jewish "remnant" to which he claimed to belong *and* the salvation of converted Gentiles (Rom. 8–11). In describing himself as a "son" of Jonson's "Adoption, not his lust," the playwright Randolph (c. 1628–35) profanely jests on Paul's assurance to the Gentiles that while they may not be God's children "in the flesh," they are his in "the Spirit of adoption."[82] Jonson's "Elegy" (c. 1633) on Venetia Digby offers a more sober treatment of this inclusivist tenet, giving thanks that Christ should "adopt us Heirs, by grace, who were of those / Had lost our selves." Liberally vague in its vision of salvation, the "Elegy" replaces "tribe" with what Jonson seems to regard as a more open and capacious yet still cohesive unit of fellowship: according to the poem, Heaven is where "all the happy souls, that ever were, / Shall meet with gladness in one *Theater*."[83]

With *The Staple of News* (1626), whose fourth act is set in the Apollo

Room of the Devil, Jonson opened his tribal council chamber to his theater audience, and with *The Magnetic Lady* (1632) he strove to incorporate his audience into his Tribe not only by adapting his rhetoric to them but also by promoting the cause of Christian unity among them. Speaking almost autobiographically for Jonson (as a "Scholar" and "Soldier" who has "been employed, / By some the greatest Statesmen o' the kingdom"), the character Compass begins *The Magnetic Lady* by describing the social arena in which he exercises his "wit":

> I'm lodged hard by,
> Here at a noble Lady's house i'th' street,
> The Lady *Loadstone's* (one will bid us welcome)
> Where there are Gentlewomen, and male Guests,
> Of several humors, carriage, constitution,
> Profession too: but so diametral
> One to another, and so much oppos'd,
> As if I can but hold them all together,
> And draw them to a sufferance of themselves,
> But till the Dissolution of the Dinner;
> I shall have just occasion to believe
> My wit is magisterial.[84]

According to Master Probee in the play's opening chorus, such harmonizing of "humors" is an undertaking not only conducive to "the reconciliation of both Churches" but "far greater" than that project, "the quarrel between humors having been much the ancienter, and, in my poor opinion, the root of all Schism and Faction, both in Church and Commonwealth." However whimsical it may sound to the modern reader, this reductive "medicalization" of religious controversy would become thoroughly conventional by the time of the Restoration, when fractiousness would be dismissed as the ravings of "enthusiasm."[85] The prologue to *The Magnetic Lady* thus asks us to see Compass as achieving more than one might otherwise think when he pacifies his dinner mates, and we quickly learn that he accomplishes his ultimately antischismatical work in familiar fashion, by making himself all things to all men:

> suiting so myself
> To company, as honest men and knaves,
> Good-fellows, Hypocrites, all sorts of people,
> Though never so divided in themselves,

Have studied to agree still in the usage,
And handling of me.

That Compass should regard himself rather than his "company" as the beneficiary of their consensus seems to highlight a limitation to Jonson's imitation of Paul, who stressed that in pleasing all men in all things he was "not seeking mine own profit, but the profit of many, that they may be saved" (1 Cor. 10.33). Tension between Jonson's accommodationism and his notorious egotism becomes an explicitly theatrical issue later in *The Magnetic Lady*, when Probee declares that "we come here to behold *Plays*, and censure them, as they are made, and fitted for us; not to beslaver our own thoughts, with censorious spittle tempering the *Poet's* clay, as we were to mould every scene anew": according to Probee, in other words, the responsibility for a successful play rests less with the playwright who fits than with the audience who must submit to being fitted. Reporting how Jonson once "fell down upon his knees" after one of his plays failed "and gave thanks, that he had transcended the capacity of the vulgar," Edmund Gayton (1654), like many another contemporary playgoer, faulted Jonson precisely for his elitist inability to suit himself to company: "men come not to study at a Play-house, but love such expressions and passages, which with ease insinuate themselves into their capacities."[86] Such criticisms, however, only highlight by contrast the intensity of Jonson's commitment to a dramaturgical theory he could not easily practice. *The Magnetic Lady* bears witness to his sense as he wrote the play that he could not justify his theatrical career without presenting Christian reconciliation as part of his purpose, and he could not lay claim to the role of reconciler without presenting himself as all things to all men.[87]

III

According to William Hazlitt (1818), Shakespeare possessed a special "power of communication with all other minds" because "he was the least of an egotist that it was possible to be": "He was nothing in himself; but he was all that others were, or that they could become." These lines echo and do not echo Paul: the difference, as Hazlitt understands it, is that when Shakespeare becomes "like all other men," he has no rhetorical designs on them because he has no particular beliefs to peddle. Thus "Shakespeare discovers in his writings little religious enthusiasm" and likewise has "none of the bigotry of his age." George Santayana (1896) pushed Hazlitt's claims to their logical conclusion: Shakespeare "is remarkable among the greater po-ets," he declared, "for being without a philosophy and without a religion."[88]

Comparison of Shakespeare to his fellow public-theater playwrights does support Hazlitt and Santayana to a degree. Little in Shakespeare's plays matches the anti-Catholic ferocity of Thomas Dekker's *Whore of Babylon* (1606), for instance, or the hatred of puritans expressed in Dekker's *If It Be Not Good, The Devil Is In It* (1611), which ends with hilarity about a deformed puritan soul burning in hell. But Shakespeare is not without polemical edge. The first two *Henry VI* plays (c. 1590) portray Cardinal Beaufort as a "scar-let hypocrite" whose corrupt ambitions help to tear England apart. Even more inflammatory, the king in *King John* (c. 1595) characterizes the pope himself as a "meddling priest" who maintains his "usurped authority" over English affairs only through the "sale" of "corrupted pardon."[89] Not even John's own mother, however, denies that John too rules illegitimately, and, as David Bevington points out, *1 Henry VI* weighs Beaufort's sins "in the bal-ance against other forms of opportunism."[90] The same balancing act occurs when Shakespeare takes aim at puritans. In *Twelfth Night* (c. 1600) the puri-tanical Malvolio is offset by the toss-pot Sir Toby Belch, while in the two *Henry IV* plays (c. 1597) the equally unsavory extremes of Malvolio and Belch meet, as it were, in the figure of the canting drunkard Falstaff.[91] If Shake-speare's plays indicate that he sided with neither papist nor puritan, they also show him striving to resist identification with antipapists and antipuritans.

Recent years have witnessed a resurgence in efforts to shed light on Shakespeare's possible religious views from biographical evidence other than the plays themselves. This new research, the work of E. A. J. Honigmann and Eric Sams in particular, has persuasively demonstrated that Shakespeare was in all likelihood raised a Catholic. Since Shakespeare was born only a few years after Protestantism had been restored as England's official religion, however, such a hypothesis is relatively unsurprising and, what's more, it tells us nothing about Shakespeare's adult beliefs: Donne too was raised a Catholic, yet he went on to become Dean of St. Paul's and a jewel in the crown of the Protestant church.[92] Extant records concerning the religious af-filiations of Shakespeare's family and friends indicate only that Shakespeare, like Compass, was able to suit himself to all sorts of people. While his father and daughter failed to attend services on occasion and were suspected of being "popishly affected," his partners and close friends Heminges and Condell were prominent officeholders in their parish church.[93] The silence of the records about Shakespeare himself suggests that he chose neither path: he seems to have conformed to the established religion, yet he also ap-pears to have kept a low profile at church.[94]

So quiet a devotional life does not make Shakespeare ipso facto an orthodox Protestant, as some scholars have maintained—many another of Shakespeare's contemporaries managed to reconcile a privately held dissenting faith with outward conformity—but it does add to the impression left by his plays that he deplored sectarianism.[95] Shakespeare's puritanical characters are typically divisive figures, longing for a separation from their moral inferiors. Thus Malvolio hopes to "wash off gross acquaintance"; the mock-puritan Falstaff continually gripes about the "villainous company" to which he is subjected; and the "precise" Angelo claims to have rejected Maria because "her reputation was disvalued / In levity." Shakespeare's Catholic bishops and cardinals are more divisive still, sponsoring factiousness on a national and even international scale: the most dangerous of them, the papal legate Pandulph, causes a truce between France and England to be broken and promises sainthood to anyone who assassinates King John.[96]

Opposition to sectarianism can seem sectarian itself, as when Dekker punishes his schismatical puritan with deformity and hellfire.[97] Such antipuritan satire figures prominently in the plays of Jonson, Cartwright, and Mayne, but Shakespeare, more careful to avoid provocation, equivocates about whether his puritanical characters are really puritans at all: in *Twelfth Night* Maria alleges that Malvolio is "sometimes" only "a kind of puritan," while Angelo in *Measure for Measure* (c. 1603) is again merely said to be "precise." The exception proves the rule: having aroused controversy by naming a comic character after the proto-Protestant hero Sir John Oldcastle, who also happened to be the ancestor of prominent puritan aristocrats, Shakespeare changed the character's name to Falstaff and ended *2 Henry IV* by insisting that the "martyr" Oldcastle was a different man. In the context of these attempts to mute his criticism of puritans, Shakespeare's reluctance to preach Christian doctrine seems a mark not of his secularism, as most scholars have claimed, but rather of his fears regarding the potential divisiveness of his religious beliefs. As the moderate puritan Sibbes put it in his *Bruised Reede, and Smoaking Flax* (1630), "In some cases peace by *keeping our faith to our selves*, is of more consequence, than the open discovery of some things we take to be true, considering the weakness of man's nature is such that there can hardly be a discovery of any difference in opinion, without some estrangement of affection." This pious discretion coincides with the advice of Shakespeare's one peace-loving bishop, Cranmer in *Henry VIII* (c. 1612), who also happens to be the only Protestant of the group: "Win straying souls with modesty again," Cranmer urges the "cruel" and "bloody" Catholic Gardiner, "Cast none away."[98]

Shakespeare's reserve signals more than his diplomacy on religious issues, however. Crediting him with what Keats called "negative capability," modern scholarship has treated the "elusiveness" of Shakespeare's "personality" as the hallmark of his secularism; yet the ability to tolerate "uncertainties, Mysteries, doubts," as Keats defined negative capability, was a virtue that Erasmus repeatedly claimed for himself as a Christian.[99] "I take so little pleasure in assertions," Erasmus assured Luther in the preface to *De libero arbitrio*, "that I will gladly seek refuge in Skepticism whenever this is allowed by the inviolable authority of Holy Scripture and the church's decrees"; thus he promised to respond to Luther "as disputant, not as judge; as inquirer, not as dogmatist." For Luther, this cultivation of disinterestedness made Erasmus seem a "Proteus," "the king of amphibology," an "eel," but Erasmus insisted on his singleminded pursuit of Christian unity. "What I write has never been in the service of any party," he assured Jonas in his letter on Luther; "I serve Christ, who belongs to us all [qui communis est omnium]."[100] Sir John Harington, nearly an exact contemporary of Shakespeare, painted a similar picture of his own religious impartiality in his *Tract on the Succession to the Crown* (MS 1602). "I am neither Papist, Protestant, nor Puritan, or a protesting Catholic Puritan [i.e., a Jesuit]," Harington declared; "*Christian* is my name, *Catholic* my surname."[101] Urging the warring sects of the day to "attempt by reason and not by rigor to win the adverse part," Harington exhorted his readers to reject hidebound sectarian thinking generally: "Let not every man imagine he sees all, but that another perhaps hath found somewhat that he hath not heard of." As evidence of his own "moderate mind," Harington professed an Atheos-like faith in fundamentals: "I do heartily believe all the Holy Scripture, and the Creed; I pray the Lord's prayer and other good prayers of the Communion book. I observe the Ten Commandments as well as I can, though not so well as I would, and I hear many sermons & am edified but by a few." In short, Harington portrayed himself as a civil Christian, an accommodationist: "I would be as St. Paul saith of himself in his Master's cause, *Omnibus omnia factus sum ut omnes facerem salvos:* I became all to all, that I might save all."[102]

The most telling evidence of Shakespeare's own accommodationism is his surprisingly sympathetic treatment of friars, who "speak with authority, within the sphere of their religious vocation, and command the respect of the other characters" in the plays they inhabit.[103] Apparent gestures of reconciliation toward the Catholic members of Shakespeare's audience, these tolerable friars also act as reconcilers in the world of their plays: Friar Patrick in *Two Gentlemen of Verona* (c. 1591), Friar Laurence in *Romeo and Juliet* (c. 1595), Friar Francis in *Much Ado about Nothing* (c. 1598), and the various friars of *Measure for Measure* all help to arrange marriages. To ponder why Shakespeare should have assigned this unitive role to friars, rather than bishops, monks, or priests, is to grasp more fully the religious aims that Shakespeare no less than Jonson seems to have regarded as compatible with his commercial efforts to "please all men." What first distinguishes friars from other Catholic clergy is their itinerancy, which, Shakespeare appears to believe, helps free them from parochialism.[104] It also links them with the itinerant players. From the 1570s theatrical companies had played in the "liberty" once occupied by London's Black Friars; Shakespeare's company acquired Blackfriars property in 1596 and opened a playhouse there twelve years later; Shakespeare himself bought the Blackfriars gatehouse. Not only did theater people thus literally take the place of friars in London, they also seem to have felt a kind of professional camaraderie with them: according to Stanley Satz, no positive representation of friars appears anywhere in Elizabethan literature after 1563 *except* in plays.[105] By making his own most important peripatetic friar a pretender—the literally "unreverend and unhallowed" Duke Vincentio of *Measure for Measure*—Shakespeare indicates that he sees friars and players as performing a similar kind of spiritual work, outside of "precise" religious boundaries. Yet Vincentio's actions also imply that Shakespeare regards players as better suited than friars to such an irregular ministry. For like Shakespeare's other friars, the "Duke of dark corners" is addicted to a secretiveness and subterfuge that go against the grain of the friar's proper excursiveness; in *Romeo and Juliet*, Friar Laurence's unwillingness to be discovered even contributes to Juliet's death.[106] Players, by contrast, enact the friars' cozenages on the open stage, in full view of the audience. This obligatory publicity appears to have made them more plausible sponsors of communal reconciliation, to Shakespeare's mind, than their hugger-mugger Catholic counterparts.

But how, aside from avoiding religious controversy, did Shakespeare think his players were to effect such reconciliation? The mere act of drawing thousands of people together on a weekly basis was unprecedented enough, outside of major church services, to make Stubbes fear the theater as the church's rival. For other writers, the relative lack of occasions for mass sociability in Renaissance England made any such event seem a churchlike gathering: so William Fennor (1619) praises even the maypole and alehouse drinking, as Atheos did, for encouraging "honest neighborhood" and "hearty fellowship," no matter what "factious" puritans may say about them.[107] As I will show in chapter 4, throughout the choruses of such plays as *Henry V* (c. 1598) Shakespeare appears to disclose his own belief that players can help forge a similarly congregational fellowship in the theater by encouraging the imaginative participation of their audiences. If community in the theater must be fashioned without the aid of preaching, so much the better, Shakespeare's reticence about religion implies. Just as Nashe urged ministers to speak within the compass of the five senses and Jonson shifted the work of Christian reconciliation from doctrinal questions to the more uncontroversial and ordinary matter of "humors," so Shakespeare seems to have conceived that players could spiritually unite audiences through a shared examination of human "frailty"—especially erotic turmoil, the carnal simulacrum of Christian fellowship. "[F]or young Charbon the puritan and old Poysam the papist," jokes the clown in *All's Well That Ends Well* (c. 1604), "howsome'er their hearts are severed in religion," their cuckold "heads are both one." What appears to have recommended friars to Shakespeare besides their itinerancy is their association with confession, which Shakespeare presents as performed in his theater the way some Protestants argued it should be: not in "private" or in "secret," but before "the open audience of the whole people."[108]

Several critics have maintained that Friar Laurence's own reticence about Christian doctrine gravely compromises him as a "ghostly confessor": for instance, Laurence counsels Romeo to regard "philosophy," not religion, as "adversity's sweet milk," while to Juliet he "utters not a word of Christian comfort in the tomb."[109] If the report of one Tribe member is to be believed, Jonson ultimately came to see his accommodationist drama as similarly misguided: George Morley (d. 1684), later Bishop of Winchester, claimed that he "often" visited Jonson in his "last sickness" and "as often heard him repent of his profaning the Scripture in his Plays, and that with horror."[110] One might plausibly view *The Tempest* as Shakespeare's indirect version of this confession, in its implicit linkage of his "art" with the magic "book" that Prospero drowns and the ale "book" that Stephano sacrilegiously substitutes for the Bible ("kiss the book," Stephano says to Caliban). But Shakespeare worried throughout his career that a religion of the book might be inherently elitist, as *The Tempest* suggests. Once Prospero renounces his "secret" textual "studies," he no longer plays the *deus absconditus* who "torments" sinners through "invisible" power. Redefining his "project" as more confessional than vengeful ("They being penitent, / The sole drift of my purpose doth extend / Not a frown further"), he reveals himself to his enemies, kenotically, in the guise of the resurrected Christ: "For more assurance that a living prince / Does now speak to thee, I embrace thy body." At the end of *The Tempest*, then, Prospero aligns himself with a "sociable" or "fellowly" Christian theology that refuses to disown "flesh and blood." This, it seems, is the religion that Shakespeare believed he had himself espoused in tying his art, as Prospero ultimately does, to bodies instead of books.[111]

The climactic proof of Prospero's new fellowly view of religion in *The Tempest* is his arranging a marriage, which he emphasizes will not be consummated until "all sanctimonious ceremonies may / With full and holy rite be minister'd," well after the action of the play is done. Shakespeare's too-worldly friars may never stage such a "full" enactment of religion; like Prospero, however, they lay the groundwork for it, and their strengths as well as shortcomings appear to be linked, in Shakespeare's mind, not only with their peripatetic liberty but with their "barefoot" lowliness as well.[112] In this respect, too, Shakespeare's friars illuminate his conception of players. If a stake in moderate reformation, doctrinal minimalism, and evangelical discretion enabled Shakespeare to adapt his theater to the restrictions that censorship placed on the staging of religion, so too did a belief in plays as performing relatively humble religious functions. This willingness to stoop low, as Ussher described catechizing, amounted to more for Shakespeare than the modesty Jonson lacked, more even than Ussher's pride in skillful foundation-building. No bishops published elegies on Shakespeare, and it may be that he kept his distance from such higher powers in order to avoid the partisan view of church affairs to which Jonson, along with an increasing number of younger playwrights, succumbed. Meaning to celebrate the era before the puritans closed the theaters, when bishops and theater people had supposedly worked together to teach religion and preserve good Christian fellowship, the Tribe member Alexander Brome (1653) instead unwittingly implicated players in the sectarianism that Shakespeare hoped his theater could help cure:

> Time was, when Plays were justly valu'd, when
> Poets could laugh away the Crimes of men.
> And by Instructive Recreation teach
> More in one hour, than some in ten do preach.
> But Times are chang'd; and 'tis worth our note,
> Bishops, and Players both suffer'd in one Vote.
> And reason good, for [the puritans] had cause to fear 'em,
> One did suppress their Schisms, and t'other jeer 'em.[113]

IV

Just as he aimed to represent true Christian faith as larger than any one sect, so Shakespeare strove to dramatize true Christian fellowship as larger than any one nation. In *1 Henry VI*, the godly young king decries the war between France and England as a civil war within Christendom: "I always thought /

It was both impious and unnatural / That such immanity and bloody strife / Should reign among professors of one faith." "The Sea divideth english men from french men," writes Erasmus in his *Querela Pacis* (1517) or *Complaint of Peace* (translated 1559), "but it divideth not the society and fellowship of religion." Events in *1 Henry VI* quickly demonstrate the naivete of Henry's supranationalism, however, for the man he chooses as peacemaker with France is the newly installed cardinal Winchester, whose first act in office is to pay a papal legate "the sum of money which I promised / Should be delivered to his Holiness / For clothing me in these grave ornaments." According to the play, it seems, a popish Christendom is united by cupidity, not faith, if it is united by anything at all.[114]

Yet throughout his plays, in pagan as well as Christian settings, Shakespeare never ceases to drive home the point that international wars "boil down to civil wars." The foreign conquest from which Caesar returns at the start of *Julius Caesar* is the defeat of his fellow Roman Pompey; in *Hamlet*, the Danish ghost risen in the arms he once bore against Norway and Poland goads his son to kill his own countrymen; Macbeth turns from slaughtering Norwegians to murdering his king. Even the comedies adhere to this scenario of warfare internalized. One of the earliest, *The Comedy of Errors*, tells a story borrowed from Plautus's *Menaechmi* of twin brothers who have made their homes in separate city-states; Shakespeare adds the twist that these cities, Syracuse and Ephesus, are at war. As Shakespeare's play opens, the Duke of Ephesus sentences the Syracusan father of the brothers to death, a verdict he blames on "the mortal and intestine jars / 'Twixt thy seditious countrymen and us." Editors of the *Comedy* generally agree with Anne Barton that the words "intestine" and "seditious" do not "fit the context," but as Erasmus notes in his *Complaint*, "Plato denied it to be called war, that the Grecians should move against the greeks. [I]t is sedition saith he."[115] Loyalty to a supranational Christendom as well as to its leader caused the papal legate Reginald Pole (1555) to rebuke Thomas Cranmer for his "seditious" reference to papal authority as "a foreign power." By changing the scene of Plautus's play from Epidamnum to Ephesus, Shakespeare gives the question of supranational allegiance in the Duke's speech a Christian resonance: as Patricia Parker has noted, the *Comedy* powerfully alludes to Paul's claim in Ephesians that Christ broke down all partition walls. Plato and Paul aside, however, a war between cities represented by twin brothers cannot help but look fratricidal, which is how Erasmus in the *Complaint* asks his readers to see all human conflict, especially among Christians: "Are they less brethren whom Christ hath coupled than they whom consanguinity hath joined?"[116]

Shakespeare's preoccupation with the idea of a fellowship that exceeds national boundaries seems all the more striking when compared to the relatively limited geographical scope of plays written by Jonson and his Tribe. Yet the Shakespearean conversion of international into civil war displaces consideration of supranational communities even as it manifests belief in them. In the chapters that follow, I will try to show how Shakespeare actually lays the basis for the seemingly more exclusive vision of fellowship in Jonson; by the same token, Jonson and his disciples concentrate rather than abandon Shakespeare's efforts to think about broad communal affiliations in the terms of narrow ones. What produced this obscurely expansive particularism in the theater of Shakespeare and his imitators, I will argue, was the espousal of an Erasmian inclusiveness by a schismatic church and a stigmatized stage. To portray the true church as larger than any nation, the theater people had first to establish that their nation and vocation even belonged in the true church. And Shakespeare was the first English playwright to offer a compelling dramatization of how these separate tasks might be combined. In the "Henriad," where Prince Hal sounds "the very base-string of humility" and then declares himself "of all humors," Shakespeare treats fraternization with scapegraces as the key to understanding England's place in the Christian world at large. While Hal's father Henry IV ineffectually struggles to resolve "intestine" conflict by reminding his people of the Crusades and their lapsed duty to Christendom, Hal finds companionship in an alehouse, and then finds a way through the alehouse to rid England of civil war, recover its empire, and strike a "Christian-like accord" with France—all as the "king of good fellows."[117]

Part One

⌒

ENGLAND AND CHRISTENDOM

Rogue Nationalism

Two Religions cannot be suffered in one kingdom: for diversities cause factions, garboils, and civil wars, which never end but with the subversion of the commonwealth. The tranquility of all estates consisteth in the union and consent of the inhabitants. Take away this union, and it is but a den for rovers and thieves.

—William Vaughan, *The Golden-grove* (1608)

Once Henry VIII had officially supplanted the pope as the head of the English church, praise of England required a special ingenuity. Propagandists used to the criticism that England was physically and culturally isolated from the rest of Christendom now had to explain why it was good for England to be spiritually isolated as well. This ideological dilemma had, moreover, two distinct yet confusable parts. The first concerned English power, and, to judge from a swiftly established conventionality of response, it proved the easier part to handle. Drawing upon a biblical discourse of paradoxes in which the lowly, weak, and foolish subdue the proud, strong, and wise, English Protestants generally did not bother to deny England's smallness in comparison to its Catholic enemies, but rather exalted the material deficiencies of their nation into signs of England's spiritual greatness. Just as David had prevailed against Goliath, so, Protestant writers maintained, England would prevail against Rome. As Joseph Hall (1613) put it, "If any nation under heaven could either parallel or second Israel in the favors of God, this poor little island of ours is it."[1]

When the issue thought to be raised by Henry's schism was not strength but community, however, a Protestant England proved much harder to defend. How, Catholics demanded, could the English possibly justify deserting the rest of Christendom? Not only had they "wander[ed] from the way of truth," they had also "departed from the company of all nations," withdrawn themselves "from the unity of the whole world." Years before the break with Rome, English writers had already begun to insist that England possessed the same right to self-rule as any other "empire," yet this nationalist-sounding doctrine remained (as the recourse to an imperial model suggests) embryonic and vague. Modern historians who exaggerate its clarity or authority at the time render us incapable of appreciating how seriously English Protestants regarded the Catholic indictment of their religious "singularity."[2] Apologists for England regularly denied the charge: England, they argued, only *appeared* to have separated itself from Christendom, when in fact it had successfully rejoined the "invisible" church from which the English had long been "wanderers, walking astray," while "under the tuition of romish pastors."[3] The truth was that English Protestants remained more detached from even the Protestant Continent than their professed devotion to a supranational church allowed them to justify; as the historian Franklin Baumer points out, "English interest in confessional agreement rarely got beyond the writing and talking stage." Surveying the state of European religion at the end of the century, the Elizabethan Protestant Sir Edwin Sandys (1599) devoted most of his time to denouncing Catholic corruption, but he also confessed that Europe's Protestants were "as severed or rather scattered troops, each drawing a diverse way, . . . without any bond to knit them, their forces or courses in one."[4]

Faced with the massive international fellowship of the papists, on the one hand, and their own "small scattered company," on the other, some English Protestants decided the best way to clear their nation from the charge of wandering was first to admit it, and they were aided in this task, once again, by a biblical emphasis on the disparity between worldly appearances and otherworldly reality. Anthony Gilby (1547) defended the English by insisting that God had always given light "only to a few whom he had chosen and long afore appointed, even to the weak abjects and castaways in the sight of the world." Bishop Hooper (1547) likened the true church to "Daniel sitting among the lions": "Deliver it out of the cave yet shall it wander upon the earth as a contemptible thing, of no estimation, not knowing where to rest her head." The most famous formulation of this Protestant self-defense appeared at the end of the century in the first half of Spenser's *Faerie Queene* (1590), which depicted the one true church as an "*Errant damozell*" reduced to "wandring in woods and forrests," wherever "wilde fortune" would lead her.[5]

When the castaways under consideration were English Protestants and the settled multitude were foreign Catholics, such championing of vagrancy blended nicely with the national interest; even England's detachment from foreign Protestants could appear less troubling. But what happened when the relevant multitude were Protestant and English, and the castaways were an internal matter? The problem was not simply the unsettling presence within England of a large number of alienated papists. From the start of the Reformation, Catholic writers had warned the English that by breaking "the unity of Christ's Church," they would soon be "cumbered with infinity of sects and opinions pernicious to the state"; having "neither head, order, obedience, neither yet certain rules or grounds whereon to stay," the English were doomed to "run headlong ye wot no more than your guides whither." As early as the Admonition Controversy in the 1570s, English Protestants could not easily deny that such gloomy prognostications were coming true; by 1589 the future Archbishop of Canterbury, Richard Bancroft, had to concede that "so many sectaries and schismatics" were now plaguing England "as that in very deed diverse do revolt daily to Papistry, many are become merely Atheists, and the best do stand in some sort at a gaze."[6]

With the church in such frightening disarray, the very fabric of English society seemed to many Elizabethans in danger of unraveling too. Protestant preachers may have denounced those malcontents who blamed a felt increase in social disorder on "the new learning and preaching of the gospel," but they rarely denied that such a deterioration had occurred. Catholic polemicists only swelled the ranks of Protestants inveighing against the most visible sign of trouble: "the Infinite numbers of the Idle wandering people and robbers of the land." Never before, complained writers of every persuasion, had the highways been "so replenished with thieves & robbers," nor had there ever been "such numbers of beggars in all parts of the realm."[7] Although modern research has tended to confirm that the number of "masterless men" in England did indeed rise throughout the sixteenth century, recent historians of nationalism have continued to gloss over the fears of national disintegration expressed in Elizabethan social criticism, just as they continue to ignore the strong investment of many Elizabethans in the old ideal of a supranational Christian church.[8] Yet even so fervently Protestant and chauvinist an Elizabethan as John Norden (1596) called the final decade of the sixteenth century "the time of trial" for England: while in Norden's view an ever growing mass of idle drifters were roaming the countryside ("to the great detriment of our quiet abiding in this standing house of our common-weal"), "swarms of false prophets" were at the same time flying "everywhere" throughout England, inciting the people to join them as "vagabonds from the church of God."[9]

Our anachronistic assumptions about English nationalism have blinded us not only to such misgivings about the nation in Renaissance England but also to the search for answers these misgivings produced. Both trends figure prominently in the English history play *1 Sir John Oldcastle* (1599), where an opening clash between Catholics who denounce Wycliffe as "a knave, a schismatic" and proto-Protestants who support Wycliffe "'gainst the Papacy, / And the religion catholic, maintained / Through the most part of Europe at this day" leads to one dramatization of vagabondage after another. In the play's second scene, for instance, Catholics condemn the "Protestants" as "thieves and rebels" who "meet in fields and solitary groves"; but then one of the Protestants' most vocal enemies, the priest Sir John, turns out to be a drifter and thief himself, a rogue. The third scene presents "a crew of seely knaves / And sturdy rogues" who are begging alms of Oldcastle; according to his servant Harpoole, Oldcastle "maintains more vagabonds / Than all the noblemen in Kent beside." Next, a Protestant fleeing from the play's initial brawl arrives at Oldcastle's gate in the guise of "some desperate rogue," and Oldcastle, a Protestant in "conscience" rather than action, is soon caught up in religious controversy against his will. "Turned out of doors" by his Catholic adversary the Bishop of Rochester, Oldcastle wanders ever further from the settled life his name once epitomized: on the run, he and his wife are forced to disguise themselves in the clothes of a Lancashire "carrier" and his wife, who exclaim that "rogues" have robbed them; Harpoole switches clothes with a "bloody rogue" of an Irishman, who has killed and robbed his English master, only to be robbed in turn by Sir John; the Oldcastles are then arrested for the murder committed by the masterless Irishman, who has since been mistaken for Harpoole as Harpoole has been mistaken for him; and finally, the discovery of the true culprit notwithstanding, Oldcastle retains his disguise as carrier and flees from England to Wales in the company of the Protestant to whom he had earlier given refuge. Even the king of *Oldcastle's* England, we learn, has descended to "roguery." Although Henry V swears that he has "reclaimed" himself from the "villainous" company of Falstaff, he still takes to the road in disguise, and his enemies consider him to be more deeply enmeshed in crime than before: a "false intruder" who has usurped the crown, they believe, Henry now "spoils" the goods of his subjects.[10]

So pervasive is the taint of roguery throughout *Oldcastle* that it strangely comes to represent the grounds for a new sort of fellow feeling in England. A fight between Harpoole and Sir John is averted when Sir John admits he is a thief but then points out that Harpoole and Henry V were once thieves too; Harpoole, tickled, calls Sir John "the madd'st priest that ever I met with," and Sir John replies, "Give me thy hand; thou art as good a fellow." This amalgamation of the good fellow with the roving thief is reinforced in a later confrontation between Sir John and Henry himself.[11] Traveling the "walk" his "old thieves" were "wont to keep," the disguised king is waylaid by the highwayman-priest, who identifies himself as "a good fellow"; "So am I, too," Henry replies. Sir John robs the king, but afterward the king fleeces Sir John at a dice game that the still disguised Henry hosts "for all good fellows' companies," and the counterstroke ends up reconciling the two. As much as these scenes deepen the impression that an England torn by religious strife is disintegrating before our eyes, they also secure the king's place at the head of an odd new English coalition, a fellowship crossing party lines—the assortment of rogues we meet throughout the play. Some Catholics allowed that the schismatic English had indeed achieved a certain measure of cohesiveness; as Thomas Harding (1565) put it, "such unity is oftentimes in thieves." Yet if *Oldcastle* seconds Harding, it also mitigates the force of his critique. After all, the fugitive Oldcastle only looks like a knave, in an England run by Catholics. By first supporting Oldcastle's request for freedom of conscience and then posing as a harmless "night-walker" himself, Henry helps sympathetic spectators distinguish the *appearance* of roguery from inward reality and actual faith.[12]

A penchant for disguise assimilates disparate characters in *Oldcastle* as much as shared thievery and vagabondage do, making theatricality as well as roguery seem hallmarks of the new English society that religious upheaval has generated in the play. And *Oldcastle* is only one of many plays during the Renaissance to link the cause of religious reformation with the interests of rogues and players. In their struggle to resist the Catholic view of the Reformation as a wandering from Christendom that had promoted wandering within England, English Protestants began around the 1590s to receive ideological support from what Norden would have considered the unlikeliest quarter—that breeding ground of "idleness and loitering," the theater. As advocates for a nation accused of vagrancy, players had one great advantage over most of their compatriots: they were accustomed to the charge. And now that some players had settled, for at least part of the year, in permanent theaters, they had new arguments available to them for differentiating themselves from mere rovers. By the end of the sixteenth century, dramatists such as Marlowe and Shakespeare had powerfully correlated the professional itinerancy of players with larger issues of religious as well as social errancy. In the decades to follow, such playwrights as Dekker, Jonson, Fletcher, Middleton, and Brome came to envision the theater as a special means not only of elucidating English vagrancy but of celebrating it too. With increasing boldness, theater people urged their audiences to view themselves as members of a better "rogue" society, one that was more civil and godly than the vagabonds but less strict and intolerant than puritans.

There were other, competing theories of England as well as of rogues at the time, and during the ascendancy of the puritans some of these theories prevailed over the views that theater people had touted. But for the admirers of the hitherto unrecognized theatrical tradition that I will outline in this chapter, England's homeless had been transformed into the symbolic sponsors of a reformed yet also antisectarian nation.[13]

I

Perhaps the clearest indication that English Protestants feared the Reformation had too radically disrupted traditional notions of community in England was the growing belief among Elizabethans—unprecedented in England before the Reformation—that England's vagrants had not only risen in number but, paradoxically, assembled a society of their own.[14] In 1565 John Awdeley published an exposé of this secret "fraternity of vagabonds," which he also termed a "brotherhood" or "company" or "profession." The next year Thomas Harman's *Caveat for Common Cursitors* described the structure of the vagabonds' "fleeting Fellowship" in more detail, even supplying a brief vocabulary of the cryptic language they were said to have developed, their "cant." By the turn of the century, pamphlets on the vagabonds had become a staple of the English book market, and claims about their social organization had grown still more extravagant: soon the playwright Thomas Dekker (1608) could speak of vagabonds—or, in the "cant" terminology, "rogues"—as a separate "people."[15] Another playwright, John Webster (1615), bolstered this stronger view: in his account the rogue seemed part of a "commonwealth" not only separate from England's but more stable and uniform: "His Language is a constant tongue; [our] Northern speech differs from the South, Welsh from the Cornish: but Canting is general, nor ever could be altered by Conquest of the *Saxon, Dane,* or *Norman.*"[16]

Despite the vividness and popularity of this belief in a rogue underworld, even those scholars who accept that vagrancy increased throughout the sixteenth century insist that "the literary image of the Elizabethan vagrant evaporates as soon as court records are examined." According to J. A. Sharpe, for instance, the only associations formed by the homeless in Elizabethan England appear to have been "loose" and "informal."[17] Yet Sharpe and his fellow historians never ask why Elizabethans bothered to invent a rogue underworld, or why they granted a greater cohesiveness to these most desperately poor castoffs of English society than to English society itself. Again, the oversight seems attributable, at least in part, to our anachronistic treatment of nationalism as a fundamental, rather than a sketchy and disputable, Elizabethan ideological position. If many Elizabethans interpreted the growing vagabondage in England as an effect of the Reformation, then why should we not also consider the Reformation to be a probable source of the Elizabethan scare about organized roguery? For the notion of a vagabond underworld embodied the worst of English fears about the Protestant schism. Not only, it seemed, had the national integrity and solidarity that the break with Rome was supposed to provide the English nightmarishly arisen among England's thriving vagabonds instead, but it had taken a thoroughly profane form: like his fellow rogue critics, the playwright Robert Greene (1591) declared that the vagabonds were "in religion mere atheists."[18] If weak abjects and castaways had achieved an invisible community in England, they had done so at the cost of the one thing Gilby, Hooper, and Spenser believed could justify vagrancy—their faith.

The literature on England's new rogue nation did more, however, than expose Protestant anxiety about the Reformation's effects on England; it also enabled a productive response to such self-doubt, in stigmatizing vagabonds as culprits, not casualties, as the active promoters of national disintegration rather than its passive victims. Along with shifting the blame for English vagrancy to the vagrants themselves, the demonization of rogues provided a splintered England with a valuable common enemy. In the preface to his *Caveat*, Harman represented his pamphlet as the first salvo in a more comprehensive battle against rogues: "Faithfully for the profit and benefit of my country I have done it," Harman declared, "that the whole body of the realm may see and understand their lewd life and pernicious practices, that all may speedily help to amend that is amiss." "The whole body of the realm": rogues were so organized, hidden, and pervasive a threat that only the entire kingdom combined could root them out. This national appeal became, for rogue writers, the standard by which the production and consumption of rogue literature was to be judged: "Nascimur pro patria," Greene (1591) and his followers proclaimed, while Dekker (1608) dedicated a rogue pamphlet "to my *own* Nation."[19]

The utility of rogues in establishing one's devotion to the common good made them an especially attractive subject for one group of Englishmen in particular—the personnel of England's theaters. Touring had always rendered players vulnerable to the charge of vagrancy and the penalty of the whipping post. Yet distinctions had also always been made between licensed and unlicensed players: between some amateur or else well-placed actors, that is, and their poor professional counterparts.[20] Theater historians agree that by tightening the requirements for licenses and thus subjecting more players to the charge of vagrancy, the 1572 Acte for the Punishment of Va-

cabondes actually provided certain acting companies with the status and security they needed to found London's permanent theaters.[21] Famously, however, these more privileged players quickly discovered that the assurances of
settled venues and official protection had failed to silence their critics. On
the contrary, for many Elizabethans the new high profile of such "roguing
stagers" constituted a national scandal.[22] What better evidence of organized
roguery could there be, after all, than an acting company—a fraternity of
vagabonds indeed? And where better could one behold the makings of a
rogue society than in the permanent theaters, "the ordinary places of meeting," a Lord Mayor protested in 1594, "for all vagrant persons & masterless
men that hang about the City, . . . where they consort and make their
matches to the great displeasure of Almighty God & the hurt and annoyance
of her Majesty's people." According to the theaters' enemies, even those
playgoers who were not originally rogues were liable to become so, because
the theaters inspired "more truants, and ill husbands, than if open Schools
of unthrifts & Vagabonds were kept." Unable to shake the stigma of vagrancy, the new professional players thus had a vested interest in persuading
the English people to fear another form of organized vagabondage more
harmful and also more clandestine than their own.[23]

So it was that around the turn of the century the production of rogue literature came to be dominated by two playmakers, Greene and Dekker, who
claimed to have devoted their lives to England's safety. The novelty of their
pamphlets had little to do with their supposed detective work, most of which
they pilfered from earlier writers. What *was* new about the rogue literature
of Greene and Dekker was the way both dramatists represented themselves
within it; their literary self-portraits show how well the notion of a rogue
underworld helped theater people excuse their seeming vagrancy and capitalize on it too. Harman had described his campaign against rogues as ne-
cessitating a very roguelike ranging "about and through all parts of this
noble realm," yet he made clear that his *book* was the rover; the reason Harman himself possessed a potentially compromising familiarity with rogue
society, he explained, was that an illness had forced him to stay home, where
he spent his time interrogating the vagabonds who came begging to his
door.[24] A quarter-century later Greene recast the inherited lore on vagabondage as a racy personal confession: he himself, he announced, had once
led a rogue's life, which he now extenuated as both a youthful excess and a
special access to knowledge about roguery. Greene's admission of vagrancy
thus amounted to a repudiation as well; in his posthumous *Repentance* (1592),
he went so far as to renounce all his writings, including his plays, except his
rogue pamphlets, which he hoped would prove "very beneficial to the Com-

monwealth of England."[25] Fifteen years later Dekker took a further step in defending the knowledge of roguery. In *The Belman of London* (1608) Dekker claimed to have been wandering in a mood of *contemptus mundi* through the English countryside when he stumbled upon evidence of a vagabond underworld; the discovery gave him a new sense of purpose, which was to roam London's streets like a bellman, warning its more sheltered citizens of the danger they could otherwise neither see nor know. Unlike the detectors of rogues before him, then, Dekker managed to represent vagrancy as a vocation—and, not coincidentally, instead of renouncing the theater as Greene had, Dekker retained his theatrical connections for another two decades.

The overt fancifulness of Dekker's *Belman* marks a further departure from Harman and Greene, both of whom had taken pains to present their works as true stories: Greene (1592), for instance, claimed that his pamphlets had so angered the rogues that "some fourteen or fifteen of them" had tried to kill him at "the Saint John's head within Ludgate." Rogues were cheats and liars, "counterfeit" beggars addicted to every sort of "cozenage"; the early rogue writer insisted on a veracity that distinguished him from his faithless opponents. This stake in truth-telling encouraged Greene to disown the theater along with vagabondage, yet Dekker's rogue literature manifests as little shame about his fiction-making as it does about his wandering. The pamphlet to follow the *Belman*, Dekker's *Lanthorne and Candlelight* (1608), repeatedly goes out of its way to comment on the likeness between rogues and players. For Dekker, it is a likeness that clarifies differences: even if players are vagrant and counterfeit, the *Lanthorne* suggests, they still serve the cause of stability and truth, insofar as they help display the truth about lying rogues.[26] A version of this argument that plays are *openly* false had long figured in defenses of the theater, but no one before Dekker had so elaborately balanced the player against the crooked drifter.[27] The protheatrical consequences of such rogue work became clearer in a play Dekker co-wrote a few years after the *Lanthorne*: *The Roaring Girl* (1610), which turned a well-known denizen of London's streets and theaters, Mary Frith, into a stage character, Moll Cutpurse, and a devastating informant against the "commonwealth of rogues."[28]

Thanks to the notion of a vagabond underworld, then, Dekker proved remarkably fluent at rationalizing the theater's seeming errancies; but Dekker's stake in professional self-justification hardly explains the great popularity of his rogue works, nor does it exhaust his motives in producing them. Around the same time as *The Belman* and *The Roaring Girl*, Dekker also authored a militantly Protestant play that explicitly addressed the larger vagrancy problem in England with which I began—England's estrangement, as one Catholic character in *The Whore of Babylon* (c. 1606) puts it, from "all the world."[29] The rogue underworld may have appeared a crisis in itself, but it was also capable of seeming to reflect deeper English crises, and this ideological commerce between England's rogues and its other troubles meant that, for Dekker and his readers, the vagrancy of the theater could seem serviceably related to more than one national scandal at once. I have elsewhere argued that the traditional reputation of poets as marginal triflers specially inclined England's poets to defend the sublimity and power of England *as* a marginal little island.[30] Once English "stagers" had established permanent theaters, their traditional reputation as degenerate vagabonds specially inclined *them* not only to detect a criminal organization of rogues within England but also to treat England's seeming vagrancy from Christendom as the means to a higher civility and community.[31]

Although the full development of this "rogue" nationalism was to come later, a faith in the broader resonance of theatrical vagrancy made its unmistakable appearance on the English stage in the play that arguably commenced the golden age of English drama. Marlowe's *Tamburlaine* (c. 1587) concerned a Scythian "troop of thieves and vagabonds" who surprise the world not only with their cohesiveness but also with their all-conquering power. A few years later, during the time Greene was publishing his rogue pamphlets, the anonymous *Lamentable Tragedy of Locrine* (c. 1592) brought the nomads of *Tamburlaine* closer to home by dramatizing a supposedly historical Scythian invasion of England.[32] Representations of vagrancy and English history were still more intimately blended in Shakespeare's history plays, which associated two princely English figures—Hal in the Henriad (c. 1596–99) and Edgar in *King Lear* (c. 1605)—with roguish companions, disguises, or behavior.[33] And the history plays of other writers as well, among them *George a Greene* (c. 1592), *Edward IV* (c. 1599), *Oldcastle* (1599), and *When You See Me, You Know Me* (1604), joined Shakespeare in linking English kings with thievish "out-riders."

While these plays thus made the vagabond seem a figure nearly as consequential for the nation as a king, they also manifested considerable skepticism about the societies in which rogues could come to possess such significance. *Tamburlaine*'s vagabonds, for instance, have power but little civility; in *Locrine* and *Lear*, vagabondage is tied to a pre-Christian world; in *Locrine*, *Henry IV*, *Oldcastle*, and *Lear*, roguery becomes important to the nation only during a time of national division, which the kings in each play have only a limited success in repairing.[34] A more patently satirical impulse often surfaced in the rogue pamphlets, which defended rogues by treating them as scapegoats for a general English depravity: as one writer in 1592 said of the "cozenage" that rogues practice, "there is no estate, trade, occupation, nor mystery, but lives by [it]."[35]

Yet just as Dekker in his pamphlets seemed less troubled by his association with vagrancy and thus better able to exploit it than Greene had been, so later Jacobean playwrights appear to have been more invigorated than disturbed by uncovering vagrancy at the heart of a nation's affairs. Both Fletcher's *Beggars' Bush* (c. 1613–22) and Middleton's *Spanish Gypsy* (1623) tell the story of exiled aristocrats who manage to return to their society and right its wrongs only by first impersonating rogues. Gone is the pretense to historicity in these plays; it fades as the act of consorting with vagabonds grows more restorative. So little trepidation does the closeness of theatricality to roguery excite in Fletcher and Middleton that they embrace it as a plot device: at the end of both *The Beggars' Bush* and *The Spanish Gypsy*, the exiled nobility regain their place and power by means of a play they stage while in their roguish disguises.

Perhaps the most striking development in later rogue plays is also the best evidence that theater people thought of themselves as specially capable of addressing concerns about the legitimacy and integrity of the nation. In play after play as the tradition matures, a group of rogues exhibit a comic rather than a demonic solidarity that makes their society seem not only sturdier than the more conventional or licensed communities from which they have wandered but even, for a time, preferable to them. A song in *The Beggars' Bush* strikes the keynote of these comedies: "Where the Nation live so free, and so merry as do we?" So lighthearted do rogues become that they happily accept strangers (such as exiled aristocrats) into their company; and it is this charitable openness or flexibility that most distinguishes the rogues from their inevitable foils in these plays, the "precise" puritans.[36]

An early, hence more skeptical representation of such a comic underworld figures in Jonson's *Bartholomew Fair* (c. 1613). As Anne Barton has noted, the rogues in *Bartholomew Fair* "display a remarkable and touching loyalty to one another," while the more socially respectable "visitors to the Fair have a vastly inferior record" on the same score. For all his talk about "the *Brethren*" to whom he is allied, none of these visitors is so profoundly antisocial as the puritan Busy, who continually spurns other characters in the play on the grounds of their supposed devotion to "rags of *Rome*." Such divisiveness, *Bartholomew Fair* insists, is true roguery: expanding on the prologue's condemnation of puritans as England's "*Faction*," one character declares that puritans are "the second part of the Society of *Canters*, Outlaws to order and *Discipline*, and the only privileg'd *Church-robbers* of *Christendom*." Yet Jonson never allies Busy with the play's more ordinary rogues; on the contrary, it is one of the ordinary rogues who finally succeeds in quelling Busy, exposing his love of contention for contention's sake by tempting him into a debate with a puppet. Significantly, this debate begins with a claim borrowed from the antitheatrical assault on players: Busy proclaims that the puppet has no "*Calling*." While the ensuing squabble further stigmatizes puritans as the promoters of schism in England, it implicitly elevates players along with the ordinary rogues into the defenders of community.[37]

Of *secular* community, one might gather from the *Fair*; for in mocking Busy, the puppet also ridicules doctrinal controversy. Jonson's friend John Selden later praised the debate scene as a witty commentary on the "vain disputes of Divines." It would be a mistake to conclude, however, that Selden or Jonson imagined *Bartholomew Fair* as satirizing religion also. To a puritan such as Busy, it is true, only "a halting *Neutral*," a temporizer "without any certain religion," would shrink from scriptural disputes.[38] But the terms of Busy's defeat indicate that Jonson had a more positive conception of religious neutrality in mind. The lower class rogues of the *Fair* cannot fully exemplify it: even at their comic best they remain rogues, and thus never represent more than a limited, negative image of some better society. They come closest, however, when unmasking puritan cant. At the climax of his battle with Busy, the puppet disarms Busy of his Old Testament scruples about cross-dressing on the stage by lifting his skirt and citing the New Testament text that "we have neither *Male* nor *Female* amongst us." To the puppetmaster, this exposure of his puppet's literal neutrality may signify nothing more than a parody of Busy's pseudo-scripturalism, yet the joke ironically discloses a scriptural countervision to Busy's that allies neutrality not with atheism or indifference but with spiritual inclusiveness: "There is neither Jew nor Greek, there is neither bond nor free, there is neither male nor female: for ye are all one in Christ Jesus."[39] (Tellingly, one of the first English writers to treat the idea of religious "neutrality" in a straightforwardly positive way was the Jonson disciple and playwright Jasper Mayne, whose *Sermon Concerning Unity & Agreement* [1646] paraphrases Paul on the factiousness of the Corinthians: "one says, *I am of Paul*, another, *I am of Cephas*, a third, *I am of Apollos*, only a few neutral men, *We are of Christ*.")[40]

Whatever the intensity of Jonson's religion at the time he wrote *Bartholomew Fair*, the same investment in rogues as neutralizers of religious controversy can be seen animating the literature of avowedly zealous Protestants. All of John Awdeley's other extant publications beside *The Fraternity of Vagabonds*, for instance, express the most militant Protestant patriotism, characterizing England as "God's Fort," under assault from papists who have falsely labeled the English "heretics." It would not be hard to treat the *Fraternity*, or for that matter any other rogue pamphlet, as an extension of this overtly sectarian work. Like the vagabonds described in the *Fraternity*, Awdeley's papists employ "vicious pranks" against the English, while a cant name for one "order" of rogues in the *Fraternity*, the "Fraters," is of course also a name for one branch of the Catholic clergy, friars. Building on a centuries-old contempt for friars, Protestants had from the start of the Reformation routinely labeled all Catholic churchmen a pack of "beggars and vagabonds," "sturdy, idle, holy thieves" whose shared allegiance to the pope bound them together into a kingdom within the kingdom.[41] If anxieties about the English Protestant schism fueled belief in a vagabond underworld, so too did anxieties about English Catholic loyalism to Rome. These concerns were powerfully intensified in the 1570s when a new "order" of "wandering *Romanists*"—the "roguing *Jesuits*"—began to infiltrate England, raising nearly hysterical fears of an underground English Catholic conspiracy.[42] Yet astonishingly, neither Awdeley nor any of the rogue writers to follow him directly claimed some hidden connection between the rogue and papist underworlds. To do so, it seems, would have been to undermine much of their purpose in establishing that a rogue society existed: what one might call the *introversion* of England's spiritual nonconformity with Catholic Christendom. Rather than depict England in oppositional terms that would open the door to charges of English vagrancy and schism, rogue writers turned from their Roman Catholic adversaries to an internal, vagabond, and irreligious enemy who were just as divided from the Continent as the English were—"*Savages*," Dekker calls them, "yet living in an Island very temperate, fruitful, full of a Noble Nation, and rarely governed."[43]

II

The very plot of an early rogue play such as *Locrine* bespeaks this desire to internalize and thereby neutralize the problem of England's schism. At first, it is true, *Locrine* seems committed to reminding England of its foreign enemies: the play's Scythian invaders raise the specter of the Catholic powers that England had successfully repelled only a few years earlier. But Albion's defenders in the play are themselves recent arrivals to the island, Trojan fugitives who have fled Greece and "fair Italy" as they had once been driven from Troy. For these "exiles," led by Brutus, invasion is only part of the threat posed by the Scythians: as wanderers who also hail from "barbarous Asia" and who treat Trojan history as if it were their own heritage, the Scythians embody the shameful past that the Trojans had hoped to leave behind them.[44] The audience of *Locrine* was capable of feeling this shame, too.

"We glory much to be called Britons," Bishop James Pilkington (1560) sermonized, "but if we consider what a vagabond Brutus was, and what a company he brought with him, there is small cause of glory. . . . So that of Brutus we may well be called brutes for our brutish condition."[45] According to Edwin Sandys, modern Italians thought worse of the English than their ancestors had of Brutus: Roman Catholics believed that "the English nation since their falling away from their Church is grown so barbarous that their Soldiers are very Cannibals, and eat young children."[46] In *Locrine*, however, war makes it possible for the Trojans to shatter the Scythian mirror of vagabondage, barbarism, and defeat. Given a second chance to resist invasion, the Trojans can now stigmatize another people as "stout fugitives" and "rascal runagates," in the process reinventing themselves as British natives. The first battle with the Scythians is indeed the first time in *Locrine* that any Trojan is called a "Briton"; thus the disgrace of exile begins to die as the Scythians do. "So perish they," proclaims the Trojan general Corineus, "that envy *Britain's* wealth."[47]

Indeed, the Scythians of *Locrine* prove to be such serviceable enemies that even after their rout the Trojans find it difficult to stop thinking about them. The title character—one of Brutus's three sons, the king of England, and the husband of Corineus's daughter—falls in love with the captured Scythian queen Estrild and hides her away for himself in a secret cave. Once Locrine's adultery is discovered, a civil war erupts, forcing Trojans to take the place of Scythians as the assailants of Trojans. Yet rather than undermine the Trojan effort to cast off the shame of vagabondage, these internal troubles actually advance that project, insofar as they now turn Trojan sights exclusively upon "our country." Shortly after the Scythian defeat, in a grand defiance issued to "all" other potential invaders of his island, Corineus had already betrayed a growing Trojan blind spot toward the world beyond Albion:

> If the brave nation of the Troglodytes,
> If all the coal-black Ethiopians,
> If all the forces of the Amazons,
> If all the hosts of the barbarian lands,
> Should dare to enter this our little world,
> Soon should they rue their overbold attempts.

There is no mention here of the civil powers at the center of the larger world Corineus knows, the Greeks and Italians who had forced the Trojans into exile. Not only are Corineus's imagined invaders all barbarians, they are also all from the ends of the (Ptolemaic) earth. According to Roman writers, that is the sort of company in which the ancient British belonged—among

Scythians and Africans, peoples wholly cut off from the civilized world.[48] Yet *Locrine* seems less troubled by this Roman association of the British with outcasts than by the prospect of open hostility toward the Italians who had cast Brutus out: what good would it do to defy Italy, after all, when it is the space separating Britain from Italy that helps make the Trojan-British seem fugitives and runagates in the first place? Hence Corineus's militancy fastens on barbarians with the force of an incantation. And when this strange craving surfaces as an adulterous love—a scandal transforming the difference between civil and barbarous into a domestic, even a "private" matter— the Trojans are still more powerfully distracted from worrying about the world they have fled.[49]

Locrine ends by directing the audience's attention to some traces of Scythia that supposedly still linger in "our little world." After Locrine's overthrow, the Trojans give the names of Humber and Severn to the rivers where Humber, the king of the Scythians, and Sabren, the daughter of Locrine and Estrild, drowned themselves. These names signify more than the Trojan desire to perpetuate the memory of Scythian barbarism as it was mastered in Britain. Before his death in act 1, Brutus divided his island among his sons: by tradition, the Humber marks the boundary he traced between England and Scotland, the Severn the boundary between England and Wales.[50] In thus lending their names to borders that distinguish England from its equally British but (for *Locrine*) less powerful and interesting neighbors, the Scythians continue to provide the island they invaded with an internal standard against which civility can be defined.

Yet the constant succession of tragic veils that *Locrine* must draw over the world east of England—the disintegration of Brutus's empire, the Scythian invasion, Locrine's adultery, civil war—suggests a felt need in the play for "rascal runagates" who could assume the burden of English vagrancy without forcing the English to oppose any external enemy. For Christians, the very paradigm of a vagabond "nation" in one's midst was the Jews, "scattered over all Countries, but nowhere planted," as Sandys writes, using language that recalls his pessimistic characterization of Protestants. According to Luther in 1528, the cant of German beggars had in fact "come from the Jews, for many Hebrew words occur in the Vocabulary."[51] But Jews were too scarce in England to be counted as a serious internal threat. English writers worried instead about the Jews' erstwhile neighbors: gypsies or, as the English called them, "Egyptians." In his "Description of England" (1577), William Harrison claimed that English vagrants had first come to devise their cant "in counterfeiting the Egyptian rogues." While the numbers of the gypsies made them a more conspicuous vexation to the English than English Jews, their comparative insignificance as bearers of religious meaning also made them less portentous enemies. Bishop Sandys (1585) reminded his congregation that Christians believed the Jews wandered for a reason: God had "marked" the Jew "like Cain to be known as a murdering vagabond upon the earth, to be a byword, and an example of God's justice to all the world, throughout all succeeding ages." Sandys cautioned his audience that the sinful English might just as easily suffer the same fate.[52] But no English writer pointed to a similarly religious explanation for the wandering of the Egyptians; like *Locrine*'s conquered Scythians, it seems, gypsies could absorb the stigma of English vagabondage without reflecting that shame too directly upon the schismatic English.

The term *Egyptian* was not without any religious charge, however. English Protestants habitually maligned English Catholics as "Egyptians" laboring to return the nation "to the old obedience of the great *Pharaoh* of Rome," while separatists used the same language to denounce the Romanism of the established church: John Greenwood (1593), for instance, spoke of "the parishes of Protestants" as still "in bondage to the Egyptians." And yet the so-called Egyptians who openly wandered through these parishes were never implicated in the papist threat.[53] What gave them such immunity? The answer seems to lie in a striking change of attitude toward the gypsies during this period: although originally classified by law as foreigners, the gypsies were increasingly treated only "*as if* they were Egyptians." By 1607 the lawyer John Cowell could flatly state that gypsies were nothing more than "a counterfeit kind of rogues, that being English or Welsh people, accompany themselves together, disguising themselves in strange robes, blacking their faces and bodies, and framing to themselves an unknown language, wander up and down."[54] If the rogues thus helped domesticate the Egyptians, the Egyptians helped exoticize the rogues—or rather, helped the rogues *play* at being foreign. Whereas even in death the Scythians of *Locrine* remained outlandish markers of English civility, the "counterfeit" Egyptians could serve as foils to England without any weighty reference to the world beyond England.[55]

After the turn of the century the theater's increasingly comic dramatizations of rogue societies seem to embody a more confident strategy for helping England rethink its break with Rome. What made the difference were two historical developments after Awdeley and Harman's time: first, the rising though still lowly status of players stationed in permanent theaters, who were professionally inclined to dramatize a community of wanderers positively; and second, the growth of a nonconformist (and largely antitheatrical) faction of "brethren," who could take the rogues' place as an internal source of national disintegration while also taking society's place as the broader target of rogue satire. The derisive image of the puritan as one who "loves God with all his soul, but hates his neighbor with all his heart" helped make the supposedly profane yet sociable vagabond a more suggestive ideological vehicle: rogues could now comically adumbrate the unitive spirituality of the English not merely as Protestants but as antisectarians too. English audiences were increasingly urged to view the commonwealth of vagabonds as the crude image of a "free" society committed to moderation and organized on the most basic principles of Christian faith—communion and charity. As Jonson frames it, the very enactment of *Bartholomew Fair* associates the theater with the formation of such a society: although the play begins by representing the audience as rigidly stratified along economic lines, in the end this decidedly unspiritual and divisive perspective has been replaced by an invitation to festive communion.[56]

A still greater conviviality marks the rogue society of Jonson's disciple Richard Brome in his *Jovial Crew* (c. 1641). Like its Jacobean antecedents, Brome's play depicts the mingling of higher class characters with vagabonds and the triumph of "good fellowship" over severity; both designs culminate in a play staged by the mixed rogue company. But the specter of religious controversy—raised in the prologue to *A Jovial Crew* by a reference to "these sad and tragic days"—is more lightly exorcised from Brome's play than it had been from Jonson's. The closest Brome comes to satirizing puritans directly is when the vagrant Springlove promises to fetch a curate "so scrupulous and severely precise" that he will marry a couple only if they have slept together. So intent is Brome on distinguishing playing from religious polemicizing that he causes the beggars' first attempt at a play, a proposed dramatization of a utopian commonwealth, to be broken off as soon as the vagabonds turn their attention to representing "Divinity."[57] Brome's "poor strolls" are no atheists, however; "the only free men of a commonwealth," as a higher class character claims, they "observe no law, / Obey no governor, use no religion, / But what they draw from their own ancient custom, / Or constitute themselves, yet are no rebels." This last report that the rogues are conservative and peaceable nonconformists suggests that the charity for which they beg includes toleration as well as alms.[58] Brome makes a stronger case for toleration at the end of the play when, in romance fashion, a seemingly trivial token reveals the kinship of some previously alienated characters. This token turns out to be a Catholic "holy relic": "The *Agnus Dei* that my mother gave me / Upon her deathbed! Oh, the loss of it / Was my sore grief; and now with joy it is / Restor'd by miracle!"[59] Daringly, Brome reconciles the wanderers of the play at the same time as he resurrects England's

Catholic past. It would be reductive to conclude, however, that Brome thus recommends a return to Catholicism as the solution to English errancy, because the characters in the play have to embrace rather than renounce vagabondage before any relic of Catholicism can appear. Selecting the rogues' "patrico" or clergyman as the character who preserves and then reveals the Agnus Dei, Brome implies that the larger "strife" in English society can be turned into "a comedy" not with the restoration of Catholicism but rather with a shared wandering from the precise sectarianism that has divided one otherwise "civil Christian" from another.[60]

The very recurrence of plays that pitted vagabonds against precisians suggests that theater people found popular support for their roguish alternative to a sectarian England. Even King James was in some sort a fan: his favorite masque appears to have been *The Gypsies Metamorphosed* (1621).[61] Retrospectively, however, the problem with the players' attempts to render their vagabondage invaluable to the English commonwealth seems all too clear. Unlike the homeless, the puritans were no easy scapegoats: they had money available to them, as well as social position, learned defenders, able leadership—and above all, religious solidarity. Rather than acquiesce in the players' satirical exposés of their fellowship, they soon rose to power and pulled the stages down. (Ironically, a production of *The Jovial Crew* appears to have been the last performance at the theater for which Brome wrote.) It is largely the success of the puritans that has led historians to overvalue the strongly nationalist view of the English Reformation against which I have been arguing.[62] To the personnel of English theaters, the puritan victory meant more than a defeat for their positive conceptions of English vagrancy, however, more even than the closure of the theaters where those conceptions had been enacted. After ordering that the theaters be shut down, the puritan-led Parliament decreed that "*all* Stage-Players" were now to be considered "Rogues, and punishable, within the statutes" against rogues, "whether they be wanderers or no."[63]

III

How closely did the players' ideal of a rogue nation approximate the modern conception of a nation-state? One might think that the vagabonds of Renaissance pamphlets and plays helped modernize England merely by traversing it. To become nationalists, after all, the English had to lift their sights beyond their parishes just as vagabonds did, like Harman tracking his rogues as they passed "through and by all parts of this famous isle." If a rogue "were learned," the playwright Webster claimed, "no man could make a better description of *England;* for he hath travel'd it over and over." In *1 Sir Thomas Oldcastle* vagabondage does more than unite people whom religious controversy has divided; it becomes the vehicle for an ever more expansive picture of the realm. Having confessed to the king that he has "but one parsonage," the roving Sir John nonetheless adds that "there's ne'er a hill, heath, nor down in all Kent, but 'tis in my parish." The once settled Oldcastle crosses this same wide territory, and continues past it. Yet national borders no more limit his excursiveness than county lines do: by assuming the identity of a Lancashire carrier, becoming entangled in the crimes of an Irishman, and finally absconding to Wales, Oldcastle traces a new image of "home" that is not even confined to England at large.[64] In similar fashion, the Scythians of *Locrine* make the Trojans feel domesticated in Albion only as they also mark the division of the island into three separate nations. As I will show in chapter 3, the early exemplars of the rogue tradition in English drama generally treated England's schism as the basis for a new *inter*nationalism. According to such plays, the English would prove capable of resolving their religious controversies only if they transcended national as well as sectarian boundaries. But to renew Christendom this way, they would also have to wander ever farther from the Christendom of old.

This Blessed Plot

Our Fairy groves are green; our temples stand
Like goodly watchtowers, wafting passengers
From rocks, t' arrive them in the Holy Land.
— Thomas Dekker, *The Whore of Babylon* (c. 1606)

the free spirit of God . . . blows where it pleaseth, not tied nor imprison'd to any place, or person.
— Donne, *Pseudo-Martyr* (1610)

The rise of the English history play in Elizabethan England has long
seemed the strongest proof that the Elizabethans were nationalists. But
were Elizabethan histories actually devoted to what Irving Ribner calls the
"nationalistic glorification of England"? A simple test is to follow the plot
of a history that Ribner describes as "intensely nationalistic and patriotic,"
George Peele's *Edward I* (c. 1591). At the start of the play, Edward's mother
triumphantly announces her son's return from the Crusades:

> Illustrious England, ancient seat of kings,
> Whose chivalry hath royalized thy fame:
> That sounding bravely through terrestrial vail,
> Proclaiming conquests, spoils, and victories,
> Rings glorious Echoes through the farthest world.
> What warlike nation train'd in feats of arms,
> What barbarous people, stubborn or untam'd,
> What climate under the Meridian signs,
> Or frozen Zone under his brumal stage,
> Erst have not quaked and trembled at the name
> Of Britain, and her mighty Conquerors?
> Her neighbor realms as Scotland, Denmark, France,
> Aw'd with their deeds, and jealous of her arms,

Have begg'd defensive and offensive leagues.
Thus Europe rich and mighty in her kings,
Hath fear'd brave England dreadful in her kings:
And now to eternize Albion's Champions,
Equivalent with Trojans' ancient fame,
Comes lovely Edward from Jerusalem,
Veering before the wind, plowing the sea,
His stretched sails fill'd with the breath of men,
That through the world admire his manliness.

According to Ribner, the "intensely patriotic tone" of this speech "is sustained throughout the play." Yet even the briefest glance at *Edward I* shows how drastically Ribner has simplified the story. For a start, the queen mother proves incapable of sustaining the patriotic tone of her speech throughout the rest of her first scene, let alone the rest of the play: as soon as Edward arrives on the stage, she swoons, and Edward exclaims, "O ingrateful destiny, / To welcome Edward with this tragedy." As it happens, the queen mother soon recovers, but the seemingly gratuitous dark note struck by her fainting spell grows more and more oppressive as the play continues. Ingrateful destiny does indeed welcome Edward with one genuine tragedy after another: the rebellion first of Wales, then of Scotland; the treachery of a close adviser; the confession by Edward's queen that she had not only slept with Edward's brother before her marriage but later committed adultery with a French friar—who is the true father of Edward's supposed daughter Joan; and finally the queen's death, along with the death of the now bastardized Joan, who collapses from shame. Troubles come so thick and fast for Edward by the end of the play that Peele himself seems to lose a grip on the action. As Edward bemoans the deaths and disgraces he has just suffered, and a messenger informs him that the recently vanquished Scottish king has renewed his rebellion, Edward confusingly declares that the Welsh rebel Lluellen—beheaded some five hundred lines earlier—is also back up in arms. If anything in the play could be said to be sustained, it is Edward's troubles: "one affliction," as he laments in his final speech, only "calls another over."[1]

A comparable flood of troubles in Shakespeare's *Richard II* (1595) overwhelms the most famous paean to England in the language:

This royal throne of kings, this sceptred isle,
This earth of majesty, this seat of Mars,
This other Eden, demi-paradise,
This fortress built by Nature for herself
Against infection and the hand of war,

This happy breed of men, this little world,
This precious stone set in the silver sea,
Which serves it in the office of a wall,
Or as a moat defensive to a house,
Against the envy of less happier lands;
This blessed plot, this earth, this realm, this England,
This nurse, this teeming womb of royal kings,
Fear'd by their breed, and famous by their birth,
Renowned for their deeds as far from home,
For Christian service and true chivalry,
As is the sepulcher in stubborn Jewry
Of the world's ransom, blessed Mary's Son.

The enthusiastic speaker is another fragile parent, John of Gaunt, although this time the parent is really dying, and instead of rejoicing in England's renewed strength, he is bitterly lamenting its decline:

This land of such dear souls, this dear dear land,
Dear for her reputation through the world,
Is now leas'd out—I die pronouncing it—
Like to a tenement or pelting farm.
England, bound in with the triumphant sea,
Whose rocky shore beats back the envious siege
Of wat'ry Neptune, is now bound in with shame,
With inky blots and rotten parchment bonds;
That England, that was wont to conquer others,
Hath made a shameful conquest of itself.

Soon after Gaunt dies, England is plunged into even worse miseries than he had just bewailed: his son Bullingbrook invades England, usurps the throne, has his rival King Richard murdered, and in subsequent plays finds himself battling not only Welsh and Scottish rebels, as Edward I had, but English ones too.[2]

Even when modern critics take seriously the tragic context of patriotic set-pieces such as Gaunt's "blessed plot" speech, they often portray the internecine warfare in Elizabethan history plays as little more than a nationalist object-lesson: fear of division, they say, is what motivates the dramatization of division. This apologetical approach to the histories has recently been refined by Peter Womack, who maintains that a true Elizabethan nationalist could not have helped but encourage some measure of civil dissension, because to forge a nation one had first to kill the king. As Womack explains, "the unity of the realm" in a monarchy amounts to little more than "a reflection of the person of the monarch. The land is what Gaunt famously called it in *Richard II:* a royal throne of kings, its history an aspect of the history of the ruling family." But for a nationalist "the true object of patriotic loyalty" is "the *corpus mysticum* of the nation." Consequently, Womack argues, a history play that ends tragically for kings must be good news for the nation: "So long as the dynastic legitimation of the monarch and the nobility is more or less working, the stage does not afford any space for anyone else. The community of the nation is not needed, so to speak, and so there is no call to imagine it. It is only when that hierarchical order fails that the undifferentiated totality of the realm appears, as *that which is harmed by its failure.*"[3] In his *Forms of Nationhood* Richard Helgerson finds a similar opposition between king and nation at work in a wide variety of Elizabethan and Jacobean literature; he too believes that England began to be understood as a nation only when writers began to liberate England from a reductive identification with its king.

Given the penchant of Elizabethan histories for satirizing, unseating, and even assassinating their kings, the basic premise of Womack's and Helgerson's arguments seems hard to deny. But why should evidence of a declining respect for monarchs in English drama indicate, as Womack and Helgerson assume it does, a corresponding rise of faith in nationalism? Elizabethan antitheatricalists would have been appalled by the notion that Elizabethan players were intent on building any "imagined community": to the antitheatricalists, after all, plays were instead diabolical provocations "to murther, slay, kill, pick, steal, rob, and rove."[4] Many recent scholars have supported the antitheatricalists to a degree in arguing that Elizabethan history plays exposed various incoherencies in English society—especially disparities of gender, class, and race.[5] Neither Renaissance theater haters nor modern literary critics mention, however, that even if Renaissance theater people did regard themselves as defenders of community, such a self-image might well have committed them to a program of *antinationalist* propaganda. For instance, they might have shared the nostalgia of the Catholic pamphleteer Robert Parsons (1599), who spoke of a time when "one God [was] worshipped and adored after one and the self same manner, not only throughout this little Island of England, and Scotland, but also of the whole body of Christendom, one faith, one belief, one form of service, one number of sacraments, one tongue in celebration, one sacrifice, one head of the Church, one obedience, one judgment in all." "But now in these points," Parsons continues, speaking the part of the Protestant, "we English . . . are not only different & divided from the general body of Catholics in Christendom (with whom we were united before) but also among ourselves and with other new sectaries sprung up with us or after us, we have implacable wars and are divided in opinions." Although Protestant polemicists labored to represent England's spiritual difference from the Continent as a second insular wall keeping England safe and whole, Parsons and his sympathizers believed that English separatism and English civil war went hand in hand: to speak of "our divided realm" was to describe an England divided from Christendom and therefore divided within itself.[6]

The possibility that some Elizabethan playwrights might have intended the wars of their history plays as a critique of English insularism makes conspicuous a recurrent feature of the Elizabethan history play that has received little critical attention: England's present troubles are repeatedly set against its past heroic part in the Crusades. Thus, as he is about to lay siege to the king's fortress in Marlowe's *Edward II*, the rebellious Mortimer Junior proclaims that "This tattered ensign of my ancestors, / Which swept the desert shore of that dead sea, / Whereof we got the name of Mortimer, / Will I advance upon this castle walls."[7] In *Richard II* the Crusades unsettle Gaunt's patriotic vision of England's distinctiveness even before he begins to complain about current events. At first Gaunt claims that England is "happier" than other countries because it is insulated from them, a "little world" unto itself. But then Gaunt celebrates England by way of the larger world it insularly shuns: England's kings are said to be "renowned . . . far from home," for "deeds" accomplished far from home and in the "service" of the Christian world from which England is supposedly divided. To Gaunt's eyes, the road toward seeing England as its own "blessed plot" also leads back toward the Holy Land.

Gaunt's inability to disentangle his English insularism from his Christian internationalism might seem to be a confusion that would come naturally to an English patriot whose very name recalls his birth elsewhere (that is, in Ghent).[8] But just as Gaunt's speech turns from praise of England to blame of King Richard, from a nation "bound in with the triumphant sea" to one "bound in with shame," so the play in general transforms the insular "plot" of Gaunt's speech into a tale of diminishment and woe. Over the course of the play, national "division" is what marginalizes the Crusades as an English interest and therefore marginalizes English participation in Christendom as well. Owing to England's dissensions, the only character to uphold its crusading reputation in *Richard II* is the nobleman whom Richard exiles at the play's start; as the Bishop of Carlisle reports of this expatriate after his death,

Many a time hath banish'd Norfolk fought
For Jesu Christ in glorious Christian field,
Streaming the ensign of the Christian cross
Against black pagans, Turks, and Saracens,
And toil'd with works of war, retir'd himself
To Italy, and there at Venice gave
His body to that pleasant country's earth,
And his pure soul unto his captain Christ,
Under whose colors he had fought so long.

Gaunt's son Henry does end *Richard II* promising to travel to the Holy Land, but in subsequent plays he never acts on his promise, which, he eventually confesses, was made in bad faith anyway, as an attempt to divert attention from the home crises that truly concerned him. While these crises may paradoxically help to realize Gaunt's insularism, as Womack might claim, they do so only at the cost of internalizing the warfare that Gaunt had celebrated insularism for warding off. Late in *Richard II* England's escalating divisiveness leads the Bishop of Carlisle to predict that "disorder, horror, fear, and mutiny / Shall here inhabit, and this land be call'd / The field of Golgotha and dead men's skulls." The allusion to the scene of Christ's crucifixion suggests that the England of Gaunt's son will go uncannily far toward realizing both Gaunt's insularism and his ambivalence about it: if England will take the place of the Holy Land, it will be as an apocalyptic-sounding battlefield.[9]

In chapter 2 I showed how the break with Rome aroused such anxieties about England in English Protestants as well as Catholics. Protestants censured "Roman" Catholics for having "confined the whole Church of Christ within themselves, and excluded all others that were not under the Roman obedience, as aliens from the Common-wealth of Israel, and strangers from the covenants of promise." The Crusades, in the standard Protestant account, exemplified the popish misbelief that some lands were holier than others, while Jerusalem's occupation by "pagans & infidels" proved instead "that God's church and the true religion is not limited to any certain place." And yet the English schism had effectively insularized the English church; how were English Protestants to differentiate this isolation from Romish particularism, or maintain that, by breaking with Rome, they had helped to restore a properly supranational church? In the late Elizabethan period theater people began to capitalize on such worries not merely by dramatizing them but also by correlating them with questions about the propriety of their own profession. Catholics might regard English Protestants as no better than vagabond players, roving with their false religion like outlaws from the rest of Christendom, but theater people staged play after play in which thievish wanderers proved to be more charitable and cohesive than the ostensibly legitimate societies they had abandoned. Thus in the history plays that follow *Richard II*, Shakespeare appears to sketch a comic countervision to English civil war in the "good fellowship" of Falstaff and his "rogues." Such "rude society" was hardly the remedy to England's schism that Catholics had in mind; in the first and second parts of *Henry IV* there seems to be no more "room for faith" among Falstaff's thieves than Prince Hal finds in Falstaff himself. By *Henry V*, however, Hal emerges from this debauched company seemingly "full of grace" and capable of welding formerly antagonistic Christian nations into a united front. My goal in this chapter is to show that other Elizabethan history playwrights joined Shakespeare in presenting a morally questionable fellowship as a rough foretype of the *supranational* Christian society that should follow upon English "reformation."[10]

To illustrate the Elizabethan theater's simultaneous investment in England and in a Christendom that transcended both geographical and sectarian boundaries, I will closely examine several Elizabethan histories in which the Crusades figure prominently: *Edward I*; the two Robin Hood plays of Anthony Munday and Henry Chettle; and Shakespeare's later histories, beginning with a play that Shakespeare wrote before he hit upon roguery as a national issue, *King John*. All these plays unfold what I call a countercrusading plot: a narrative in which English characters turn against the Crusades and also turn them around, to search for a new Holy Land in the English isle. Such a reversal would seem at first glance to indicate a Protestant nationalist design, but in *Edward I* Peele actually opposes an insularist conception of England to a Christian one: Edward's crusading at home assimilates him in the play to the pagans he used to battle abroad. *Edward I* also tentatively sketches a "rogue" solution to England's schism, which the later Robin Hood plays more confidently elaborate: in Munday and Chettle's version of the story, Robin and his followers are exiled from a corrupt crusading society and then, by virtue of their outlawry, see their way toward reviving the true Christian values upon which the rest of Christendom is only nominally based. But the second of the two Robin Hood plays proves to be a tragedy; the rogue renewal of Christian fellowship quickly founders on the underlying paradox of a schismatical demand for inclusiveness. Finally, for all its grand speeches about the English isle, *King John* portrays an English schism as having tragic national as well as international consequences. Such skepticism about English separatism does not mean that Shakespeare was a Catholic; *King John* endorses the Protestant critique of Rome while applying the same objections to a breakaway England.

Yet how can Shakespeare be thought to have opposed the celebration of England as its own "little world," when nearly half of his dramatic output by the time he finished *Henry V* consisted of English history plays—a commitment to representing England that no other Elizabethan dramatist even came close to matching? Shakespeare would not have been alone in attempting to reconcile a belief in English exceptionalism with a desire for an international Christian fellowship. Like many Elizabethan Protestants, Edwin Sandys (1599) judged that England's distinctive *via media* in religion made it "fitter and able to work Unity" among Christians than any other Christian community; more aggressive Protestants such as John Dee (1577) envisioned Queen Elizabeth as a conqueror "at the Helm of the Imperial Ship, of the most part of Christendom."[11] Encouraged in part by their professional ties to itinerancy, Elizabethan theater people tended, however, to favor a more diffusive conception of Christian unity than either Sandys or Dee promoted. Shakespeare, for instance, seems to have believed that both England's insularity *and* its civil wars were providential. Just as Christ had long ago risen from the sepulcher for which the crusaders fought, so, Shakespeare's histories suggest, God had long ago distinguished Christianity first from Palestine and then from the Rome that encouraged crusading in Palestine. As that faith continued its progress westward from the supposed holy lands of the past, a reformed England might have looked to some like a possible destination, but for Shakespeare England's civil wars and insular littleness exceptionally clarified the difference between Christendom and any narrow bounds that would lay exclusive claim to it. What the history plays of Peele, Munday, Chettle, and Shakespeare all suggest is that the plot of Christian history is unfolding westward still—away from Rome *and* England, on a spiritual Crusade for a new Christian world altogether.[12]

I

One potentially nationalist explanation for the king's troubles in *Edward I* is that he has brought disaster on himself, by marrying a Spaniard. The Spanish Queen Elinor is, to say the least, a disruptive force in the play. She is so proud of her Spanish heritage, and so scornful of her new country, that at one point she advises Edward to cut the beards off every Englishman and the right breast off every Englishwoman; later, the cheerful and charitable Lord Mayoress of London proves to be such an irritation to Elinor that she has her bound, stripped, and then murdered with asps. The climactic sign of Elinor's inassimilable foreignness, however, is her confessed adultery with a French friar. Significantly, Edward learns of his wife's infidelity only when he replaces the French confessors she had requested with English ones—a switch that Edward represents, moreover, as an act of chauvinism: "I'll have no ghostly Fathers out of France, / England hath learned Clerks and Confessors, / To comfort and absolve as men may do."[13] Instead of sending English clergymen to Elinor, however, Edward surprisingly decides to disguise himself as his wife's confessor. The implication of this stratagem seems clear: if Edward truly wants to free England from entangling foreign alliances, he must dispel the enchantments not only of Spain and France but of a still more invasive foreign power—the Roman Catholic Church.

This Protestant slant to the play's confession scene casts an interesting light, retrospectively, on the inauguratory action of the play, Edward's return from the Crusades. Peele is reticent about both the purpose and the outcome of Edward's exploits in the Holy Land. They are described merely as "Christian wars," fought "for Christ and country"; Peele never mentions the traditional crusading goals of reconquering the Holy Land or of preserving Christendom. Indeed, Peele never mentions any other Christian force involved in Edward's Crusades besides his own English troops; revealingly, the only Christian foreigner said to have accompanied Edward on his holy wars is the awful Elinor, who describes Edward as having been "my fellow soldier, and compeer in arms." This link between the Crusades and Edward's abortive marriage suggests that the Crusades were an equally misguided foreign venture, which distracted Edward from his true sphere of interest, his island home. Certainly Edward's island enemies view his crusading as a boon to their cause: "Whilst he wins glory at Jerusalem," the Welsh leader Lluellen advises, "Let us win ground upon the Englishmen."[14] Even the domestic rebellions that plague Edward, therefore, seem related to his foreign entanglements, so that his returning from the Crusades looks conversely like his undertaking the properly nationalist objective of consolidating his domestic power.

That is the way Peele's contemporary John Davies of Hereford, writing in his *Microcosmos* (1603), described Edward's career: Edward "wisely weigh'd how incommodiously / The *Conquests* stood achiev'd the *Land* without," and "therefore he bent his *power*, and *industry*," to "reduce" his own island into one "entire *Monarchy*." Edward's mother expresses a similar view at the start of Peele's play. "And now to eternize Albion's Champions, / Equivalent with Trojans' ancient fame, / Comes lovely Edward from Jerusalem": it is Edward's return from the Holy Land, not his conquests there, that Edward's mother heralds as an imperial *renovatio*. Her only mention of Edward's accomplishments as a crusader is a disquieting reference to "the poor remainer of the royal fleet"; the rest of the first scene, strangely devoted to the display of Edward's maimed soldiers and to promises about their future maintenance, further implies that the Crusades have done nothing but weaken England gravely. And yet the phrase "the poor remainer of the royal fleet" also uncannily reinforces the queen mother's equation of Albion with Troy, insofar as it links Edward's returning fleet to Aeneas's scattered ships at the start of the *Aeneid*, "the sely poor remain of Troy that Greeks had laid so low." Rather than count as the first in a series of imperialist conquests, then, the Crusades figure in *Edward I* as the epic fall or diaspora from which a new Troy—and perhaps a new Jerusalem—will arise.[15]

By the end of the play, however, this early image of England as Edward's true desideratum has been considerably tarnished. The play's initial presentation of Edward as a warrior "for Christ and country" invidiously colors the later dramatization of his wars against his fellow islanders, the Welsh and the Scottish. During their first battle, the Welsh leader Lluellen denounces Edward as both a "traitor" who "seeks thy country's sack" and a vagrant renegade, "the famous runagate of Christendom." Edward's defiant rejoinder only bolsters Lluellen's charges. To certify, on the contrary, just "how great, how famous, and how fortunate" he is, Edward recounts his acts of crusading homicide: "this sword unsheath'd hath shined oft, / With reeking in the blood of Saracens"; "setting before the gates of Nazareth, / My horse's hoofs I stain'd in Pagans' gore, / Sending whole centuries of heathen souls, / To Pluto's house." Instead of renouncing the Crusades, Edward seems to have converted them into a model for his domestic expansionism—proving Lluellen's point that, like a runagate, Edward can neither live quietly at home nor keep his sword sheathed in the company of fellow Christians.[16]

While Edward's turning away from the Holy Land and Christian service is thus compromised by his turning domestic life into a kind of inverted Crusades, Edward does not remain the only possible representative of an exclusivist nationalism among the characters Peele presents. Elsewhere in the play, Peele speaks directly, not just allusively, of "the true remains of glorious Troy," and the nation he so describes turns out to be not the English but the Welsh. The opening scene of Edward's homecoming is immediately countered in the play by a scene set in Wales, where the Welsh Lluellen matches the patriotic fervor of the queen mother by exhorting his men to rouse themselves "for thy country's good":

Follow the man that means to make you great:
Follow Lluellen rightful prince of Wales,
Sprung from the loins of great Cadwallader,
Descended from the loins of Trojan Brute,
And though the traitorous Saxons, Normans, Danes,
Have pent the true remains of glorious Troy,
Within the western mountains of this Isle,
Yet have we hope to climb these stony pales,
When Londoners as Romans erst amaz'd,
Shall trembling cry Lluellen's at the gate.

In Lluellen's eyes, Edward is as much an invading foreigner as the Spanish or French are, and surprisingly, no Englishman in the play ever disputes Lluellen's claim that the Welsh are the only true islanders and thus the only authentic Trojans around. Their presence in *Edward I*—so irrepressible, as I have said, that the dead Lluellen and his quashed rebellion eerily revive at the play's end—relegates the English king Edward to a curious middle ground: he can never escape the embattled position of a man torn between foreign and domestic ties.[17]

As Lluellen's own aggressive plans suggest, however, the Welsh themselves are not free from the taint of warring against fellow Christians, nor does their insularism so readily distinguish them from the ostensible rootlessness of Edward. To be pent within the mountains, after all, is to seem a barbarous and fugitive "runagate" oneself. The Welsh effort to shake off this outlaw image by reconquering Britain does not prosper in *Edward I*: instead of storming London, Lluellen spends most of the play cavorting in the greenwood as a new Robin Hood. Peele further travesties the supposed purity of the Welsh by having Lluellen fraternize with a wandering representative of the Catholic Church, a "good-fellow" friar who at one point declares that he will defend his claim to his "wench" "Contra omnes gentes." Edward may make English expansionism look questionable, but Lluellen and his band do little good for the Welsh insularist alternative.[18]

In his less bellicose moments, it is Edward and not Lluellen who points a way out of this impasse in the play, along a *via media* made possible by the same cosmopolitan streak in Edward that had earlier linked him, disastrously, with the Crusades and his Spanish wife. Having learned that the Welsh would submit to a ruler who, if not Welsh by blood, was nevertheless born in Wales, Edward forces the pregnant Elinor to travel westward. After the birth in Wales of the future Edward II, Edward honors the Welsh still further by swaddling the child in a mantle of lowly Welsh frieze. Preferring to rule "with familiar majesty," Edward has as little stake in princely as in English snobbery; conversely, the most nationalist-sounding character in the play is Edward's proud Spanish queen, who bitterly complains about Welsh wit, manners, clothes, even about the "base" Welsh ground.[19] Once he renounces the standoffish yet adulterous Elinor, Edward frees himself, it seems, to continue altering his foreign policy in two related respects: as he curtails his relations with the Christian powers—France, Spain, and Rome—to the east, he can now ally England more closely with its insular neighbors—the Welsh, the Scottish—in the west. Elinor's disgrace and death at the end of *Edward I* thus transform while they recapitulate the diaspora that opens the play. Having left Palestine and Christendom in order to become a domestic crusader, Edward finds that he must turn his back not only on his old conception of Christian service, but on an English separatist alternative as well. To gain a Holy Land at home without also turning runagate and shedding Christian blood, Edward needs to fashion a new Christendom, which he can accomplish only by embracing the *internationality* of his island.

II

In recent decades, historians such as J. G. A. Pocock, Hugh Kearney, and Norman Davies have profoundly discredited the English version of Manifest Destiny as a principle for explaining the history of Wales, Scotland, and Ireland. Encouraged by this revisionist interest in the multinational context of the British Isles, some literary historians, among them David Cairns, Shaun Richards, David Baker, and Philip Schwyzer, have treated Renaissance English nationalism as effectively inseparable from an island imperialism.[20] Differentiating the insular internationalism of *Edward I* from English imperialism would indeed be a difficult task, and *Edward I* does not make clear how far Peele would be willing to pursue the distinction. Edward's failure to unify the island could be seen as Peele's compliment to the Tudors, who did successfully absorb Wales, but it could also register Peele's dismay at the continuing chauvinism of English policy regarding Scotland as well as Wales, and then again it could reflect Peele's satisfaction with Elizabeth's restrained Scottish policy (which Bacon, for one, favorably contrasted to Edward's expansionist "forwardness").[21] What makes the ambiguity of Peele's stance particularly hard to resolve is his vagueness about the nonimperialist corporate identity that could develop from a peaceful confederation between the Welsh and English—whether that identity would be understood as Christian or "British" or both. This vagueness seems necessitated by Peele's refusal to face, more directly than he does, England's break with the older international identity, Christendom, that Edward begins the play by leaving behind him.

A telling sign of Peele's confusion is his half-hearted attempt to portray the Welsh Lluellen and English Edward as comrades in a single "Commonwealth" of "good fellows." Lluellen only pretends to be a Robin Hood, while, in reality, his thievings go to the "maintenance" of his "wars," not to the poor. By the same token, one of Edward's noblemen may wish that "some good fellows" would "take in hand to cudgel Robin Hood," and Edward may resolve to venture on this "merry flirt," but when Edward and Lluellen actually meet as "irregulars," they try to kill each other. "I could love and honor the man for his valor," Lluellen says of Edward after their greenwood duel, "were it not that rule and sovereignty sets us at jar." If the later Robin Hood plays of Munday and Chettle seem more nationalist in Womack's paradoxical sense than *Edward I* does, that is largely because the plays avoid depicting the English as enemies to any other insular or even Continental Christian nations. In *The Downfall of Robert, Earle of Huntingdon, Afterward Called Robin Hood*, England is a team player; here, more emphatically than in *Edward I*, England's participation in the Crusades is what plunges the country into misery. While Richard the Lion-Hearted is off battling the heathen, England suffers depredations first from Richard's deputy the Bishop of Ely and then from Ely's supplanter, the no less corrupt Prince John. One of Richard's crusading henchmen, the Earl of Leicester, lauds Richard for his eastward excursion in defense of the "true religious faith," but the events of the play, along with its heavy anti-Catholicism, support John's counter-claim that Richard has in effect sold his own nation to buy the Holy Land: "*Richard* is a king, / In *Cyprus, Acon, Acres*, and rich *Palestine*: / To get those kingdoms England lent him men, / And many million of her substance spent, / The very entrails of her womb was rent." In personifying England's misfortunes, the hero of the play—"the banisht, beggar'd, bankrout *Huntington*"—dramatizes those troubles as a form of exile: Richard, the play implies, has banished England from his thoughts. And when we learn that Huntington has been excommunicated as well as dispossessed during Richard's absence, England's exile from its king comes to seem, by analogy, also a banishment from Christendom, which like Richard has shunted England aside in its obsession with "the glorious East."[22]

The nationalist appeal to this marginalization of England in the play is that it throws the English upon their own resources. First the deposed Bishop of Ely, then the equally disgraced Prince John, and finally almost every other character in the play find themselves exiled to the woods along with Huntington (now called Robin Hood); once apart from civilization, they appear to stumble upon a better mode of Christian fellowship than the one they have left behind. The older society is epitomized by the Crusades, which Leicester describes in even more appalling terms than Edward I had: "O still me thinks I see king *Richard* stand, / In his guilt [sic] armor stain'd with Pagans' blood, / Upon a galley's prow, like war's fierce God, / And on his crest, a Crucifix of gold." Such bloodthirsty and even blasphemous carnality—for Protestants, the predictable complement to Richard's lust for "the blessed land"—has no place in Sherwood Forest. Acquisitiveness is not an option for roving outlaws who give their plunder to the poor. In the eyes of the law, Robin and his men may count as nothing better than good fellows who "revel, waste and spend, and take no care," but Robin views his carefree life as a way to recover the civil Christian values, the "true charity, / Good dealing, faithful friendship, honesty" that England has lost. Thus Robin forgives all the former enemies who end up sharing his banishment, and this "perfect charity" converts them.[23]

When Richard finally returns home, he too undergoes a greenwood reeducation. Meeting Robin, the king at first praises him as the "true pillar of my state, right Lord indeed, / Whose honor shineth in the den of need," but Robin immediately corrects the carnal eastern bias in Richard that has led him to correlate England with a needy den:

> Do not, dread Lord, grieve at my low estate:
> Never so rich, never so fortunate,
> Was *Huntington* as now himself he finds.
> And to approve it, may it please your Grace,
> But to accept such presents at the hand
> Of your poor servant, as he hath prepar'd,
> You shall perceive, the Emperor of the East,
> Whom you contended with at *Babylon*,
> Had not such presents to present you with.

Robin's gifts to Richard are the banished Earl of Fitzwater, the Bishop of Ely, Prince John, and Robin's own beloved (yet still virginal) Matilda; eschewing the ultimately bloody materialism that pervades the rest of Catholic society, Robin has come to see England's wealth not as its land or riches but rather as its people, now met "as combined friends."[24]

The *Downfall* thus elaborates an early version of the "rogue" nationalism that develops on the Tudor and Stuart stage in response to England's break with Catholic Christendom—a nationalism that treats the "outlawed" English as a sodality more charitable and cohesive than the supposedly legitimate Christian fellowship from which they have been expelled. The clearest sign that the *Downfall* does indeed represent an early version of this paradoxical nationalism is that the utopian community of the greenwood quickly falls apart: in the next installment of Robin's story, as one character warns us at the end of the *Downfall*, Robin will be poisoned, Richard will die while on a further Crusade, and Matilda will enter a nunnery, where she too will be poisoned. Like *Edward I*, but far more boldly, *The Death of Robert, Earle of Huntington* seems to blame these renewed troubles on the continued Romish presence in England. Robin's murderers are a prior and priest (who set off every imaginable alarm for Robin when they offer him a "precious drink" "from *Rome*" with "*Syrian Balsamum*" in it); Matilda is betrayed by a corrupt Abbess and her lover, a "lewd shaveling" Monk.[25] Only when the English take the cue from their figurative excommunication in the *Downfall* and truly cast off papist shackles, the play seems to imply, will they permanently reinvent themselves in the image of Robin's merry band.

Richard's successor, King John, appears to lay the groundwork for just this schismatical process when, still under the influence of his greenwood sojourn, he renounces the foreign lands that Richard had conquered:

> *Ambition*, that had ever waited on king *John*,
> Now brings him *Austria*, easy to be ta'en,
> Being wholly tam'd by *Richard's* warlike hand,
> And bids him add that Dukedom to his crown:
> But he puts by *Ambition*, and contemns
> All other kingdoms, but the English crown.

Pardoning the former rebels Richmond and Leicester, John further manifests the good effects of his exile: "I do embrace ye both, and hold my self / Richer by a whole Realm, in having you." But if John knows that he ought to reject foreign possessions and embrace his own people instead, he proves incapable of maintaining the charitable inclusiveness that Robin had tried to foster during his exile. Instead, John spends most of the play lusting after the person of Matilda, whose sight he is said to hold "dearer than England, or earth's Empery." What John lacks, apparently, is any spiritual account of England's difference from Christendom, which would enable him to care about England as an estimable community.[26]

Leicester is so revolted by John's lust and the internal dissensions it produces that he begins to speak of England as "the den of cruelty" and urges his fellow lords to fly for aid to the "Christian" arms of the invading French. But persuaded in part by the recollection that the French king had abandoned Richard in Palestine, the lords decide against such treason: they are caught between the carnal particularism of their king, on the one hand, and, on the other, a Christian internationalism they can no longer trust. This impasse in the play might be thought, again, to underscore the historical prematurity of the nationalism that Robin and his contemporaries dimly outline, or more precisely the urgent need for a full-scale Reformation that would rationalize and also idealize English "outlawry." Neither Robin nor Matilda, for instance, ever questions Catholic doctrine. Yet their conspicuous devotion to beads and crucifixes also makes it difficult to separate Robin and Matilda's heroic charity from their Catholicism—especially when that charity constitutes, again, a plea for inclusiveness.[27] Convinced that an England estranged from Christendom can revive the spirituality on which Christian fellowship should be based, Munday and Chettle nevertheless cannot take the nationalist step of assuming that this purified English community ought then to be defined against the rest of Christendom.[28] Robin may be exiled in the plays to an elsewhere that is domestic, not foreign like Lluellen's Wales, but the reformation of England that takes place in this internal utopia proves to be as short-lived as Robin's stay there: the Robin Hood plays ultimately fail to find an alternative to Christendom that can do without other Christian nations.

III

In its simultaneous criticism and defense of an English schism, *King John* intensifies the apparent confusion that seems to plague the representation of England in *Edward I* and the Robin Hood plays. But the seeming contradictions in the play are not a function of Shakespeare's oft-celebrated skepticism or ambivalence; they are too systematic for that. Instead, they point to Shakespeare's hope that religious corruption in Protestant England as well as Catholic Christendom might ultimately lead to a reformation of Christianity in fact.

Even more than the second Robin Hood play, Shakespeare's *King John* depicts a postcrusading England as a shadow of its former self: without Richard the Lion-Hearted, England in *King John* is ravaged not only by civil wars and French hostilities, but by the pope, too. The second act of the play is set in France, before the walls of the English-held city Angiers, where the armies of John and the French king Philip have met to decide whether John or Philip's candidate, John's nephew Arthur, should succeed the dead Richard as England's king. By the start of act 3, this international rendition of English civil war appears to have been peacefully concluded. John has agreed to marry his niece Blanch to Philip's son Lewis, and he supplies Blanch a dowry that includes all his French possessions except Angiers, which, to "heal up all," he relinquishes to Arthur; in exchange, Philip has agreed to treat his mission for Arthur as successful. Yet, as soon as the marriage knot is tied, the papal legate Pandulph enters the play and demands that John adopt the pope's choice for Archbishop of Canterbury, a candidate whom John has rejected. The result is that John defies the pope, Pandulph excommunicates John, Philip under threat of excommunication is forced to sever his league with the English "arch-heretic"—and the war between France and England begins anew.[29]

In so openly dramatizing English resistance to what John calls the pope's "usurped authority" over English affairs, Shakespeare appears to align his play with a Protestant polemical tradition that had long regarded John as a reformer *avant la lettre*.[30] In response to Pandulph's demands on the pope's behalf, Shakespeare allows John a stirring defense of royal supremacy; when Philip accuses him of blasphemy, John broadens his attack on the pope to include a denunciation of Roman Catholicism generally:

> Though you and all the kings of Christendom
> Are led so grossly by this meddling priest,
> Dreading the curse that money may buy out,
> And by the merit of vild gold, dross, dust,
> Purchase corrupted pardon of a man
> Who in that sale sells pardon from himself;
> Though you, and all the rest so grossly led,
> This juggling witchcraft with revenue cherish,
> Yet I alone, alone do me oppose
> Against the Pope, and count his friends my foes.[31]

The trouble with the anti-Roman reading of *King John* that seems to follow from this speech is that Shakespeare strongly criticizes John, too. If no character in the play ever rebuts John's attack on papist carnality, none ever denies that Arthur is the rightful heir to England's throne. The most heroic English figure in *King John*, the bastard son of Richard, goes so far as to disparage Philip for renouncing the "zeal and charity" that had brought him to the field "as God's own soldier" on Arthur's behalf, and a guilty Philip himself admits that, as "God knows," he has allowed political expediency to take precedence over Arthur's "right." This correlation of legitimacy and Christian charity with the international candidate Arthur makes a nationalist reading of John's schism difficult to sustain, especially when, in the same scene, the Bastard reproaches John for trying to secure his shaky claim to the throne by selling off England's overseas possessions.[32]

Shakespeare's insistence that John isolates and diminishes England for his own worldly gain gives the play a Catholic edge and raises the sort of questions about an English monarch that Catholic polemicists loved to ask about Elizabeth. In his *Admonition to the Nobility and People of England and Ireland* (1588), written to justify the impending Armada, William Allen lists three major reasons why Shakespeare's queen lacks the "right" to England's throne, and they all have relevance to Shakespeare's play. First, Allen points out, Elizabeth is an excommunicate; second, she is only the bastard issue of Henry VIII; and third, she never received the pope's approbation, a condition of legitimacy confirmed by English kings themselves when Henry II and then John surrendered their crowns to the pope. In Allen's view, Elizabeth's illegitimacy has forced her to undertake the sort of "*Machiavellian*, godless, and conscienceless course" for which Protestants condemned the pope: to prop up her lawless title, Elizabeth has not only separated England from the Christian community but become "the first & principal fountain" of all the rebellions now troubling Christendom. Such considerations, Allen explains, are what have led the pope to exhort "the chief and greatest princes of his Christian Catholic communion" to "give succor to their afflicted brethren & confederates, & join together with him their supreme pastor, for chastisement of that wicked woman, the bane of Christendom and all their kingdoms."[33] Just as an earlier pope had ordered the king of France "to invade the realm of England, and revenge him of the manifold injuries done to the universal church, by that cursed Turk or Pagan, King John," so now a second westward Crusade has been launched against the new English "bane of Christendom," Elizabeth.[34]

Yet Shakespeare's emphasis on John's illegitimacy does not cancel out the strong grounds that John cites for defying the pope, too. How is one to reconcile the play's apparently mixed polemical signals? An earlier King John play on which Shakespeare closely modeled his own effort, the anonymous *Troublesome Raigne of King John* (c. 1590), managed to concede that John was not an ideal ruler without having to abandon the Protestant interpretation of John's struggles: in the *Troublesome Raigne*, John confesses to himself that "Thy sins are far too great to be the man / T'abolish Pope, and Popery from thy Realm: / But in thy seat, if I may guess at all, / A King shall reign that shall suppress them all."[35] For all its cynicism about John, Shakespeare's play appears to adopt this prophetic vein when, after John's death, the Bastard sketches out the heroic vista of a self-sufficient English nation:

This England never did, nor never shall,
Lie at the proud foot of a conqueror,
But when it first did help to wound itself.

Now these her princes are come home again,
Come the three corners of the world in arms,
And we shall shock them. Nought shall make us rue,
If England to itself do rest but true.

England's suffering has apparently opened the Bastard's eyes just as it opened Robin's in the *Downfall*. Having begun in *King John* by expressing pride in his illegitimacy—"a good blunt fellow," John condescendingly calls him—the Bastard now ends the play by transforming John's earlier outlawry from Christendom into a nationalist chauvinism.[36]

What this prophetic reading of the play fails to explain, however, is why the first character in *King John* to paint a heroic picture of English separatism should be a shady figure on the pope's side. Before the battle at Angiers, the duke of Austria, pledging his support for the international candidate Arthur, promises Arthur

That to my home I will no more return
Till Angiers, and the right thou hast in France,
Together with that pale, that white-fac'd shore,
Whose foot spurns back the ocean's roaring tides
And coops from other lands her islanders,
Even till that England, hedg'd in with the main,
That water-walled bulwark, still secure
And confident from foreign purposes,
Even till that utmost corner of the west
Salute thee for her king.[37]

What makes Austria's evocation of English insularity particularly strange and unsettling is that he has just been introduced in the play as the man who killed King Richard and thus helped plunge England into civil war in the first place. The murdered Richard was hardly a separatist enemy to the Christian community; on the contrary, as Philip recalls only a few lines before Austria's speech, he was a crusading hero, who "fought the holy wars in Palestine." An early spokesman for a holy war against England, Austria gives that war, by association, a revealing set of motives. Having turned inward the conflict between Christendom and its external enemy the Turk by murdering an English crusader, Austria misrepresents internal dissension within Christendom as a product not of English victimage but of English aggression: in his speech England "spurns back the ocean's roaring tides / And coops from other lands her islanders," willfully dividing her people from the rest of Christendom. When the French ambassador subsequently announces John's impending arrival before Angiers, and remarks that "a braver choice of dauntless spirits / Than now the English bottoms have waft o'er / Did never float upon the swelling tide / To do offense and scathe in Christendom," the English are once again made to seem both indomitable and perverse, as if they will leave their island only when they can widen the wound to Christendom already inflicted by their insularism. John may think himself heroically defiant when he later decides to "spurn" the Catholic Church, but the fact remains that his schism conveniently fits Austria's bill for transforming England into Christendom's new scapegoat.[38]

King John thus goes further than *Edward I* and the Robin Hood plays in complicating the nationalist interpretation of England's exodus from Palestine: if England in *King John* has become the new object of crusading desire, that is because John has effectively conspired with the pope to substitute himself for the Turk as the bane of Christendom. "All form is formless, order orderless," Pandulph warns Philip, "save what is opposite to England's love."[39] But why has a papal Christendom chosen England as the site of its new holy wars? The answer seems to lie in Austria's vision of England as literally divided from the Christian community: England, "that utmost corner of the west," can be represented as geographically distinct from a Christendom that, in both the thirteenth and sixteenth centuries, found the Turk knocking at its eastern gate. Yet, if Pandulph's hyperbole is any indication, the exceptional capacity of England to provide a contrasting form and order to the Christian community that excludes it also seems to make England too useful, as though Christendom would be "formless" and "orderless" were there no island nation to hate.

Both the appeal and the danger to Christendom of an insular Christian scapegoat come clearer in a unusual moment of the play, when the Bastard exhorts John and Philip to suspend their differences for a time and turn their aggression instead against the city, Angiers, that has shut them out: "Do like the mutines of Jerusalem, / Be friends awhile, and both conjointly bend / Your sharpest deeds of malice on this town."[40] The Bastard refers to a famous episode from Josephus's *Jewish Wars* in which the civil warriors of first-century Jerusalem belatedly combined forces against a Roman army that would soon destroy their city; the episode came to be moralized again and again as plain evidence for the view that internal divisions are what make a nation conquerable.[41] The obvious upshot of the Bastard's analogy is that John and Arthur are civil warriors who have exposed their nation, England, to foreign intervention, although the comparison of the international forces outside Angiers to the Jewish fighters within the Holy City suggests still larger implications—that John and *Philip* are civil warriors, who have exposed the greater state to which they belong, Christendom, to the threat of Jerusalem's current conqueror, the Turk. Not even the most zealous Elizabethan Protestants were immune to the anxiety that Christian strife would open the door to Turkish invasion: John Foxe, for instance, explains to the Christian community at large that he has included a history of Turkish atrocities in his book of martyrs so that "the consideration of this horrible persecution of the Turks rising chiefly by our discord and dissension among ourselves, may reduce us again from our domestical wars, in killing and burning one another, to join together in christian patience and concord."[42] Yet if the Bastard intends something like Foxe's plea for Christian "concord," why is he recommending that "malice" be turned against a Christian and, what is worse, an English city? Even for an English hero, it seems, the physical segregation of an English populace recommends that populace over the Turks as the enemy against which Christian cooperation is required. The Bastard's loyalties thus seem to be as confused as the king's in *Edward I*, and his comparison of his fellow soldiers to the citizens of Jerusalem suggests a further blurring of affiliations, because the comparison is almost pointedly inapt. After all, England and France are the besiegers, not the besieged; the Bastard takes his cue for order from the city he recommends attacking, and by analogy reduces the English and French forces to the size of another embattled city, Jerusalem—which, notoriously, lost its war. Though the Bastard's proposal frightens the citizens of Angiers into proposing the marriage settlement and thus leads to a temporary truce, it also shows how Christendom in the play has come to require for its unity a self-division that both diminishes the Christian community and threatens to destroy it.

When over the course of *King John* Angiers is replaced as scapegoat by the English island, this confusion of besieged and besieger, excluded and excluder, grows more conspicuous. In act 4, under prompting from Pandulph, Philip's son Lewis invades England, while John as always plays into the pope's hands by seeming to have murdered Arthur and thus alienating the English nobility. Now, as the civil warriors outside the walls of Angiers enter England's water-walled bulwark, Christian factiousness is physically displaced to the English island. Yet the introjection of a larger Christian division into England goes, as it were, too far: not only does England become the exclusive scene of division in the play between itself and an invading France, but the English themselves begin to edge out the French as England's most prominent enemies. After defecting from John to the French, a leader of the English nobility, the Earl of Salisbury, laments to his fellow noblemen

That we, the sons and children of this isle,
Were born to see so sad an hour as this,
Wherein we step after a stranger, march
Upon her gentle bosom, and fill up
Her enemies' ranks.

Providing Christendom some form and order by taking upon itself the divisions internal to Christendom, England in filling up the French ranks even begins to take over Christendom's internationality. The name of England's dead crusader, Richard Cordelion, had always implied the Frenchness of an England ruled, after all, by Normans, but it is not until Lewis invades a now insular England that the English actually speak French and in the act represent their foreign ties as treasonous to England: "Have I not heard these islanders shout out / 'Vive le roi!,'" Lewis brags to Pandulph, "as I have bank'd their towns?" Growing more distressed at the thought of his own treachery, Salisbury longs for a more traditional alternative to Christian division, the Crusades; but the outlines of the crusading venture he envisages at this point in English history are strikingly novel

O nation, that thou couldst remove!
That Neptune's arms, who clippeth thee about,
Would bear thee from the knowledge of thyself,
And gripple thee unto a pagan shore,
Where these two Christian armies might combine
The blood of malice in a vein of league,
And not to spend it so unneighborly![43]

It may be thoroughly conventional for Salisbury to wish that international Christian "mutines" would unite themselves against the Turks, but he envisions an England *internally* international, not Christendom, as so uniting itself. Similarly, Salisbury may take the side of Catholic polemicists, such as Parsons and Allen, in thinking that England's divisive insularity should be eliminated, but the "shore" to which he wants England's island joined is, surprisingly, not Christian but "pagan." In Salisbury's imagination, the Continent dividing England from the Turks disappears, replaced *as* Christendom by its insular scapegoat. So thoroughly has England assumed the burden of Christendom's troubles in the play that Christendom, not its troubles, begins to be forgotten.

With one important catch: Salisbury may wish that England could recapture Jerusalem by "removing" its "mutines" to Palestine and thus encouraging them to turn their aggression outward against the Turks, but his wish to conjoin England and the Holy Land is, as he knows, physically impossible. This material impediment is crucial, and underscores the difficulty in the play of idealizing any polity as an embodiment of Christian unity—a difficulty that had already figured in the Bastard's self-defeating reference to a walled holy city he forgot had lost its war. Shakespeare's audience need not have been sectarian Protestants to have sympathized with *King John*'s persistent critique of attempts to organize Christendom in terms of some old or newly designated Holy Land. After all, the fall of Jerusalem, the failure of the Jewish civil warriors to save their city from physical destruction, was regularly hailed by Christians as one of the most productive events in history. It signalled, among other things, the universalization of God's promise. As Samuel Purchas explained in 1625, once Jerusalem had been "demolished by the Romans, the Church became truly Catholic, not looking any more to walls of a Temple, to carnal Sacrifices, to the petty pinfold of one Nation, to one City, as the Mart & Mother of Christian Religion and discipline." Purchas meant to chastise those Christians who still believe the church to be shut up, if no longer in Jerusalem, then in the "great metropolis and see" that Pandulph speaks of as if it were synonymous with "the holy church"—Rome.[44] In *King John*, however, such criticism of Rome is for the most part deflected onto another city, Angiers, and then onto a nation "walled" like a city, off in the utmost corner of the Christian map. As this marginal island nation becomes increasingly important to Christendom and to the plot of the play, however, England's spiritual insignificance in relation to Rome starts to look, paradoxically, significant. Far from the lands of the New Testament, England has no persuasive grounds for claiming, as Jerusalem once had and Rome now does, an exclusive relation to God's promise; at the same time, the insularity that "spurns" and "coops" makes England look more obviously exclusive than a Rome lying in the center of Christendom. Shakespeare may want England to take the place of a divided Christendom in the play, but only insofar as England can then help differentiate Christendom from the sort of exclusive physical boundaries that, as definitive spiritual criteria, fell with the walls of Jerusalem.

IV

What I called the mixed polemical signals of the play might seem to suit this critique of exclusivity only negatively, insofar as they suggest that Shakespeare would rather call down a plague on both Catholics and Protestants than take sides with either faction. But once the scene of *King John* shifts to the English island, religious conflict diminishes as a dramatic issue: John, for instance, never theologizes about the pope again. Instead, John's own failings take center stage; just as the Catholic scapegoating of England is both underwritten and undermined by the transferral of Christian dissension exclusively to the English stage, so John in embodying the corruption of an absent pope eventually shoulders aside the pope as a dramatic issue. If John thus wins the debate over royal versus papal supremacy, he also loses any claim to royal stature; conversely, if the play bears out the accusations of the pope's party, it also empties them of their sectarian content.

In Shakespeare's later histories, when the pope drops out of the action altogether, the sort of criminal behavior that Protestants associated with Rome will increasingly crop up in England's kings. For instance, the Protestant sources of *King John* like to complain how the pope uses the Crusades only as a ruse either to divert attention from his own illegitimate title or to steal kingdoms from crusader-kings while they are away.[45] Such hypocritical commitment to the Crusades is, again, a prominent attribute of Shakespeare's Henry IV, who on his deathbed confesses to his son that, to disarm his enemies, he "had a purpose now / To lead out many to the Holy Land, / Lest rest and lying still might make them look / Too near unto my state." Henry never succeeds in launching this diversion; the pilgrims who do appear in the *Henry IV* plays are traveling only as far east as Canterbury, and even that reduced, intranational excursion is brought to an abrupt halt when the pilgrims are robbed along the way by the roguish associates of Prince Hal. One might argue that this theft—Shakespeare's ironic version of the Robin Hood topos—merely preempts the larceny that awaited the pilgrims in Canterbury anyway, where they would have lost their "rich offerings" to a thieving Catholic clergy. (As I will detail in chapter 4, Protestant polemicists typically claimed that "the Bishops of Rome, with the marts of their purgatories and pardons, have both tormented men's consciences and picked their purses"—which helps explain why Shakespeare had earlier characterized Hal's thieves as mock-clergy, "Saint Nicholas' clerks.")[46] But the incorporation of papist carnality into English authorities has made the pope practically irrelevant to England's concerns. This process of displacement is neatly epitomized in *2 Henry IV*, when the Holy Land indeed becomes English territory, but only in such a way as to minimize larger Christian concerns. Having had it prophesied to him for "many years" that he "should not die but in Jerusalem, / Which vainly I suppos'd the Holy Land," the spurious crusader Henry learns that he will instead die in what is merely a room called Jerusalem. The name of his son Hal's residence in this play—the thieves' den, Eastcheap—seems another odd, allegorical pun meant to signify the debasing introjection of the eastern world into England, that utmost corner of the west.[47]

When he learns how the prophecies regarding his death have been fulfilled only by being deflated, Henry IV is nonetheless moved enough to exclaim, "Laud be to God!" In *King John* Shakespeare similarly appears to regard England's secularizing internalization of Christendom as somehow a providential process. Consider the fate of Arthur in the play. When John imprisons Arthur in the England that John has just insularized, he unintentionally represents England's water-walled bulwark as confining a truer, more internationally oriented English sovereignty, but at the very moment when John relents toward Arthur, Arthur jumps from the prison walls to his death—as if to show that John has the power to confine Arthur and England but not to liberate them.[48] Later, in response to the French invasion and the defection of his own nobility, John tries to save his crown by submitting himself to Rome, but Pandulph's subsequent revocation of the pope's curse fails to assuage the English nobles or to turn back the invading Lewis; not even the pope can halt the introversion of Christian dissension into England. Finally, and most tellingly, reinforcements to Lewis's invading army are shipwrecked on an English shoal, while shortly thereafter much of the defending English army is also drowned, the victim of "unexpected" tides in an English bay: "Neptune" appears willing to defeat England's invaders (just as he will later disperse the Spanish Armada), but he also refuses to allow the English to interpret the French disaster as a sign that he supports English insularism. In line with the double edge of all these events, the strongest assertion of England's spiritual bankruptcy in the play comes paradoxically from England's staunchest defender throughout, the Bastard. Lamenting how England's hopes have shrunk to the size of Arthur's dead body—"How easy," he observes upon Hubert's lifting Arthur's corpse, "dost thou take all England up"—the Bastard exclaims that "the life, the right, and truth of all this realm / Is fled to heaven." No other character in the play offers a more positive account of England's spiritual health; yet by the end of *King John* the Bastard has embraced the view of England that has been thrust upon him by the course of events, which in his eyes irresistibly demand that England's separateness from the rest of Christendom be preserved.[49]

As it sharpens the general ambivalence regarding England in the play, the bleak picture of Arthur's corpse also begins to explain why the now spiritless "clay" of a schismatical England should come to seem so providentially important. What arouses the Bastard's despair as he looks at Arthur is the dramatic contrast between England's life, right, and truth, on the one hand, and the mere "*morsel* of dead royalty," on the other: it is the *littleness* of Arthur's corpse that makes the division between present matter and absent spirit in England seem to the Bastard so telling.[50] In his final words, John similarly refers to his own dying body as "but a clod / And module of confounded royalty"; he too transforms the originally international dissension between English kings into the quite different discrepancy between an ideal "royalty" and the meager embodiment that "confounds" it. This insufficiency of both kingly corpses to English royalty is, as the Bastard emphasizes, shared by "all England," the island nation that has lost its international stature along with its kings: thanks to the alienation of England's overseas possessions and then its banishment to a corner of the Christian map, England in *King John* has itself been reduced to a "morsel" or "module" of its former self.[51] What's more, England's belittlement dramatically reduces Christendom in size and dignity, not only because a separate England diminishes the territory belonging to Christendom, but also because, in scapegoating the English, Christendom inadvertently turns the English island into the exclusive theater of Christian operations in the play. This irony receives perhaps its most straightforward notice in *King John* when the Bastard tells the invading Lewis how John intends "To whip this dwarfish war, this pygmy arms, / From out the circle of his territories": to the Bastard's mind, Lewis has diminished rather than augmented his own power by conveying it to the restricted "circle" of insular England. Shakespeare's Catholic contemporaries loved to insist that what Protestants called the "most worthy spectacle" of Reformation in England actually dramatized the inability of Protestants to agree even within the boundaries of "one little Island."[52] While *King John* may similarly present little England as an exemplary theater of dissension, Shakespeare gives the spectacle a far less divisive moral than Catholics did. Separated from Christendom and from the spiritual components of its identity that have fled with Arthur to heaven, England in *King John* has only the material boundaries of its island to define it; yet this reduction of England's meaning to a separate little world underscores, without sectarian reference to the rest of Christendom, the restrictive inadequacy of any materially exclusive conception of Christianity—whether that conception depends on the pardons one sells or, more saliently, on the lands one possesses.

In one of the most popular of Elizabethan sermons, his *Sermon of Christ Crucified* (1570), John Foxe moralizes recent losses of Christian territory into a lesson that his auditors should separate their affections from a world torn by dissension. "Sometimes a rich church, a large church, an universal church, spread far & wide through the whole compass of the earth," Christ's "poor Church militant," Foxe laments, has in recent times been "driven into a narrow corner of the world." Not only have Asia and Africa fallen from the Christian fold, but "now in *Europa* a great part also is shrunk from thy Church. All *Thracia* with the Empire of *Constantinople*, all *Grecia*, *Epyrus*, *Illyricum*, and now of late all the kingdom almost of *Hungaria*, with much of *Austria*, with lamentable slaughter of Christen blood is wasted and all become *Turks*. . . . Only a little angle of the west parts yet remaineth in some profession of thy name." (What the duke of Austria belies in reducing England to a westward "corner," Foxe helps us see, is not only his own crimes but also Christendom's accelerating losses on its eastern front, including "much of Austria.") "But here, alack," Foxe continues, "cometh an other mischief as great, or greater than the other"—the pope, whose usurpations have brought "such dissension and hostility . . . amongst us, that *Turks* be not more enemies to Christians, than Christians to Christians, Papists to Protestants: yea Protestants with Protestants do not agree, but fall out for trifles." "For as much as thy poor little flock can scarce have any place or rest in this world," Foxe concludes, "come Lord, we beseech thee, with thy *Factum est*, and make an end, that this world may have no more time nor place here, and that thy Church may have rest for ever."[53]

The sight of Arthur's corpse tempts the Bastard toward a similar *contemptus mundi*, but he quickly decides to fight instead; his lament over England's diminution is transformed into a battle cry: "Come the three corners of the world in arms / And we shall shock them!" The perception of Christendom's littleness that turns Foxe otherworldly had once served as a rallying point in launching the first Crusades. According to William of Malmesbury, Pope Urban II had inspired his Christian warriors by reminding them "how small is the part [of the world] inhabited by us Christians," and then how "even this fragment [portiunculam] of our world is attacked by the Turks and Saracens." For Urban, the diminished bounds of Christendom meant that Christians needed to turn their eyes eastward as well as upward, and fight to regain their earthly patrimony.[54]

By the time of *Henry V* England's insular littleness similarly provokes expansionism, although now on the part of England alone. After three plays of the claustrophobia induced by dissension at home, Henry V takes up the French threat that opens his play as it had opened John's, but in revealingly new terms: he wittily assures the French ambassador that he "never valu'd this poor seat of England," which is why he looks forward so eagerly to "ruling in large and ample empery / O'er France." Once having left his "poor" island to spread his "sail of greatness" and conquer France, Henry proves still more ambitious. In the play's final scenes, he is betrothed to a French princess and foresees a child from their marriage who will begin restoring Christendom to "Christian-like accord": "Shall not thou and I," he asks his future wife, "compound a boy, half French, half English, that shall go to Constantinople and take the Turk by the beard?" For Henry, at least, the perceived littleness of England in the histories that follow *King John* seems to have excited a Christian desire not to abandon the world but to reclaim it—with the difference from the original Crusades that the pope has been replaced as Christendom's leader by a man better able to appreciate the limitations of narrow boundaries.[55]

Of course, Henry the imperialist soon dies, with disastrous results for England: in the epilogue to *Henry V,* the "small time" (5) that Henry V reigned shrinks to the "infant bands" constraining his son, which in turn inspire such dissension among the child's "many" regents "that they lost France, and made his England bleed." The epilogue concludes by linking this return to both an externally and internally divisive insularity with a similar closing of a circle in the course of Shakespeare's histories: the story of Henry VI, the epilogue reminds us, is one "which oft our stage hath shown."[56] For reasons just as mysterious and yet inescapable as Neptune's in *King John,* neither England nor Shakespeare has proven able to shake off England's insular constraints.

At this point in Shakespeare's histories, however, it becomes very difficult to argue, as some critics have, that Shakespeare believes England must settle for an insularist nationalism *"faute de mieux."*[57] The effect of the epilogue's recourse to the first tetralogy by way of Henry V's lost empire is to undermine the happy, implicitly insularist conclusion of *Richard III,* which had brought Shakespeare's Elizabethan histories closest, in their represented time, to his own day: in *Richard III* the prayer of the future Henry VII that "peace" would now "long live here" goes quite against the grain of his predecessor Henry V's "sword," "By which the world's best garden he achieved / And of it left his son imperial lord." Having reenclosed England in insularity only after first dramatizing the expansive effects of insularity, *Henry V* may suggest that England must forego an imperialist interpretation of its littleness, but that does not mean England should forego all forms of expansionism whatsoever. When Bishop James Pilkington in 1585 denounces Urban II for having "stirred up all princes to recover the holy land again, more like a superstitious Jew, putting holiness in the place which then was inhabited with wicked people, than like a true preacher of true holiness," his point is not that Christendom should stop trying to expand its worldly bounds, but that it must first eschew materialism in order to expand. As an earlier work of Pilkington's (1562) explains,

> Worldly princes, when they go to conquer a country, they go with fire and sword to destroy all that withstand them: but in Christ's kingdom there come saviours to preach salvation to rebels, his enemies and haters, if they will repent. Earthly princes come with guns, horses and harness: Christ's disciples come to conquer the devil and his members without bag, staff, or money. Mortal princes come with might and power of men: the preachers of Christ's kingdom come in the might of God's Spirit, which opens the eyes of the blind, and softens stony hearts, and turns them to the Lord. . . . So in all points, as heaven and earth are contrary, so are the kingdoms, the ministers and subjects of them both, the way to conquer and compass them both, the means to enjoy them both, and the pleasure in them both when we have gotten them.

To believers such as Pilkington, the failure of Henry's imperialist Crusades might well have illustrated by contrast the properly spiritual nature of true Christian warfare.[58]

But Shakespeare's histories suggest that Henry's reliance on fire and sword is only one of the reasons his expansionism fails: another is his traveling in the wrong direction. I have already remarked upon the apparently providential forces behind the narrowing of Christian sights in *King John*, but I have yet to discuss another noteworthy indication of providence in the play: the westward movement of Christian warfare from the Holy Land to the campaign outside Angiers and then to conflict within England. If England truly were the utmost corner of the west, as Austria claims, there would be no further battlefield left for Christendom beside England. But beyond the Continent lay Wales, Scotland, and Ireland, countries that figure far more prominently in Shakespeare's second tetralogy than in his first. *Richard II* and *1 and 2 Henry IV* show these countries at war with England; in *Henry V* all four nations maintain a provisional united front as they battle a common enemy, but the aggression that unites them also continually flares up among them (chapter 4 will look more closely at this uneasy partnership between fellowship and violence in the play.)[59] Throughout the second tetralogy, one might conclude, not even providence can lead Christianity away from carnal warfare, except that farther westward than the British isles, as Shakespeare knew, lay a "pagan shore" that could fulfill the conditions of Salisbury's envisaged Crusade without England's having to turn back, literally or spiritually, to the Christendom of old. *Richard II* twice evokes it, in the most distant fashion: a nobleman in the play speaks of the "new world" that Richard's crimes and Henry's usurpation have produced, while the fallen Richard later tells his queen that instead of striving any longer for worldly power, "our holy lives must win a new world's crown." In the divided England that Shakespeare depicts, a nation newly separated from a corrupt Christendom and yet unreformed itself, it hardly seems possible that Christianity can regain the sense of spiritual unity and purpose it has lost, but the very expressions of skepticism regarding England in these plays are capable of suggesting a radical alternative for Christianity: a New World in fact, complete with the pagans who could motivate the extroversion of crusading zeal once again.[60]

Westward longings figure prominently in the other counter-crusading plays I have discussed. In *Edward I* the western course of Edward's voyage home is continually mirrored and underscored by references to the posthistory of Troy, or to the Roman, then Saxon, Danish, and Norman invasions of England, or to Wales, where more than half the play's scenes are set. The final movement of Elinor's life and of the play begins when Elinor rises from the earth at Queenshithe and hears boatmen calling, "Westward ho." The whole scene of Christian history, Peele seems quietly to insist, is shifting westward; no longer can the Holy Land, or even Europe, be considered the battleground on which the fate of Christianity will be decided. The Robin Hood plays begin with a framing scene in which the fictional author of the plays, John Skelton, and a second, supposedly historical figure, Sir John Eltam, discuss a geographical conference with Henry VII or VIII from which Eltam has just returned:

> These two hours it pleas'd his Majesty
> To use my service in surveying Maps,
> Sent over from the good king *Ferdinand*,
> That to the *Indies*, at *Sebastian's* suit,
> Hath lately sent a Spanish *Colony*.

The play we are about to witness turns out to be a rehearsal for another command performance, another few hours spent educating and delighting the king—who, we are told, has "survey'd the plat" of the *Downfall* also.[61] So emphatic a correlation between Henry's viewing first a map of New World colonization and then a play on English outlawry suggests that the king is studying two versions of the same story.

But how exactly, for Munday and Chettle, do a rogue nation and a new world blend into a single "plat"? Peele's stress on the imperial destiny of the scattered Trojans provides one possible answer; similarly, Richard II's advice to seek a new world's crown follows a speech in which his queen twice refers to England's Trojan heritage.[62] Yet, as Richard's despair over worldly crowns reflects, the *translatio* enacted by Shakespeare's histories traces the westward course of division, not empire, while the ground for whatever is moving westward increasingly shrinks, until not only eastward conquest but ground itself, as Pilkington might say, seems an erroneous goal. A contemporary voyager to America, Edward Hayes (1583), identified another kind of *translatio* that was just beginning to gain attention in England—"the revolution and course of God's word and religion, which from the beginning hath moved from the East, towards, & at last unto the West, where it is like to end, unless the same begin again where it did in the East, which were to expect a like world again. But we are assured of the contrary by the prophecy of Christ, whereby we gather, that after his word preached throughout the world shall be the end."[63] To Hayes's mind, the spirit's revolution would indeed produce the end for which Foxe prayed, but not until the English strove to close the spiritual circle by transporting religion to America. Purchas drew the same conclusion from the fact of Christendom's diminution alone: nothing had more pointedly demonstrated "how little to the rest of the World is all that which is called Christendom, or that also which in any settled flourishing estate of a Church hath ever yet been Christian," than the discovery of pagan America, and thus nothing more poignantly summoned Christians to "that dilating the Church's Pale, and a more Catholic enlarging of her bounds" that would proceed by America's conversion.[64]

For Purchas's contemporary Thomas Cooper (1615), England's own smallness would stimulate New World evangelism. By having "wonderfully preserved this little Island, this Angle of the world," which "in former Ages was not known, or accounted to be any part of the world," God intended not to pamper the English, Cooper insisted, but rather to inspire their twice-otherworldly labor of conveying the gospel still farther westward: for Cooper, "the Church of God in this life dwelleth in Tents," so that it may "be spread over the face of the earth."[65] Taking a more critical look at the English church, the New England preacher Robert Cushman in 1621 represented the religious strife devastating the Old World as the very engine that might carry Christianity to the New. Wondering whether God had decided to "punish his people in the Christian countries of *Europe*, (for their coldness, carnality, wanton abuse of the Gospel, contention, &c.) either by Turkish slavery, or by Popish tyranny," Cushman found comfort in the thought that "here" in America "is a way opened for such as have wings to fly":

> and as by the dispersion of the Jewish Church through persecution, the Lord brought in the fullness of the Gentiles, so who knoweth, whether now by tyranny, and affliction, which he suffereth to come upon them, he will not by little and little chase them [i.e., the converted Gentiles], even amongst the Heathens, that so a light may rise up in the dark, and the kingdom of heaven be taken from them which now have it, and given to a people that shall bring forth the fruit of it.[66]

No character in Shakespeare's Elizabethan histories could possibly share these views on the American trajectory of true religion; in the historical time they dramatize, the histories come to a halt at just the era when English kings first began to inspect New World maps.[67] Restless Englishmen in these plays have little choice but to look backward toward Christendom as Henry V does, or westward toward Ireland as the conquering Richard II does, or, as the conquered Richard does, upward to heaven.[68] Yet Salisbury's conception of the Crusades as driven by the "blood of malice" suggests that Shakespeare may have viewed Catholic England's ignorance of the New World as a providential boon for America's (northern) inhabitants. Shakespeare resists making any relatively direct reference to the New World in his histories until, historically, the speaker can be a Protestant, and an irenic one at that: in Shakespeare's final history play, *Henry VIII* (1613), Archbishop Cranmer foresees Shakespeare's own era as a time when "God shall be truly known," "peace" (three times invoked) shall reign in England, and England shall "make new nations."[69] A westward future for England: that would seem to be the lesson of the first tetralogy, which ends with Henry Tudor's westward voyage of conquest to the English isle; it would also seem to be the lesson of the second tetralogy, which ultimately demonstrates both the expansive power of insularity and the dead end of eastward quests. What Shakespeare consistently avoids in his histories, as I hope I have shown, is any identification of true religion with an insular England: he suggests the providentiality of English civil warfare far more strongly than he does the providentiality of America's discovery or of Christianity's rediscovery because, it seems, he does not want his audience to mistake England for anything other than the latest prison in which Christians have tried to confine God's supranational church. If Shakespeare thus refuses to support the view that Christianity had found a new holy land in England, neither does he endorse the *contemptus* claim of Richard II that the spirit should seek a new world's crown in heaven alone. England in Shakespeare's histories may not be the blessed plot that Gaunt thinks it is, the throne, the isle, the earth, the seat, as a nationalist Protestant might maintain, of a resurrected Christendom, but then England, as Shakespeare's Cranmer reminds us, is not the end of the world.

Part Two

Church and Theater

CHAPTER 4

—

Preachers and Players

> The temple is despised, to run unto Theaters; the Church is emp-
> tied, the yard is filled; we leave the sacrament, to feed our adulterous
> eyes with the impure, & whorish sight of most filthy pastime.
>
> —Anthony Munday, *A Second and Third Blast of Retrait from
> Plaies and Theaters* (1580)

To many a godly Elizabethan, the new public theaters and the newly purified church were enemies in a war that the theaters seemed to be winning. Such pious antagonism toward the English stage marked a revolutionary change from the time of miracle and morality plays, when the Catholic
church had welcomed the services of players; it even marked a change from
earlier days in the Reformation, when Protestant clergymen had embraced
the English stage so wholeheartedly as to appear its "driving force."[1] John
Foxe (1563), perhaps the most influential figure among these earlier reformers, and a playwright himself, had gone so far as to assert that "players, print-
ers, [and] preachers" were "set up of God, as a triple bulwark against the
triple crown of the Pope, to bring him down"; yet only a few years after the
construction of the first permanent playhouses, Anthony Munday in *A Second and Third Blast of Retrait from Plaies and Theaters* (1580) called upon "every
true soldier of Jesus Christ" to join him in his assault upon "the chapel of Satan, I mean the Theater," "to the suppressing of those which fight against
[God's] word."[2]

What was it about the new theaters that suddenly made plays seem capable of teaching the people nothing "but that which is fleshly and carnal?"
The vast concourse of people drawn to these theaters, and the opportunities
for idleness, debauchery, and sedition that such mass audiences generated,
were of course high on the list of reasons why the stage was now said to be
inimical to true religion. Even more outrageous to theater haters than the
playgoers, however, were the players themselves. Not only were they said to

engage in every imaginable vice, both on and off the stage, but they had begun staging their plays, or rather "waging their battle," "on the Sabbath day the more conveniently to destroy the souls of the children of God." The resulting competition between player and preacher could at times seem outrageously direct. In 1596, for instance, a group of citizens from the Blackfriars district of London petitioned the Privy Council to stop construction of a playhouse to be built "so near" their church "that the noise of the drums and trumpets will greatly disturb and hinder both the ministers and parishioners in time of divine service and sermons." Munday claimed the players had already taken their attack much further, and actually invaded "every Temple of God, and that throughout England," with their performances, "so that now the Sanctuary is become a players' stage, and a den of thieves."[3] But the most oft-cited evidence in Elizabethan England that the players had set out to undermine the church was the sheer popularity of the players in comparison to the church. "Woe is me!" one scandalized observer (1587) among many exclaimed: "The play houses are pestered, when churches are naked; at the one it is not possible to get a place, at the other void seats are plenty."[4]

For the reformed clergy (many of whom took up the attack on the stage in their sermons), the mortification produced by this outrush of patrons from church to theater must have been acute.[5] Preachers may always have fretted about the size of their audience; yet these were exceptional days, when the Word, buried for centuries beneath the "dumb" show of Catholic ritual, had at last been restored to a "miserable and hungry people." Why then were there so few takers? To the author of the first printed attack (1577) on the public theaters, the preacher John Northbrooke, the paradox is stunning: "There was never more preaching, & worse living, never more talking and less following, never more professing, and less profiting, never more words and fewer deeds, never truer faith preached and less works done, than is now." For Northbrooke as for other pious commentators, this deplorable state of affairs was not to be imputed "unto the preaching of God's word," but rather "unto the wickedness and perverse nature of man's corruption." The fact that "many can tarry at a vain Play two or three hours, when as they will not abide scarce one hour at a Sermon," proved to Northbrooke only how "great is our folly, to delight in vanity, and leave verity, to seek for the meat that shall perish, and pass not for the food that they shall live by for ever." Indeed, the greater passion of the English people for players rather than preachers was, Northbrooke concluded, only one of the many signs "whereby we may easily gather, that the day of judgment is not far off."[6]

Other Elizabethans put more of the blame on the preachers. After all, the Reformation did not uproot Catholicism or even "heathenism" from Elizabethan England overnight; many parishioners loathed their preachers (especially their puritan preachers) precisely for the new religion they were preaching.[7] But to a remarkable extent the hostility of parishioner to preacher appears to have been fueled by a hatred of preaching per se. Puritans such as Northbrooke may have associated this resistance to sermons with unregeneracy—"If the Preacher do pass his hour but a little," Atheos is told in George Gifford's *Briefe Discourse* (1582), "your buttocks begin for to ache, and ye wish in your heart that the Pulpit would fall" (Atheos replies, "Ye may guess twice before ye guess so right")—but others recognized the need to moderate the godly fixation on sermonizing. Some divines, as we saw in chapter 1, turned to catechism for help. The failure of preachers in this duty, writes the catechist Robert Cawdrey, "is in very deed the cause why their preaching taketh so little effect amongst their parishioners." To Cawdrey's mind, the difference that catechism made was rhetorical: it could feed people the sort of "meat" that "their nature and capacity was able to digest and conceive." The conservative minister Leonard Wright (1589) thought a more basic accommodation to the carnality of one's flock was in order. Far less disdainful than Northbrooke of his parishioners' appetite for "the meat that shall perish," Wright observed that Christ "did both feed the souls of his sheep, with heavenly doctrine, and example of virtuous living, & their bodies with material food of barley loaves and fishes"—and, according to Wright, it was Christ's material food that "did more win the people's hearts, than all his wonderful miracles and divine Sermons which they saw & heard." Hence, Wright concludes, we "shall find that a mean learned Parson of an honest conversation, keeping a good house in his Parish, shall persuade and profit more in coming to one dinner, than the best Doctor of divinity which keepeth no house shall do by preaching a dozen solemn sermons."[8]

Along with these milder supplements to preaching came the more direct solution of reforming the preacher. For the godly, this meant ridding England's pulpits of the "dumb dogs" who could do little more than read prepared services; the true preachers were those dedicated ministers, in lamentably short supply, who sermonized their flock "as the spirit moved them."[9] Yet critics of the puritans argued that the preacher should rightly be moved by the plight of his parishioners' buttocks as well. When Wright complains of those preachers who "stand so long about instructing the souls, as though they had forgotten the people had any bodies, who do not so much edify as tedify," he may well be recalling the advice of the influential rhetorician Thomas Wilson (1553), who similarly cautions sermonizers not to think that their zeal alone will suffice to spread the gospel.[10] Wilson recommends that the preachers take a more rhetorical—indeed, a more theatrical—approach to their calling:

> except men find delight, they will not long abide: delight them, and win them: weary them, and you lose them for ever. And that is the reason, that men commonly tarry the end of a merry play, and cannot abide the half hearing of a sour checking Sermon. Therefore, even these ancient preachers, must now and then play the fools in the pulpit, to serve the tickle ears of their fleeting audience, or else they are like some times to preach to the bare walls, for though the spirit be apt, and our will prone, yet our flesh is so heavy, and humors so overwhelm us, that we cannot without refreshing, long abide to hear any one thing.

"They are like some times to preach to the bare walls": for those Elizabethans who shared Wilson's sentiments, the theater's power to empty the church might well have seemed to stem just as much from the preachers' intemperate spirituality as from the wanton carnality of the people.[11]

Renaissance comedies frequently underscored their own appeal by joking about the soporific effect of sermons, but Wilson's comparison of play to sermon suggests that such vying with preachers need not have been profanely motivated.[12] Northbrooke would agree that players had become more popular than preachers because the players and not the preachers were willing to "play the fools"—but what if some players intended their folly to be edifying, as Wilson had recommended?[13] What if, in other words, some Elizabethans came to prefer the theater to the established church because they believed the player had *subsumed* the preacher's role? Surprisingly, Northbrooke himself suggests this possibility, though he treats it with contempt. So ardent for playgoing have the people become, he writes, "that they shame not to say and affirm openly, that Plays are as good as Sermons, and that they learn as much or more at a Play, than they do at God's word preached." Munday in the *Blast* raises and rebukes the same argument: try to withdraw playgoers "from the Theater unto the sermon, [and] they will say, By the preacher they may be edified, but by the player both edified and delighted."[14] Yet after all, nothing could have been more traditional for the English stage than to serve as a platform of religious instruction; why, with the rise of permanent theaters, should that function have simply vanished without out a trace?

At one point in modern literary criticism, when it seemed to some scholars as if any reference to religion in a Renaissance play disclosed a Christian polemic, the answer was easy: the theaters never really had abandoned their religious roots; plays truly had been as good as sermons. Over the past four decades, however, in reaction against the simplifications and also the piety of this critical school, literary historians have generally responded to the problem of the Renaissance theater's religious heritage by tracing the merely formal or histrionic survival of religious plots, themes, and types upon an increasingly naturalistic stage. As Bernard Spivack (1958) put this now conventional view, the Tudor play "gradually freed itself from its homiletic purpose, whereby it was essentially the dramatized exemplum of a sermon, and acquired autonomous life and justification as dramatic spectacle. The stage ceased to be a pulpit or the audience a congregation."[15] Even scholars who balk at Spivack's rhetoric of liberation reach the same conclusions: it was censorship, Glynne Wickham argues, that "effectively divorced" the theater "from religion." Insofar as critics have traced any devotional continuity between early and late Tudor plays, they have generally claimed that the theater continued to satisfy not a religious but a ritualist craving in its audience. According to Louis Montrose, as I noted in my introduction, the Elizabethans found a "substitute" for the "ritual practices and popular religious festivities of late medieval Catholic culture" in the new secular theaters; for Stephen Greenblatt, Shakespeare's plays may have exposed "religious ideology" as a fiction, but audiences embraced the "evacuated rituals" of Shakespeare's theater as "preferable to no rituals at all."[16]

In this chapter I will argue, however, that neither an increasing naturalism on the Elizabethan stage nor an evacuation of religious mystique by that stage need have been secularizing operations. As for the state censorship to which the players were subjected, such repressiveness may simply have had the effect of driving the theater's "homiletic purpose" underground. But there is no reason to assume with Spivack that if a play were not a sermon it could not be religious, or that if the stage were not a pulpit the audience could not be a congregation. Even in so bloody a play as Shakespeare's final Elizabethan history, *Henry V,* I will show, the spectacles of the theater are presented as better than demystifying: they are made to seem sacramental. That is, Shakespeare appears to believe that his audience can draw spiritual strength from their experience of the theater, and *Henry V* shows that this belief has strong affinities with orthodox English Protestant conceptions of the eucharist.[17] Catholics claimed that Christ's "natural" body was physically present in the consecrated host and that the priest in breaking holy bread thus re-created Christ's sacrifice; the majority of English Protestant writers argued that Christ's sacrifice could only be remembered and imitated, not repeated, and that Christ was spiritually, not physically present in the eucharist. Shakespeare alludes to this controversy in *Henry V* when one character pessimistically asserts that "men's faiths are wafer-cakes"; according to an army of Protestant writers, papist faith was not only as brittle as wafer-cakes but as small, reduced to an idolatrous belief in a "wafer god." Following those Protestants who instead treated the petty materiality of the wafer as proof that it *represented* Christ, *Henry V* suggests that the carnal spectacles of the theater sacramentally highlight, rather than obscure, the operations of the spirit precisely because those spectacles are so conspicuously inadequate to the tales of "*Non nobis* and *Te Deum*" they represent.[18]

Given the theater's popularity in comparison to the church, this professed insufficiency of the stage to its grand subject might undermine not only Catholic idolatry, Shakespeare seems to have believed, but the clerical elitism that encouraged Protestant churchmen to climb "up the Pulpit tower" and make "tedious Preachments, of no edifying power." *Henry V* begins with scenes of a church that will share its "cup" with Harry only in supporting his war efforts; such exclusivity allows the clergy and even the king to treat French and English soldiers as "sacrifices" to their own carnal interests. Conversely, the Chorus to the play insists that Shakespeare's players could not so much as represent king and clergy without the communal participation of the audience. For Munday in the *Blast*, the only communion enactable in the theater was a diabolical one: "Those unsavory morsels of unseemly sentences passing out of the mouth of a ruffenly player doth more content the hungry humors of the rude multitude, and carrieth better relish in their mouths, than the bread of the word, which is the food of the soul."[19] Yet, by framing his play as a sacrament whose real power lay in the minds of its spectators, Shakespeare represented his theater as a means not to "fight against [God's] word" but to save it from papists and preachers.[20]

I

If asked to compare Shakespeare to such outspokenly religious contemporaries as Spenser and Donne, even those critics who detect a spark of religion in Shakespeare would have to admit that he did not like to preach. In one important respect, of course, the comparison is unfair: neither Spenser nor Donne faced the kind of censorship regarding their religious views that by 1606 prevented Shakespeare from even mentioning "the holy Name of God or of Christ Jesus, or of the Holy Ghost or of the Trinity" in his plays. Nonetheless, to most recent critics Shakespeare's apparent reticence about Christian doctrine has seemed a matter less of state imposition than of personal choice. Roland Mushat Frye crystallized this view four decades ago in his *Shakespeare and Christian Doctrine* (1963), which claims that not a thread of religious polemic can be found anywhere in Shakespeare's plays. According to Frye, the plays not only fail to "furnish us evidence of Shakespeare's religious orientation," but the little theology they do invoke always proves "contributory to the drama, and not vice versa." Speaking for generations of Shakespeare critics, Frye concludes that "the mirror of Shakespearean drama was held up to nature, and not to saving grace."[21]

Not once in his exhaustive study, however, does Frye consider the most obvious textual evidence for Shakespeare's "religious orientation"—his representations of churchmen. The higher ranking the clergyman in Shakespeare's plays, the more suspect he tends to appear. The opening scene of what is possibly Shakespeare's first history play, *1 Henry VI*, sets the antiprelatical pattern for the rest. In the midst of a funeral procession for Henry V, the Duke of Gloucester accuses the Bishop of Winchester of having prayed for Henry's death, and when Winchester in turn charges Gloucester with greater obedience to his wife than to "God or religious churchmen," the exasperated Gloucester exclaims, "Name not religion, for thou lov'st the flesh, / And ne'er throughout the year to church thou go'st / Except it be to pray against thy foes." The audience does not have long to wait before learning whether Gloucester's attack is justified. In the scene's final speech, after the lay noblemen have hurried off the stage on state business, Winchester like the medieval stage-Vice turns to the audience to protest,

> Each hath his place and function to attend:
> I am left out; for me nothing remains.
> But long I will not be Jack out of office.
> The King from Eltam I intend to send,
> And sit at chiefest stern of public weal.

One could hardly imagine English history introduced with a more antiprelatical slant.[22]

Why does Shakespeare make perhaps his first historical villain a bishop? Some scholars would assign *1 Henry VI* to the late 1580s, the very period in which the bishop-hating "Martin Marprelate" waged his pamphlet war. Winchester, moreover, was the bishopric held by one of Martin's prime targets, Thomas Cooper, whom Martin accused of "most godless proceedings." While David Bevington is right to observe that Shakespeare's criticism of churchmen was "notably mild" for its day, an affinity between Shakespeare and the outrageously derisive Martin is not unthinkable. The next installment of Shakespeare's histories, *2 Henry VI*, paints an even fiercer portrait of Winchester than the first: he is shown helping to arrange Gloucester's murder and then dying, terrified and unrepentant, in the same bed as his victim. Marprelate would have been hard pressed to match the grotesque mixture of foolery and repugnance that Shakespeare inscribes on the very face of his expiring prelate: "See how the pangs of death do make him grin!"[23]

Of course, the mere fact of Shakespeare's satirizing one particular bishop (and a Catholic bishop at that) does not in itself demonstrate that Shakespeare had any religious objections to bishops. In explicit support of Frye, Bevington claims that on the contrary Shakespeare's attitude toward Winchester is essentially "non-theological," because Shakespeare "attacks the bishop for moral crimes and political meddling, not for doctrine." Yet one might just as easily argue that Shakespeare excludes specific doctrinal complaints against his bishop so as to include both past (Catholic) and present (Protestant) irreligious Winchesters within the scope of his satire. Winchester's lack of enthusiasm for theology is in any case part of Gloucester's opening grievance against him; when Gloucester and Winchester once again wrangle in *2 Henry VI*, it is the king who tries to pacify them with doctrine—"blessed are the peacemakers on earth"—only to have the bishop characteristically pervert that doctrine: "Let me be blessed for the peace I make / Against this proud Protector with my sword!"[24]

Shakespeare may drop this element of downright caricature from his later representations of English bishops, but he never abandons the dark comedy of episcopal militarism. The first speech by the Bishop of Carlisle in *Richard II* sounds far more pastoral than any lines of Winchester, as Carlisle offers heavenly encouragements to a king faced with rebellion:

> Fear not, my lord, that Power that made you king
> Hath power to keep you king in spite of all.
> The means that heavens yield must be embrac'd,
> And not neglected; else heaven would,
> And we will not. Heaven's offer we refuse,
> The proffered means of succors and redress.

And yet another lord, interpreting for Carlisle, immediately highlights the element of mystification in Carlisle's otherworldly rhetoric: "He means, my lord, that we are too remiss, / Whilst Bullingbrook, through our security, / Grows strong and great in substance and in power."[25] What the bishop counsels when he speaks of heavenly aid, in short, is nothing other than swift military action.

In the later *2 Henry IV*, so much more audaciously bellicose is the rebellious Archbishop of York that many of the passages concerning him in the play appear to have been censored. The first of these passages begins with familiar irony: "The gentle Archbishop of York is up / With well-appointed pow'rs." In *Richard II*, Henry IV had praised Carlisle for the "high sparks of honor" he exhibited, for his gentility rather than his religion; thus even if York's gentleness is understood as aristocratic rather than benevolent, it cannot palliate the incongruity of a bishop in arms. "Fine pairing of words, these," Erasmus writes in his "Sileni Alcibiadis": "bishop and warrior!" Yet Shakespeare is no longer content simply to correlate a prelate's militarism with his high social position. For the first time in the history plays, he has a character articulate a theory of episcopal warfare. The speaker in question, a retainer of Hotspur's father Northumberland, explains why he thinks York will succeed in his rebellion where Hotspur had failed. Hotspur

> had only but the corpse',
> But shadows and the shows of men, to fight;
> For that same word, rebellion, did divide
> The action of their bodies from their souls,
> And they did fight with queasiness, constrain'd.

York, on the other hand, "turns insurrection to religion."

> Suppos'd sincere and holy in his thoughts,
> He's follow'd both with body and with mind;
> And doth enlarge his rising with the blood
> Of fair King Richard, scrap'd from Pomfret stones;
> Derives from heaven his quarrel and his cause;
> Tells them he doth bestride a bleeding land,
> Gasping for life under great Bullingbrook,
> And more and less do flock to follow him.

From *1 Henry VI* to *2 Henry IV*, Shakespeare has charted a steady progression in episcopal support for violence: first Winchester the faithless brawler, then Carlisle the sanctifier of war, then York the sanctifier of war who himself engages in warfare.[26]

Yet if in one respect the bishop in *2 Henry IV* who leads troops "not to break peace" but to "establish" it represents only a more sophisticated version of the bishop in *1 Henry VI* who clownishly threatened to make peace with his sword, in another respect York is strikingly different from his predecessors. With no apparent interest in their flocks, both Winchester and Carlisle promoted violence only before the aristocracy, whereas York when he is up in "ill-beseeming arms" climbs his pulpit to address the common people. As Prince John complains to him,

it better show'd with you
When that your flock, assembled by the bell,
Encircled you to hear with reverence
Your exposition on the holy text
Than now to see you here an iron man, talking,
Cheering a rout of rebels with your drum,
Turning the word to sword and life to death.

Yet this new urge in a bishop to "publish" the blessings he bestows on war does not indicate some new episcopal populism: in another, probably censored passage, York derides the common people as, among other things, "sick," "giddy," and "unsure," a "beastly feeder," or "common dog" that "wouldst eat thy dead vomit up / And howl'st to find it." Episcopal warfare remains a "gentle" business; York only shows how a bishop can employ the "vulgar heart" against one's aristocratic rivals.[27]

The final play in the sequence of Shakespeare's Lancastrian histories, *Henry V*, opens by partially recapitulating this transition from an episcopal militarism that is personal and overtly elitist to one that is public and covertly elitist. The action of the play begins with a private conference between two prelates, the Bishop of Ely and the Archbishop of Canterbury, who bemoan a parliamentary bill that would "strip" the clergy of "all the temporal lands, which men devout / By testament have given to the Church." The only hope that the "commons" will not have their way with the clergy turns out to be the king, "a true lover of the holy Church," whom the archbishop has bribed by pledging Harry an enormous sum to help him finance his planned conquest of France. The next scene takes place at court, and turns this shabby backroom deal into a pious public spectacle. Canterbury delivers a learned disquisition on French legal history that ends by assuring Harry of his just title to the French crown; both Canterbury and Ely then exhort Harry to "forage in blood of French nobility" as his warlike ancestors have, "in aid whereof" the clergy will provide him with the "mighty sum" already mentioned in the previous scene.[28] Once again Shakespeare's bishops have gone from secret conspirators to open propagandists for war, though this time the same characters fill both roles and thus conspicuously fuse the interests of the church with the bloodshed it promotes.

Yet the bishops of *Henry V* do not entirely synthesize the disparate characters of their predecessors. Although they continue to "incite" their king to violence, they no longer preach war, as York once had, to the common people. That office passes to the king. So zealously does Harry absorb both the church's money and its sanctifications of violence that after the second scene the bishops drop out of the play altogether. Immediately following Canterbury's final lines, Harry begins to speak of conquering France "by God's help," "by God's grace," with "God before"—a theme he never tires of reiterating throughout the play. It is now the king who counsels his courtiers to "deliver / Our puissance into the hand of God, / Putting it straight in expedition"; once the wars in France are under way, it is again the king who inspires his soldiers: "Follow your spirit; and upon this charge / Cry, 'God for Harry, England, and Saint George'!" After the triumph at Agincourt, Harry's public acknowledgments of God's part in the war effort grow even stronger. As soon as the French herald tells him that the English have carried the day, Harry exclaims, "Praised be God, and not our strength, for it"; he then has it "proclaimed through our host" that it is death "to boast of this, or take that praise from God / Which is his only." The night before, during a debate with common soldiers, Harry had already made the best case in the histories for believing that God approves of war—the biblical argument that war is God's "beadle" or "vengeance," His scourge for punishing sin. But of course this theory does not let Harry off the hook for leading his soldiers into war; as Christ explains in a warning often quoted by Elizabethan writers to explicate the moral status of a scourge, "it must needs be that offenses shall come, but woe be to that man, by whom the offense cometh."[29] The bishops begin the play by confessing their interest in war to be self-serving; while Harry may sound and truly be more devoutly inclined than they, both he and his fellow debaters agree that the war he elsewhere calls "well-hallow'd" is "his cause" and "his quarrel" alone.[30]

Earlier in the play, Harry had himself underscored the need to mistrust "glist'ring semblances of piety"; but then Shakespeare throughout *Henry V* takes every opportunity to highlight the monstrous incongruity of yoking "blood and sword and fire," as the bishops do, to professions of "spirituality." The Duke of Burgundy, for instance, likens soldiers to "savages" who do nothing "but meditate on blood." The Chorus puts a better face on this monomania when he claims that "honor's thought / Reigns solely in the breast of every man" in the English army. Yet even this idealization of their militarism allows the English soldiers no room for thoughts of religion: as Harry's disputant Williams says of his comrades, "how can they charitably dispose of any thing, when blood is their argument?" If Harry's piety gilds over such bloodymindedness, the paint cracks and peels in the scenes of the lower classes that Shakespeare continually intersperses with scenes of their betters. To the braggadocio Pistol, for example, the point of war is only "to suck, to suck, the very blood to suck!" His fellow lowlife Nim "scorns to say his prayers, lest 'a should be thought a coward." The captains of Harry's army, an intermediate class in the play, make such brutality look if anything more appalling by their crude appeals to religion. "God's plud" —that is, "by God's blood"—are the first words of the Welsh captain Fluellen, though the past master at this sort of blasphemy is the Irish captain MacMorris: "I would have blowed up the town, so Chrish save me law"; "there is throats to be cut, and works to be done, and there ish nothing done, so Christ sa' me law"; "So Chrish save me, I will cut off your head." Pistol's version of these oxymoronic oaths pares them to the bone. When Bardolph blocks an impending duel between Pistol and Nim, promising "by this sword" to kill the first man who draws, Pistol remarks, "Sword is an oath, and oaths must have their course." The joke is that Pistol translates *sword* into *'s word*, "by God's word," and thus literally enacts the sacrilege of which Prince John in 2 *Henry IV* had accused the Archbishop of York—"turning the word to sword."[31]

The most straightforward demystification of Harry's holy war in the play, however, is a war crime that ironically reflects Harry's absorption of both the bishops' money and their piety: Harry's old companion Bardolph robs a church. Pistol cannot believe that Fluellen would let Bardolph be hanged for such a crime; the only thing Bardolph stole, Pistol protests, was a minor accessory of Catholic ritual, a "pax of little price."[32] Whatever the rules of military discipline, the marked contrast between Bardolph's petty theft and the enormous sum that Henry wrung from the church does make Bardolph's punishment seem excessively harsh. That a "pax," of all things, should become grounds for hanging only strengthens Pistol's case. It is not just that *pax* means "peace," or even that, as a component of the mass, the pax helped celebrate the heavenly pardon won for humanity by Christ's sacrifice; the irony of Bardolph's theft is that he steals what already in some sense belongs to him, though not to him exclusively—a share of communion.

This aspect of Bardolph's crime links him both with Harry and, more plainly, with Harry's bishops, who regard the "temporal lands" of the church as their own "possession."[33] According to Protestant polemicists, the reason such "merchandise" as Bardolph's pax had been invented in the first place was to facilitate the clergy's plunder of the church. In one antipapist tract after another, Protestants attacked the "thievish" Catholic mass as a travesty of communion, "a sacrament rather of hate and dissension than of love and unity," designed to secure "a certain special privilege" for the Catholic priesthood.[34] According to Thomas Becon in 1563, these "massmongers" were not content to wear special robes, stand behind rails, and conduct their service in a language the people did not understand; they actually barred the people from fully partaking of the eucharist, instead offering them only an inedible pax to kiss: "while the boy or parish-clerk carrieth the *pax* about, ye yourselves alone eat up all and drink up all."[35] Bardolph may have stolen a pax, and Harry may have pocketed "a greater sum / Than ever at one time the clergy yet / Did . . . part withal," yet the worst "church-robbers" in *Henry V* are the clergy themselves, who have not only expropriated the church from the people but sponsored the "hate and dissension" of war with its resources.[36]

Oddly enough, Harry's more refined church-robbery thus turns out to be an old trick of his, the kind of roguish "good jest" he had supposedly repudiated upon becoming king—that is, to "rob the thieves." Though thwarting the will of the commons, his confiscations from the bishops do after all confer some benefits on his people, by helping to break the episcopal monopoly not just on church wealth but on church piety as well.[37] We have already seen how Harry adopts York's public religiosity in preaching war to his soldiers, but Harry takes his populism a good deal further than York had. The Chorus is inspired to his highest commendation of the king ("Praise and glory on his head!") when the night before Agincourt Harry "goes, and visits all his host, / Bids them good morrow with a modest smile, / And calls them brothers, friends, and countrymen." Twice in the play we hear Harry himself voice this egalitarian regard for his soldiers: "For there is none of you so mean and base / That hath not noble luster in your eyes"; "For he today that sheds his blood with me / Shall be my brother; be he ne'er so vile, / This day shall gentle his condition." The deaths in battle of two noble Englishmen, the Earl of Suffolk and the Duke of York, seem not only to realize this promise of a blood brotherhood but to cast a spiritual glow over it: as an English lord recalls it, the dying York takes the already dead Suffolk

> by the beard, kisses the gashes
> That bloodily did yawn upon his face.
> He cries aloud, "Tarry, my cousin Suffolk!
> My soul shall thine keep company to heaven;
> Tarry, sweet soul, for mine, then fly abreast,
> As in this glorious and well-foughten field
> We kept together in our chivalry!"

What Harry gives his soldiers, the bloody mouths of this set piece appear to avow, is a communion liberated from the confines of the church to the open battlefield.[38]

The less "pretty" the picture of a warrior "fellowship" in the play, however, the more egalitarian and also bloodthirsty it looks. The French herald speaks of aristocrats who "lie drown'd and soak'd in mercenary blood" while "our vulgar drench their peasant limbs / In blood of princes." What the herald sees as mixing "nobles" with "common men" is the same power that for Harry turns mean and base soldiers noble or in Exeter's eyes makes heaven as much a "yoke-fellow" to chivalry as York is to Suffolk: violence.[39] Even England's king is threatened with such degradation when Williams challenges him to a duel, but Harry dodges the peril by causing Fluellen to act as his substitute. Other English characters, too, use scapegoats to displace the leveling effects of violence. Bardolph reminds the dueling Nim and Pistol that "we must to France together; why the devil should we keep knives to cut one another's throats?" A companion of Williams employs the same logic on Williams and Harry: "Be friends, you English fools, be friends, we have French quarrels enow." Only the vanquished in the play prove capable of envisioning a peace or unity that is not realized through some bloody sacrifice. In the play's closing moments, the French king and queen foresee an end to even larger structures of exclusion than class: the queen prays for ties so close between the French and the English "that English may as French, French Englishmen, / Receive each other," a communion the French king calls a "Christian-like accord." Yet Harry's final words in the play make little reference to these internationalist pleas. Though heroically capable of forging bonds between piety and egalitarianism, Harry never transcends the warmongering that enables him to forge those bonds in the first place. The only occasion on which he approaches an inclusive vision of French-English relations is when he playfully tempts his future wife, the French princess Katherine, with the thought of a renewed Crusade: "Shall not thou and I, between Saint Denis and Saint George, compound a boy, half French, half English, that shall go to Constantinople and take the Turk by the beard?" The antiprelaticalism of the history plays may suggest Shakespeare's longing for a religion that would be inclusive and pacifist rather than elitist and bellicose, but the last of these plays seems to leave us with the image of a communion broadened from clergy to congregation, from paxes to peace, only when first sanctified by violence.[40]

II

Harry's wartime egalitarianism, however, is not the only alternative to a prelatical church in the play. Although the movement from church to court in the opening scenes of *Henry V* has long been a major topic of scholarly discussion, critics have given far less attention to the remarkable transition from prologue to play that precedes it. Perhaps that is because this transition is so much more jarring: instead of the heroic military struggles that the prologue's Chorus leads us to expect ("O for a Muse of fire!"), the first scene of *Henry V* places us in the midst of an episcopal conspiracy. Yet, when compared to the smooth modulation of this conspiracy into Harry's war effort, the very discontinuity of prologue and first scene seems to speak well of the Chorus; and indeed throughout the prologue the Chorus expatiates on an institution holding so little in common with either the church or the court that over the course of the play it will come to represent a moral standard against which both episcopal and kingly piety can be judged. This alternative institution is the theater.

The most striking difference between the theater as the Chorus manifests it and the church as the bishops manifest it is the theater's openness. In the prologue, this amounts to both a literal and a figurative feature: literal, because the theater is open-air, a "wooden O"; figurative, because the Chorus openly confesses that the theater is nothing more substantial than a wooden O. Both forms of openness reverberate throughout the prologue, as the Chorus repeatedly apologizes for the "unworthy scaffold" upon which "flat unraised spirits" have presumed to stage Harry's story. These are the sort of derogatory terms that antitheatricalists loved to apply to the theater, belittling players as "poor, silly, hunger-starved wretches" who "are so baseminded, as at the pleasure of the veriest rogue in England, for one poor penny, they will be glad on open stage to play the ignominious fools for an hour or two together." Yet in similarly depreciating the players of *Henry V* as mere "ciphers" to the "great account" they will dramatize, the Chorus actually supplies the audience with reasons for preferring the players to the bishops whom the audience will meet in the first scene: as secretive and covetous aristocrats who translate the great account of Harry's story into a "mighty sum" of hoarded treasure, the bishops make "poor" and "open" sound like virtues.[41]

Indeed, the characteristics of the stage for which the Chorus apologizes are subjects of praise in a later protheatrical tract (c. 1635–37) by Sir Richard Baker, who also celebrates a further supposed shortcoming of the theater: Baker argues that playgoing "is a *general* delight, general to *Sex*, to *Age*, to *Quality*; it is a *cheap* delight, it ventures nothing, and spends but little; it is a *sociable* delight, many do at once enjoy it, and all equally." The heterogeneity of *Henry V*'s spectators is as much a source of professed regret for the Chorus as his flat players and unworthy scaffold are: he claims that the tale of Agincourt deserves not only "a kingdom for a stage" and "princes to act" upon it, but an audience composed exclusively of "monarchs." This is nearly the class of persons the bishops come to address in scene 2, with an earl their lowest ranking auditor, but the same inclusive mixture of "mean and gentle" that "behold" Harry before Agincourt is presumably what fills the seats of the theater that now beholds him anew.[42]

As "the king of good fellows," Harry himself helps sharpen the contrast between the theater and the church throughout the play. He even points the way toward seeing the theater as an alternative site of spiritual edification. Half of the bishops' first scene is devoted to their astonishment at the extraordinary "reformation" in Harry's character since his accession to the throne. "Never was such a sudden scholar made," exclaims Canterbury, who considers this change in Harry a nearly miraculous "wonder,"

> Since his addiction was to courses vain,
> His companies unletter'd, rude, and shallow,
> His hours fill'd up with riots, banquets, sports;
> And never noted in him any study,
> Any retirement, any sequestration
> From open haunts and popularity.

The members of the audience who have previously witnessed the two parts of *Henry IV* know better than to think that Harry's "addiction to courses vain" allowed him no time for "study," but then as spectators of Harry's time spent in "open haunts" and as frequenters of such haunts themselves, the audience has a double advantage over the bishops, who not only differentiate "study" from "popularity" but never deign to mix with the people.[43]

On several occasions in *Henry V* Harry himself expounds the lessons that "courses vain" have taught him. The most basic of these lessons is to view anyone and anything, no matter how contemptible, as a possible source of edification. "God Almighty!" Harry exclaims on the morning of Agincourt, "There is some soul of goodness in things evil, / Would men observingly distil it out." The immediate example Harry has in mind is his enemy, a "bad neighbor" who "makes us early stirrers"; more important, Harry says, the French "are our outward consciences / And preachers to us all, admonishing / That we should dress us fairly for our end." "Thus," Harry concludes, "may we gather honey from the weed, / And make a moral of the devil himself."[44]

If the French and even the devil can be seen as "preachers," then surely so can the denizens of "open haunts." But what does Harry think they preach? His debate with Williams and his companions leads Harry to soliloquize on what is by this point in his story an old theme for him, the surprising lack of difference between king and commoner: "What have kings, that privates have not too, / Save ceremony, save general ceremony?" Harry speaks as dismissively of this "idol Ceremony" as Protestants did of the idolatrous ceremonies that obscured the Truth while exalting the Catholic (and, to Marprelate, the episcopal) clergy above the people. The balm, the scepter, the ball, the sword, the mace, and all the rest of royal pomp are for Harry so many disguises that fail to hide not only how "the King is but a man," but also how much better off the common man is in comparison to the king. For the commoner's "gross brain" allows him to sleep, whereas Harry the scholar-king must always keep the sort of "watch" that this very meditation of Harry's exemplifies.[45] Yet here of course is the royal difference Harry had first seemed to question. The comparison between king and commoner, a moral Harry gathered from the weeds of popular haunts, has taught him to discount as little more than props not only the ceremonial accoutrements that distinguish the king from the commoner, but also the mortal body that assimilates him to the commoner. What really sets the king apart from the commoner, Harry thus implies, must be the king's uncommon brain, his marvelous capacity for watching and learning.

Again and again in the play Harry sermonizes on the unimportance of all but immaterial distinctions. Offering a lighter version of his ceremonial catalogue in the preceding act, Harry reminds his future wife Katherine that "a good leg will fall, a straight back will stoop, a black beard will turn white, a curl'd pate will grown bald, a fair face will wither, a full eye will wax hollow; but a good heart, Kate, is the sun and the moon." What makes the body less valuable to Harry than the "brain" or "heart" is not only the body's mutability but the mind's power to exploit this mutability: comforting Sir Thomas Erpingham on the subject of his listless troops, Harry assures him that "when the mind is quicken'd, out of doubt, / The organs, though defunct and dead before, / Break up their drowsy grave, and newly move / With casted slough and fresh legerity." This is the basis of Harry's appeal to his army throughout the war—"All things are ready, if our minds be so"—and it easily modulates for Harry into the piety that leads him to declare, after the outnumbered English at Agincourt defeat the French, "O God, thy arm was here; / And not to us, but to thy arm alone, / Ascribe we all."[46]

Such antimaterialism is famously anticipated by the Chorus, who repeatedly exhorts the audience to translate the obvious material deficiencies of the theater into an "imaginary puissance." Yet if Harry and the Chorus both derive a lesson in the power of the immaterial from their experience of open haunts, the audience served by the Chorus seems better able to appreciate this lesson than Harry's subjects can.[47] The only king in the play to have mixed with commoners, Harry is in a unique position to compare classes, and he capitalizes on his special knowledge so successfully that he comes to be regarded with awe: "when he speaks," Canterbury marvels, even "the air, a charter'd libertine, is still." Although Harry's surprising ability to "reason in divinity" may help liberate such power and its attendant mystique from the clergy, Harry alone remains, as his precursor York was said to be, "the very opener and intelligencer / Between the grace, the sanctities of heaven" and the "dull workings" of his auditors. The theater, by contrast, makes the mixture of king and commoner a sight for all the audience to see; it even turns Harry's soliloquy on the subject into a public spectacle. Just as Harry demystifies the bishops' privileged relation to spirituality, so the theater demystifies the seemingly esoteric scholarship of the king.[48]

This new communal access to a previously restricted knowledge has, as Joel Altman has shown, specifically eucharistic overtones in the Henriad. The audience of the plays "participates" in Harry's experience, as communicants were said to "participate" in Christ; the exclusive hold of the clergy on a spiritual power commodified into lands and paxes gives way, it seems, to the more inclusive and also immaterial communion enabled by the play. If Harry's antimaterialism sets this reformation in motion, the antimaterialism of the Chorus advances it even further along Protestant lines. Especially in the context of clergymen desperate to save their privileges, the Chorus's Harry-like insistence on "imperfections" that the audience must "piece out" with their "thoughts" recalls standard Protestant explications of the Lord's Supper. Just as the Chorus claims that Harry's soldiers at Agincourt were "pining and pale" wretches before Harry inspired them, and that the theater's representation of Agincourt will amount to only "four or five most vile and ragged foils" unless the audience agrees to "eke out" such props with their "working" thoughts, so reformers claimed that the church and its sacraments would be of little price (as Pistol says of the pax) without the spiritual investments of God and each individual worshipper. "I so make division between the Spirit and sacraments," writes Calvin in a work translated in 1561, "that the power of working remain with the Spirit, and to the Sacraments be left only the ministration, yea and the same void and trifling without the working of the Spirit: but of much effectualness, when he inwardly worketh and putteth forth his force."[49]

Catholics objected to this Protestant denial of any intrinsic efficacy to the sacramental "elements" in the same terms that Greenblatt applies to Shakespeare's representations of Christian ceremonies: they argued that the Protestants "do evacuate and make of none effect the sacraments." "This is not my body," says the Protestant version of Jesus in a typical Catholic pamphlet, "but the figure of my body, being absent in substance, and only present to your imaginations, by the sight of the bread."[50] Protestants routinely countered that it was rather the papists who had robbed the sacraments of their true substance, turning the Lord's Supper, as John Jewel (1562) argued, into "a stage-play, and a solemn sight; to the end that men's eyes should be fed with nothing else but with mad gazings, and foolish gauds."[51] The prologues to *Henry V* suggest that Shakespeare wants to help redeem the spirituality not only of the sacraments but of stage-plays too. Under examination by his Marian inquisitors, Archbishop Cranmer (1554) imagined Christ as enjoining communicants to "consider and behold" not "that which is set before your bodily eyes" but rather the "mystical matter" it signifies, "my body crucified for you; *that* eat and digest in your minds." When the Chorus similarly advises the spectators of *Henry V* that they should be "minding true things by what their mock'ries be," he too exhorts them to invest bare elements with something more substantial—to treat ragged foils, pale wretches, and open haunts, in other words, as vehicles for an inward power.[52]

Shakespeare apparently expects that this reformed hermeneutics will be facilitated not only by the audience's participation in Harry's extraclerical piety, but also by the Chorus's repeated belittlement of the stage. From the first prologue of *Henry V*, the Chorus subordinates both Harry and the players who represent his story to the imaginative capacities of the audience, "for 'tis your thoughts that now must deck our kings." This sort of self-deprecation was, in principle, the job of every Protestant preacher: to make plain, as Bishop Pilkington (1560) cautions, that "it is not we that speak, when we speak any truth: but it is the Holy Spirit of God that speaks in us, whose instruments we be." Yet the manifest alternative in *Henry V* to the bishop or king who encourages his auditors to treat him idolatrously is the player, not the preacher, as the Chorus shows. He humbly asks the audience to "admit" him to a public office that, unlike "king" or "bishop," lasts only as long as the run of the play; and he relegates himself, along with every other stage-herald of "true things," to the status of a mockery.[53]

But then Harry is just as self-deprecating as the Chorus, and, what's more, he employs his humility, as the Chorus does not, for overtly pious ends. The Chorus himself tells us how Harry, "being free from vainness and self-glorious pride," refused to have his war-worn armor paraded through London, "giving full trophy, signal, and ostent / Quite from himself to God." If even this ostensibly modest king proves committed to retaining a privileged hold on spirituality, why should we believe that the far less religious-sounding Chorus is not at least as interested in self-aggrandizement? After all, although he may appear, like a good Protestant, to place the burden of spiritual action where it belongs—onto the "working" thoughts of each auditor—the Chorus also occasionally stresses, like a good Catholic, the mediatory power of the players. Having claimed in the first prologue, for instance, that his auditors must fill in the play's temporal gaps with their thoughts, the Chorus nevertheless adds that he himself will "supply" this function; in his second prologue he declares that the players, not the thoughts of the audience, will "convey" the audience to France and back, "charming the Narrow Seas / To give you gentle pass." Most revealing, *Henry V* is hardly as unsatisfactory a play as the Chorus makes it out to be, a fact Shakespeare highlights for his audience when, in likening Pistol to the "roaring devil i'th' old play," he contrasts the primitive religious stage to his own more sophisticated and naturalistic theatrical illusions.[54] Why then shouldn't we regard the Chorus's abasement before the mental power of the audience as simply a means of flattering his auditors and absorbing them in his play? This is certainly the view of players that the antitheatricalists favored; they insisted that one should respond to any player's intimations of piety just as Gloucester had responded to Shakespeare's first episcopal villain: "Name not religion, for thou lov'st the flesh."

Henry V provides at least the outlines of a defense of the theater's carnality, for the whole thrust of Shakespeare's stage-religion is to reject the violent opposition between spirit and flesh that the bishops promote from one side and Harry from the other. Harry's spirituality may be egalitarian, allowing him to glimpse a noble luster even in the eyes of the mean and base, but as we have seen, the inclusiveness of his piety goes only so far: it thrives on a warfare waged between the spirit and the flesh as well as between the English and the French. Comparing Harry to his forebears, the Archbishop of Canterbury treats these two conflicts as if they were one: he exhorts Harry to "invoke" the "warlike spirit" of the Black Prince, who "play'd a tragedy" at Crécy "whiles his most mighty father on a hill / Stood smiling to behold his lion's whelp / Forage in blood of French nobility." One act later, the French king Charles eerily echoes this characterization of Edward III as a god well pleased with his son, but his aim is to depict the English victory at Crécy as a kind of sacrilege: Edward, "up in the air," "smil'd to see" his son not mingle flesh and spirit but "mangle the work of nature, and deface / The patterns that by God and by French fathers / Had twenty years been made." According to Charles, an English spirit "flesh'd" is one that has been given a taste for murder.[55]

If the Chorus also belittles the flesh in comparison to the spirit, he does not encourage the same murderous opposition between the two. In one respect his more moderate approach reflects the fictionality of the violence he introduces: unlike Harry's Agincourt, of course, Shakespeare's "brawl ridiculous" causes no physical harm. Conversely, the persuasive naturalism of

Shakespeare's fictions suggests that, no matter how paltry the theater and, by analogy, the flesh may be, the audience requires both in order to sustain its "imaginary puissance." The difference between Shakespeare's theatricalism and Harry's militarism runs still deeper, however. When Harry encounters the "lank-lean cheeks and war-worn coats" of his "poor" troops, he extols the ability of spirit and Spirit to crush the opposing French; but when the Chorus considers the four or five most vile and ragged foils of his players, he is led only to pray for the audience's "pity."[56] In other words, the Chorus regards the material inadequacies of the theater as forming the basis of a plea for spiritual aid and fellowship. Insofar as Shakespeare's theater succeeds in catering to the carnal impulses of the audience, this plea grows only more persuasive: with its own money and pleasure at stake, the audience has, after all, a vested interest in pitying the players' weak efforts.

Yet the fellowship between flesh and spirit that Shakespeare aims to encourage through the experience of *Henry V* depends on more than a matching fellowship between stage and audience: it depends as well on a fellowship encouraged *within* the audience. In the play, the English achieve a Christian-like accord among themselves only by venting their pitiless antagonisms onto the French; in the theater, Shakespeare may accept that his audience requires a scapegoat for its own pacification and unification, but he denies that the audience's relation to this scapegoat need be violent. Once again he appears to imagine his auditors as playing the communicants to the eucharist of his historical drama. In other words, he seems to think that as a stage for two kinds of immaterial violence—the represented violence of Harry's wars and the violence done to Harry's wars in representing them— *Henry V* provides the audience as "unbloody" a sacrifice as the eucharist was thought to supply in recalling Christ's death.[57]

That Shakespeare believed his audience could achieve some form of communion through his play is implied by the Chorus's first apology. We have already seen how the Chorus begins *Henry V* with a wish for a fully royal theater; the reason he desires such a theater, he explains, is that he wants "the warlike Harry" to appear "like himself"—that is, as a god of violence, who would "Assume the port of Mars, and at his heels / (Leash'd in, like hounds) should famine, sword, and fire / Crouch for employment." "But pardon, gentles all." This brief line epitomizes the sort of moral adjustment the audience is asked to make throughout the play. Confessing himself unable to stage Harry's superhuman violence, the Chorus at the same time begs the audience to forego its own aggression. What's more, he offers this very self-sacrifice of the audience as precisely its compensation for the players' shortcomings. Unlike an all-royal theater, the audience may be socially diverse, and unlike Harry it may lose the opportunity for murder; here, as in the rest of Shakespeare's histories, aristocracy and warfare go hand in hand. Yet, the Chorus suggests, the audience gains by these losses a fellowship transcending class, in which "all" come to share a gentility that embraces rather than excludes, that pardons rather than kills. In ending the prologue on this same communal note, beseeching his auditors "gently to hear, kindly to judge, our play," the Chorus prepares those auditors to regard the theater as not only a more open, cheap, and egalitarian site of "participation" than the church they will next encounter, but, above all, a more *peaceable* institution.[58]

Why then does the Chorus not say so much outright? Apparently, his indirection is, for Shakespeare, one more sign of the saving difference between players and preachers. In defense of the bitter dissensions sparked by their sermonizing, many puritans proudly recalled the scriptures that Winchester deforms, about Christ's coming to bring not peace but a sword; the author of *A Dialogue, Concerning the Strife of Our Churche* (1584) maintains that in any case godly preachers never disrupt more than "a cursed unity and a wicked love, which is in the flesh."[59] Yet Shakespeare so values the communality of the theatrical experience—values it, indeed, before any particularity of doctrine—that he has the Chorus explicitly address no more controversial or spiritual an issue than the powers of the imagination. This is not the supposed transcendence of dogma, the displacement of religion by literature, for which modern critics have praised Shakespeare; what gives the appearance of an aestheticizing skepticism in Shakespeare's plays is rather his increasing conviction that, for religion's sake, doctrinal controversies must be muted. Sacrificing preacherly goals to what he considers the necessarily prior objective of fellow-feeling, Shakespeare even allows the hawkish members of his audience a provisional confidence in his militarism, and offers his play as a (pardonable) scapegoat when that confidence is repeatedly betrayed.[60]

Such faith in communion as the strongest basis for edification pits Shakespeare against the elitism as well as the sectarianism that godly preaching could generate. The reformer Miles Coverdale (1593) extolled the sacraments for distributing Christ's power to teach as well as love to all participants: "Christ with these outward tokens thought to couple and knit together the members of his holy church in obedience and love one towards another; whereby they knowing one another among themselves, might by such exterior things stir and provoke one another to love and godliness." In presenting *Henry V* as an "outward token" that is nondoctrinal and thus obviously free of the need for any "exposition on the holy text" like York's,

Shakespeare seems intent on fostering a communion even more liberated from clerical pride than Coverdale perhaps envisioned. Indeed, much of the theater's beauty for Shakespeare seems to lie in its plain *inadequacy* to the task of edification. Gone is the didactic religiosity "i'th' old play." With the aid, not the impediment, of a state censorship that keeps preachers off the stage, the theater as Shakespeare sees it now helps register the difference between the Spirit and any vehicle that would lay some privileged claim to it. No longer must the people wait for a bishop, king, or even Chorus to play the preacher and, in the process, assume the port of Mars; rather, Shakespeare suggests, the people can learn how to edify themselves—stirring and provoking one another to love and godliness.[61]

From a modern perspective, this extraclericalism might seem to place Shakespeare back in the company of radical, Marprelatean Protestants. The separatist Henry Barrow argued (1590) that the "exercise" of preaching "belongeth to the whole church, and ought not to be shut up . . . amongst the priests only." Another separatist, John Dove (1589), insisted that "public ministers" were unnecessary, since "every man in his own calling was to preach the gospel."[62] By "every man," however, Dove meant every man who was "a brother"; his brand of extraclericalism would thus only have confirmed Shakespeare's sense that a zeal for preaching was inherently factious. Paradoxically, Shakespeare's apparent desire in *Henry V* to free Christianity from the preachers more nearly approximates the views of conformist clergy such as Bishop Sanderson (1640), who maintained that sermonizing may be "a necessary part" of the church's work, "yet is it not the whole work though, no, nor yet the chiefest part thereof. Our Apostle expressly giveth charity the preeminence before it: *Knowledge puffeth up, but charity edifieth*. And for once he speaketh of edification in his Epistles with reference to knowledge, I dare say, he speaketh of it thrice with reference to peace and brotherly charity or condescension." Puritans, in Sanderson's view, had therefore seriously impoverished Christianity by confining the process of edification "wholly to the understanding":

> whatsoever thing any way advanceth the service of God, or furthereth the growth of His Church, or conduceth to the increasing of any spiritual grace, or enliving of any holy affection in us, or serveth to the outward exercise or but expression of any such grace or affection, as joy, fear, thankfulness, cheerfulness, reverence, or any other, doubtless every such thing so far forth serveth more or less unto edification.[63]

So liberal an interpretation of Christian ministry, authorized by an Erasmian devotion to charity over doctrine, had earlier led Tyndale (c. 1533) to regard even the sort of lay pardon for which the Chorus pleads as a literal communion: because it transpires "in our own selves," Tyndale argued, forgiveness represents "more sensible and surer" a sacrament than either baptism or the Lord's Supper.[64] "Still be kind, / And eke out our performance with your mind": to pardon is both the first and the master "work" that the Chorus asks of the audience. Thus *Henry V* seems to identify the real presence of a theatrical sacrament not only with the inward participation of the audience but also with the sense of charity and communal endeavor that such participation is supposed to inspire.[65]

Catholic writers took this congregational theory of sacramental presence to be the English view generally. In their eyes, English communions had become indistinguishable from any other social gathering: according to Robert Parsons (1603), for instance, the church as John Foxe understood it amounted to "a multitude of men bearing the name of Christians, that have no external work of Religion at all among them after their baptism, but only to meet now and then at the *Lord's Supper,* which is nothing in effect, but eating of bread, and drinking of wine." The Catholic Queen Anne (1593) reportedly described the Protestant communion as "a tavern breakfast"—like the "breakfast" that Bardolph offers his fellow "ale-wash'd wits" Nim and Pistol in order to "make" them "friends." And that is nearly the form communion took for the Marian martyr George Tankerfield (1555), who, shortly before his execution, as Foxe records, "desired the wine-drawer that he might have a pint of Malmsey and a loaf, that he might eat and drink that in remembrance of Christ's death and passion, because he could not have it ministered unto him by others in such manner as Christ commanded." Parsons could only note with amazement, "Tankerfield takes his communion with a pot of Malmsey."[66]

Protestants, too, worried that their reforms might end up desacralizing communion. An imaginary interlocutor in Roger Hutchinson's *Faithful Declaration of Christes Holy Supper* (1560) claims that "we may receive [Christ's] body without the sacrament, wheresoever we be, if we believe upon him; whether we be in the field, or in the town, or in our beds." Hutchinson responds to such extraclericalism with the strongest defense of church sacraments in the English Protestant arsenal: "It is not enough to receive [Christ's body] spiritually, we must receive it also sacramentally; for both receipts be required and commanded, and Christ himself with his apostles used both for our erudition, example, and instruction."[67] Shakespeare may have accepted this argument from scriptural authority and agreed that the spiritual receipt of Christ's body in the field, tavern, or theater was "not enough," but he also seems to have believed that the fellowship achievable in the theater was at least a better start for Christians than the communion practiced in either a popish or a preacherly church. *Henry V* implies that authentic reform must in any case proceed gradually, almost imperceptibly: broadening Christian fellowship by degrees, Harry steals communion from the clergy, and the theater steals communion from Harry, without anyone's remarking the thefts. Many conformist clergymen argued that the sacraments themselves worked gradually, and the sacraments were the church's primary engine for converting sinners. Even among the first Christians, Marprelate's enemy Cooper (1562) declared, "their earnest zeal did not so much cause them to come often to the Lord's Supper, as the often frequenting thereof did increase their so great zeal and charity."[68]

Whether or not Shakespeare preferred a theatrical to a clerical communion, the same inclusiveness that underwrote his extraclericalism would have militated against his rejecting a preacherly church altogether. If, in Shakespeare's view no less than Hal's, anyone or anything could edify, then preachers could edify, too. Even the "cockpit" of the theater, so small that "the very casques" of Agincourt cannot be "crammed" into it, could be thought to have an edifying effect, in helping to forge a communal intimacy among a socially diverse audience. At one point the Chorus appears to suggest that the physical limitations of England, too, "model to thy inward greatness, / Like little body with a mighty heart," might have this same incorporating effect. Yet the Chorus evokes this conception of England just as he is about to inform us of some treasonous Englishmen who had been hired by the French to murder Harry; one of these assassins was Harry's occasional "bedfellow." Clearly the intimacy encouraged by physical limitations has its limitations. But then the Chorus had called England only a "model" to its inward greatness; like the theater, in other words, the little body of the English isle is no more than a "mockery," an outward and unworthy token that does not measure up to the spiritual truth it signifies. Insofar as the "little place" of the theater takes the part of little England in *Henry V,* it helps equate the real presence of England with an imagined community, not an island, while also differentiating that community from the island: thus the Chorus can urge the audience to "suppose within the girdle of these walls / Are now confin'd *two* mighty monarchies." In chapter 3 I outlined the Christian supranationalism that Shakespeare encourages in *King John* by replacing insular "walls" with theatrical ones. As I have tried to demonstrate in this chapter, however, Shakespeare stops short of insisting that such material "imperfections" as the English isle possess no spiritual significance whatsoever. In resisting what he considers the clerical and kingly tyrannies that would turn the word to sword, Shakespeare in his history plays supports a "gentler" moral: one in which the "fleshly and carnal" cannot be excluded from the project of redemption ("so Chrish save me"), even if they must always remain as "ciphers to this great account."[69]

CHAPTER 5

Pseudo-Christianity

There was lately a great Dispute between some *Actors* of *Tragedies* and other new-sprung *Sects*, which were the greatest *Impostors?* The Players alleged, That the disguise of the *mind* was far worse than that of the *body*; and that they did really seem to be *Actors*, and when their *Vizards* and brave *Apparel* was taken off; they would appear to be at best but hired to Act their Parts for a little silver; but such *Sects* wearing their *disguises* inwardly, cannot (as the *Players*) put them off and on at Pleasure.

—*The Laughing Mercury* (1652)

Among the many vices Spenser assigns to the corrupt Protestant clergy-man of *Mother Hubberds Tale* (1591)—illiteracy, ambition, dereliction, lechery, avarice—is a love of the theater: "All his care was, his service well to saine, / And to read Homilies upon holidays: / When that was done, he might attend his plays." Spenser means playgoing to say more about the clergyman than his irresponsibility: as a "formal Priest" or priest in outward form only, the clergyman is himself a pretender, able to "fashion" a "godly zeal." Even his preference for reading over preaching is supposed to betray his playerlike hollowness: as the puritans Field and Wilcox maintained in their *Admonition to the Parliament* (1572), merely reciting the set liturgy "is as evil as playing upon a stage, and worse too. For players yet learn their parts without book," while many non-preaching ministers "can scarcely read within book."[1]

Writing some thirty years after *Mother Hubberds Tale*, the puritan Thomas Scott (1622) applies the terms of Spenser's satire to the mass of English Protestant worshippers. According to Scott, the "Puritan" is the only true re-former, while the "Protestant" is nothing better than a "Formalist"—that is to say, a timeserving conformist:

A Protestant is an indifferent man,
That with all faiths, or none, hold quarters can:
So moderate and so temperate his passion,

As he to all times can his conscience fashion.
He at the Chapel can a Bishop hear,
And then in Holborn a Religious Frear:
A Mass ne'er troubles him, more than a play,
All's one; he comes all one from both away.

Spenser's formal clergyman claims to oppose "deep learning" because of the "doubts" and "controversies" it breeds.[2] No less averse to doctrinal "troubles" is Scott's "moderate" Protestant, who treats religion with the same detachment he treats a play: "he comes all one from both away." Or rather, Scott's Protestant treats religion *as* a play, and his "conscience" as a part he can "fashion" to fit any sect. His toleration and his playgoing are equally signs of his merely pretended faith.

"Counterfeit Christians," the preacher John Walsall (1578) called such dissemblers: "If these good fellows meet with Papists, they resist not: if with Atheists, they strive not: if with temporizers and servers of time, their humors are fed: if with zealous & true Christians, they become key cold, and yet hollow pretenders of love and good will to the Gospel. These honest men can with the Chameleon transform themselves into every color." Given the world's "carnal love" for such accommodating "good fellows" and its derision of zealous "saints," it hardly surprised Walsall to learn that "vain players have had about this city of London far greater audience, than true preachers." A sure sign of a merely "formal" Christian, the puritan Robert Bolton (1611) observed, is a willingness to "offer" oneself to "profane and obscene Plays." But Phillip Stubbes (1583) blamed the hollow pretense of religiosity in England on the plays as well as the playgoers: theaters, he wrote in his *Anatomie of Abuses*, are "Schools o[r] Seminaries of pseudo christianit[y]."[3]

The accusation climaxes Stubbes's angry response in the *Anatomie* to the protheatrical claim that plays "be as good as sermons, and that many a good Example may be learned out of them." In my previous chapters, I considered the potential for rivalry between preachers and players one glimpses in this remarkable comparison. I outlined the attractions for theater people of a reformist tradition, identifiable with the "semi-Christian" Erasmus (as Bellarmine called him), that elevated Christian fundamentals and fellowship over doctrinal precision and sectarian zeal. I argued in chapter 4 that Shakespeare drew on this Erasmian tradition to distinguish the sacramental communitarianism of players from the homiletic elitism of preachers. For the theater lovers Stubbes describes, however, plays are just as good at *teaching* as sermons are, and it is this homiletic conception of the theater that provokes Stubbes's wrath—not because he doubts that plays can teach, but rather because he thinks they teach pseudo-Christianity all too well. Above all, Stubbes believes, plays school their audiences to care less for the truth than for show. "If you will learn falsehood, if you will learn cozenage: if you will learn to deceive: if you will learn to play the Hypocrite": so begins Stubbes's long list of the "good Examples" he claims a spectator will actually "see painted before your eyes in interludes and plays." By absorbing audiences in dissemblance and display, the "bawdy, wanton shows" of players do worse than illustrate all "kind of sin and mischief," Stubbes concludes; they "renew the remembrance of heathen idolatry."[4]

Such antitheatrical commonplaces appear nearly fifty years later in Thomas Randolph's comedy *The Muses' Looking Glass* (1630) as the refrains of two fanatically puritan spectators, Bird and Mistress Flowerdew, who oppose themselves to the player and the "formalist" both. Equating a "Masque" with the "Idolatry" of the "Mass," Randolph's zealots worry whether the pleasing shows of the theater will "unsanctify" their "eyes, and make 'em Carnal." But the actor Roscius counters that a play's shows are the very things that make it spiritually so valuable:

> On the stage
> We set an Usurer to tell this age
> How ugly looks his soul: A prodigal
> Is taught by us how far from liberal
> his folly bears him: Boldly I dare say
> There has been more by us in some one Play
> Laugh'd into wit and virtue, than hath been
> By twenty tedious Lectures drawn from sin
> And foppish humors.

It is because they so forcefully engage the audience's senses, Roscius insists, that plays edify better than "tedious Lectures" do. Instead of merely reciting an instructive "Example," a player *performs* one, and thus shows how a vicious "soul" "looks" in the flesh. "Men are not won by th' ears," Roscius concludes, "so well as eyes."[5]

Bird and Flowerdew agree that the "sights" of plays win audiences; their objection is that plays win audiences to sin. The theaters, they claim, are "Colleges of Transgression, / Wherein the seven deadly sins are studied"; as London's authorities put it to the Privy Council in 1597, plays "move wholly to imitation & not to the avoiding of those faults & vices which they represent." Strikingly, Randolph does little to counter such accusations. Instead of depicting virtue in action, for instance, the *Looking Glass* parades one pair of vices after another as the "Extremes" from which the "Mean" of a virtue must be deduced; if men are won by the eyes, as Roscius claims, why should Randolph insist on teaching virtues sight unseen?[6] Or again, to dispute the puritanical charge that playing is "irreligious," Randolph has Tragedy declare that she was once considered "a fit ceremony of Religion," but then Comedy points out that Tragedy's original "Benefactors" were "the reeling Priests of *Bacchus*," while Tragedy retorts that Comedy's priests were "such / As chanted forth religious, bawdy sonnets, / In honor of the fine chaste God *Priapus.*" Bird and Flowerdew might have complained that Roscius seems to equate "wit" with "virtue" and "sin" with "foppish humors," but the puritans are far more appalled by Roscius's apparent inability to distinguish virtue and true religion from false religion and vice. To the eyes of the formalist, Scott would say, "all's one."[7]

Yet the very equivocality of Randolph's apologies for the stage is itself polemical: it underscores Randolph's belief that the wheat cannot be separated from the chaff as easily as "the sanctified fraternity" pretend. In Randolph's view, it is the puritans, not the players, who are obsessed with appearances; Bird and Flowerdew condemn playgoers as "the wicked" and the theater as a "den of spiritual thieves" without ever having seen a play. The problem is not simply that "just Judges" must never, as Roscius says, be "prejudicate." According to official church doctrine (as I will shortly show), only God knows if a person is as truly "pure" and "good" as Bird and Flowerdew claim themselves to be.[8] In line with this orthodoxy, the *Looking Glass* urges "mildness" not only toward its "offending" scenes but toward all those whom puritans would scorn as "Reprobate" on appearance alone. And that is precisely the effect the play has on Bird and Flowerdew. At the end of the *Looking Glass*, Flowerdew confesses that her "eyes" have hitherto been "blinded" by "ignorance," while her companion Bird promises "hereafter" to "visit Comedies, / And see them oft, they are good exercises!" Learning to appreciate plays is only part of the "reformation" these puritans undergo, however. Once they drop their professed abhorrence to carnal scenes, their sectarianism begins to vanish too: Bird vows to "teach devotion now a milder temper."[9] According to the *Looking Glass*, in other words, the theater's shows encourage the very toleration that Scott and Walsall despise.

But Randolph's play is a late instance of the protheatrical logic it exemplifies. In this chapter I will show how the connections that Scott and Walsall draw between formalism, religious toleration, and playgoing were as important to the defenders of the stage in Renaissance England as to its attackers. I will begin by outlining established-church policy on the question of outward conformity to religion and then try to show how the apologetical tradition to which the *Looking Glass* belongs portrayed the theater as a source of spiritual guidance about the question. The first play I will consider, *Sir Thomas More* (c. 1594), dramatizes a matter of tremendous religious controversy, More's martyrdom, yet hardly mentions religion at all, stressing instead the "merry" elements of More's story; the next play, Thomas Middleton's *The Puritan* (c. 1606), turns religious controversy into scurrilous city comedy; while the third play, Jasper Mayne's comedy *The City Match* (1637), appears to acknowledge the religious controversy that would soon overwhelm England only by incidentally satirizing puritans. For the Bird-like critic, these three plays would seem to mark the theater's increasing secularization, but I want to argue that, on the contrary, they manifest an increasing confidence, even arrogance, about the theater's ability to "teach devotion a milder temper." Players, in the early view of the protheatrical tradition I will analyze, taught their audiences how to comport themselves in a time of religious controversy, how to bear the thought of a possible spiritual hypocrisy in others and in themselves, how to recognize that a tolerant acceptance of such pseudo-Christianity was the practice of true religion. With their task of allying church and theater simplified by the shared threat of puritanism, however, later protheatricalists grew emboldened about the social as well as moral dubiousness of acting and presented that dubiousness itself, paradoxically, as both more palatable and more edifying than puritanical zeal. In the words of one such writer (1653), "there is more gain / In seeing men act vice than virtue feign; / And he less tempts a danger that delights / In profess'd players than close Hypocrites."[10] What good was the "art" of feigning virtue if the puritans too were experts at it?[11] And how were libertine playgoers to be attracted to virtue when its pretense in puritans disgusted them? Having begun, in support of church and theater, by promoting a toleration of outward conformity, apologists for the stage found themselves increasingly identifying the true Christian less with the feigning of virtue than with the profession of vice.

I

During the reign of Elizabeth, religious toleration, or a limited form of it, became a highly touted feature of the English church. Although from the 1580s English citizens who refused to attend state-sponsored church services were liable to severe fines, apologists for the church regularly stressed that no Christian complying with English law would ever be subjected to an inquisitorial examination of his or her actual faith. In the famous words of Sir Francis Bacon (1593), Elizabeth refused "to make windows into men's hearts and secret thoughts, except the abundance of them did overflow into overt and express acts and affirmations"; "utterly disliking of the tyranny of the Church of Rome," the queen (according to Bacon) sought to repress papists "in faction" only, not "in conscience." For the Elizabethan orthodoxy, in other words, toleration depended on the distinction between a private world where Christian dissidents might live free, "reserving their consciences to themselves," and a public world where they lived according to the rules, "conforming their outward demeanor no further, than is needful for the common tranquility of all."[12]

The consequent admission by established churchmen such as Hooker (1597) that dissidents could "satisfy law in *pretending* themselves conformable" outraged stricter Protestants, who believed that by instituting conformism the church had licensed, indeed encouraged hypocrisy. To these critics, common tranquility in England was merely the outward face of a church rotten at its core. As one character in Arthur Dent's *The Plaine Mans Path-way to Heaven* (1601) put it, "This age indeed aboundeth with many hollow hearted Hypocrites, dissemblers, and time-servers: which, howsoever they make a face, and bear a countenance, as though they loved the Gospel, yet their heart is not with it. Their heart is with Atheism: their heart is with Popery. They have a Pope, in their belly: they be Church-papists."[13] More agitated opponents to conformism argued that such double-dealers were secretly ready "to bury their poniards in our breasts."[14] And some dissidents went still further, accusing church authorities of a hidden atheism, too, for how else could one explain the church's willingness to receive "profane and ungodly people" into its fold? The Brownist Francis Johnson (1594) reported that an Elizabethan official who was pressuring one of Johnson's brethren to conform had finally exclaimed to him in frustration, "Come then to church, and obey the Queen's laws, and be a dissembler, be an hypocrite, or a devil if thou will be."[15]

Even in the face of such damaging criticism, the defenders of conformity refused to take a stronger stand against hypocrisy, because they claimed that it was inevitable. To judge oneself capable of exposing and expelling dissemblers from the church was, conformists argued, to arrogate a power that belonged to God alone. As Edward Aglionby (1571) declared in Parliament, "the conscience of man is internal, invisible," and therefore it is "not in the power of the greatest monarch in the world"; "in the eye of God," stated Hooker, "they are against Christ that are not truly and sincerely with him," but "in our eyes they must be received as with Christ that are not to outward show against him."[16] For conformists, such agnosticism about the true state of any particular soul did not mean that the church was helpless to save souls. By requiring the hollow-hearted to attend church service and thus be exposed to weekly doses of the truth, conformism could gradually be productive as well as expedient. According to Richard Bernard (1608), "many that for fear of law were first brought to the Church, & outward profession of the truth, have been and are effectually converted by the ministry of the word." The task of the church, as Hooker reminded his readers, had always been "to build wheresoever there is any foundation, to add perfection unto slender beginnings." If the clergy were to require stricter tests of piety from its congregation than conformism allowed, the church would "lose or willfully hazard those souls from which the likeliest means of full and perfect recovery are by our indiscretion withheld. For neither doth God thus bind us to dive into men's consciences, nor can their fraud and deceit hurt any man but themselves." Indeed, a more coercive policy than conformism, as William Chillingworth (1638) explained, would only exacerbate the problem of inward rebellion from church authority, "for human violence may make men counterfeit, but cannot make them believe, and is therefore fit for nothing, but to breed form without, and atheism within."[17]

Yet if carnal weapons were either useless or self-defeating in spiritual warfare, as one conformist after another claimed, what justified the enforcement of conformity? Along with invoking the Pauline ordinances that Christians should obey "the higher powers" and conduct their worship "decently and in order," conformists tried to palliate this seeming contradiction to their general policy of moderation by treating church attendance as no real constraint at all. "Christian liberty," maintained George Downame (1609), "is wholly spiritual, being a liberty of the conscience and inner man, which may stand with the outward servitude of bondslaves, much more with the subjection and obedience of free subjects. For though the outward use of the liberty be moderated by the Magistrate, and confined; yet the inward liberty of the conscience is not impaired." In the view of nonconformists, this argument only weakened the conformist case: if, as conformists claimed, the substance and reality of the spirit lay within, in a private realm open to God yet hidden from human sight, while outward forms of worship were like all human inventions merely *adiaphora*, "things indifferent," then why should the magistrate be concerned to regulate outward forms at all? Called before Archbishop Whitgift in 1587, the Brownist Henry Barrow refused to swear an oath on the Bible as Whitgift demanded, and when Whitgift tried to placate Barrow by explaining that the required oath was "but a ceremony," "a thing indifferent," Barrow replied, "if it be indifferent, as you say it is, then do I well in not using it."[18]

Conformists strengthened the positive case for regulation by grounding that case in the essentially social nature of the church. Particular forms of worship had, for the conformist, no intrinsic spiritual value; as adiaphora, they mattered only insofar as they helped unite Christians in the cause of sincere worship. "That edification which is ascribed to ceremonies," cautioned Richard Bancroft (c. 1583–85), "is but *per accidens:* as when men being brought through order and decency in the Church to a more reverent behavior and opinion of divine Service, they are by God's spirit the sooner edified. For ceremonies therefore to be orderly and decent, is their tending to edification: and none other edifying can proceed from them, but as they be both decent and orderly." It followed from this instrumental account of ceremonies that just as no form of worship could be considered inherently edifying, so none could be considered inherently decent. "Diversity of times, of manners, and of people," explained Bancroft, "requireth as occasion shall serve, a diverse manner, kind, or form of government."[19] To aid devotion, in other words, a ceremony had first to suit decorum; and, while "a private *Spirit* knows what best agrees / With his own fancy," the poet George Wither (1628) wrote, "the *Church* best sees / What fits the *Congregation.*"[20]

Protestants were thus in the conformist view certainly right to condemn those, such as Jews and Catholics, who claimed a spiritual necessity to their ceremonies, but the "private" worshipper who despised all set forms of worship betrayed a similarly idolatrous obsession with outward things, and more important revealed an uncharitable disregard for the rest of his congregation, especially the weak in faith. "The godly man," it was true, as one conformist wrote, "must always retain & keep safe in his mind" the knowledge that his conscience cannot "be holden & tied with any religion in external things, but when he cometh to the use & action of them, then must he moderate and qualify his liberty, according to charity toward his neighbor, and obedience to his Prince. So though by this knowledge his mind and conscience is always free: yet his doing is as it were tied or limited by law or love."[21] In requiring compliance with its outward practices, the church had demanded nothing more of its members, conformists insisted, than shouldering their basic social responsibilities—and it had led the way by example. For so indulgent was the church to its weaker members that it had charitably retained certain popish ceremonies and apparel in order to make compulsory church service more palatable to the unreformed—a moderation, according to Bancroft, that would gradually "win" more and more converts among church papists, "when they shall not only see in us, the lawful practice of such things, as they had superstitiously abused, but also a most charitable intention, and meaning to bear what we may, and to reject, mislike or alter nothing, which hath of long time been continued in the Church without most urgent and necessary causes."[22]

These conformist theories of toleration—in particular, the notion that the mere performance of conformity would at worst do no harm to the individual conscience and at best help to unite a community of believers—often figure in Renaissance English drama as a central, even a constitutive feature of plays.[23] One prominent and hitherto misunderstood case in point is the Elizabethan history play *Sir Thomas More* (c. 1593), to which Shakespeare almost certainly contributed some revisions. Scholars have long viewed More the Catholic martyr as an unlikely hero for the popular Elizabethan stage; citing the heavy cuts made to the extant manuscript of *Sir Thomas More* by the Elizabethan censor Edmund Tilney, they have generally concluded that the play's "subject was simply too controversial to be dramatized at all." Yet, while Tilney does indeed command the players of *Sir Thomas More* to alter various potentially inflammatory scenes and passages as he specifies "& not otherwise at your own perils," he never objects to depicting More's life per se, nor does he seem to mind a considerable portion of the celebratory treatment that More receives in the play.[24] Conformism encouraged such ideological flexibility. A decade before *Sir Thomas More* was written, so high a church official as the Bishop of London had urged Protestants to "bear what we may" about More by publicly distinguishing between More's "zeal," for which More should "be honored," and his "religion," for which he should "be abhorred."[25] *Sir Thomas More* goes further, presenting the Catholic martyr as an acid test for conformity: how, More's life enables the play to ask, can an Englishman maintain both his freedom of conscience and his obedience to authority?

At the start of *Sir Thomas More*, More is himself a magistrate, an undersheriff who rises to the position of Lord Chancellor by pacifying a dangerous group of lower class rebels. He assures these rebels, as the established church assured its own dissidents, that insubordination is "a sin, / Which oft th'apostle did forewarn us of, / Urging obedience to authority."[26] This initial presentation of More as an exemplary subject makes his refusal to sign some unspecified articles from the king a puzzle to many commentators on the play and to most characters within it, who marvel that More, of all people, would thus shirk the "duty that the law of God bequeaths / Unto the king." But More recognizes no inconsistency in his behavior, and the play tries to illustrate the logic of his position by contrasting it to the blunter resistance of his fellow conscientious objector, the Bishop of Rochester. Rochester frankly protests that he would make himself a "hypocrite" if he were to sign the articles, and he later boasts that "in this breast / There lives a soul, that aims at higher things / Than temporary pleasing earthly kings." More himself obviously shares Rochester's scruples, but apart from oblique references to his conscience and a satirical Latin apothegm on his situation, he never *says* he shares them. Instead, he consistently frames his disobedience as compliancy—"I will subscribe to go unto the Tower / With all submissive willingness"; "I'll satisfy the king even with my blood" —and these quibbles appear, in his mind, to render his resistance to Henry consonant with his service to him.[27]

The reason such wordplay can make a difference for More is that even in his most orthodox moments he had never committed himself to the view that submission to the higher powers must be absolute. When persuading the rebels to lay down their arms, More had preceded his exhortation to "obey the magistrate" by explaining to the rebels that they must "give up" themselves "to *form*" only. More, in short, is a conformist; he believes the law should regulate not how people think but rather how they act.[28] Later in the play, when the issue of signing the king's articles arises, we learn that Henry VIII wants the law to do more, but More himself appears to share the view of conformists such as Aglionby, who argued that "neither Jew nor Turk do require more than the submission to the outward observance and a convenient silence, as not to dislike with what is publicly professed. But to enforce any to do the act which may tend to the discovery of his conscience, it is never found." At his execution, More indicates that he holds just as high an opinion of inner freedom as Rochester had: skeptically appraising the guard placed on him, More speaks of "a thing within me, that will raise / And elevate my better part 'bove sight / Of these same weaker eyes."[29] Yet by constantly equivocating about his disobedience, More also shows that, like Bacon, he believes the free conscience of a dissenter must never be allowed to overflow into overt and express acts and affirmations; such outright contempt for authority is the crime to which More objects in the rebels' case and, presumably, in Rochester's too.

This crucial reservation is the topic of an earlier comical scene in *Sir Thomas More* about a malcontent named Falkner whom More punishes for the seemingly innocuous crime of having long hair. Falkner had vowed not to cut his hair for six years, and More decides to imprison him till the expiration of his vow "because I will not have ye walk the streets / For every man to stand and wonder at."[30] In the eyes of More the conformist, private fancies must give way, or at least seem to give way, to the public interest. Falkner quickly repents "his rude behavior," promising henceforth to "conform himself / To honest decency in his attire"; at the same time, he insists that his newfound obedience stems from inward illumination, not abjection. Inspired, as he claims, by More's charge that he has been "cherishing a loathsome excrement," Falkner reports that he has abandoned his vow because he has now "looked into [him]self with more respect" than he had before. For Falkner, in other words, conformity proves to be consciousness-raising: by redefining hair length as a question of decorum rather than of conscience, conformity helps free his conscience from enslavement to external things. As More jests in a revised version of the same scene, the submissive Falkner now has "less hair" but "more wit."[31]

The final scene in *Sir Thomas More* before the pivotal one of More's own disobedience translates this lesson about true inwardness from a juridical to a theatrical context. A company of players arrives at More's house to entertain him, but they discover they are missing a beard for the young actor who will play the part of Wit, and ask if they might delay their entertainment. More, urbanely carrying forward the terms of his anti-excremental discussion with Falkner, reassures them that "wit goes not all by the hair": "we'll rather allow a beardless Wit," he adds, "than wit all beard to have no brain." The players agree to begin, but when the actor sent to find a new beard fails to return, the play is once again delayed, and now More, to avoid having "our audience disappointed," "extempically" takes the missing actor's place. Earlier in *Sir Thomas More*, we had witnessed More the magistrate either persuading or coercing dissidents to preserve decorum; now we see the lessons of conformity magnanimously exemplified by the magistrate himself, playing his part as the occasion demands and for the greater good. After the show is over, one of the actors admiringly suggests that the Lord Chancellor would "make a rare player," which unsettles the nerves of another actor, the erstwhile Wit, who exclaims, "do you know what ye say? My Lord a player? Let us not meddle with any such matters." True to his conformism, however, More shows no similar anxiety about having disgraced himself by joining the players, because he believes that his outward performances bear no essential relation to his inward self. This moral is just the advice that More extemporaneously offers Wit in his part as Good Counsel: "judge not things by the outward show."[32]

The climax to his career as a prosperous magistrate, More's playing thus helps illustrate and vindicate his conformism, but one could just as easily say that his earlier acts of conformism had been quietly laying the groundwork for a defense of his playing. All of More's scenes before his disobedience are concerned to anticipate the criticism that More the conformist and conscientious objector is no better than a player—or, as the antitheatricalist would say, a "dissembling hypocrite."[33] In his first scene, More tries to enlist the services of a cutpurse named Lifter to help play a trick on a justice named Suresby, and Lifter worries that More is trying to entrap him; one of the rebels next warns More that if More does not secure them the king's pardon as he has promised, she will call him "a plain cony-catcher"; when Erasmus first comes to visit More, More commands his servant to pretend that the servant is More; and even during the play within the play, Wit worries whether More, in his part of Good Counsel, is a "deceiver." As these scenes run their course, however, More ends up not only vindicating his honesty but also proving that his deceptions have a moral, indeed an edifying purpose. By dressing his servant as himself, for instance, More hopes to put Erasmus to a moral test: "I'll see if great Erasmus can distinguish / Merit and outward ceremony." This is, once again, a conformist lesson, but *Sir Thomas More* also represents it as a theatrical one. More's characterization of his disguised servant as "a formal player" could equally well describe every rebel whom More persuades to observe "form"; "act thy part / With a firm boldness," More exhorts his servant—although he could just as easily be addressing Falkner or Wit—"and thou winst my heart."[34]

In sum, *Sir Thomas More* equates conformity with theatricality: the toleration of pretense in one context supports the toleration of pretense in the other. And More's "merry" tricksterism in the play amounts to a running appeal for such toleration, because it tries to inveigle the audience of *Sir Thomas More* into acknowledging the existence of a socially acceptable form of deceit. At its best, the play hopes to show, More's urbane detachment from outward things encourages rebels to lay down their arms and magistrates to temper their pride, or it inspires an exceptional generosity to the poor, or it strengthens More to face with equanimity the loss of his rank, fortune, even his life. At its worst, as Hooker might say, More's deceit hurts no one: "I think there lives not a more harmless gentleman in the universal world," a Tower butler comments during the final act of the play, to which the Tower brewer replies, "Nor a wiser, nor a merrier, nor an honester."[35]

II

In his own lifetime, the principal author of *Sir Thomas More* was also famous for his tricksterism, but harmless is hardly the word one would have applied to Anthony Munday. By the time *More* was written, Munday had been working for over a decade as an informer specializing in the entrapment of religious dissidents. In 1588, for instance, while acting as a pursuivant for Whitgift, Munday had employed his talents at make-believe to draw out the puritan Giles Wigginton on the subjects of church government and Martin Marprelate; after promising Wigginton that he would never betray his confidence, Munday immediately reported Wigginton's views to the archbishop. Wigginton described Munday that day as "a great Dissembler"; in print, another Marprelatean called Munday a "Judas." Ostensibly defending Munday against these attacks, his fellow playwright Thomas Nashe (c. 1589) effectively underscored the deadly relationship between Munday's theatrical talents and his treachery: "Beware *Anthony Munday* be not even with you for calling him Judas, and lay open your false carding to the stage of all men's scorn."[36]

Critics have found Munday's penchant for treachery difficult to reconcile with his seeming moderation toward Catholics in *Sir Thomas More*, but Munday began his career as an informer by pretending sympathy with the English Catholics in Rome, and even after having achieved some notoriety for helping capture and execute some of these Jesuits a few years later, he still managed to impress Wigginton as one "who seemeth to favor the Pope." At the same time, it is hard not to see Munday's positive portrayal of More as a kind of professional courtesy to a fellow inquisitor: the play never mentions the whippings, rackings, and burnings that led John Foxe to denounce More as "a bitter persecutor."[37] One could imagine Munday's replying to these grim readings of his authorship that neither playing nor conformity requires good intentions: each practice sets aside the question of conscience in the interest of outward decency and social order. What's more, Munday might say, dissidents such as Wigginton and the Jesuits ought never to have shared their heterodox opinions with him, as *Sir Thomas More* could have helped them appreciate. Yet the English Catholics whom Munday betrayed were not voicing dissident views when they originally spoke with him (if indeed they ever voiced such views at all): they were in Rome, conforming to the government of the pope. And there was little in the nature of overt acts or affirmations to Wigginton's disclosures: if a dissident could not safely express his true opinions even in confidence, it is hard to see what substantive freedom of conscience English authorities could claim to allow. As the Congregationalist Henry Jacob asked King James in 1616, turning the social argument for conformism against itself, what faith can exist solely inside a person's head? "Meetings of a Congregation to the joint and common exercise of God's worship are necessary parts of religion, and duties in conscience, as being Christ's very ordinance and commandment. Your Majesty's wisdom understandeth perfectly that without such meetings, common prayers, and other acts of a religion in a Congregation, God neither is nor can be served, as he ought to be."[38]

Munday's spying for the church raises as serious questions about the theater as about conformism. In his remarkable book on Christopher Marlowe, *The Reckoning*, Charles Nicholl has shown that close ties between the theater and espionage in Renaissance England were not limited to the figure of

Munday; on the contrary, playwrights were favorite tools of English spy-masters, who appear to have regarded theater people as experts at "pretending themselves conformable" to religious dissidents.[39] In their plays, after all, theater people must often have seemed the *least* conformist members of English society. *Sir Thomas More* represents the ability to detach one's inward self from outward forms as an aid to conformity, but players regularly exploited this distinction between outward fiction and inward truth to license the expression of far more outrageous opinions to audiences of thousands than Wigginton was safely able to communicate in private to one man. Consider these lines on the origins of religion spoken by the actor in the title role of *Selimus* (c. 1592):

>   some sage man, above the vulgar wise,
> Knowing that laws could not in quiet dwell,
> Unless they were observed: did first devise
> The names of Gods, religion, heaven, and hell,
> And gan of pains, and feign'd rewards to tell:
> Pains for those men which did neglect the law,
> Rewards, for those that liv'd in quiet awe.
> Whereas indeed they are mere fictions,
> And if they were not, *Selim* thinks they were:
> And these religious observations,
> Only bug-bears to keep the world in fear,
> And make men quietly a yoke to bear.
> So that religion of it self a bauble,
> Was only found to make us peaceable.

As if his atheism were not scandalous enough, Selimus confirms the worst fears of those who claimed that conformists feigned their religion in the interest of the status quo. Yet *Selimus* was licensed to be printed as well as performed; only when the speech surfaced a decade later as "Certain Hellish Verses" ascribed to "that atheist and traitor Ralegh"—only, that is, after it had been removed from the special protections that English society granted to theatrical discourse—did its heresy become a serious liability to its supposed expresser.[40]

When antitheatricalists such as Stubbes described the theater as the place to go to learn falsehood, hypocrisy, and cozenage, they probably had more in mind, then, than the actor's necessary pretenses or the fact that play after play dramatized elaborate ruses and hoaxes. The disturbing religious equivocality of such figures as Munday and "Selimus" lent considerable fuel to the antitheatrical fire; when these proofs that "players get their living by craft and cozenage" were combined with arguments consigning the theater to the social level of the brothel and alehouse, it was no wonder that apologists for the theater regularly felt compelled to supplement their more high-minded defenses of playgoing with the admission that plays were not entirely free of vice.[41]

In his protheatrical *Kind-Harts Dreame* (1592), for instance, Munday's occasional collaborator Henry Chettle confesses that "plays are not altogether to be commended"; indeed, Chettle presents the *Dreame's* defense of plays as having occurred to him one afternoon while he lay at a tavern in a drunken stupor. Over the course of the *Dreame*, however, Chettle turns the acknowledged disreputableness of the theater into a special virtue. It is because players are perhaps too familiar with London's demimonde, Chettle argues, that they can expose crimes of which the more respectable elements of society are unaware: as a bawd in *Kind-Harts Dreame* complains, players "open our cross-biting, our coney-catching, our trains, our traps, our gins, our snares, our subtleties: for no sooner have we a trick of deceit, but they make it common, singing Jigs, and making jests of us, that every boy can point out our houses as they pass by."[42] Furthermore, while theater haters might castigate the idler who would spend "two-pence" in "an afternoon" to "see treachery set out, with which every man nowadays useth to entrap his brother," Chettle asks such critics to consider what the idler would be doing if "our moderate merriments" were no longer available to him: according to Chettle, the recent closure of the theaters for the duration of the plague had meant "no small profit" to "the Bowling-alleys in Bedlam and other places, that were wont in the afternoon to be left empty, by the recourse of good fellows unto the unprofitable recreation of Stage-playing."[43]

Sir Thomas More broadens this strangely creditable association of playing with petty criminality to include conformism in the mix. The conformist More is first introduced to us in the play as an authority on petty crimes: having announced at a Court of Sessions that the court's attention will now turn from "our weightier businesses" to "petty felonies," the Lord Mayor calls on More to present the cutpurse Lifter. What at first seems to be nothing more than a juridical relationship between a sheriff and his prisoner quickly turns into a working partnership: More suborns Lifter into cutting Justice Suresby's purse and proves to be so conversant with Lifter's thieving ways that he is able to apply the accurate term from rogues' cant—"I'll be thy setter"—to his own role in the coming robbery. Antitheatrical literature regularly depicted players as the willing or at least unwitting accomplices of cutpurses; posing for a time as a theater hater, Munday (1580) himself had claimed of players that their "chief end" was in any event "to juggle in good earnest the money out of other men's purses into their own hands." As Chettle indicates, however, theater people routinely boasted that their proximity to cutpurses put them in a unique position to detect and then expose the rogues who plagued church congregations no less than theater audiences. Plays, the protheatricalists claimed, "discover *Thefts*, and *Cheatings*." Admitting that cutpurses are "always about the playhouse door" when a new play opens, the dramatist Thomas Dekker (1607) detailed the modus operandi of these criminals so as to help "keep honest men's money in their purses." This was only a more sophisticated version of the claim made by the comedian William Kemp in 1600 that players often tied cutpurses "to a post on our stage for all people to wonder at." Like the player in an antitheatrical tract, Munday's More may conspire with Lifter to steal a purse, but then like the player in a protheatrical tract, he aims in truth only to *stage* a crime. "See that thou diminish not / One penny of the money," More cautions Lifter; "It is the cunning *act* that credits thee." This counterfeit theft does more than show audiences how pickpocketing works; it also teaches Justice Suresby a conformist lesson. Suresby had boasted that "wise men" never lose their purses; when he finds his own purse missing, however, he like Falkner is forced to contemplate the "folly" of confusing inward substance with outward things.[44]

Sir Thomas More defends players, then, by asking its audience to accept the notion not simply of a harmless deception but of a tolerable crime, and the play surprisingly underwrites this apology for the petty vice in theaters by invoking the pious logic of conformism. Taking Munday's sordid life into account, one might be tempted to write off such an ingenious amalgamation of theatrical disreputability with ecclesiological orthodoxy as a particularly egregious sort of special pleading: if playing and conformism help excuse the cutpurse of *More*, the cutpurse absorbs the shame that in Munday's case would otherwise seem proper to the conformist and player. But later dramatists similarly interwove church, theater, and petty vice with increasing frequency, and they were encouraged by a phenomenon that only marginally figures in *Sir Thomas More*: the opposition of religious dissidents to plays and conformism both.

Throughout the commendatory poems to Thomas Heywood's *Apology for Actors* (1612), for instance, Heywood's admirers support playgoing in conventional fashion as an innocuous amusement that would be justifiable even if it did nothing more than "keep gallants from misspending of their time," yet this standard call for moderation is now conspicuously linked to the vilification of puritanical theater haters. Claiming to prefer the "modest mirth" of plays to the greater evils of gaming or whoring, the actor Richard

Perkins confesses (somewhat disingenuously, in light of his profession) that he not only goes to see plays but also makes sure "that all may see me" once he has arrived at a theater: "I love no public soothers, private scorners, / That rail 'gainst lechery, yet love a harlot. / When I drink, 'tis in sight, and not in corners: / I am no open Saint, and secret varlet." Players are not the hypocrites, Perkins maintains: puritans are, and they only aggravate their vices (as secret varlets) by denying them (as open saints). In the same vein, the theatrical impresario Christopher Beeston portrays the foes of "modest pastimes" as dissemblers who "pretend more strictness than the rest"; Heywood subsequently declares himself "moved" to write his *Apology* "by the sundry exclamations of many seditious Sectists." This antipuritanical stance encourages a certain theological directness to Heywood's defense of plays. If "in all their holy doctrines, books, and principles of Divinity," Heywood argues, Christ and his apostles "were content to pass [Theaters] over, as things tolerated, and indifferent, why should any nice and over-scrupulous heads . . . take upon them to correct, control, and carp at that, against which they cannot find any text in the sacred Scriptures?" Echoing the conformist attack on puritans as those who "quarrel against Ceremonies, neither idolatrous, nor superstitious, and which have no real relation to the soul and conscience by any sacred ordinance of God in the rules of his Word," Heywood insists that a morally "harmless" pastime is also a doctrinally "indifferent" one.[45]

This was no sudden or revolutionary transformation in terms, as *Sir Thomas More* shows us. From the start of the Vestiarian Controversy in the 1560s, puritan writers had themselves associated the church ceremonies they deplored with the theater. The author of *An Answere for the Tyme* (1566), for instance, attacked the surplice as "playerlylike apparel" and refused to "place order in these trifling pomps, which have nothing but a vanishing show."[46] Some Elizabethan antitheatricalists had allowed that plays might be things indifferent, but they had argued (in nonconformist fashion) that "if indifferent things give offence to the weak, they ought to be removed."[47] Conversely, the protheatrical assault on puritanical hypocrisy in Heywood's *Apology* was anticipated by Nashe's *Pierce Penilesse* (1592), which claimed that plays expose "all cunning drifts over-guilded with outward holiness." Yet Nashe had not specifically identified puritans as the overguilders in question; the crackdown on players that had begun a few years before *Pierce Penilesse*, when Nashe and Munday had helped involve the theater in sectarian brawls with Martin Marprelate, must certainly have encouraged such discretion.[48] The decision by Heywood and his friends to defend the theater in openly sectarian terms would seem to mark a change less in attitude than in political climate: as a playwright working for Queen Anne's Men, Heywood could, after all, point to royal backers—who also happened to loath puritans.

In his own apology for players, addressed to the antitheatrical puritan preacher Thomas Sutton, the actor and dramatist Nathan Field (1616) makes sure to exploit this royal connection: "Our Caesar, our David, that can vouchsafe amongst his grave exercises some time to tune hymns, and harken unto harmless matters of delight, our Joshua that professeth, howsoever other nations do, he and his household will serve the Lord, holds it no execrable matter to tolerate them." For Sutton to condemn what the king allows is a sign, Field shrewdly implies, not only of poor judgment but of nonconformity too: "and how ungodly a speech it is in a public pulpit to say that he [i.e., King James] maintains those whom God hath damned, I appeal to the censure of all faithful subjects, nay, all Christian people." Since conformists regarded royal authority as a kind of shorthand for the church en masse, this emphasis on Sutton's disagreement with the king helps Field portray Sutton's antitheatricalism as anticommunitarian too: "none repines" at the profession of player, Field continues, except "some few whose curiosity [i.e., scrupulosity] overweigheth their charity." It is charity, Bancroft had said, that makes the conformist bear with things indifferent; thus Field maintains it must be a lack of charity that causes Sutton to abominate harmless matters of delight. Of course, reproaching someone for "uncharitable dealing" can itself seem uncharitable, a danger Field acknowledges when he begs Sutton to believe "that I enter not the list of contention, but only take hold of the horns of the altar in mine own defense."[49] By challenging the conformity of antitheatricalists, theater lovers such as Field and Heywood raised a difficult question about themselves as well: how successfully could they represent themselves as the promoters of tolerance, decency, and good order if they now based this self-defense no longer on the quiet moderation of a play such as *Sir Thomas More*, but rather on their violent clashes with "seditious Sectists"?

The paradox looms large in Thomas Middleton's comedy *The Puritan* (c. 1606), a play so antagonistic to "uncharitable" puritans that it drew fire from the pulpit and may even have led to the suppression of the playing company that enacted it.[50] Throughout *The Puritan*, however, Middleton tries to distance himself from his own sectarianism by placing it in the mouths of disreputable characters. Early in the play, the dissolute Corporal Oath informs the puritan Nicholas St. Antlings that Captain Idle, Nicholas's cousin, has been condemned to hang for highway robbery. "Thou Church-peeling, thou Holy-paring, religious outside thou," Oath exclaims to Nicholas, "if thou hadst any grace in thee, thou wouldst visit him, relieve him, swear to get him out." This attribution of a hypocritical hollowness to Nicholas continues even after Nicholas agrees to visit Idle in prison: "thou gap'st upon me comfortably, and giv'st me charitable faces," the Captain himself now scoffs, "which indeed is but a fashion in you all that are Puritans"; or again, "I'll sooner expect mercy from a Usurer when my bond's forfeited, sooner kindness from a Lawyer when my money's spent: nay sooner charity from the devil, than good from a Puritan." Though clearly tendentious, these diatribes against puritans are not therefore shown to be untrue, as Nicholas indicates when he questions whether "thou shalt love thy Neighbor" actually appears in the bible. Instead, Middleton asks us to believe that the sharply drawn vices of the chief rogue in the play, the playmaker Pieboard, give him a privileged insight into the crimes of the puritan whose funeral has just taken place as the play begins, a man who, the eavesdropping Pieboard discovers, "cozen'd the right heir" of the lands that his son will now inherit. Pretending to be a fortune-teller, the streetwise Pieboard in turn cozens the dead man's rich widow, the Lady Plus, with an accurately deduced picture of her husband's secret varletry: "he thought it Sanctity enough, if he had kill'd a man, so 'tad been done in a Pew, or undone his Neighbor, so 'tad been near enough to th' Preacher. Oh,—a Sermon's a fine short cloak of an hour long, and will hide the upper-part of a dissembler.—Church, aye, he seem'd all Church, & his conscience was as hard as the Pulpit!"[51]

A common fraudulence thus brings rogues and puritans together in Middleton's play, but the disparate magnitude of their vices works to separate them again. Whereas the Captain is to be hanged for "the poor purchase of ten groats," the obscenely felonious Plus has died a wealthy and respected citizen; as Pieboard observes to the Captain, "your greatest thieves are never hang'd." Though equally dishonest, the rogues seem less offensive than Plus because they are only petty and, ultimately, ineffectual criminals. Pieboard even justifies his chicanery as the life taught him by his betters, "for since the law lives by quarrels, the Courtier by smooth God-morrows, and every profession makes itself greater by imperfections, why not we then by shifts, wiles, and forgeries?" In practicing upon the widow and her family, moreover, Pieboard confines himself to duping only fellow dissemblers and to profiting only from pretense. (*'Tis No Deceit to Deceive the Deceiver*, as the title of a lost Chettle play declares.) Although his scheme to free the Captain appears to involve the theft of a valuable chain from the widow's brother-in-law Sir Godfrey Plus, the chain is actually merely hidden on Sir Godfrey's premises so that Pieboard can appear to recover it with the help of a conjurer—the Captain, whom Sir Godfrey is persuaded to deliver from prison. Later in the play, when the liberated Captain wants to know whether he has played his conjuring part well, Pieboard replies, "better than any Conjurer, for here was no harm in this."[52]

Without contrasting rogues to puritans, *Sir Thomas More* had staged a similarly harmless crime and even solicited the audience's tolerance for actual petty thefts. To prove that he intended to play no trick on Lifter in the planned purse-snatching of Justice Suresby, More had reminded Lifter that

> Thou knowest there are such matters in my hands
> As, if I pleased to give them to the jury
> I should not need this way to circumvent thee.
> All that I aim at, is a merry jest:
> Perform it, Lifter, and expect my best.

As we have seen, *More* promotes such indulgence toward petty criminality at the outset to prepare the audience to accept the later appearance of deceit in More's conformity and theatricality, an apologetical strategy that Middleton also seems to have in mind when he makes the Captain speak of performing "a little conjuring ceremony" that he has borrowed from the actions of "a stalking-stamping Player." Yet in scene after scene Munday had felt compelled to dramatize just how unlike a deceiver More truly was, while Middleton never bothers to delineate the character of a good player or a good conformist; for Middleton, apparently, this task is already fulfilled by the play's invidious comparison of roguish to puritanical deceit. Antipuritanism has thus both revised and condensed the conformist apologetics of *Sir Thomas More:* now, incongruously, a "religious outside" has become a badge of shame, while, to occupy the position of the theater lover and conformist, one need only tolerate dissembling rogues.[53] When first resolving to aid the Captain, the crooked playmaker Pieboard gives this strange new theatrico-conformist logic a proverbial ring: "a charitable Knave is better than a soothing Puritan."[54]

The petty criminals of *The Puritan* serve, then, a positive as well as a negative function for Middleton: they allow him not simply to distance himself from his sectarian attack on puritans, but also to display the charitable inclusiveness that his puritans lack. Quite apart from any protheatrical incentive, Hooker had encouraged conformists to extend their charity even to outright knaves, whose potential for reclamation only God could know: "The Church of God may therefore contain both them which in deed are not his yet must be reputed his by us that know not their inward thoughts, and them whose apparent wickedness testifieth even in the sight of the whole world that God abhorreth them. For to this and no other purpose are meant those parables which our Savior in the gospel hath concerning mixture of vice with virtue, light with darkness, truth with error, as well an openly known and seen as a cunningly cloaked mixture." Conversely, it was a popular slur against puritans that they restricted their brotherly love only to their fellow "saints," as the puritan Dryfat in Middleton's *Family of Love* indicates when he protests, "I live in charity and give small alms to such as be not of the right sect."[55] Conformist preachers such as Hooker might condemn such uncharitableness, but they could hardly confess the potential roguishness of their own profession as sanguinely as Middleton does in making Pieboard a playwright (and a famous playwright at that, insofar as Pieboard's character and actions recall the figure of George Peele).[56] This frank admission of the close ties between theater people and rogues further distinguishes Middleton from his play's hypocritical puritans, who hate nothing so much about theater people as their commitment to exposing hypocrisy: Nicholas says that his parson "rails against Players mightily, I can tell you, because they brought him drunk upo'th' Stage once—as he will be horribly drunk."[57]

Midway through *The Puritan*, Middleton offers playgoers a model of how they too might confess their sympathies with rogues. Pieboard has been arrested for debt by some serjeants, who despise scholars for the same reason Nicholas's parson does, because "they will publish our imperfections, Knaveries, and Conveyances upon Scaffolds and Stages."[58] To keep his "poor carcass" from "these Puttocks," Pieboard hits on the "device" of claiming that he was just about to collect "five pound of a Gentleman, for the Device of a Masque." He leads the serjeants to the home of a man he gathers is a wealthy justice of the peace, bluffs his way to the owner, and then throws himself on the gentleman's "understanding and pity": "may it please your good Worship then but to uphold my Device, which is to let one of your men put me out at backdoor, and I shall be bound to your worship forever."[59] "By my troth," the gentleman responds, "an excellent device," which the serjeants in a sense accurately misconstrue as a reference to Pieboard's phantom masque. Pieboard had worried that the justice might prove "a formal Citizen," but instead of standing on forms, this magistrate, like Sheriff More before him, expresses his appreciation for the inner substance, the "good wit, brave wit, finely wrought," glimpsed beneath a rogue's shifting disguises. The gentleman thus exemplifies the charitable posture that Middleton believes we should all adopt toward wayward souls: "Alas poor wretch, I could not blame his brain / To labor his delivery." Yet charity is only half the moral of the scene. *Sir Thomas More* had suggested that faith in the inward goodness of a person should grow in proportion to that person's urbane detachment from outward things, and now *The Puritan* pushes that conformist logic in an even more paradoxical direction, toward the view that charity is specially inspired by the spectacle not simply of detachment but of outright cozenage, too.[60]

Middleton's puritans license this extreme interpretation of conformism because they enable him to characterize any strong investment in forms as hypocritical, uncharitable, and ridiculous. On one side of the issue, Pieboard complains that "words pass not regarded nowadays unless they come from a good suit of clothes"; he and his fellow cozeners will shortly illustrate why More had taught Wit not to judge things by the outward show. The puritan Simon St. Overies, on the other hand, praises a barber because "he washes the sins of the Beard clean"; it was against such faith in excrements that More had called for less hair and more wit. The accusation of "Fopster" that Pieboard levels at Nicholas thus bears a specific sectarian charge: it is intended to underscore Nicholas's formalism in religion; and long after *The Puritan* an obsession with clothes remained a prominent feature of antipuritan satire on the stage.[61] In Randolph's *Hey for Honesty* (c. 1627), for instance, the puritan Ananias Goggle proves to be so thoroughgoing a formalist that he regards his cloak as "well-affected" and his shoes as "zealous." This fanatical conflation of inward and outward makes the thought that an enemy might wear his cloak almost intolerable to Goggle: "No, good cloak, ne'er turn / Apostate from the faith of *Amsterdam*. / Good cloak, be not akin to *Julian's* jerkin: / Though thou be threadbare, thou shalt ne'er be turn'd." Nonetheless, Goggle is in the end persuaded to exchange his cloak for another garment that had at first seemed "profane" to him until he had "sanctified" it by "thrice" wiping his nose on it: his idolatry proves to be the outward, indeed excremental sign of his inanity.[62]

The most extensive theatrical attack on puritan clothes-mongering appears in Jasper Mayne's comedy *The City Match* (1637). The maid Dorcas, a student of puritans, so deplores the popish "surplice" worn by established ministers that she blames it (along with the equally malevolent force of "powders") for dry summers and the plague. And she is no less agitated about lay clothing: her mistress Aurelia complains that "I am never dressed / Without a sermon"; "her whole service / Is a mere confutation of my clothes." Puritans are not the only characters in the play, however, to invest clothes with such importance. As *The City Match* begins, the merchant Warehouse recalls how the "daily suits" of his prodigal nephew Plotwell once cost him "more than the stock that set me up." Plotwell now seems "quite transfigur'd," yet Warehouse, worrying that "this reformation may but be" his nephew's "part," devises a plot whereby he will pretend his own drowning and then return in disguise to see whether Plotwell reverts to his spendthrift ways. The audience learns the truth long before Warehouse does. Plotwell's wastrel friends—"bright Offsprings / O'th' female silkworm, and Tailor male," as Plotwell calls them—arrive on the scene, mock him for the "Pagan dress" of merchant he now wears, tear that "old velvet" off him, and then lead him merrily to the tavern. Viewed in the light of these earlier scenes, Dorcas may seem to be no more obsessed with clothes than any other character in the play, but her vestiarian harangues insist, Goggle-like, on a fixity to clothes that Plotwell's metamorphoses belie. When the disguised Warehouse subsequently learns that Plotwell regards the report of his drowning as "good news," he disinherits the hypocrite, and Plotwell comes to appreciate what had already been implicit in his conversion from "plush to pennystone" and back again: that clothes are "transitory pelf." If he is now to restore his good fortune, he must rely on the inner resources that Mayne insists scrupulous puritans lack: as Plotwell's sister Aurelia exhorts him, "since / We are left wholly to our wits, let's show / The power and virtue of 'em."[63]

Only at this point in *The City Match*, when he has come to appreciate the difference between form and substance, does Plotwell begin to live up to his name. Warehouse is keen to ensure Plotwell's disinheritance by his own marriage, and Plotwell consequently arranges for his uncle's faked nuptials with Dorcas, who, we discover, has only pretended to be influenced by puritans and who now, for Plotwell's benefit, persuades her supposed husband that she is a whore acquainted with "all *Tongues* and *Nations*."[64] Warehouse had originally undertaken his plot because he believed it would enable him to learn the truth about his nephew, but now he finds himself so subjected to transformations and deceit that, when Plotwell reveals to Warehouse that he was married to Dorcas "but in jest," Warehouse is actually relieved by the thought of his nephew's dissembling. "I / Grieve not I am deceived," he confesses to Plotwell and his accomplices: "Believe me, *Gentlemen*, / You all did your parts well." Instead of fretting whether his nephew "may act his virtues," Warehouse has been humbled into the conformist toleration exemplified by Pieboard's gentleman-savior: he has come to appreciate the wit that Plotwell discloses in so ably manipulating "forms."[65]

What seems starkly absent from the implied conformism of *The City Match*, however, is any pretense of a spiritual dimension to Warehouse's cozenage. The victims of Pieboard's deceptions had at least been cheats themselves, hiding their own crimes behind a veil of "sanctity"; while Warehouse may have been wrong to test Plotwell, his discovery of Plotwell's joy at his reported death seems an overly harsh corrective, and Plotwell never apologizes for it. In *Sir Thomas More*, More's jests had bespoken both his freedom of conscience and his obedience to authority; in *The Puritan*, Pieboard helped place wit on the side of charity, if not of law or conscience; but in *The City Match* wit appears to be the *sole* good toward which Plotwell gestures in his detachment from puritan formalism. From Munday to Middleton to Mayne, the spirituality suggested by cozenage has come to seem increasingly restricted, although nonconformists would never have granted the validity of such a negatively imputed spirituality in the first place. "Inward intents," as Barrow (c. 1587) argued, "will not excuse outward, yea, obstinate, transgressions."[66]

The various prologues and epilogues to *The City Match* suggest that Mayne himself worried about the possible spiritual bankruptcy of his play. They go well beyond the standard tropes of modesty, "holding works of this light nature to be things which need an Apology for being written at all." Mayne's self-defense is that he composed the play "merely out of Obedience," and "the same / Power that makes Laws" not only "redeem'd this from the flame" but "made" *The City Match* "public," too. Insofar as the play might remain his work alone, Mayne "confesseth," it would amount to "nothing" more than a bald copy of low life, or "what was first a Comedy i'th' street." Yet if his sponsor the king applauds *The City Match*, the play will rise above its roguish origins and become something truly appreciable— a kind of religious ceremony, though one far more questionable than a surplice:

> as the Gods refin'd base things, and some
> Beasts foul i'th' Herd grew pure i'th' Hecatomb;
> And as the Ox prepar'd, and crowned Bull
> Are Offerings, though kept back, and Altars full:
> So, Mighty Sir, this sacrifice being near
> The knife at Oxford, which y' have kindled here,
> He hopes 'twill from you, and the Queen, grow clean,
> And turn t' Oblation, what He meant a Scene.

Lacking any intrinsic spiritual merit, in Mayne's portrayal, *The City Match* can nevertheless be made suitable for "altars" by royal authority.[67]

That substituting wit for conscience, tolerance for scrupulousness, and roguery for piety might leave Christianity little more than an Erastian pseudo-religion occurred at the time to playwrights no less than puritans. James Shirley's comedy *The Sisters* (1642) depicts a "commonwealth" practicing religious toleration, but these latitudinarians are bandits compelled to a sham piety by their rogue "prince" Frapolo:

Frapolo.	I will not have you thieves among yourselves.
Longino.	How's that, and please thy Excellence, not thieves?
Frapolo.	Not thieves one to another; but Religious—
	There is a kind of a Religion
	We Outlaws must observe.
Strozzo.	I never knew
	Religion yet, and 'twill be now unseasonable
	To learn.
Rangino.	I'll be of no Religion.
Frapolo.	Who was so bold
	To say he would have no Religion?
	What man is he, hopes to be drunk, to whore,
	To 'scape the wheels, the Galleys, and the gallows
	And be of no Religion?
Longino.	He says right.
Frapolo.	Ye shall be of what Religion I please.
Pachequo.	'Tis fit we should, *Frapolo* is our monarch.
Frapolo.	And yet I must consider of some fit one
	That shall become our trade
	And constitutions; hum! Silence.
Strozzo.	Nay, nay Prince, take time to think on't,
	There's no haste.
Frapolo.	I have thought,
	And you shall be no *Pagans, Jews,* nor *Christians.*
Longino.	What then?
Frapolo.	But every man shall be of all Religions.
Rangino.	I like that well.
Frapolo.	Why should I clog your Conscience, or confine it?[68]

By Mayne's own account, what feature of *The City Match*—aside from its anti-puritanism, which Shirley shared—suggests that Mayne cared about religion any more than Pachequo, or for that matter Selimus, does?

One answer might be seen to lie, again, in the play's clothing, which characters repeatedly invest with religious sentiment and value. There is Dorcas, of course, who sews "such holy embroideries" onto Aurelia's "smock-sleeves" that Aurelia fears her "apparel" will in time "be quoted by / Some pure Instructor." But Plotwell too weaves religion and clothing together when he shudders at the thought of growing prosperous enough "to sleep the sermon in my Chain and Scarlet," or when he jokes that the mercer who supplied Newcut and Bright with their attire must have "the patience of a burnt Heretic": "The very faith that sold to you these silks / And thinks you'll pay for 'em is strong enough / To save the Infidel part o'th' world, or Antichrist." The more Plotwell treats clothes as mere theatrical "properties," however, the more effectual his wit becomes, and this transferral of felt "power and virtue" from outsides to insides suggests that a spiritual capacity has potentially been unlocked within him. Nothing Plotwell says or does in the play directly indicates such newfound piety, but then *The City Match* relentlessly mocks the idea that a person can undergo any sudden "reformation" other than a pretended one.[69] Dorcas does manage to "convert" a parrot in an instant, but human sinners, Mayne implies, need the more gradualist program that conformists advocate—the very antithesis to Frapolo's religion by fiat in *The Sisters*.[70]

The strongest evidence that Mayne viewed his play in this gradualist light is his own evolution as a roguish wit. Shortly after *The City Match* was first performed, Mayne took holy orders. He was far from the only clergyman-playwright of his day, as we have seen: William Cartwright, Peter Hausted, and William Strode, among many others, all composed for the stage before ascending to the pulpit. Mayne and Cartwright came to be highly regarded (in conformist circles, at any rate) as preachers of moderation and charity: offering a sermon in "Dr. Mayne's and Mr. Cartwright's Style," Abraham Wright in 1656 espoused "no holiness of the Separation," but rather the holiness that "is diffusive, and holds communion with all."[71] Like *The City Match*, such clergyman plays as Cartwright's *The Ordinary* (c. 1635), Hausted's *The Rival Friends* (1632), and Strode's *The Floating Island* (1636) laid claim to this spiritual inclusiveness contrarily, through the satire of puritans and a show of debauched wit. Refusing to "huff, puff, and snuff" at the delights of the flesh as Randolph's Mistress Flowerdew would, Mayne and his colleagues apparently saw themselves as charitably bearing with carnality in order to attract even the reprobate to a gradual conversion.[72]

As a new clergyman, Mayne in the prefatory letter to *The City Match* nevertheless seems to have felt compelled to mark the distance he had traveled from the stage: he claims to have been "one of the severest Spectators" when the *Match* was first performed, and to have shown no "other Sign whereby it might be known to be his, but his liberty to despise it." Yet when reflecting on the works of other dramatists, Mayne treated the playwright's liberty from his own disreputable "scenes" as opening space for a kind of pious dissemblance, what Mayne in his elegy on Cartwright calls a "holy Cozenage." My first chapter traced this paradoxical phrase to its roots in the *pia vafricie* or pious guile of the Erasmian evangelist whom charity inspires to become all things to all men. The continuity between such accommodationism and the conformism of Mayne is underscored by an English Catholic satire from the 1630s, which seizes on *vafer* as the perfect label for the "*Proteus*-like" "Rover" who can "suit his religion unto every place."[73] But *The City Match* helps clarify the difference between Erasmus's and Mayne's conceptions of godly pretense: "holy Cozenage" epitomizes the case for the theater's powers of spiritual edification from Munday to Middleton to Mayne because it flaunts the theater's associations with criminality and vice. As one T. C. puts it in commendation of John Ford's *The Queen* (1653), plays "cheat / Men into virtue." Not content to excuse the apparent roguery in plays as "harmless mirth," T. C. maintains that such roguery teaches and that such teaching is itself a form of roguery. So high a conception of playerly cozenage depends for T. C., as one ought by now to expect, on a contrastingly low evaluation of puritans, who "in melancholy zeal admit / Only a grave formality for wit." Unable to appreciate the difference between form and substance, the puritan in T. C.'s account can only condemn roguish appearances, while the gradualist play-wit recognizes how such appearances can be made to serve holy ends: thus, T. C. concludes, "in the Theater men are easier caught, / Than by what is in clamorous pulpits taught."[74]

Mayne ultimately chose the pulpit over the theater, but his printed sermons indicate that he never quit the stage entirely. Throughout his *Sermon Concerning Unity & Agreement* (1646), for instance, he continually exhorts his congregation to become as "harmlessly unscrupulous" as T. C.'s witty theater people. The greatest trouble in England has arisen, Mayne laments, from the most trivial grounds: "a little, slight, indifferent Ceremony." If only English worshippers could regard church service as Thomas Scott feared they would, with the detachment of a playgoer! Does the puritan oppose using the Book of Common Prayer "because it prescribes a Ring in marriage, or a Cross in Baptism? over-scrupulous man! who would'st rather choose to make a rent, and schism, and division in the Church, than be spectator to things so harmless, and indifferent." What real cause had any puritan to denounce the English church, "where everyone was left to the full use and exercise of his Christian liberty, where nothing was blameable among us, but the ridiculous, over-acted postures and gestures of some few busy, fantastical men, whose Popery lay in making discreet men laugh, to see them so artificially devout, and so affectedly ceremonious"?[75] Combine a spectatorial detachment with a commitment to toleration, Mayne suggests, and one can even distinguish a false from a true prophet. Should a minister "preach

Charity, and banish strife from his Pulpit," embrace him; but if "on the contrary" "the Preacher's Sanctity and Religion consist, merely in the devout composure of his looks and carriage," then be sure he is a hypocrite. In his preface to *The Rival Friends* (1632), the future clergyman Hausted has a simple name for such "formal outsides," the puritanical "tribe" his play has "brought to open view": he calls them "mock-Christians."[76]

Viola. Dost thou live by thy tabor?
Clown. No, sir, I live by the church.
Viola. Art thou a churchman?
Clown. No such matter, sir. I do live by the church;
         for I do live at my house, and my house doth
         stand by the church.

—Shakespeare, *Twelfth Night*

"We *Priests*, and *Poets*": so Jonson (1629), near the end of his life, conceived his Tribe. How seriously are we to take such Renaissance theater people who posed as churchmen, or the churchmen who posed as theater people? In the dedicatory epistle to his *Tragedie of Lodovick Sforza* (1628), published a few years after he had joined the clergy, Robert Gomersall acknowledged that some readers would think "sermons had been fitter for my setting forth, and to preach more proper than to write." "But," he added, "is not this to preach?"[1] I hope that my book has made Gomersall's question harder, not easier, to answer. While expressions of religious purpose were far more prevalent in Renaissance drama than scholars have previously supposed, it generally takes some strain to uncover the purpose, and still more strain to credit it. When theater people laid claim to pious intentions, I have tried to show, they did so for the most part paradoxically—in their capacity as drunkards, as vagabonds, as dissemblers, temporizers, chameleons, hypocrites, cheats. At best, they professed their religion by refusing to profess it outright.

Perhaps the central claim of this book has been that such indirection was, to a surprising extent, in conformity with the Erasmian spirit of the English religious settlement—a spirit of uncontentiousness and impartiality, according to its defenders, of apathy and evasiveness, to its enemies. Addressing one of the first English Protestant martyrs, John Frith, shortly before Frith's death, the Erasmian William Tyndale counseled his friend never to stand his ground on religious issues, whenever possible: even "if you be sure that your part be good, and another hold the contrary," Tyndale maintained, "yet if it be a thing that maketh no matter, you will laugh and let it pass, and refer the thing to other men." Foxe printed this advice in his *Acts and Monu-*

ments, and praised Frith for having remained faithful to it even when Frith felt compelled to polemicize on the most controversial religious topic of the period:

> I cannot choose, but that I must need earnestly and heartily embrace, the prudent and godly moderation, which was in that man, which maintaining this quarrel of the sacrament, no less godly than vehemently amongst the English nation[,] . . . yet he did it so moderately, without any occasion of contention, that he would never seem to strive against the Papists, except he were driven to it even of necessity. In all other matters, where necessity did not move him to contend, he was ready to grant all things for quietness' sake.

"In all other matters . . . to grant all things": Foxe's account of Frith has a Pauline, accommodationist ring to it. If we could but imitate "this most meek martyr," Foxe continued, how easily might the "seditious divisions or factions of these our days . . . be brought to a unity and concord, and there should be much more concord and love in the church, and much less offence given outwardly."[2]

Moderation and martyrdom are not often thought to go hand in hand, and yet to Foxe's mind Frith had indeed died "for quietness' sake." According to Frith himself in another document Foxe printed, "The Articles Wherefore John Frith Died, Which He Wrote in Newgate the 23d Day of June, the Year of Our Lord 1533," the martyr may not have agreed with his inquisitors, but he did not entirely disagree with them either. Frith was asked whether he believed that Christ's "very natural body, both flesh and blood, is really contained under the Sacrament, and there actually present, besides all similitudes? No, said I, I do not so think. Notwithstanding, I would not that any should count that I make my saying (which is the negative) any article of faith." Frith's point, later echoed by Hooker and other prominent English theologians (including Foxe), was that it finally didn't matter which theory people used to explain the presence of Christ in the sacrament: for that reason, we should "leave it indifferent for all men to judge therein, as God shall open his heart, and no side to condemn or despise the other, but to nourish, in all things, brotherly love, and to bear others' infirmities."[3]

Yet if the moderate Frith regarded his own theory of Christ's presence as adiaphoric, a thing indifferent, why did he choose martyrdom rather than bear others' infirmities and profess a different theory? Near the end of his open letter, Frith himself acknowledged the apparent contradiction: "I think many men wonder how I can die in this article, seeing that it is no necessary article of our faith."[4] To account for the necessity not of his beliefs but of his martyrdom, Frith offered his readers three rationales, seemingly in the order of increasing strength. First, he explained, he "verily" regarded the sacramental theory of his inquisitors as "false." But this objection could hardly have required his death, because, as his letter takes pains to emphasize, such disagreements were in Frith's view of no consequence. Frith's second justification for his martyrdom was that he would "not bind the congregation of Christ (by mine example) to admit any necessary article beside our Creed, and specially none such as cannot be proved true by Scripture." In other words, his fatal disagreement with his inquisitors concerned not the correctness of their sacramental theory but its necessity: thus Frith had earlier pointed out that he would not have endorsed transubstantiation as "an undoubted article of the faith necessary to be believed" even if it "were indeed true." Yet why should Frith have felt any "necessity," as Foxe put it, to dispute the necessity of transubstantiation? Although the absence of sacramental theories from the Creed might seem to imply that they are adiaphora, the Creed never states that any unspecified religious issue should be regarded this way, nor does it ever specify that adiaphorism should itself count as an article of faith. By Frith's own logic, in short, a belief in the adiaphorism of sacramental theory would itself seem adiaphoric.[5] Frith's third justification for his martyrdom appears to get closest to the heart of his resolve:

> I dare not be so presumptuous in entering into God's judgment, as to make the prelates in this point a necessary article of our faith; for then I should damnably condemn all the Germans and Almains with infinite woe, which indeed do not believe nor think that the substance of bread and wine is changed into the substance of Christ's natural body. And surely I cannot be so foolish-hardy as to condemn such an infinite number, for our prelates' pleasure.[6]

What necessitated a noncommittal approach to sacramental theory, Frith believed, was the preeminence (as Bishop Sanderson would later assert) of charity over knowledge. To have agreed with his inquisitors would for Frith have meant to condemn "an infinite number" of other Christians, thereby "damnably" dividing the very fellowship that the sacraments ought to "knit" together.[7]

Theater people, I have argued, tended to profess a similar regard for charity and fellowship over doctrinal precision, but rarely with such straightforwardness, and never with Frith's life-and-death commitment to remaining noncommittal. Simply put, their religion would seem to have lacked the seriousness of Frith's. Yet Frith himself believed that his accommodationism demanded a certain lack of seriousness, as Tyndale's exhortation to laugh one's way out of contention indicates. In a noteworthy instance of his unstinting "good humor" and inclusiveness to boot, Frith in 1533 did not scruple to compare the proper celebration of the sacrament to a gathering of good fellows: he joked that those who believe "health" may be found in the mere "outward sign" of a sacrament are like the "fond fellow" who,

> when he is very dry, and an honest man show him an alepole and tell him that there is good ale enough, would go and suck the alepole, trusting to get drink out of it, and so to quench his thirst. Now a wise man will tell him that he playeth the fool, for the alepole doth but signify that there is good ale in the house where the alepole standeth; and will tell him that he must go near the house, and there he shall find the drink, and not stand sucking the alepole in vain, for it shall not ease him, but rather make him more dry; for the alepole doth signify good ale, yet the alepole itself is no good ale, neither is there any good ale in the alepole. And likewise it is in all sacraments; for if we understand not what they mean, and seek health in the outward sign, then we do suck the alepole, and labor in vain.[8]

This is the "merry" approach to religious controversy that figures so prominently in *Sir Thomas More* (ironically, because More was, in Foxe's words, "a deadly persecutor of Frith"). As I have shown in chapter 5, *More* recommends a genial and "harmless" religiosity to its audience, who supposedly enjoy a luxury that was not afforded to More: the religious toleration exemplified by the play's laudatory treatment of a Catholic martyr. Had More too lived under a monarch who respected "liberty of conscience," the play implies, he would not have felt any "necessity . . . to contend" (as Foxe said of Frith), and therefore might have appeared no more seriously committed to religious controversies than the authors of *More* do.[9] This faith in moderation came to dominate the portrayal of true religion on the Renaissance stage, so much so that by the 1630s a play such as *More* might well have seemed not light enough, its accommodationist ideals vitiated by the martyrological context in which they are dramatized. Jasper Mayne's *City Match* (1637) repeatedly pokes fun at the notion that one should die for one's faith. There is Plotwell's waggery about the mercer with "the patience of a burnt Heretic," Dorcas's comic lament about the good book that "suffer'd Martyrdom / By fire in Cheapside," and, most outrageously, Aurelia's description of the puritanical Dorcas's cooking:

She can't preserve
(The gift for which I took her) but (as though
She were inspir'd from *Ipswitch*) she will make
The Acts and Monuments in sweet-meats; Quinces
Arraign'd and burnt at a stake; all my banquets
Are persecutions, and *Dioclesian's* days
Are brought for entertainment, and we eat Martyrs.[10]

Even this mockery of martyrology, however, remains surprisingly consistent with Frith, who, like More, tried to put a jolly face on his death. Foxe (1583) reports that, while en route to his final trial, Frith was urged by his guards to escape, but he replied "with a smiling countenance" that "if you should both leave me here, and go to Croydon, declaring the bishops, that you had lost Frith, I would surely follow after as fast as I might, and bring them news that I had found and brought Frith again"—"and so," Foxe concludes, "with a cheerful and merry countenance he went with them." Although equally merry on the subject of martyrdom, *The City Match* strikes a different tone: its sarcasm about burning suggests that Mayne would have considered a smiling martyr to be a contradiction in terms, a kind of fanatical moderate, who perverted a suitable laughter at unnecessary religious disputes into a suicidal laughter at unnecessary death. The true moderate Christian, Mayne indicated in his *Sermon Concerning Unity & Agreement* (1646), was "the free, sociable, affable, open, harmlessly unscrupulous man": the man who carried his lack of seriousness lightly.[11]

Given the concerted efforts by Renaissance theater people such as Mayne to lessen the burden of religion, as Frith had attempted to do, it seems almost gratuitous to accuse them of a frivolous Christianity. The year he published *Lodovick Sforza*, Gomersall praised a fellow clergyman-playwright for preaching "sermons that at the same time make us devout and witty."[12] The puritans in their ascendancy may have enforced a graver religious ethos: thus Mayne (martyred only to the extent of being expelled from his Oxford pulpit and rusticated to Devonshire) complained in 1654 that "all my *public Poetry* hath [been], and still is, *objected* to me as a piece of *Lightness*, not befitting [my] *Profession*." But with the Restoration, moderation was hailed once again as "the proper glory of the *Church of England*"—"*not only the best, but the best natured institution in the world*," the churchman Timothy Puller (1679) declared—and this ultimate triumph of the "affable" Christianity favored by Renaissance theater people makes it difficult to dismiss even their most facetious expressions of religious purpose as idle posturing merely.[13]

Throughout this book, I have tried to give weight to the opposite criticism: that frivolity on the Renaissance stage became a vehicle for the aggressive sectarianism it claimed to dissolve. Shakespeare raises this objection to merrymaking in the play of his that most overtly addresses the problem of divisiveness among English Protestants, *Twelfth Night* (c. 1601). Overtness in Shakespeare is a relative concept, of course; as Donna Hamilton observes, "*Twelfth Night* displays its connection to the issues of religious controversy with a disarming playfulness. The characters do not talk directly about religion, but religion and church politics often provide the language for what they do talk about." Thus the asinine Sir Andrew Aguecheek declares that he would "as lief be a Brownist as a politician"; Olivia calls the "divinity" and "doctrine" of Orsino's love "heresy"; Maria says of Malvolio that "sometimes he is a kind of puritan" ("O, if I thought that," Sir Andrew responds, "I'd beat him like a dog!"); and Maria later jokes that the gulled Malvolio has "turn'd heathen, a very renegado; for there is no Christian that means to be sav'd by believing rightly can ever believe such impossible passages of grossness." These incidental references to religious controversy become dramatically actualized, however, during the scene in which the clown Feste, dressed as a churchman, torments the quasi-puritanical Malvolio, bound and sequestered as a madman. It is a scene of "sportful malice," as one of Malvolio's enemies later observes, a disconcerting mixture of the light comedy and scurrilous cruelty about puritans that later English comedies would more facilely blend.[14]

Hamilton persuasively interprets Malvolio's predicament as "a demystifying satire" on the "exclusionary tactics" and "demonizing strategies" that church conformists directed against puritans.[15] But this is also her account of the play generally, and to arrive at such a reading she must employ some exclusionary tactics of her own. First of all, she must downplay the satirical thrust of Malvolio's resemblance to "the caricature of the puritan developed in anti-puritan polemic." *Twelfth Night* may take conformists to task for their antisocial behavior in "scapegoating" puritans, but the far more salient target of criticism in the play is the antisocial puritan. Second, in order to place Shakespeare squarely in any one polemical camp, Hamilton must ultimately ignore her own initial point about the "disarming playfulness" with which *Twelfth Night* treats religious controversy.[16] This is not to say that, for Shakespeare, merriment is incompatible with serious religious purpose: the very holiday title of the play suggests otherwise. Although the mourning Olivia seems at first to insist that "godliness" requires "gravity" when she responds to Feste's greeting, "God bless thee, lady," scornfully—"Take the

fool away," she says—Feste soon redeems folly in her eyes by sportively offering to play the minister and "catechize" her:

Clown.   Good madonna, why mourn'st thou?
Olivia.   Good fool, for my brother's death.
Clown.   I think his soul is in hell, madonna.
Olivia.   I know his soul is in heaven, fool.
Clown.   The more fool, Madonna, to mourn for your brother's
          soul, being in heaven.

Malvolio denounces the fool along with any who would "minister occasion
to him," Olivia accuses Malvolio of "self-love," and the belief, shared by both
characters, that foolery is inherently social and adaptive becomes a fundamental doctrine in the play: as Viola later notes, a clown "must observe their
mood on whom he jests, / The quality of persons, and the time."[17] This supposedly dialogic character of wit suits it, ideally if not reliably, to the inclusivism that Shakespeare faults conformists as well as puritans for violating.
True to such inclusivism, Shakespeare even sanctions a Malvolian distrust
of wit to a degree, insofar as he refuses ever to make clear in the play when
he is being serious. Yet, by keeping his allegiances ambiguous in this way,
Shakespeare resists any party's efforts to claim a monopoly not only on true
religion but on the foolery that could help enforce such claims. In *Twelfth
Night*, wit lives "by" the church—that is to say, it pursues a ministry that lies
in a determinedly approximate and equivocal relation to the church.[18]

The tonality of the scene in which Feste actually disguises himself as a
clergyman is indeed equivocal enough to suggest concerns about the English church that run in opposite directions: not only toward the church's
possible cooptation of the theater, but also toward the theater's possible
cooptation of the church. Stephen Greenblatt has brought this second anxiety of Shakespeare's before our eyes with uncanny force, although he never
describes it *as* an anxiety. With Edgar's pretense of demonic possession in
King Lear, Greenblatt has argued, Shakespeare "moves to appropriate" the
"social energy" of Catholicism "for the greater glory and profit of the theater"; *Hamlet*, according to Greenblatt, enacts a further "appropriation" of
Catholicism, as "the space of Purgatory becomes the space of the stage."[19] In
my chapter on *Henry V*, I tried to show how a more pious notion of appropriation informs the play: through the vehicle of Harry's story, I claimed,
Shakespeare attempts, Robin Hood–like, to steal religion back from the
prelates and preachers who had stolen it from the people in the first place.
"*Cucullus non facit monachum*," the cowl does not make the monk, Feste

reminds Olivia before catechizing her: in the context, Shakespeare's point seems to be that people can minister to each other without having to take holy orders. It is only when Feste opts to "dissemble" his lay status and don the "gown" of a curate, in fact, that his ministry grows sectarian and malicious.[20] By the same token, *Henry V* may applaud the king for helping to differentiate "the Church" from "the clergy," yet the play also manifests Shakespeare's concern that Robin Hood might keep his plunder for himself, as Harry does in using the clergy to help fund and extenuate his wars, or as Henry VIII did in selling off monastic properties and declaring himself head of the church.[21] Always alive to the corruptibility of any good intention, Shakespeare seems to have worried that he himself might be posing as a churchman for his own "greater glory and profit." Thus, in *Measure for Measure* and again in *The Tempest*, Shakespeare recurred to the *Henry V* plot of a weak ruler made strong by the theft of godlike power and mystique, demonstrating both his desire to expose such expropriations and his belief that his theater too was capable of perpetrating them.

Duke Vincentio and Duke Prospero differ from King Henry in some significant respects, however: they are foreigners, not Englishmen, for example, and their quasi-sacrilegious machinations are more implausible than Harry's. To explain these changes, one might point to the controversy sparked by Oldcastle/Falstaff in the Henriad, and note that neither Vincentio nor Prospero is a killer as Harry was: in other words, the changes might indicate that Shakespeare wanted to distance his later plays from any applications to contemporary Protestant dissension, and distance himself from any celebration of violence. Yet, since such buffering produces a greater emphasis in these plays on fancifulness as well as inclusiveness, *Measure for Measure* and *The Tempest* end up, even more than *Henry V* had, linking Shakespeare's theft of the church from its thieves to a self-referential absorption in theater. That these two drives in Shakespeare—toward the promotion of his religion, on the one hand, and of his profession, on the other—only partially cohered seems underscored by the modern reception of Shakespeare. In the eyes of admirers such as Harold Bloom, as I noted in my preface, Shakespeare has succeeded in appropriating and thereby differentiating religious power and mystique not only from the clergy but from Christianity generally. His plays have acquired "the status of a secular Bible"—and "the worship of Shakespeare," Bloom asserts, "ought to be even more a secular religion than it already is."[22]

Although Bloom attributes the veneration of Shakespeare as a kind of "mortal god" to the "last two centuries" only, Renaissance writers praised Jonson along with Shakespeare in similarly exalted terms. Nicholas Oldisworth (1629) went so far as to exhort Jonson to "die" so that his devotees would not turn "superstitious":

> Thy works make us mistake
> Thy person; and thy great Creations make
> Us idol thee, and 'cause we see thee do
> Eternal things, think Thou eternal too.

A decade after Jonson complied with Oldisworth's request, Robert Herrick published his "Prayer to Ben. Jonson" (1648): "When I a Verse shall make, / Know I have pray'd thee, / For old *Religion's* sake, / Saint *Ben* to aid me." A few years later, Herrick's fellow Tribe member Samuel Sheppard (1651) insisted that "*Ben*" would henceforth "be / A Saint" to his "Verse" also, although the idea of Jonson as a kind of tutelary deity had already been broached the year of Jonson's death (1638) by Richard West: "*Poet* of Princes, Prince of *Poets* (*we* / If to *Apollo*, well may pray to *thee*)." Bloom and the rest of his visionary company might see this reverence for Jonson as dimly prefiguring the literary religion that would later find its true messiah in Shakespeare; however unintentionally, Jonson and Shakespeare did encourage such secularizing aestheticism, as I have suggested. Yet Oldisworth, Herrick, Sheppard, and West either were or became churchmen: it seems improbable that these clerical "*Adorers*" of Jonson would have risked appearing sacrilegious merely to advertise their literary tastes. They must have believed that, by worshipping their "Patriarch" in the terms of overtly false religion, they had struck a "harmlessly unscrupulous" compromise between the weightiness of his Christianity and the lightness of his profession. Not imagination over faith, but a *via media* between piety and wit: that is what Jonson himself urbanely sketched for his Tribe when he claimed to honor Shakespeare's memory "on this side Idolatry."[23]

—

Rogue Frequencies

Drawing on the Chadwyck-Healey database (http://lion.chadwyck.com) for English plays, I can offer a roughly quantified basis for claiming that Shakespeare's history plays were seminal in the development of rogue nationalism. Shakespeare was the first playwright to use the word *rogue* and its variants more than once or twice in a play. The term crops up 6 times in *The Taming of the Shrew* and then flourishes in Shakespeare's history plays, appearing 20 times in *1 Henry IV,* 13 times in *2 Henry IV,* and 8 times in the remaining Falstaff play, *The Merry Wives of Windsor.* Only four other Elizabethan plays use *rogue* with similar frequency, and they are all history plays that postdate *1 Henry IV,* in my estimation: *1 Sir John Oldcastle* (1599), 12 times; *Look About You* (c. 1599), 11; *1 Edward IV* (c. 1599), 18; and *1 Blind Beggar of Bednal Green* (1600), 11. Whatever the actual chronology of these works, it is clear that *rogue* first gains currency in English drama as a property of history plays—that is, as a tool for conceptualizing England.

Although crude, Chadwyck-Healey's categorization of plays by period also indicates that *rogue* became even more prominent as a feature of Restoration drama than of Renaissance drama. Among Shakespeare's later contemporaries, the three playwrights to use *rogue* and its variants most frequently are Fletcher, Jonson, and Massinger: Fletcher uses the word 283 times in 39 of his plays, or 7.3 times per relevant play, on average; for Jonson the figures are 121 times over 18 plays, or 6.7 times per play; for Massinger, 129 times over 23 plays, or 5.6 times per play. Yet Aphra Behn uses *rogue* 290 times in 17 plays, or 17 times per relevant play—more than double the frequency in Fletcher. Comparison by period rather than author yields similar figures. For plays in the "Jacobean and Caroline" period (1603–60, according to the monarchists at Chadwyck-Healey), the database lists 1,874 occurrences of *rogue* or its variants over 355 plays, or 5.3 hits per play, on average. The "Restoration" period (1660–1700) has 4,063 occurrences over 321 plays, or an average of 12.7—once again, more than double the "Jacobean and Caroline" frequency. Incidences drop off in the century following the Restoration: the period "1700–1749" has 1,627 hits over 233 plays, or 7 per play, on average; while "1750–99" has 1,295 hits over 380 plays, or only 3.4 per play. In the English theater, it appears, the golden age for rogues was the Restoration.

Behn's play *The Roundheads* (c. 1682; 27 hits), set during the final days of the Commonwealth, suggests one possible explanation for this Restoration renewal of interest in roguery: according to the play, the puritans had actually succeeded in reducing England to a commonwealth of rogues. At the start of *The Roundheads,* the Cavalier Loveless defines the puritans' "Good Cause" as "Roguery, Rebellion, and Treason" (1.1.127–28); "I'd rather beg where Laws are obey'd and Justice perform'd," he bitterly declares, "than be powerful where Rogues and base born Rascals rule the Roost" (162–63). In *The Rover* (1677; 32 hits), also set during the Commonwealth, three "banished cavaliers" (epil.1), who have been made sturdy vagabonds by the king's defeat and the sequestering of their estates, speak of rogues 18 times. Roguery is equally prominent in plays of Behn set at other times and places, however. In *The Lucky Chance* (1686; 29 hits), for instance, set in contemporary London, the term never carries an overtly sectarian charge; rather, it is largely a verbal tic of the lecherous old alderman Sir Feeble Fainwould. But then none of Behn's plays allows *rogue* to be monopolized by any one character or sect. For Behn, it seems, the religious differences that sparked civil war are not so much transcended as undermined by the roguery that her characters generally share.

Autolycus

And when I wander here and there,
I then do most go right.
—*The Winter's Tale* 4.3.17–18

The character in Shakespeare who most obviously resembles the pamphlet rogue is Autolycus of *The Winter's Tale*, as William Carroll and Barbara Mowat have recently reminded us.[1] But neither Carroll nor Mowat notes that Autolycus also differs from the pamphlet rogue in one crucial respect: he does not belong to a rogue society, as his very name ("Lone Wolf") indicates. Autolycus's singleness might suggest that Shakespeare wanted to distance himself from the rogue nationalism that his histories had helped generate, but what Shakespeare actually repudiates in *The Winter's Tale* is an *exclusive* nationalist conception of the fellowship that rogues help define. Autolycus plays a far more conspicuous part in uniting divided peoples than the rogues of the Henriad had: by the end of *The Winter's Tale*, he has unintentionally helped reconcile the previously estranged nations of Sicilia and Bohemia. This reconciliation, moreover, has a distinctly religious resonance in the play, which critics have also overlooked.

Throughout *The Winter's Tale*, the "great difference" between Bohemia and Sicilia (1.1.3–4) evokes Renaissance sectarian controversies in the buried fashion that Shakespeare characteristically prefers. Bohemia, home of the early reformer Jan Hus, was a center of Protestant activism at the time *The Winter's Tale* was written, and Sicily was of course Catholic.[2] Although the play is set in an unspecified pagan era, markers of the contemporary religious orientations of each country are nonetheless legible in the *Tale*. The Sicilian emissaries to the oracle at Delphos speak in reverential Catholic terms of the "sacrifice" performed there (3.1.6–7) and the "celestial habits" worn by the officiating priests (3.1.4), just as the Sicilian Antigonus dreams of Hermione dressed "in pure white robes / Like very sanctity" (3.3.22–23). In Bohemia, however, where there is anachronistic mention of a "Puritan" (4.3.44), Autolycus demystifies white robes: they become the "white sheet" (4.3.5) he steals or the "lawn" he peddles, "as white as driven snow" (4.4.218). Autolycus even borrows the language of anti-Catholicism to mock the people who "superstitiously" (3.3.40) covet his wares: "They throng who should buy first, as if my trinkets had been hallow'd and brought a benediction to the buyer" (4.4.600–602).[3] As for his own clothes, Autolycus considers them to be nothing more than an "excrement" (714) that he can shift at will; it is one such costume change that enables Florizel and Perdita to escape Bohemia and begin the process of international peacemaking.

That unitive process is completed in the final scene of the play when Paulina takes the place of Autolycus as at once the peddler and debunker of idolatry.[4] After Paulina reveals the "statue" of Hermione, Perdita worries that her attraction to it will be regarded as "superstition" (5.3.43). Paulina seems to engage in superstition herself when she claims that she can make the statue come to life; but this miracle, she insists, will require the assembled Sicilians and Bohemians to "awake" their "faith" (95), just as reformers claimed that faith alone would enable communicants to experience the living Christ.[5] In *Henry V* Shakespeare had hoped to promote a sacramental community in the theater by imploring his audience to awaken their imaginations and employ them charitably. Yet the "faith" required to bring Hermione back to public life means more than imaginative fellow-feeling; in *The Winter's Tale*, Shakespeare treats erotic love too as a sacrament his theater can encourage, through "an art / Lawful as eating" (110–11).[6]

Autolycus's absence from this final scene implies that rogues may prefigure and unwittingly promote a reformed sacramental fellowship that cannot be equated with them. But players are not absent from the scene; they enact it, and their comparative refinement as Paulina- or Hermione-like cozeners makes it possible to imagine them by implication as the *intentional* facilitators of religious reconciliation.[7]

Poetry as Cozenage

Erasmus's depiction of Paul as a cunning trickster, a *vafer*, suggests that his own notion of accommodationism has a literary as well as scriptural basis. To Renaissance
readers trained in the classics, the term *vafer* would most likely have recalled the wily
slave of Roman comedy. A more precise analogue to Erasmus's usage, however, appears in Persius's description of Horace's poetic method: "Omne vafer vitium ridenti
Flaccus amico / tangit et admissus circum praecordia ludit" (*Satires* 1.116–17). Here
are the lines in the principal seventeenth-century English translation (1616), by the
future dramatist and clergyman Barten Holyday:

> So subtle *Horace* laughing with his friend
> Would cunningly his vices reprehend,
> And lying in his bosom, in his heart,
> Would bitterly deride him with great art.
> (*Persius*, B7r)

Sidney quotes the Latin in his *Defence of Poesie* (104); it suits his general claim that
poetry alone can insinuate its lessons into resistant readers, just as Aesop's "pretty
Allegories, stealing under the formal tales of beasts, make many, more beastly than
beasts, begin to hear the sound of virtue" (97). But there is a scriptural as well as classical component to Sidney's poetics. The *Defence* also characterizes poetry in the accommodationist terms of 1 Cor. 3.2, Heb. 5.12–14, and 1 Pet. 2.2, as "food for the
tenderest stomachs": "in the noblest nations and languages that are known, [poetry]
hath been the first light-giver to ignorance, and first Nurse, whose milk by little and
little enabled them to feed afterwards of tougher knowledges" (*Defence*, 97 and 84).
The Persius reference helps Sidney assimilate this image of poet as catechist to a potentially competing image of poet as rogue:

> even those hard-hearted evil men who think virtue a school name, and know
> no other good but *indulgere genio*, and therefore despise the austere admoni-
> tions of the Philosopher, and feel not the inward reason they stand upon, yet
> will be content to be delighted, which is all the good-fellow Poet seemeth to
> promise; and so steal to see the form of goodness (which seen they cannot but
> love) ere themselves be aware, as if they took a medicine of Cherries. (102)

Although quickly converting the good-fellow poet into a physician, Sidney does
not try to hide the stealth or guile that he sees as common to the practices of both
figures. With its special power to edify the wicked as well as the ignorant, poetry in

Sidney's view has a rightful place in "the Church of God" (87); but for Sidney it gains that place, paradoxically, through cozenage.[1]

The most influential English characterization of the poet as an Erasmian *vafer* appears at the start of Herbert's *Temple* (1633):

> Thou, whose sweet youth and early hopes enhance
> Thy rate and price, and mark thee for a treasure;
> Harken unto a Verser, who may chance
> Rhyme thee to good, and make a bait of pleasure.
>> A verse may find him, who a sermon flies,
>> And turn delight into a sacrifice.

In Greene's *Notable Discovery of Coosenage* (1591), a "verser" is not a poet but a coney-catcher, the accomplice of the "setter" mentioned in *Sir Thomas More*.[2] Herbert emphasizes this cant connotation to "verser" by referring to his poetry as "bait"; in commenting on *The Temple*, Herbert's admirer Josua Poole (1657) makes the correlation between poet and cozener even clearer:

> Many have been, which Pulpits did eschew,
> Converted from the Poet's reading pew,
> And those that seldom do salute the porch
> Of Solomon, will come to Herbert's Church;
> For as that English Lyric sweetly sings,
> Whilst angels danc'd upon his trembling strings,
> A verse may find him who a Sermon flies,
> And turn delight into a sacrifice.
> Then let the Poet use his lawful bait,
> To make men swallow what they else would hate,
> Like wise Physicians that their pills infold
> In sugar, paper, or the leaves of gold,
> And by a virtuous fraud and honest stealth,
> Cozen unwilling Patients into health.
> (*English Parnassus*, A7v–A8r)

In large part, it was the condemnation of poetry as deceit that thrust cozenage into poetic as well as dramatic theory in the Renaissance. Yet ostensible criminality was given far more play in Renaissance drama than in Renaissance poetry for two reasons this book has discussed at length: first, the plots of Renaissance drama typically involved acts of cozenage; and second, criminality seemed to theater haters and theater lovers alike an inescapable part of the theatrical demimonde. Like Renaissance dramatists, Renaissance poets did surprisingly embrace the terms in which their art was denigrated, yet, as I have argued in *An Empire Nowhere*, the criticism that most absorbed the poets was the charge that poetry amounted to trifling. Sidney and Herbert do show that poets could nonetheless characterize themselves as rogues, just as theater people could characterize themselves as triflers. Shakespeare's plays are called "trifles" on the first page of the First Folio (1623), while, in his prefatory epistle to the *Three Excellent Tragedies* (1656) of the clergyman-dramatist Thomas Goffe (d. 1629), Richard Meighen associates plays with accommodationism and trifling both: "He that gave them birth, because they were his *Nugae* [trifles], or rather recreations to his more serious and divine studies, out of a nice modesty (as I have learnt) allowed them scarce private fostering. But I, by the consent of his especial friend, in that they show him rather *Omnium scenarum homo* [a man for all scenes], to his glory than disparagement, have published them" (A2r).

Unless otherwise noted, all citations from classical authors refer to Loeb Classical Library editions.

Abbreviations

AM   Foxe, *Acts and Monuments*
CW   Erasmus, *Complete Works*
ES   Chambers, *Elizabethan Stage*
HM   Prynne, *Histrio-Mastix*
HS   Herford and Simpson, eds., *Ben Jonson*
JCS   Bentley, *Jacobean and Caroline Stage*

Preface

1. Knight, *Wheel of Fire*, 87; cf. Coghill, "Comic Form," 21. Knight maintained that *Measure for Measure* "must be read, not as a picture of normal human affairs, but as a parable, like the parables of Jesus" (106); Coghill preferred to think of his reading as "anagogical," which in his view did not remove "a particle of the Duke's humanity on the literal plane" (21). Lawrence, "Why the Novel Matters," 196.

2. Lawrence, ibid.; Hulme, "Romanticism," 768; Bloom, *Shakespeare*, 3, 717; Bloom, *Western Canon*, 56, 75. "If the world indeed can have a universal and unifying culture," Bloom argues, "such a culture" will have to "emanate" not "from religion" but from Shakespeare (*Shakespeare*, 717–18).

The extravagance of Bloom's bardolatry might tempt readers to dismiss his views on Shakespeare as unrepresentative of modern scholarship, but at the opposite end of the current critical spectrum, Lisa Jardine (1999) also describes Shakespeare as "all things to all people" ("Much Ado," 3). Inevitably, the Pauline characterization of Shakespeare has itself come to mean different things to different people: thus Linda Colley (1999) treats Jardine's formulation as newfangled, a "fashionable postmodern stress on a persistently multivalent Shakespeare" ("Shakespeare," 23), while Jardine herself concludes that Shakespeare's proteanism makes him "the perfect foil for our consensus-politics and focus-group driven age" ("Much Ado," 3). Nevertheless, both Colley and Jardine share with Bloom the conventional notion of Shakespeare as mysteriously "nothing and everything."

3. Greenblatt, *Renaissance Self-Fashioning*, 3, 222–54; *Riverside Shakespeare*, 95.

Introduction

1. *HM* 934. I have modernized spelling throughout, with the exception of titles, which library catalogues generally index by original spelling, and the deliberately archaic Spenser. Wherever they do not cause unnecessary confusion, I have also retained the italicization, capitalization, and major punctuation of the original texts, because they often indicate an author's emphases. These features of Shakespeare's texts are so commonly modernized, however, that I have not included them in citations of his plays.

2. See Duffy, *Stripping*, 579–81. As Whitfield White observes, censorship cannot be the whole story of the demise of the miracle plays: see his "Theater and Religious Culture," 135.

3. Stubbes, *Anatomie*, L5r–L6r.

4. See *ES* 4.306–7, 4.338–39. For a challenge to the conventional view that the Marprelate ruling "ushered in a new era of strict regulation" of the stage, see Dutton, *Mastering*, 77ff.

5. Harsnett, *Declaration*, 114; *ES* 4.279. Unless otherwise indicated, the dates given for plays refer to their first performance, not publication.

In her *Biblical Drama under the Tudors* (160–61), Ruth Blackburn lists only fourteen plays on biblical subjects performed in the public theaters between 1587 and 1602; all but two of these—the *Looking Glass* and George Peele's *David and Bethsabe* (c. 1587–94)—are lost.

6. Recent scholarly attempts to associate Shakespeare with Catholicism strike me as stopgap measures: if Shakespeare must have religion, the feeling seems to run, at least let that religion be heterodox.

7. *HM* 935, 979; Milton, *Works*, 3.1.300; Corbet, "A Certain Poem," in *Poems*, p. 15, ll. 86–88. A marginal note in one manuscript copy of the poem reads "Actores omnes fuere theologi" ("all the actors were theologians"; quoted, p. 111). Gager, *Works*, 4.273.

8. By counting the clergymen-playwrights noted in Bentley's *Jacobean and Caroline Stage* and Harbage's *Annals of English Drama*, I estimate that there were nearly half again as many clergymen writing plays from 1583 to 1632 as from 1533 (the year the schism officially began) to 1582. Most of the prominent clergymen-playwrights throughout the English Renaissance were connected to Christ Church, Oxford, a "playing" college from the days when Nicholas Grimald dedicated his biblical tragedy *Archipropheta* (published in 1548) to the college's first dean. Other clergymen-playwrights associated with Christ Church include Robert Burton, James Calfhill, William Cartwright, Richard Edes, Richard Edwards, Gager, Goffe, Barten Holyday, Henry Killigrew, Jasper Mayne, and William Strode.

9. Field was the son of the puritan firebrand John Field and the brother of Theophilus Field, bishop of Llandaff; Fletcher's father had been bishop of London.

10. Buc wrote this information c. 1600 on the cover of his copy of the play; see Nelson, "George Buc."

11. The sole exception I can find is a Latin play, John Hacket's *Loyola* (1623), which was twice performed before James I.

12. *JCS* 4.843–44; Cartwright, *Ordinary*, 2273.

13. Marprelate, *Hay*, 226–27; Barrow, *Brief Discoverie* (c. 1590), in *Writings . . . 1587–1590*, 349. Cf. the puritan Gilby (1581) on the "pageant" that conformist ministers "play" (*Pleasant Dialogue*, A2v).

14. Calderwood, *Altar*, 216; John Canne quotes this passage in *A Necessitie of Separation* (1634), 103. Puritans simply transferred the Protestant attack on "the playerlylike apparel, which the papists use in their service," to the established clergy who continued to wear such apparel: see, e.g., *Answere*, 39–40.

15. The term *puritan* had a wide range of reference during the Renaissance. In its broadest sense, it denoted a scrupulous English Protestant. Most "puritans" also de-

sired a further reformation of the English church; a large number refused to conform in some fashion with church liturgy; and some even felt the need to separate from the church. But all "puritans" were understood as abhorring libertines—which helps explain why their enemies loved to equate them with libertines; see Poole, *Radical Religion*. For a useful bibliography of recent efforts to define *puritan* or else reject the term entirely, see Walsham, "Glose," 200–202.

16. Parker, *Discourse*, 4; Hutchinson, *Memoirs*, 44. Cf. John Bastwick (1637), who complained that puritans were being "brought upon every stage, and into the pulpit, *as fittest for ludibry by the Players[,] Priests, and Prelates*" (*Answer*, A4r).

17. Ridpath, *Stage*, 4, 9.

18. See also Donna Hamilton's *Shakespeare and the Politics of Protestant England* (1992). In *The Cambridge Companion to English Renaissance Drama*, the sole essay to deal at any length with religious issues is Margot Heinemann's "Political Drama." Russ McDonald's recent *Bedford Companion to Shakespeare* (1996) is only superficially different. Of the eleven "Illustrations and Documents" included in his chapter on "Politics and Religion," only two are intended to represent religion, and they have clearly been chosen for their political charge: one is an excerpt from the foundational puritan tract, *An Admonition to the Parliament*, while the other is an excerpt from the church's *Homily against Disobedience and Willful Rebellion*.

Marcus does note that "most of the Laudian proponents" of recreations such as playgoing "would not have seen themselves as operating on a purely political level," but she finds only "inklings" of a "sacramentalizing strain" in one play, Jonson's *Bartholomew Fair*, and she adds that Jonson "was clearly wary of the trend even as he half espoused it" (*Politics*, 17).

19. HS 1.180; Ridpath, *Stage*, 11 (paraphrasing *HM* 935), 214, 12.

20. Stubbes, *Anatomie*, L8r. Prynne added that printed plays also lured people from the church: "there are at least a dozen Play-books vented for one printed Sermon," he complained, while "Shakespeare's plays are printed in the best Crown paper, far better than most Bibles" (*HM* 532r, **6v).

21. On the conventionality of the protest "that the churches were empty and places of entertainment full," see Collinson, *Religion*, 203ff. Drawing on the evidence compiled by the *Records of Early English Drama* series, Andrew Gurr maintains, however, that "the strength of the hostility in most local authorities, including London, to professional playing was notably greater than it was to other crowd-pulling enterprises such as bear- or bull-baiting, or even to the smaller groups of entertainers like tumblers and acrobats" (*Shakespearian Playing Companies*, 7).

22. Stubbes, *Anatomie*, L7v, L6r; Northbrooke, *Treatise*, 66.

23. [Munday? and] Salvianus, *Blast*, 89; Baxter, *Christian Directory*, 878. For the case that Munday authored the third part of the *Blast*, see Turner, *Anthony Mundy*, 39–41; I will henceforth refer to Munday as the author in fact. Stephen Gosson in *Plays Confuted* (1582) states that "Stage Plays are the doctrine and invention of the Devil" (*Markets*, 151); William Rankins, in *A Mirrour of Monsters* (1587), that players "are sent from their great captain Satan . . . to deceive the world, to lead the people with enticing shows to the devil" (2v). Daniel Dyke in his *Two Treatises* (1616) declares that "many are led by the Devil as dogs in a string, and carried from the Church to the Alehouse, the Stews and the Stage" (216; cited in Sasek, *Literary*, 92).

And finally Prynne claims that stage-plays *"never issued from God, or from his Children; but from the Factors, and Minions of the Devil, who only did frequent, and Act them heretofore,* and applaud, perform, and haunt them now" (*HM* 43).

24. *Mercurius Britanicus*, no. 12 (9–16 November 1643), 89; cited in Hotson, *Commonwealth*, 9. In September 1644 Mercurius Britanicus responded in similar fashion to the royalist charge that parliamentary soldiers had cut to pieces the library of an established-church minister: "Those were only some Lady Psalters, and *Cosin's* Devotions, and *Pocklington's* Altar, and *Shelford's* Sermons, and *Shakespeare's* Works, and such Prelatical trash as your Clergy men spend their Canonical hours on" (quoted in Sirluck, "Shakespeare and Jonson," 94).

25. John Cook, *King Charls*, 13; cited in Bradley and Adams, eds., *Jonson Allusion-Book*, 293.

26. See, e.g., Collinson, "Elizabethan and Jacobean Puritanism," 32–57; White, "Theater," 139. The sectarian opponents to lecturers often labeled them "roguish persons" or vagabonds, which further assimilated lecturers to itinerant players: see, e.g., *Second Parte of a Register* 1.291; Stubbes, *Anatomie*, pt. 2, M5a–b; Barrow, *Writings . . . 1590–1591*, 243–45; and Ainsworth and Johnson, *True Confession*, C1r.

27. *TN* 2.123. *A Satyre Against Seperatists* (1642), possibly by the clergyman-playwright Peter Hausted, describes the "Brownist" preacher as a "Christian" version of the Marlovian character *"Bajaset"*: "His stretch'd-out voice sedition spreads afar, / Nor does he only teach but act a war" (4).

28. Hooker, *Works*, 2.107–8; Shepard, *Parable*, 2.97, cited in Webster, *Godly Clergy*, 97. Cf. Shepard, *Parable*, 100: "Books are but a carcass of the living Word." Crockett, *Play*, 14, cites Samuel Hieron in his *Preachers Plea* (1605) on the special power of "the word being urged and pressed by preaching" (123).

29. *Epicoene*, in *HS* 2.2.32–36. Cf. a character in Shackerley Marmion's *Hollands Leaguer* (1631) on the age before "so many Plays, and Puritan preachings," when "women might be chaste; now 'tis impossible" (B2r).

30. Anderton?, *Epigrammes*, 9; Scott, *Two Notable Sermones*, quoted in Marshall, *Catholic*, 227; Dorman, *Proufe*, 5v and 123v; *AM* 6.433, cited in Marshall, *Catholic*, 233n.3; and Gilby, *Pleasant Dialogue*, C3v.

31. Holinshed, *Chronicles*, 1.235; Cooper, *Admonition*, 11. Cf. Thomas Adams, *The Gallants Burden* (1612): "no jest in such laughter, as that which is broken on a Priest [i.e., clergyman]; the proof is plain in every Tavern and Theater" (14r); cited in Crockett, *Play*, 49. Cooper's complaint is somewhat belied, again, by its conventionality: he is quoting the church father Gregory of Nazianzus (who incidentally wrote a biblical tragedy, *Christus Patiens*). For a careful assessment of the claim that the laity showed a "growing disrespect" toward the clergy in Reformation England, see Marshall, *Catholic*, especially 211–36.

32. Montrose, *Purpose*, 30–32; Greenblatt, *Shakespearean Negotiations*, 125–27. Greenblatt characterizes his criticism as "anthropological" in the introduction to *Renaissance Self-Fashioning* (4). Montrose's argument first appeared in his 1980 *Helios* essay, "The Purpose of Playing."

33. Huston Diehl makes this point about both Montrose (94–95) and Greenblatt (108–9) in her *Staging Reform*. Commenting on claims similar to Greenblatt's and Montrose's in Michael O'Connell's "The Idolatrous Eye" (1985), Crockett observes

that O'Connell overlooks "the ways in which the Protestant movement itself incorporated and transformed Roman Catholic ritual" (*Play*, 33).

While C. L. Barber also sees the theater as appropriating the sacred, he argues that Renaissance tragedies derive their pathos in large part from the failure of the theater to make good the loss of Catholic ritual. See especially "Family," 196–97. This view is elaborated in Barber and Richard Wheeler's *Whole Journey* (1986) and *Creating Elizabethan Tragedy* (1988), where Barber describes Shakespeare as "post-Christian" (122).

34. White, "Theater," 146; Shuger, "Subversive," 46.

35. See, e.g., Hamilton, *Politics*; Diehl, *Staging Reform*; Crockett, *Play*; McEachern, *Poetics*, 83–137; Poole, *Radical Religion*; and Targoff, "Performance."

36. This is true even of Diehl's *Staging Reform*, which only appears to repudiate a secularist reading of Renaissance plays when it argues that the plays were "both a product of the Protestant Reformation—a reformed drama—and a producer of Protestant habits of thought—a reforming drama." Like Greenblatt and Montrose, Diehl bases her thesis on "the insights of symbolic anthropologists who believe that religious practices help shape both individual consciousness and cultural forms." In other words, she does not think that Renaissance playwrights consciously intended to comment on the religious issues their plays "symbolically replicate and mediate" (1, 3n.6).

Crockett similarly asserts that "the Renaissance stage play and the Reformation sermon perform the same work—helping audiences adjust to and control the peculiar ambiguities of the early modern period." Yet he unites church and theater only on the most abstract plane: they both provide "performative resolutions to paradox" (*Play*, 3, 37).

37. Battenhouse, *Shakespearean Tragedy*, 374. A thorough selection of christianizing criticism may be found in Battenhouse's *Shakespeare's Christian Dimension* (1994).

38. Laud, *Works*, 6.236. Cf. Laud's comments in Star Chamber the same month, in Gardiner, ed., *Documents*, 26–28. Nonetheless, Laud went further than the attorney in the proceedings, who would "not make any apology for stage plays, for *Amamus tollerare multa, quae non amamus*" (2). Another member of Star Chamber avowed that it was "not his intention nor meaning, nor (as he thinks) is it the meaning of any of their lordships, to apologize for stage plays" (22).

39. John Taylor, "To my approved good friend M. Thomas Heywood," in Heywood, *Apology*, A3v.

40. For Rosseter, see Fripp, *Shakespeare*, 2.750 (my thanks to Kenneth Fincham, Judith Maltby, and the late Karl Wentersdorf for helping me track down this reference).

41. HS 1.195; Honigmann and Brock, *Playhouse Wills*, 3; Barish, *Antitheatrical*, 121.

42. Stubbes, *Anatomie*, L7v; Barish, *Antitheatrical*, 127. Montrose too asserts that protheatrical arguments in the period "remain constrained within the terms of the dominant antitheatrical discourse" (*Purpose*, 44).

43. Bentley, *Professions*, 1.43 and 1.47; Bayly, *Practise*, e.g., A2v–A3r. Martin Butler paints a different picture in his *Theatre and Crisis* (1984). He sees a supposed scarcity of puritan writing against the theater in the 1630s (*Histrio-Mastix* aside) as

evidence that the theater was no longer a particularly controversial institution; the closure of the theaters shortly thereafter amounted to "an act of public safety rather than of puritan reform" (138). But Butler is hard pressed to explain why the theaters stayed closed till the puritans fell from power. His later article, "Ecclesiastical Censorship of Early Stuart Drama" (1992), strikes me as a persuasive revision of his earlier position. Now an absence of discourse—in this case "the rarity of direct comment on religion" in plays from the 1620s and 1630s—signals "religious censorship of the drama," which Butler concludes "may have been significantly more rigorous than censorship of other media" (479) in Laudian England.

44. Cf. *ES* 1.309ff. *Histrio-Mastix* denounces "the Profession of Play-poets, of Stage players" on its title page.

45. The most useful introduction to these different types of theater work remains Bentley's *Professions of Dramatist and Player in Shakespeare's Time: 1590–1642* (1971 and 1984). Bentley himself uses the expression "theater people" (e.g., 2.64).

46. Bentley, *Professions*, 1.30; the eight "attached" dramatists, according to Bentley, were Richard Brome, Dekker, Fletcher, Thomas Heywood, Massinger, William Rowley, Shakespeare, and Shirley.

47. See *ES* 1.376–86.

48. Jonson was not alone in defining the term *tribe* imprecisely. For most writers throughout the Renaissance, *tribe* primarily denoted a unit of social classification once used in Israel and also Rome, but outside of those contexts the term became unclear. When John Davies (1611) refers to a person's "*Country, name*, and *Tribe*" in his *Scourge of Folly* (93), he seems to be thinking of a tribe as a genealogical group, which might be the definition that George Wither (1643) has in mind when his *Campo-Musæ* calls on "ev'ry *Canton, Province, Tribe*, and *Nation*" (66). But a similar list from John Taylor's *Sieges of Jerusalem* (1616)—"every *Kindred, Kingdom, Tribe*, and *Nation*" (D6r)—either differentiates tribe from kindred or else equates tribe with nation. An earlier text, Arthur Kelton's *Chronycle* (1547), does directly equate "tribe" with "Welshmen" (C4v).

Seventeenth-century authors were more likely than sixteenth-century ones to use *tribe* figuratively, especially in the theater. Thus *Othello* (1604) invokes "all the tribe of hell" (1.3.357); Fletcher's *Women Pleas'd* (c. 1619–23) speaks of cobblers as "the old tribe of toe-piercers" (4.1.176); Joseph Beaumont's *Psyche* (1648) mentions "our *Female Tribe*" (32) and "the Tribe of Oriental Rubies" (71); while Sir William Vaughan in *The Church Militant* (1640) calls the Church itself a "Tribe" (65–66).

49. Greene's notorious remark is quoted in the *Riverside Shakespeare*, 1959. Jonson briefly returned to bricklaying after he had begun writing plays: see Riggs, *Ben Jonson*, 53–55. For the critics who never let him forget his manual labor, see *HS* 1.164n.241.

50. G[ainsford?]., *Rich Cabinet*, 117r.

51. Heinemann, *Puritanism and Theatre* (1980); Butler, *Theatre and Crisis* (1984). The other two major antitheatricalists, John Northbrooke and John Rainoldes, seem to have been conforming puritans. The prefatory material to Northbrooke's *Breefe and Pithie Summe* (1571; rev. ed., 1582) and *Poore Mans Garden* (1571; rev. ed., 1573 and 1582) portrays him as a "godly" minister in constant conflict with the "envious and spiteful Papists and Neuters" in his congregations: see, e.g., *Poore*, ¶7r–v. Rainoldes, a widely respected university professor, was chosen by James I to help repre-

sent puritan views at the Hampton Court Conference. For an illuminating discussion of Stubbes's ambiguous "profession," see Walsham, "Glose."

52. Heinemann cites the apologies of Sidney and of Thomas Heywood, but the most she herself can claim of these authors is that they "had some Puritan sympathies" (*Puritanism*, 30). A stronger case can be made for Heywood, who late in life (1641) wrote a pamphlet attacking the episcopate, although he hoped that the "offenders" might simply be "remov'd" and "the function might remain" (*Reader*, 2). Yet three years before the *Apology for Actors* (1612), Heywood published a harshly critical portrait of puritans in his *Troia Britanica* (1609), 89–90; the portrait ends with condemnation of the puritan assault on plays.

53. Thus a character in Robert Tailor's *The Hogge Hath Lost His Pearl* (1613) states that "words and deeds are now more different than Puritans and Players" (1.1.111–12). For other plays that treat the opposition of puritans to the theater as proverbial, see, e.g., Lording Barry, *Ram Alley* (1607–8), prol. 25–32; George Chapman, *The Revenge of Bussy D'Ambois* (c. 1601–12), 1.1.351–54; Thomas Middleton, *Hengist King of Kent, or The Mayor of Queenborough* (c. 1618), 5.1.184–85; and Shackerley Marmion, *The Antiquary* (1634–36), D1r–v.

Opposing the tendency of literary critics to treat the demonization of puritans in Renaissance plays as merely reactive or self-defensive, Collinson argues (with uncharacteristic exaggeration) that theater people scapegoated puritans ("Ben Jonson's *Bartholomew Fair*"). For a striking illustration of what one might call the puritanization of antitheatricalism, see Walsham on Stubbes ("Glose," 203–6).

54. Stubbes, *Anatomie*, L8r and L7r; for Prynne's many comments on the subject, see his index at *HM* Qqqqqq3v. The antitheatricalists cited precedent for the ban on players: "It was decreed under Constantinus the Emperor, that all Players of Interludes should be excluded from the Lord's table" (Northbrooke, *Briefe and Pithie Summe*, 70). Cf., e.g., Munday, *Blast*, 116; and Ames, *Conscience*, 4.217. Lake, *Probe*, 268–69; according to Lake, "none, but of rare grace and gift can be present at, or actors in them [i.e., plays], without going away spotted from them" (271).

55. Crosse, *Vertues Common-wealth* (1603), Q1r. "For a Play is like a sink in a Town," Crosse continues, "whereunto all the filth doth run: or a bile in the body, that draweth all the ill humors unto it."

56. *HM* 3–4. Thus, e.g., Heywood begins his *Apology* by characterizing theater haters as "seditious Sectists" (B1r), while the antitheatrical puritan Richard Rogers (1603) is forced to explain that he does not advocate "the breaking off of Christian fellowship," as his critics contend, but only "the cutting off of ungodly fellowships" such as those at "stage-plays" (*Seven Treatises*, 578).

57. The most compelling recent contributions to this tradition are Richard Helgerson's *Forms of Nationhood* (1992) and Claire McEachern's *Poetics of English Nationhood* (1996). Although confining itself to nondramatic Renaissance English literature, Andrew Hadfield's *Literature, Politics, and National Identity* (1994) also maintains that the authors he studies shared a "desire to help constitute and participate within a national public sphere" (5).

58. Holinshed, *Chronicles*, 4.262; the victory at Lepanto led Holinshed to call for Christian unity, which he maintained could be promoted by granting subjects "liberty of conscience, concerning matters of faith," and by using "the word" rather than "the sword" to decide religious controversies (4.264).

59. I refer, of course, to the influential definition of nationalism in Benedict Anderson's *Imagined Communities*.

60. So writes the future archbishop of Canterbury, Richard Bancroft, in "Certain Slanderous Speeches Against the Present Estate of the Church of England" (MS c. 1583–85), in *Tracts*, 153.

61. Montagu, *Appello Caesarem* (1625), 113; cf. 116–17. The *Appello* sparked such controversy at the time not because of its stand on essentials but rather because it turned that stand into a sectarian platform, as Stuart theater people increasingly did also.

62. I[ohn]. G[reene]., *Refutation* (1615), 65 [misnumbered 59]; More, "Eruditissima Epistola," 296–301 (my thanks to Sonja Albrecht for this reference).

63. Perkins, *Workes* (1612[-13]), 1.755. The reference is cited by Christopher Hill in his influential essay, "William Perkins and the Poor" (1958). As Hill notes, Perkins repeatedly declared that vagabonds belong to no "Corporation, Church, or Common-wealth": see *Workes*, 2.145 and 3.92, 3.191, and 3.539.

64. Jonson, *Bartholomew Fair*, 5.2.42–44; for Jonson on the preciseness of puritans, see *Volpone* 1.2.43, *Alchemist* 1.1.164, and *Every Man In his Humour* (1616 version), 3.3.88. In *Epicoene*, Truewit assures Morose that if he marries a "precise" wife, he will have to "entertain the whole family, or wood" of puritans (2.2.80–82; cf. *Alchemist* 3.2.95): Herford and Simpson gloss "wood" as a latinism for a group or crowd, but the term also suggests the barbarity underscored in *Bartholomew Fair*.

65. Crompton, *Mansion* (1599), M1r; Maxwell, Prospectus (1604), 8v. In *King James VI and I and the Reunion of Christendom* (1997), W. B. Patterson has shown that King James remained seriously committed to the cause of international Christian unity throughout his reign.

66. *Booke of the Common Prayer*, 4 and 268.

67. HM 529r; Cooper, *Apologie* (1562), 68, 213; Bradford, *Writings*, 1.262; Bayly, *Practise*, A3r; Musculus, *Temporisour* (1555; rpt., 1584), A6r.

68. Bale, *Chief Promises*, 2; Grimald, *Christus Redivivus*, 114–15 ("quidem non externis tantummodo / Luminibus, intimo sed & haustu pectoris"); *Henry V*, prol. 28, 18, 17. For a still later exemplar of the tradition, see "The Prologue for the Court" in Jonson's *Staple of News* (1625), which offers the play "as a *Rite*, / To *Scholars*, that can judge, and fair report / The sense they hear, above the vulgar sort / Of Nut-crackers, that only come for sight" (5–8). The elitism that differentiates this prologue from Shakespeare's will be discussed in chapter 1.

69. *Henry V*, prol. 23; Bale, *Three Laws* (1538; rev. c. 1547 and 1562), in Happé, ed., *Complete Plays*, 2.66.

70. John Jewel, *A Treatise of the Sacraments*, in *Works* 2.1100.

71. Bayly, *Practise*, A2v–A3r; Spurr, *Restoration Church*, 297 (although Spurr is paraphrasing criticism of the Restoration church, he rightly sees "much in the general tenor of sixteenth-century English Protestantism" that was already "potentially 'moralist'" [298]). Wigand, *De Neutralibus et Mediis* (1562), B1r; Sandys, *Sermons*, 192.

72. In his attack on the theater, Stubbes demanded to know how one could be called "a just man, that playeth the part of a dissembling hypocrite?" (*Anatomie*, M1r). Even the theater's defenders used the term *hypocrisy* to describe theatrical pretense: in his *Theatrum Redivivum* (c. 1635–37), Sir Richard Baker argued that "some *Hypocrisy* is no *evil*, if it be without *Deceit*" (21).

73. Munday et al., *Sir Thomas More*, 3.1.140; *HM* 100; Hooker, *Works*, 2.351–52; Middleton, *The Puritan*, 1.3.49–50.

74. *HM* 100; Hooker, *Works*, 2.351–52; Middleton, *The Puritan*, 1.3.49–50.

75. In Consistory Court, Frith (1612) confessed that at the Fortune theater she "sat . . . upon the stage in the public view of all the people there present in man's apparel & played upon her lute & sang a song" (quoted in Dekker and Middleton, *Roaring Girl*, 262). Although John Chamberlain (1612) refers to Frith as "Mall Cutpurse" (*Letters*, 1.334), it is unclear whether *The Roaring Girl* borrowed that alias from Frith or conferred it on her. For more information on Frith, see Mulholland, "Date"; and Dawson, "Mistris."

76. *The Stage Acquitted*, 82, 79, 57, 17, 56–57, and 86–87. By the 1690s the ploy of lifting the stage over the pulpit while claiming to lower it had a long history. A decade after the puritans had closed the theaters, the playwright Richard Flecknoe (1654) acknowledged that English drama had grown scurrilous and needed reforming; a first step in the right direction, he maintained in the preface to his closet drama *Love's Dominion*, would be for the stage to regard itself as merely a "humble coadjutor of the Pulpit, to teach *Morality*, in order to the other's *Divinity*." Adapting the gradualist bias of the established church to his protheatrical purpose, however, Flecknoe went on to characterize the moral teachings of plays as "molding and tempering men's minds for the better receiving the impressions of Godliness." Indeed, he contended, "Devotion" could *not* stick to "rough and unpolish'd minds, unless they be first prepared with politeness of manners, and the tincture of good education, for the receiving it"; for him, this necessary foundation was "best taught" not in the church but in "the *Theater*, by how much those precepts move the mind more forcibly and efficaciously, which besides the allowance of the *Ear*, have a powerful recommendation of the *Eye*." "The main reason why *Virtue* is no better followed," Flecknoe concluded, "is, because 'tis no more delightfully persuaded"—"which also may be the reason," he added, "why more sleep at *Sermons* than at these Representations" ("Preface," *Love's Dominion*, A4v–A5r, A7r–v).

In *Love's Dominion* itself, the character Philostrate similarly declares that "Music and Poetry"

> Are the Language, and the Accent of the Gods,
> Speaking unto us in a diviner strain,
> And moving our minds with far more Energy,
> Than plain dull Rhetoric. Religion
> Still ent'ring easilier, and penetrating more
> Profoundly, those hearts th'ave soft'ned before.
> (13–14)

The preface distances itself from such hints that plays are better than sermons by attacking *puritan* preachers: "And now having reformed the Stage, we may justly expect they should reform the Pulpit too, who preach so much against it, where of late there has been uttered more scandalous and libelous stuff, than ever yet was uttered on the Stage, (especially against those in Authority, I know not from what spirit, but I am sure not from the Spirit of *God*, who commands us to obey our Superiors, without exceptions) a spirit so much the more dangerous, by how much it pretends more Scripture and Religion, than the Stage, for what it does" (A5v–A6r).

Ostensibly, the final clause means that puritans have neither scripture nor religion to support their nonconformism, but it also insinuates that players are preferable to preachers insofar as their teachings make no pretense to godlike authority.

Chapter One

1. Prynne, *Perpetuitie*, *4v–**1r. For the conventionality of identifying the taverngoer with the theatergoer and opposing them both to the churchgoer, see, e.g., Henry Smith's *Sermons* (1592), 634; and Thomas Adams's *The Gallants Burden* (1612), 5r.

2. Gurr, *Shakespearean Stage*, 119.

3. Harvey, *Fowre Letters*, 8, 13; Wood, *Athenae Oxoniensis*, 1.196; John Ward (c. 1661–63), quoted in Bradley and Adams, *Jonson Allusion-Book*, 324. Charles Nicholl maintains that the house where Marlowe was killed was probably a private home licensed to sell food and drink rather than a tavern (*Reckoning*, 35). Whether or not this distinction is a significant one, Marlowe died during what Prynne would have considered a good-fellow meeting: according to William Vaughan (1600), Marlowe's companions were "playing at tables" when the fatal fight erupted (quoted in Nicholl, *Reckoning*, 77).

4. Heywood, *Apology*, E3r; *TN* 1.287, 323, 288. When protheatricalists distinguished theatergoing from taverngoing, it was usually to insist only that one was a less serious vice than the other. Thus Robert Pallant in a prefatory poem to the *Apology* states that he has known men who "would not for any treasure see a play, / Reel from a Tavern" (A7v), and Richard Brathwait (1635) claims to "prefer a pleasant Comedy / Before a Tavern, where so many sit / To drench down care without a drop of wit" (*Anniversaries*, A7r). I will address this issue of playgoing as a lesser, even prophylactic vice in chapter 5.

5. Heminges, *Elegy*, pp. 2 and 11; ll. 153–54, 197, 176–78, 192–94, 197–98.

6. Heminges's puritans "Quak'd at Jonson as by him they pass / because of Tribulation Holesome and Ananias" (183–84; Moore Smith thinks that Heminges meant the puritans "quacked," cried out against, rather than "quaked").

7. Aubrey is quoted in *HS* 1.179. For the Sun, Dog, and Triple Tun, see *HS* 11.375 and 416. For Wilde, see Bradley and Adams, *Jonson Allusion-Book*, 294. Ames?, *Search*, 1. For Jonson as "Genius," see *HS* 11.506; for the *Preparative* (misdated in *HS*), see 505–6; for Ben Jonson's Head, see 506–7; and Bradley and Adams, *Jonson Allusion-Book*, 373.

8. Jonson, *Every Man Out*, Induction, 334–38.

9. *HS* 5.17–18, 1.141, 1.113.

10. *HS* 1.141; see Wood, *Athenae Oxoniensis*, 1.508. For a famous alehouse anecdote concerning Jonson, Corbet, and "*sack*rifice," see L'Estrange, "Merry Passages" (c. 1640), 29–30. For poets who link Jonson with urbanely sacramentalized drinking, see *HS* 11.374–76 and 505–6.

11. *HS* 11.438–39. The current or future clergymen were William Bew, Ralph Brideoake, William Cartwright, James Clayton, Samuel Evans, Henry King, Jasper Mayne, Thomas Terrent, and Richard West; Bew, Brideoake, and King later became bishops. For evidence of a close relationship between Jonson and Duppa, see Probst and Evans, "Bishop Duppa."

12. Robinson, *Works*, 2.257. For the variety and complexity of English Protestant

theories about "the Cohabitation of the Faithful with the Unfaithful," see Collinson's essay bearing that title (Collinson quotes Robinson on p. 59).

13. Ainsworth, *Counterpoyson*, ***3b; Crosse, *Vertues Common-wealth*, Q1r.

14. Bernard, *Two Twinnes*, 3; Sibbes, *Bruised Reed*, 64; 1 Cor. 9.22, 10.33, as translated in Tyndale, *New Testament*, 252–53; Gainsford?, *Rich Cabinet* (1616), 116v.

15. *Two Wise Men*, ll. 55, 104; Sidney, *Defence*, 122; Heywood, *Gunaikeion*, A4v (I thank Paulina Kewes for this reference).

16. Gardiner, *Letters*, 403, also in *AM* 6.47; Parsons, *Treatise*, 577, cited in Thompson, *Erasmus*, 63.

17. Dickens and Jones, *Erasmus*, 212. The eight translators are Thomas Artour, William Burton, Thomas Chaloner, Nicholas Grimald, Thomas Heywood, Thomas Key, Thomas Norton, and Nicholas Udall (John Rastell is a possible ninth: see Devereaux, *Translations*, 65). This list excludes later interesting figures, such as John Wilson, author of the influential Restoration comedy *The Cheats* (1663), who published a translation of *The Praise of Folly* in 1668.

18. Brome, *Weeding*, 4.2.18–21, 134–35, and 5.3.150. "Vain imaginations" is a standard phrase in puritan polemics, as when Anthony Gilby (1581) refers to "the ministration [of the sacrament] in the wafer cake, whereby the people hath been brought into vain imaginations" (*Pleasant*, C1r–v).

19. Gifford, *Countrie Divinitie*, 7r (further editions were published in 1582, 1583, and 1598). Robert Cawdrey (1604) similarly condemns the "civility" of the know-nothing Christian (*Short*, *8v–A1r). Cf. Perkins, *Workes*, 1.A2r; Sclater, *Commentary*, 201; and Bolton, *Generall Directions*, 300–301, cited in Lake, "Charitable," 162.

20. Gifford, *Countrie Divinitie*, 1v, 2r, 29r. He seems to have had a specific "carnal" minister in mind—his rival at Maldon in Essex, Robert Palmer; see Collinson, *Birthpangs*, 57.

21. Gifford, *Countrie Divinitie*, 30v.

22. Ussher, *Briefe Declaration*, 25; Erasmus, *Paraclesis*, n.p.; *Enchiridion*, 11; Verkamp, *Indifferent*, 36.

23. Bernard, *Christian Advertisements*, 174–75, noted in Jordan, *Religious Toleration*, 2.38; Bunny, *Treatise*, 107.

24. Ussher, *Briefe Declaration*, 52–54, 26; Bernard, *Two Twinnes*, 4, 19.

25. Bernard, *Two Twinnes*, 7. The claim was conventional: see Green, *Christian's ABC*, 1.

26. Bernard manifests some anxiety on this score: having cited various scriptures in which "catechism" is synonymous with "teaching," he weakly adds that "catechizing is not only, and alone, the duty of a Minister, but also other ways of instructing and teaching" (*Two Twinnes*, 3). Thomas Gibson (1584) takes a harder line: some "can Catechize, & lay the grounds of Religion," he writes, "yet this will not serve the turn, there must be building after the foundation, there must be a leading to perfection" (*Fruitful Sermon*, C7v). For the opposite extremism, see, e.g., John Selden: "Preaching for the most part is the glory of the preacher to show himself a fine man. Catechizing would be most beneficial" (*Table-Talk*, 107).

27. Gifford, *Countrie Divinitie*, ☞ 2r–v, 17v, 83r; Green, *Christian's ABC*, 26.

28. Bernard, *Faithfull Shepheard*, 10. According to the *Paraclesis*, Christianity is by its very nature accommodationist: "this delectable doctrine doth apply [accommodat] herself equally to all men[,] submitting herself unto us while we are children[,]

tempering [attemperat] her tune after our capacity[,] feeding us with milk[,] forbearing[,] nourishing[,] suffering[,] and doing all things until we may increase & wax greater in Christ" (*Exhortation*, n.p.; *Opera Omnia*, 5.140A). One of Erasmus's English translators, the playwright Nicholas Udall (1548), praises the writings of Erasmus himself in the same terms: "all things [are] aptly tempered to induce & train the gross & the rude multitude as well of Curates & teachers, as also of other private readers" (Erasmus, *First Tome . . . of the Paraphrase*, B5v).

29. *CW* 8.202–4; *Epist.*, 4.486–89 (the letter implies but does not directly state that Luther has such zeal for purity). Erasmus commends Paul's "civilitate," "oratione civili," and "urbanitate," while he chides Luther for choosing rather "to pile one cause of hatred on another" than "to soften a naturally painful subject by the civility [civilitate] of one's handling." For Erasmus as a self-styled "civil" Christian in his disputations with Luther, see Boyle, *Rhetoric and Reform* (1983), especially 114–15.

I have silently emended the Toronto translation in favor of word choices warranted by Thomas Elyot's *Dictionary* (1538).

30. Hooker, *Works*, 1.18.

31. Erasmus, *CW*, 8.210; *Epist.*, 4.493; *First Tome . . . Paraphrase*, Ee3v; Hooker, *Works*, 2.143–45.

32. Bury, *Moderate Christian*, 11–13; Trapp, *Commentary*, 92; Gifford, *Countrie Divinitie*, 5v; *CW* 8.205, 210; Erasmus, *Epist.*, 4.489, 493; Erasmus, *Opera Omnia*, 5.98F, quoted and translated by Bietenholz, *History*, 86.

33. Ussher, *Briefe Declaration*, 53–54; Bernard, *Terence*, ¶2r; Bernard, *Two Twinnes*, 18. In *Two Twinnes*, Bernard portrays Christ and Paul as renouncing sophisticated teaching methods in order to instruct the ignorant: "Our Savior Christ taught, but as his Disciples were able to learn, not after his skill, but after their measure of conceiving: so did the Apostle the *Corinthians*" (20). At the same time, however, Bernard calls Christianity itself an "Art" (4, 8). For the plain style as an ostensibly artless accommodationism, see Auksi, *Christian Plain Style*, especially 232–303.

34. Erasmus, *Second Tome . . . Paraphrase*, EE3r–v. See Bietenholz, *History*, 86–89, on Erasmus's notion that Christ "played roles" and that his apostles, especially Paul, imitated his acting.

35. Calvin, *Commentarie*, 107v; Calvin, *Pauli Epistolas*, 178.

36. Foley, ed., *Records*, 7.2.1125; quoted in Basset, *English Jesuits*, 42. Urging his readers to become accommodationists like Christ and Paul, Sibbes noted that "the ministers of Satan turn themselves into all shapes to *make proselytes*. A Jesuit will be every man" (*Bruised Reed*, 66).

37. Cunnycatcher, *Defence* (1592), 37. Cf. Munday, *Blast*, 112: "Players can not better be compared than to the *Chameleon*." Barish notes that positive as well as negative valences were assigned to the figures of Proteus, the chameleon, and the polyp during the European Renaissance, but his positive references are all Neoplatonic: he does not mention Erasmus or his theological inheritors. See *Antitheatrical Prejudice*, chap. 4, especially 98–113.

38. Cartwright, *Comedies*, *2r, B1v, B5v–B6r; cf. **2r–v and **6r. Lloyd, *Memoires*, 424.

39. Richard Meighen in Goffe, *Three Excellent Tragedies*, A2r; Mayne, *Sermon*, 35, 18–19. Like Erasmus, Mayne compares Paul to a chameleon (19).

40. Mayne, "On the Works of *Beaumont* and *Fletcher*," in Beaumont and Fletcher, *Fifty Comedies and Tragedies*, A3r; *HS* 11.453; Mayne in Cartwright, *Comedies*, B5v.

41. *TN* 2.121–29; Bury, *Moderate*, 16–18.

42. *Staple of News*, prol. 23. Comparison of Jonson's boast with two other self-portraits at the start of the *Staple* helps illustrate his sense of how accommodation-ism should work. In the "Induction," a bibulous Jonson is said to be "rolling himself up and down like a tun" backstage, "sweating" like "a good Shroving dish" (61–66). But "The Prologue for the Court" abandons this image of the dramatist as the carnivalesque embodiment of good-fellowship and transforms him instead into a hierophant, who offers his play as "a *Rite*, / To *Scholars*, that can judge, and fair report / The sense they hear, above the vulgar sort / Of Nut-crackers, that only come for sight" (5–8). Although they seem antithetical, both the portraits depict Jonson as providing communion to his audience. Part of what Jonson seems to mean by the poet's ability to steer the souls of men, then, is this represented capacity to fashion himself differently to different audiences, and thus, as it were, conjoin those audiences through separate sacramentlike participations in the play. I will more fully explore the topic of plays as sacraments in chapter 4.

43. Chapman, Jonson, and Marston, *Eastward Ho*, 1.1.125–27, 151–52, 168–71, and 4.2.350–51. As Touchstone's bad daughter sarcastically puts it to her pious sister, "though thou art not like to be a lady as I am, yet sure thou art a creature of God's making, and mayest peradventure to be saved as soon as I" (1.2.52–55).

44. *Eastward Ho*, 5.3.117–18, 5.5.112–15.

45. Munday, *Blast*, 109; *Adagia*, 1.1.91–95, in *CW* 31.131–37 and *Opera Omnia*, 2.1.198–204. Discussing another theatrical adage, "Cothurno versatilior," "As versatile as a buskin," Erasmus associates "vafriciem" with "inconstant and equivocal behavior." The further Erasmus moves from the context of actual theater, the more positive his interpretations become. In the case of "Servire scenae," Erasmus notes that "to serve the time is indeed the part of a wise man" (*CW* 31.132), while in regard to "Cothurno versatilior" he adds that "there is no reason, however, why we should not use the proverb in a good sense" and admire Ulysses, who "could play any part [personam apte] to perfection" (*CW* 31.137; *Opera Omnia*, 2.1.204).

46. Rankins, *Mirrour*, 7r; *HM* 153.

47. Northbrooke, *Treatise*, 65; Crosse, *Vertues Common-wealth*, P3r; Gosson, *Playes Confuted*, in *Markets*, 177–78; letter from Edmund Grindal to William Cecil, quoted in *ES* 4.267; cf., e.g., Stubbes, *Anatomie*, L5r–v.

48. *HM* 929. Atkinson may be Thomas Atkinson, an Oxford man (d. 1638) who wrote a Latin tragedy, *Homo*, dedicated to Laud.

49. Collinson makes the same observation, noting that "another biblical play, the *Historie of Jacob and Esau* [c. 1550–57, published 1568], was described as 'merry and witty', an interlude on the story of King Darius [published 1565] as 'pithy and pleasant'" (*Birthpangs*, 98).

50. Garter, *Susanna*, A2r–v; Wager, *Marie Magdalene* 843–44, 1696, and 2005.

51. Wager, *Marie Magdalene* 86, title page, 31, and 52–54.

52. Bale, *Three Laws*, 124; *A. C. Mery Talys*, D2r–v, cited by Ingram, ed., *Records of the Early English Drama: Coventry*, xvii. The *Tales* were read in Shakespeare's day. According to Beatrice, Benedick has been defaming her by claiming that she has her

"good wit out of the *Hundred Merry Tales*" (*Much Ado* 2.1.129–30). A. R. Humphrey's Arden edition of *Much Ado* notes a 1603 Venetian report of Elizabeth's enjoying the *Tales* (116n.120).

53. Sandys, *Sermons*, 277; cf. 282.

54. Taylor, *Japhets*, title page.

55. Ibid., 6, citing Eph. 2.14.

56. Gainsford?, *Rich Cabinet*, 116v; Northbrooke, *Treatise*, 66.

57. Wager, *Marie Magdalene*, 17–22, 80–81, 1838–40, 1946–48, 65, 68, 1922, 38–41, 11, 24, 31, 33, and 69.

58. Gosson, *Plays Confuted*, in *Markets*, 150.

59. Sandys, *Europæ Speculum*, 214; Gilby, *Pleasant Dialogue*, A6r.

60. See Peck, ed., *Desiderata Curiosa* (1779), 1.194; cited in Walsham, *Church Papists*, 17.

61. Gilby, *Pleasant Dialogue*, F3v (for the brunt of Gilby's attack on gradualism, see E8v ff.); Bolton, *General Directions*, 331, 305.

62. Hooker, *Works*, 2.335. For other reformers who viewed theories of the eucharist as adiaphora, see my epilogue.

63. Ussher, *Briefe Declaration*, 43–44; Laud, *Works*, 2.59–60. This passage of Laud may be familiar to readers of the Cambridge Platonist Benjamin Whichcote, who quotes Laud's *Relation* nearly verbatim in his *Several Discourses* (1703); see Patrides, ed., *Cambridge Platonists*, 86.

64. *CW* 7.126; Erasmus, *Epist.*, 4.118; *CW* 9.252.

65. Donne, *Letters*, 87; Sheldon, *Sermon*, 51–52; Radford, *Short Treatise*, 587.

66. Lev. 19.19, Deut. 22.11; Sheldon, *Sermon*, 30 [31]; Sutton, *Summons*, 216. Sheldon and Sutton are cited by Walsham, *Church Papists*, 116–18.

67. Sutton, *Summons*, 216; Field, "Letter," 116. "Christ never sought the strayed sheep in that manner," Field continues, "he never cursed it with acclamation or sent a barking dog to fetch it home, but gently brought it upon his own shoulders." Thus the true Christian minister must not "bruise the broken reed" but instead stoop to the capacities of his congregation, recognizing that "children are to be fed with milk and not strong meat."

68. *Timber* (written c. 1623–35), 1046–62 (*HS* 8.595–96); "Execration" (written c. 1623), 102–4 (*HS* 8.207). For Jonson's debt to Erasmus, see Kay, "Jonson."

69. *HS* 1.151; Cartwright, *Plays and Poems*, 497–500.

70. Jonson, *Catiline* 3.1.30–31; *Devil Is an Ass* 1.1.143; *Mercury Vindicated* 108; Hausted, *Rival Friends*, "Preface to the Reader," 7. For Hausted's debt to Jonson, see Mills's edition of *The Rival Friends*, xv.

71. Ormerod, *Picture*, 72. Cf. R. C. in *The Time's Whistle* (1615): "the Puritane, / Which as the plague shuns all that are profane" (26). *Weeding* 4.2.203, 1.1.98–99. A "roarer" in the play declares to the puritan Gabriel that "we are brethren, sir, and as factious as you" (4.2.275–76). Smuts, *Court Culture*, 94.

72. Rev. 7.1–8 (King James version); Corbet, *Poems*, 52–56; Davenport, *New Trick*, F4v; Sanderson, *Works*, 3.160–61. Cf. Henry Howard, Earl of Northampton, in his *Defense of the Ecclesiasticall Regiment in Englande* (1574): "I see not what can be intended by this new devised discipline, but only restitution of the veil, and clogging men's consciences with such Jewish observation, from the which we are enfranchised already by the Gospel" (13). Howard invokes Peter's sermon in arguing that puri-

tans are wrong to oppose the ordination of former priests (19–20). Even Catholics mocked puritans as Jews: see the Catholic play *Hierarchomachia* (MS c. 1630), 181–82, 1236–37.

73. Sampson, *Vow Breaker*, 5.2.5–8, 3.2.53. The cat anecdote was a standard antipuritan joke: see Holden, *Anti-Puritan Satire*, 83.

74. *Bartholomew Fair* 1.6.93–96; Busy is called a rabbi at 1.3.116, 5.5.109, and 5.6.40.

75. Hooker, *Works* 1.18; Jonson, *Alchemist*, 5.5.96–100.

76. Gifford, *Sermons*, 144. Cf. Dent, *Ruine of Rome*, 79–80. So strongly did Jonson associate the seal of Revelation 7 with sons that it figures in the remarkable "vision" he had of "his eldest son" Ben at the time his son died of the plague. Jonson told Drummond that his son appeared "unto him with the Mark of a bloody cross on his forehead as if it had been cutted with a sword"; in Revelation, the angel "sealed the servants of our God in their foreheads." Jonson also claimed that his son "appeared to him . . . of a Manly shape & of that Growth that he thinks he shall be at the resurrection" (*HS* 1.139–40)—that is, during the event that Revelation foretells. And finally, Jonson had his vision while in the company of his spiritual father Camden, "Best Parent of his Muses" (8.662), "to whom I owe / All that I am in arts, all that I know" (8.31).

77. Jonson, *Alchemist*, 1.1.164; "Epistle," 3, 75–79, 10, 20.

78. William Cain too notes Jonson's "failure or unwillingness to identify the virtues that are to be set against vice and depravity, and that 'seal' good men in a common bond against them" ("Self and Others," 167).

79. Drayton, "Sacrifice" 1, 8, 31 (*Works*, 2.357); Jonson, "Leges," 1–4, 11, 14 (*HS* 8.656); Brome, "Ben Johnson's Sociable Rules for the Apollo," 2–4, 16, 18–19 (*HS* 11.360). The "Leges" were "engraved in gold letters on a marble tablet over the mantlepiece" in the Apollo (*HS* 11.295). Jonson's Latin, "Deseriis, aut sacris, poti, et Saturi ne diserunto," could be more clearly translated as "let's not discourse on serious or sacred things when drunk or sated." Richard Peterson notes that it is difficult to decide whether the ending of the "Epistle" associates the Tribe with "easy accessibility" or "elitism," and he finds this ambiguity reflected in the use of the Apollo Room by clubs as well as by the public (*Imitation*, 156–57).

Devil and saint were a more shocking pair at the time than one might think: in *Ben Jonson's London*, Fran Chalfant quotes a 1608 order of the Vintner's Company requiring the owner of the Devil "to reform his sign of St. Dunstan and the Devil and to put the Devil clean out of it" (66). Later references to the sign in William Rowley's *Match at Midnight* (c. 1622) and Thomas Fuller's *Church-History* (1655) suggest that it nonetheless continued to display both of the tavern's original patrons; see Sugden, *Topographical Dictionary*, 151–52.

80. Like many another clerical admirer of Jonson, the copyist was a graduate of Christ Church, Oxford; see *HS* 11.294.

81. Rev. 7.9; Bale, *Image*, 334. Donne (1624) reads the verse after the tribe of Benjamin as putting an end to papistry and puritanism both: "salvation is a more extensive thing, and more communicable, than sullen cloistral, that have walled salvation in a monastery, or in an hermitage, take it to be; or than the over-valuers of their own *purity*, and righteousness, which have determined salvation in themselves, take it to be" (*Sermons*, 6.151).

82. Randolph, "Gratulatory to Mr. Ben Jonson for his adopting of him to be his

Son" (published 1638), in *HS* 11.390–91. For other Pauline references to adoption, see Gal. 3–4 and Eph. 1–2.

83. "Elegie on my Muse," 140–41, 113–14 (*HS* 8.282–89).

84. *Magnetic Lady* 1.1.19–21, 2–13 (*HS* 6.499–597).

85. Ibid., chor.112–16; 1.1.23–28. Cf. Jonson's admirer John Collop in his *Medici Catholicon* (1655), where he defines "Controversies" as "either the Ebullitions of indigested Idleness, symptoms of distemper'd zeal, or inebriations of Passion" (A5r; cf. A2r). I borrow the notion of "medicalization" from Michael Heyd, who points out that major landmarks in the development of this discourse were Robert Burton's *Anatomy of Melancholy* (first published 1621), Meric Casaubon's *A Treatise Concerning Enthusiasme* (1654), and Henry More's *Enthusiasmus Triumphatus* (1656). See Heyd, *"Be Sober and Reasonable,"* especially 44–108.

86. Jonson, *Magnetic Lady*, 5.chor.14–17; Edmund Gayton, *Pleasant Notes upon Don Quixot* (1654), in *HS* 11.505. The "apologetical Dialogue" to *Poetaster* (1601) shows how easily Jonson could metamorphose into the sort of exclusivist he satirized: responding to criticisms of the play, the "Dialogue" denounces Jonson's audience as a "drunken rout" of "unclean birds" and derides players as a "tribe" mainly "vile" ("To the Reader," 208, 219, 146, 152 [*HS* 4.321–23]). Although the dialogue was first published in 1616, Jonson states that it was "once spoken upon the stage" and then "restrain'd . . . by Authority" (*HS* 4.317).

87. The prologue to Jonson's final, uncompleted play *The Sad Shepherd* shows him still concerned to portray himself as an accommodator, with the burden for success still falling to a considerable extent on his audience:

> He that hath feasted you these forty years,
> And fitted fables for your finer ears,
> Although at first he scarce could hit the bore,
> Yet you, with patience hearkening more and more,
> At length have grown up to him, and made known
> The working of his pen is now your own.
> (1–6)

As David Riggs points out, Jonson's surrogate in this play is Reuben the "Reconciler" (*Ben Jonson*, 345).

88. Hazlitt, "On Shakspeare and Milton," in *Collected Works*, 5.47, 56. Cf. Coleridge (1811) in *Shakespearean Criticism*, ed. Raysor, 2.66–67. Santayana, "The Absence of Religion in Shakespeare" (1896, revised 1900), 100.

89. *1 Henry VI* 1.3.56; *K. John* 3.1.149–71.

90. *K. John* 1.1.40–43; Bevington, *Tudor Drama*, 202.

91. In her discussion of Falstaff in "Saints Alive," Kristen Poole is certainly right to point out that puritans were often caricatured as drunkards: thus Marmaduke Joshua in *The Vow Breaker* confesses, "I was converted in my drink, and so are most of my brethren" (5.1.108–9). But it seems reductive to claim that Shakespeare presents Falstaff as a puritan: the stage puritan was generally a secret or hypocritical libertine, while Falstaff in *1 Henry IV* does not seriously attempt to hide his vices from anyone.

92. For Donne's early Catholicism, see Bald, *John Donne*. Neither Honigmann nor Sams makes the case that Shakespeare was Catholic when he wrote his plays.

93. See Honan, *Shakespeare*, 38–40, 354.

94. The many echoes of the English liturgy in Shakespeare's plays are strong but not definitive evidence of his attending church: he might simply have owned a copy of the prayer book. For instances of Shakespeare's allusions to the liturgy, see Milward, *Shakespeare's Religious Background*, 104–25; and Rowse, *William Shakespeare*, 41–46.

95. The most zealous exponent of Shakespeare's orthodoxy is A. L. Rowse: see his *William Shakespeare*, 43.

96. *Twelfth Night* 2.5.162–63; *1 Henry IV* 3.3.10; *Measure* 1.3.50, 5.1.221–22.

97. "Alack! / How can I choose but halt, go lame, and crooked? / When I pull'd a whole church down upon my back" (Dekker, *If It Be Not Good*, 5.4.281–83).

98. *Twelfth Night* 2.3.140; Sibbes, *Bruised Reed*, 200; *Henry VIII* 5.2.99–100, 164. For an alternative reading of Shakespeare as a "moderate Catholic" who conceals his true beliefs because he fears persecution, see Taylor, "Forms of Opposition." My reading of Shakespeare is entirely compatible with F. W. Brownlow's speculation that Shakespeare's reticence stemmed from his childhood Catholicism, which taught him "that belief was a private matter, to be kept to oneself" ("John Shakespeare's Recusancy," 191).

99. Keats, *Letters*, 1.193–94. For the persistence of this Romanticism, see, e.g., the works of Harold Bloom discussed in my preface, and Stanley Wells's *Shakespeare: The Poet and His Plays*, 14–15, 20–21, and 229. Wells largely omits the topic of religion from his analysis of Shakespeare's life and works. Without citing the available biographical evidence on Shakespeare's possible religious views, Wells dismisses it as "tenuous and therefore useless" (12). His survey of Shakespeare's reading (12–14) does not mention the Bible; in a later list of Shakespeare's sources he places the Bible second to last, before "accounts of foreign travels" (33). But Wells does briefly refer to the presence of "Christian paradox" and "prayer" in *The Tempest* (369–70).

100. *CW* 76.7–8, 8.209. For a compendium of Luther's hostile remarks on Erasmus, see Murray, *Erasmus and Luther*, 228–29. Erasmus, *Epist.*, 4.492.

101. Harington, *Tract*, 108. So Donne in his *Pseudo-Martyr* (1610) chastises those "who think presently, that he hath no Religion, which dares not call his Religion by some newer name than *Christian*" (13–14).

102. Harington, *Tract*, 108–9, 111, 120.

103. Milward, *Shakespeare's Religious Background*, 73.

104. Shakespeare highlights the itinerancy of friars in Petruchio's song—"It was the friar of orders gray, / As he forth walked on his way" (*Shrew* 4.1.145–46)—and in contradistinction to the "strict restraint" of *Measure for Measure*'s nuns (1.4.4).

105. See Satz's "The Friar in Elizabethan Drama" (Satz himself does not raise the issue of professional identification).

106. *Measure* 5.1.305, 4.3.157.

107. [Fennor?], *Pasquils Palinodia*, B3r–B4r, D3v. Gifford was, again, only one of many writers to satirize this view: cf. the worldly Antilegon in Arthur Dent's *Plaine Mans Path-way to Heaven* (1601, rev. 1603) who insists that alehouse life is "good fellowship, and a good means to increase love amongst neighbors" (165). For more on the defense of popular pastimes in Renaissance England, see Marcus, *Politics*; and Hutton, *Rise and Fall*. Marcus associates "complaints about the decline of 'neighborhood'" during the period with "the breakdown of a communal agrarian system" (*Politics*, 146); she does not cite sectarianism as a factor.

108. *All's Well* 1.3.51–54; Jewel, *Works*, 4.361. Jewel also affirms the efficacy of lay confession (357). Cartwright's cheaters make a private confession public in *The Ordinary*, 5.3. Shuger reads *Measure for Measure* as dramatizing a "penitential" conception of society, in her forthcoming book *The King of Souls*. For the communalism shared by the Shakespearean stage and the English church, see Targoff, "Performance."

109. *Romeo and Juliet* 2.6.21, 3.3.55; see Satz, "Friar," 222–38. For the fullest exposition of the view that Friar Laurence offers "worldly nostrums rather than gospel mystery for a solution" to crises, see Battenhouse, *Shakespearean Tragedy*, 121–23.

110. Wood, *Athenae Oxoniensis*, 1.509. Morley told the same story to Izaak Walton, who relayed it to Aubrey; see *HS* 1.181–82.

111. *Tempest* 3.1.94, 5.1.57, 2.2.130 and 142, 1.2.77, 2.2.64 (e.g.), 1.2.302 (e.g.), and 5.1.1, 28–30, 108–9, 63–64, and 114. For more on "embodiment" in *The Tempest*, see chapter 6 of my *Empire Nowhere*. Prospero's pseudo-resurrection seems closest to the picture drawn in Luke: "But they were terrified and affrighted, and supposed that they had seen a spirit. And he said unto them, Why are ye troubled? and why do thoughts arise in your hearts? Behold my hands and my feet, that it is I myself: handle me, and see" (24.37–39, King James version). Christ proceeds to command his disciples to preach "repentance and remission of sins" (47).

112. *Tempest* 4.1.16–17; *Romeo and Juliet* 5.2.5. Thus Laurence consecrates the marriage of Romeo and Juliet offstage (2.6.35–37); the same is true for the marriages consecrated by Friar Francis (*Much Ado* 5.4.67–71) and Friar Peter (*Measure for Measure* 5.1.377–79).

113. Brome, "Upon the Ingenious Comedies of Mr. Richard Brome," 15–22.

114. *I Henry VI* 5.1.11–14, 52–54; Erasmus, *Querela pacis*, E6r.

115. Barish, "War," 11; *Comedy of Errors* 1.1.11–12; *Riverside Shakespeare*, 115n.11; Erasmus, *Querela pacis*, D6r. Erasmus refers to Plato, *Republic*, 5.470. To my knowledge, only T. S. Dorsch, the editor of the new Cambridge *Comedy*, credits the implication of civil warfare in the Duke's speech (41).

116. Cranmer, *Miscellaneous Writings*, 540. See Parker, "Anagogic Metaphor," 42–45; Parker, "Shakespeare and the Bible," passim. Erasmus, *Querela pacis*, D6v.

117. *I Henry IV* 2.4.5–6 and 92; 1.1.12; *Henry V* 5.2.353 and 242–43. A source play for the Henriad, *The Famous Victories of Henry the Fifth*, by Drayton and others, has Henry say to his thieves that "we are all fellows, I tell you, sirs" (1.78–79). But it was the Henriad that seems to have launched the craze for good-fellow kings in such plays as Heywood's *Edward IV Part 1* (c. 1599), Rowley's *When You See Me You Know Me* (c. 1604), and *1 Sir John Oldcastle* (c. 1599). See appendix 1.

Chapter Two

1. Hall, "An Holy Panegyric" (1613), in *Works*, 5.103. I discuss the ideology of England's sublime littleness more fully in my *Empire Nowhere*.

2. Bishop Cuthbert Tunstall, as reported in *AM* 4.666–67; Sander, *Treatise*, preface, cap. 98; Harding, *Rejoindre*, C1a. For the history of the belief that England counted as an empire, see Ullman, "Realm." Dorman, *Proufe*, 112a.

3. Queen Elizabeth (1559) in response to a petition from her Catholic bishops (Strype, *Annals*, 1.1.218); cf. Peter Moone's *Short Treatise* (1548) on the English as "wandering in the Pope's laws" (B1v). Radical Protestants maintained that the En-

glish were walking astray still. For example, Henry Barrow begins his *Brief Discoverie of the False Church* (c. 1590) by declaring that the English people "are so universally departed from the strait ways of life and peace, and are so far wandered and strayed in their own byways which they have sought out unto themselves, as they have now utterly lost all knowledge of the true way, and have no will to return" (*Writings . . . 1587–1590*, 263).

4. Baumer, "Church of England," 12. For the largely unrealized proposals by English churchmen to achieve an international confessional unity, see 12–21. Sandys, *Europæ Speculum*, 189; Sandys notes ambivalently that England is "divided from all the rest of the world." Cf. Calvin to Cranmer (1552) on the "scattered members [membris dissipatis]" of the reformed church (Cranmer, *Miscellaneous Writings*, 432). Catholic polemicists happily cited the Sandys passage as an instance of Protestants condemned "by their own judgments," as Richard Broughton put it on the title page of his *The English Protestants Recantation* (1617): see, e.g., Brereley, *Protestants Apologie*, 501 and 507; Broughton, *Recantation*, 31; and Anderton, *Epigrammes*, 76.

5. Dorman, *Proufe*, 118b; Gilby, *Answer*, 69b; Hooper, *Early Writings*, 201, quoted in Davies, "Poor Persecuted Little Flock," 83; Spenser, *Faerie Queene*, 2.1.19, 3.1.24, 1.2.9, and 1.7.50.

6. Allen, *Defense of English Catholics*, 234; Dorman, *Proufe*, 5b; Bancroft, *Sermon*, 3. Cf. Robinson, ed., *Zurich Letters*, 287; and *Dialogue*, 3. In 1590 George Gifford reported that "there are, say some, at the least fifty several sects" in England; "behold, say others, how the people are led without ground, and have no stay but are carried without end from one thing to another" (*Short Treatise*, A3v).

7. Northbrooke, *Treatise*, A1b; Edward Hext (1596), in *Tudor Economic Documents*, ed. Tawney and Power, 2.341–42; Verstegan, *Declaration*, 60, 58. King James (1616) himself later declared that "Beggars and Rogues . . . so swarm in every place, that a man cannot go in the streets, nor in the high ways, nor any where for them" (quoted in Randall, *Jonson's Gypsies Unmasked*, 55n.114). R. H. Tawney's famous remark that the Elizabethans "lived in terror of the tramp" appears in his *Agrarian Problem in the Sixteenth Century*, 268. According to Catholics, the Reformation had spawned these social problems in various ways: by precipitating a general decline in civility and morality; by ruining the monasteries, which had cared for the poor; and by allowing clerical marriage, which expanded the population while making it impossible for the clergy to afford the Catholic level of "hospitality for the poor" (Parsons, *Epistle*, 17).

8. For the apparent increase in vagrancy, see Beier, *Masterless Men*, 14–28; and Slack, *Poverty*, 43–45, 49–50, 93–94. According to both historians, the major causes of this increase were overpopulation and the displacements resulting from enclosures, but Slack agrees with contemporary assessments that the dissolution of the monasteries and holy orders along with the Protestant attack on voluntary poverty helped worsen the plight of England's poor (*Poverty*, 13, 23, 206). See also Pound, *Poverty*, 1–22.

For a recent compendium of traditional claims about the rise of English nationalism, see Liah Greenfeld, *Nationalism*, 27–87. Like most of her predecessors, Greenfeld has a Whiggish faith in the "uninterrupted" and thus "inevitable" (40) development of English nationalism that blinds her to any social problems or expressions of concern for England's internal integrity during the Renaissance. Nor does her Whiggism allow her to consider any religious stumbling blocks: she maintains that "the affinity between Protestantism and the idea of the nation guaranteed . . . the lack of religious opposition to nationalism" at the time (53). Greenfeld is untraditional, however, in her extreme secularization of the period: she argues, for instance, that by the time of the Revolution "it was the association with nationalism which made religion at all meaningful" (75).

9. Norden, *Progresse of Pietie*, 114, 116, 175–76.

10. Drayton, Hathway, Munday, and Wilson, *1 Sir John Oldcastle*, 3.110–14; 2.20–23; 3.32–33, 48–49, and 90; 6.18; 13.98; 19.67 and 55; 10.81–83; 11.152; 10.82; 7.31 and 118. For a good account of the play as picturing "a society riddled with division and injustice," see Champion, "Havoc," 169–74, although Champion does not mention the pervasiveness of vagabondage in the play.

11. *Oldcastle* 4.175–82. The equation of good fellow with thief seems to have been idiomatic at the time, although English history plays took to the idiom with particular vigor. In Heywood's *I Edward IV* (c. 1599), for instance, Hobs states that "good fellows be thieves" shortly before he mistakes the king for "some out-rider, that lives by taking purses" (C4r–v). Cf., e.g., *King Leir* 19.10–11; and *A Knack to Know a Knave* 97.

12. *Oldcastle* 10.52–53 and 40–41, 11.33; Harding, *Confutation*, 150r; *Oldcastle* 11.20 and 6.17–21.

13. Norden, *Progresse*, 178. By calling the rogue literature I discuss a tradition, I mean to suggest its limitations as well as its extensiveness. Not all theories of the nation in the theater, let alone in England, were rogue theories, and not all "rogue sentiment," as Empson called it, was antisectarian or nationalist. In his *Liberty against the Law* (1996), Christopher Hill has compellingly linked some rogue plays to a seventeenth-century struggle for a "liberty" that was not associated "exclusively with property or Parliament" (325). I differ from Hill in finding that rogue plays from Marlowe to Brome grow more conservative socially. Hill himself has trouble reconciling his allegorization of Robin Hood as anticapitalist lawlessness with his observation that the literature of the period increasingly gentrifies Robin (77–78). What's more, he never mentions that rogue plays recurrently satirize puritans.

14. For the history and literature of the Renaissance English belief in a vagabond "underworld," see Aydelotte, *Elizabethan Rogues*; Judges, *Elizabethan Underworld*; Berlin, *Base String*; Beier, *Masterless Men*; and Kinney, ed., *Rogues*.

15. Awdeley, *Fraternitie*, passim; Harman, *Caveat*, 112, 148–53; Dekker, *Lanthorne and Candle-light*, 216. The early interchangeability of *vagabond* and *rogue* is apparent in Peter Levins's *Dictionarie of English and Latin Words* (1570): Levins defines *a Rogue* as "vagabundus" and *to Rogue* as "vagari" (157). But its derivation from cant quickly made *rogue* the more complex term, connoting thievery, fraudulence, and a criminal underworld.

16. [Webster?], *Characters*, 73 (for Webster's authorship, see xvi–xxiv).

17. Sharpe, *Crime*, 101–3; see also Beier, *Masterless Men*, 57–58, 123–45. For a more qualified position on organized roguery, see Slack, *Poverty and Policy*, 102; and Pound, *Poverty and Vagrancy*, vii–viii. Beier, too, notes that there were some large gangs of vagabonds, and that "itinerant tradesfolk . . . showed occupational solidarity" (*Masterless Men*, 91). I agree with Pound that there must have been *some* truth to the rogue pamphlets: some organized roguery, some recognizable rogue types, and probably more cant.

18. Greene, *Notable Discovery*, 36.

19. Harman, *Caveat*, 114; Greene, *Notable Discovery*, 37; Dekker, *Lanthorne*, 213 (my emphasis). Cf. *Defence of Conny catching*, 11–12; and Rowlands, *Greenes Ghost*, A2b.

20. Thus the prologue to the Oxford play *Narcissus* (c. 1603) begins, "We are no vagabonds, we are no arrant / Rogues that do run with plays about the country" (5). For touring players regarded as vagrants, see Gildersleeve, *Government Regulation*, 21–31.

21. See, for example, Bradbrook, *Rise of the Common Player*, 37–38; and Gurr, *Shakespearean Stage*, 28–29. For the text of the 1572 act, see *Statutes of the Realm*, 4.590–98, and see also 4.899–902. Peter Roberts rightly cautions against viewing the act as intentionally aiding professional players ("Elizabethan," 45).

22. The phrase appears in a posthumously published work by the Elizabethan puritan Thomas Cartwright, *A Confutation of the Rhemists Translation* (1618), 75. Much to the horror of their critics, the permanent theaters replaced the vagrancy of players with a new social mobility: "*England* affords those glorious vagabonds, / That carried erst their fardels on their backs, / Coursers to ride on through the gazing streets, / Sooping it in their glaring Satin suits, / And Pages to attend their masterships" (*2 The Return from Pernassus* [c. 1601–2], ll. 1922–26). Gosson makes a similar complaint in his *Schoole of Abuse:* "Overlashing in apparel is so common a fault, that the very hirelings of some of our Players, which stand at reversion of vi. s. by the week, jet under Gentlemen's noses in suits of silk, exercising themselves to prating on the stage, & common scoffing when they come abroad, where they look askance over the shoulder at every man, of whom the sunday before they begged an alms" (*Markets*, 96). Cf. *ES* 4.303; Crosse, *Vertues Common-wealth*, Q1r; and Moryson, *Itinerary*, 4.233.

23. *ES* 4.317. For similar pronouncements by officials, see *ES* 4.307–8, 315–16, 318, 320, 322, 340. Gosson, *Markets*, 99. In *Histrio-Mastix* (1633), Prynne famously remarks that the licensing system of the Elizabethan vagabond statutes exempted players "only from the punishment, *not from the infamy*, or style of *Rogues and Vagabonds*" (496).

24. Harman, *Caveat*, 110. In *Martin Mark-all, Beadle of Bridewell* (1610), Samuel Rid observes that Dekker's "volumes and papers" on the rogues are "now spread everywhere" (in Judges, *Elizabethan Underworld*, 386).

25. Greene, *Repentance*, 26.

26. Greene, *Disputation*, 40. For rogues compared to players, see Dekker, *Lanthorne*, 228, 240, 244, 247, 250–52, 254–56, and 260. Unlike play-rogues, however, the actual rogues reveal themselves only at night: "now when the stage of the world was hung in black, they jetted up and down like proud *Tragedians*" (258).

27. Nashe (1592) claims that "in plays, all cozenages . . . are most lively anatomiz'd" (*TN* 1.213); cf. Chettle, *Kind-Harts Dreame*, E3v. For the view that the open roguery of the player makes him *worse* than other criminals, see Gosson, *Markets*, 130.

28. Middleton and Dekker, *Roaring Girl*, 5.1.131–32. Although it was the first English play to offer an extended exposé of the rogue underworld, *The Roaring Girl* was not the first to be based on the life of an actual rogue: the cutpurse Dick Evans inspired the now lost *Cutting Dick* (c. 1600). See Clark, *Thomas Heywood*, 28–29.

29. *Whore of Babylon* 1.2.129–31.

30. Again, see my *Empire Nowhere*.

31. I do not mean to distinguish sharply between poets and issues of power, on

the one hand, and players and issues of community, on the other. But playing was an inherently more communal activity than poetry writing, and players were therefore more likely than poets to treat issues of community as professionally significant.

32. Marlowe, *Tamburlaine*, 4.1.6. The same speech labels Tamburlaine a "rogue" (4). Around the same time as *Locrine*, Tamburlaine is also domesticated in the historical comedy *George a Greene*, in which the rebel Earl of Kendall threatens to become "like martial Tamburlaine" and "lay waste" any towns that resist him (A3r).

33. Although critics have long noted that Shakespeare drew on rogue literature to fashion Edgar's disguise as "poor Tom," they have generally overlooked the same basis for Shakespeare's characterization of Hal, whose ambivalent fraternizing with rogues seems directly modeled on Greene's pamphlet confessions and self-defense: "The odd mad-caps I have been mate to, not as a companion, but as a spy to have an insight into their knaveries, that seeing their trains I might eschew their snares: those mad fellows I learned at last to loath, by their own graceless villainies, and what I saw in them to their confusion, I can forewarn in others to my country's commodity" (Greene, *Notable Discovery*, 7–8).

34. According to Shakespeare's Henry IV, for instance, "insurrection" never lacks "moody beggars, starving for a time / Of pell-mell havoc and confusion" (*1 Henry IV* 5.1.79–82; cf. *Hamlet* 1.1.95–104). For other contemporary history plays that associate vagabondage with rebellion, see *The Life and Death of Jack Straw* (c. 1590); also Shakespeare's *2 Henry VI* (c. 1590–91), in which the "valiant" (4.2.53) or sturdy beggar Jack Cade proclaims his ambition to become England's king.

35. *Defence*, 64. Cuthbert is the first to complain that the rogue detectors are actually wasting their time on a relatively insignificant evil (9). Cf. Rowlands, *Greenes Ghost*, A4b–B1a; and Rid, *Martin Mark-all*, 391–92.

36. Fletcher, *Beggars' Bush*, 2.1.145.

37. Barton, *Ben Jonson*, 205–6. *Bartholomew Fair* 1.6.37, 4.6.106, prol. 4, 5.2.44–46, 5.5.52. In the theater, this association of puritans and rogues dates from perhaps the first play to satirize puritan clergymen, *A Knack to Know a Knave* (acted 1592), which presents the priest John "the precise" (l. 1759) as the brother of Cutbert Cutpurse "the *Conycatcher*" (l. 1843).

38. Selden, *Table-talk*, 119–20; *Bartholomew Fair* 4.6.112. The definition of a "Neuter" in Wigand, *De Neutralibus et Mediis*, A6r. Cf. Norden's disgust toward the Christian "that is neither hot nor cold, a key cold professor, a neuter, that is contented to run with every religion and think well of every profession" (*Mirror*, 108). The puritan Gilby thought that all church conformists were "halting Neutrals, . . . which fondly patch Christ his Religion, with the Pope's" (*Pleasant Dialogue*, F6r). And sectarian Catholics were equally contemptuous of the "neuter," whom they regarded as "not affected to either religion, and consequently of no religion" (Martin, *Treatise*, A5v).

39. *Bartholomew Fair* 5.5.104–5; Gal. 3.28 (King James version). For more on the play's relation to Galatians, see Shuger, "Hypocrites." Richard Brathwait similarly plays on the term, although for a different effect, when he calls a "*Neuter*" in religion "neither *masculine* nor *feminine* Christian" (*Whimzies*, 105). Attacks on the neuter as "not affected to either religion, and consequently of no religion" often cited the Mosaic prohibition against weaving garments of "both linen and woolen" (see, e.g., Gregory Martin's *Treatise of Schisme*, A5v–A8v). Deuteronomy 22 forbids cross-

dressing as well as "linsey-woolsey" clothing, so Jonson may have found a scriptural subtext for joining players with neuters in the language of the religious controversialists he despised. The later *Discourse Concerning Puritans* (1641) of Henry Parker explicitly links "Neuters" with "Stage-poets" as types of antipuritans (58–59).

40. Mayne, *Sermon*, 30. While some writers during the period complained that religious moderates were regularly stigmatized as "Neutrals, neither *hic*, nor *haec*" (*Differences*, D2r–v), the modern positive usage of "neutrality" in such contexts was slow in coming. An early instance appears in Richard Montagu's *Appello Caesarem* (1625). Montagu maintained that he had always been "solicitous to preserve peace" and therefore had often "suspended [his] own judgment" regarding secondary points of doctrine, opting to remain "aloof in a kind of neutrality" (37). Although Prynne unsurprisingly took this statement to be a confession that Montagu was a "Neuter" (*Perpetuitie*, 250), Montagu carefully limited his suspended judgment to an orthodox broadmindedness about adiaphora, and he called this practice only "a kind of neutrality." I have not found an unqualifiedly positive reference to "neutrality" that predates Mayne's sermon.

41. See Awdeley, *Godly Ditty* (1569?); *Cruel Assault* (c. 1560); and *Wonders* (1559). Awdeley, *Fraternitie*, 92; Fish, *Supplicacyon*, 1 and 4. Tyndale (1530) described the Catholic clergy as "one kingdom, sworn together one to help another, scattered abroad in all realms" (*Practyse*, 296); Cranmer (1555) stated that "the king is head in his own realm: but the pope claimeth all bishops, priests, curates, &c. So the pope in every realm hath a realm" (*Miscellaneous Writings*, 213). English Catholic polemicists made the same charge against Protestants, whom they called "a Confederate company of licentious and unbridled persons, dispersed in every Country (as the Jews lately were) that being limited by no law of God nor of Conscience (nor yet of man, where they be of strength to show it) are the professed enemies of all Monarchy and Kingly Dominion" (Leslie, *Treatise*, 154v).

42. Hanmer, *Jesuites Banner*, ☞ 2b, C1b. In speeches of 1581 and 1582 Sir Walter Mildmay called the Jesuits "a rabble of runagate friars" and "a swarm of lewd vagrant hypocrites" (Petti, ed., *Recusant Documents*, 10, 13). Cf. Mildmay (1591), quoted in Neale, *Elizabeth I*, 383–84; Nichols, *Plea*, 108; and Copley, *Answere*, 118. Verstegan (1593) reports that Burghley began his examination of a captured Jesuit by asking him, "[N]ow, rogue, where hast thou been a-roguing?" (*Letters*, 115).

43. *Lanthorne*, 216. The closest a rogue writer comes to identifying rogues with religious dissidents is an exception that proves the rule. In *Martin Mark-all* (1610) Samuel Rid imagines that his fellow detectors have put such pressure on England's rogues that the rogues have decided to emigrate to a vagabond utopia, "Thievigen," which Rid borrows from Joseph Hall's *Mundus Alter et Idem* (1605). Located near the South Pole, Thievigen, Rid explains, is filled with such misfits as "your idle vagabonds that after war will betake themselves to no honest course of life . . . , but especially seditious and rebellious subjects in a commonwealth, schismatical and heretical seducers in the Church, as Brownists, Papists, Jesuits and suchlike" (Judges, *Elizabethan Underworld*, 403). Even in this fictive and distanced setting, rogues and schismatics are merely compared, not conflated.

44. *Locrine* 1.2.4 and 89; 3.2.44. For Scythian references to Troy, see 2.2.89–92, 4.2.58–67, 5.6.69–72, and 2.4.29–34. The Scythians also follow nearly the same route to Britain that the Trojans had taken: see 1.2.46–50 and 2.2.5–8.

45. Pilkington, *Works*, 125. For more on Renaissance English embarrassment about England, see Helgerson, *Forms of Nationhood*; and my *Empire Nowhere*. In book 3 of *The Faerie Queene*, Paridell declares that Troy's fall "embaste" its "of-spring," "and later glory shente" (9.33).

46. Sandys, *Europæ Speculum*, 119. As Sandys continues, he implies a connection between England's supposed barbarism and its religious vagabondage: the Italians also view Geneva as "a very professed Sanctuary of roguery, giving harbor to all the runagates, traitors, rebels, and wicked persons of all other Countries." But Sandys quickly transforms Protestant roguery into a Catholic projection: "Sundry of their prigging and loose Friars, hearing *Geneva* to be a place of good fellowship . . . have robbed their Convents of their Church-plate, & repository, and brought away the booty in triumph to *Geneva*, under the color of being reformed in their Religion, where their advancement hath been straight to the Gibbet for their labor."

47. *Locrine* 2.4.11, 14; 2.5.25; and 3.6.11 (my emphasis).

48. *Locrine* 5.6.184, 4.2.28–35. In Virgil's First Eclogue, Meliboeus laments, "At nos hinc alii sitientis ibimus Afros, / pars Scythiam et rapidum cretae ueniemus Oaxen / et penitus toto divisos orbe Britannos" (64–66). For the importance of these lines to English national identity in the Renaissance, see my *Empire Nowhere*.

49. *Locrine* 5.6.197. When contemporary apologists for England did take on Rome directly, they often looked to roving barbarians for aid and comfort. Chagrined that George Buchanan should wonder how a mere pack of Trojan wanderers could succeed in conquering Britain when the Romans "*in their greatest fortune and strength*" would later fail, Richard Harvey (1593) advised Buchanan to talk with Tamburlaine: "He could tell you, that his *multitude* of *rude Scythians* and shepherds could do more Acts than all the fine gay troops and ranks of *Bajazete*" (*Philadelphus*, 3–5). Michael Drayton (1612) invoked the Scythian invasion in a similar apologetic context:

> And though remorseless *Rome*, which first did us enthrall,
> As barbarous but esteem'd, and stickt not so to call;
> The ancient *Britans* yet a sceptered King obey'd
> Three hundred years before *Rome's* great foundation laid.
> And had a thousand years an Empire strongly stood,
> Ere *Caesar* to her shores here stemm'd the circling Flood;
> And long before, borne Arms against the barbarous *Hun*,
> Here landing with intent the Isle to over-run.
> (*Poly-Olbion* Part 1, 8.37–44)

50. For the importance of Sabrine's Severn as a border in English Renaissance literature, see Schwyzer, "Purity and Danger."

51. Sandys, *Europæ Speculum*, 232; *Liber Vagatorum*, 3. For the English and ultimately even Jewish conception of the Jews as a nation during this period, see Shapiro, *Shakespeare and the Jews*, 173–93. The most famous contemporary references to Jews as a "nation" are of course Shylock's in *The Merchant of Venice* (1.3.48, 3.1.56 and 85).

52. Harrison, "Description," in Holinshed, *Chronicles*, 1.309; cf. Rid, *Art of Jugling*, 265; Sandys, *Sermons*, 349–51. Writers such as Rid state that the Egyptians were "banished" (265), without explaining the circumstances of their banishment.

53. Bale, ed., *Laboryouse Journey*, A5a–b; Greenwood, as reported in [Verstegan], *Letters*, 146. Cf. Ainsworth and Johnson's *True Confession of the Faith* (1596), which laments "the rueful estate of our poor Countrymen who remain yet fast locked in Egypt that house of servants in slavish subjection to strange LLs. & laws" (A2r)— that is, to Romish clergy and practices.

As with the rogues, the only stated connection between the gypsies and the papists at the time was one of comparison: Copley claims that the Jesuits are "*like* those ye call Egyptians" (*Answere*, 118 [my emphasis]).

54. Rid, *Martin Mark-all*, 421 (my emphasis); Cowell, *Interpreter*, Bb1r; cited in Randall, *Jonson's Gypsies Unmasked*, 60n.120. Cowell's definition is repeated by John Minsheu in his *Guide Into Tongues*, 168. Cf. Dekker, *Lanthorne:* "If they be Egyptians, sure I am they never descended from the tribes of any of those people that came out of the Land of Egypt. *Ptolemy*, King of the Egyptians, I warrant never called them his Subjects; no, nor *Pharaoh* before him" (243).

55. To protect herself, the goddess Poverty in Thomas Randolph's *Hey for Honesty* (c. 1627) organizes "an army of rogues" led by the Scottish Brun, the Welsh Caradoc, the Irish Termock, and the English Higgen. The first three rogues speak in dialect, while Higgen speaks in a cant he can turn on and off at will, thus making himself seem more domestic or artificially foreign than his fellow internal aliens.

56. Manningham, *Diary*, 219. This transformation has been overlooked by the play's most influential reader in recent years, Jean-Christophe Agnew, who claims that the Induction to *Bartholomew Fair* heralds the alliance between two secularizing forces, the theater and the marketplace (*Worlds Apart*, 119–21). In their *Politics and Poetics of Transgression* (1986), Peter Stallybrass and Allon White counter that "the very notion of contract which the Induction proposes is subverted in the play which follows" (70), but in their view *Bartholomew Fair* offers no other alternative to contractual social relations than a "grotesque, saturnalian" one (71).

57. Brome, *Jovial Crew*, 5.1.242, prol.3, 3.1.520–25. For an earlier, more Jonsonian depiction of puritans by Brome, see his *Weeding of Covent Garden* (1633?). Springlove suggests giving the part of Divinity to "the old patrico, our priest," but when the patrico arrives on the scene, it is to tell the other rogues that now "is no time to play" because "our quarter is beset" (4.2.171–224).

58. *Jovial Crew* 5.1.119 and 2.1.172–76. The rogues are Erastian, insofar as they denounce no ceremonies of others while practicing only "their own" (2.2.147–48).

59. *Jovial Crew* 5.1.432–37. For typical Protestant attacks on the Agnus Dei, see Kaula, "Autolycus' Trumpery," 289–91. The Catholic play *Hierarchomachia* (c. 1630) claims that English pursuivants "strip the clothes from maids / Under pretense to find some Agnus Dei's / Or other relics" (1049–50).

60. *Jovial Crew* prol. 14. As I noted in chapter 1, Brome uses the phrase "civil Christian" in another of his comedies, *The Weeding of Covent Garden*. Neither the Agnus Dei nor the ecumenical drift to *A Jovial Crew* figures in the critical literature on the play. Although Martin Butler describes *A Jovial Crew* as profoundly "committed" to "reflecting on the destiny of the nation" (*Theatre and Crisis*, 279), he says little about Brome's views on religion. In *Professional Playwrights*, Ira Clark also speaks of Brome's "commitment to facing sociopolitical problems" (158), without mentioning religious problems.

The patrico's role in preserving the Agnus Dei is only part of the evidence that

Brome wants to free his characters and his audience from reductive sectarian labels. Earlier in the *Crew*, Springlove is chided for linking pilgrimages with vagrancy as Protestant polemicists would (1.1.207–13), but Springlove means the association to be complimentary. And the play continues to present pilgrimage as a merrily roguish activity (2.1.93, 2.1.333–35, 4.2.62–64): thus pilgrimage is celebrated only insofar as its Catholic significations are subsumed under the more open and equivocal practice of vagrancy. Another index of the complexity of Brome's attitude toward Catholicism is the difference between the play's start and finish. *A Jovial Crew* begins with a potentially anti-Catholic tale about a necromantic monk who goes to the devil, but the play concludes with the patrico's happily leaving the beggar priesthood to become the "faithful beadsman" of his new patron (5.1.485). How literal a "beadsman" does the patrico intend to become? Brome seems to regard this ambiguity, which fits his vagueness about the patrico's religion throughout the play, as the enabling medium for comic restoration.

61. For a good introduction to the masque, see Randall, *Jonson's Gypsies Unmasked*. As Randall notes, Jonson's "Egyptians" are counterfeit rogues: the Patrico in the masque speaks of using "the noble confection / Of walnuts and hog's grease" to change his "complexion" (1120–22).

62. In his dedication to the first edition of *A Jovial Crew* (1652), Brome states that the play "had the luck to tumble last of all in the epidemical ruin of the scene" (26–27). See *JCS* 3.71–72.

On the more absolute nationalism that accompanied the civil wars, see Kohn, "Genesis"; and Greenfeld, *Nationalism*, 40–41, 73–78.

63. For the "Ordinance of the Lords and Commons against Stage-plays and Interludes" (2 September 1642), see Hazlitt, *English Drama*, 63; for the ordinances against players (22 October 1647, 9 February 1648), see 64–67. One contemporary news-book claimed that members of Parliament felt "*Plays* must be lash't down, / For fear themselves be *whipt* about the *Town*" (quoted Rollins, "Contribution," 291).

64. Harman, *Caveat*, 109; [Webster?], *Characters*, 74; cf. Saltonstall, *Picturae Loquentes*, D9r; *Oldcastle* 11.55–65. The father of the man murdered by the Irishman laments the tragic irony that his son met his death not in Ireland but at "home," "where security gave greatest hope" (20.77–90). This nostalgic conception of "home" is constantly undermined in the play.

Chapter Three

1. Ribner, *English History Play*, 24, 87–88; Peele, *Edward I*, 11–32, 42–43, 2649–58.

2. *Richard II* 2.1.40–56, 57–66.

3. Womack, "Imagining Communities," 137, 125, 136. For an impressive skeptical reading of the monarchism in Gaunt's speech, see Friedman, "John of Gaunt."

4. Helgerson does not think that Shakespeare was skeptical about kings, however; for my response to his argument, see chapter 4. Stubbes, *Anatomie*, L8v.

5. See, e.g., Rackin, *Stages*; Hall, *Things*; McEachern, *Poetics*, 83–137; Helgerson, *Forms*, 193–245.

6. Parsons, *Temperate Ward-word*, 4, 129. For English insularism, see my *Empire Nowhere*, 66–73. John Speed in his *Description of the Civill Warres of England* (1601?) celebrated Elizabeth's reign as the time "when all hostility and outrage of civil wars,

broils, and dissensions, have seemed by the power of the Almighty hand of God stretched forth in our defense, to have been transported out of this Island over the Seas into other Countries" (n.p.).

7. Marlowe, *Edward II*, 2.3.21–24.

8. Gaunt depicts his name as a title of impoverishment (2.1.73–83), and Falstaff echoes this wordplay in *1 Henry IV* (2.2.67–68) and *2 Henry IV* (3.2.324–26). I will return to the notion, suggested by Ghent's Anglicization as Gaunt, that England represents a diminished version of the Continent.

9. *Richard II* 4.1.146, 4.1.92–100, 5.6.49–50, 4.1.142–44; *1 Henry IV* 1.1.1–27; *2 Henry IV* 4.5.209–12.

10. Ussher, *Briefe Declaration*, 15; Willet, *Ecclesia Triumphans*, 38–40; *1H4* 1.2.139–40, 2.2.23, 3.2.14, 3.3.153–54; *Henry V* 1.1.22, 33.

11. Sandys, *Europæ Speculum*, 214; Dee, *General and Rare Memorials*, 53. When Sandys states that the English concur entirely "with neither side" yet are "reverenced with both," he probably means that the English can mediate between Lutherans and Calvinists, but his syntax is murky enough to allow a reading of the opposing sides as Protestants and Catholics. Frances Yates describes Elizabethan imperialism such as Dee's as "a blend of nascent nationalism and surviving medieval universalism" ("Astraea," 87).

12. Yates similarly detects hope for "the establishment of pure religion" in Shakespeare's histories, but she differs from me in claiming that Shakespeare, like Dee, thought this goal was to be achieved by "Tudor imperial reform" (*Shakespeare's Last Plays*, 70). I believe that Shakespeare was more critical of "royal-imperial power" than Yates suggests; although he supposed that England's monarchs had indeed contributed to the cause of true religion, Shakespeare considered their aid to have been for the most part unintentional. For further discussion of Shakespeare's views on kings and Christianity, see chapter 4.

13. *Edward I* 2350–52.

14. *Edward I* 54, 121, 215, 298–99.

15. Davies, *Microcosmos*, 54; *Edward I* 5. I quote Thomas Phaer's translation of the *Aeneid* (1573). Frank Hook notes the probable echo of Phaer (Peele, *Dramatic Works*, 2.175), but only in reference to a later line from *Edward I* that, for reasons I will shortly discuss, echoes the queen mother's speech.

16. *Edward I* 835–36, 838, 843–44, 849–52.

17. *Edward I* 274, 268–78. Edward's position is nonetheless favorably contrasted in the play to the more treacherously divided loyalties of his Welsh friend David of Brecknock, Lluellen's brother, who appears to have betrayed Lluellen but who actually betrays Edward.

18. *Edward I* 385, 438–39.

19. *Edward I* 250; scenes 6 and 10.

20. For Schwyzer's argument that sixteenth-century English writers conceived of the English nation as British, see his remarkable unpublished dissertation, "Narratives of Nationhood."

21. Bacon, "Certain Observations," in *Works*, 8.155. Earlier in the same work, Bacon conventionally praises Elizabeth for her "firm resolution to content herself with those limits of her dominions which she received, and to entertain peace with her neighbor princes" (157).

22. *Edward I* 1172–73, 1848, 1525–26, 1549, 1181, and 1918–19; *Downfall* 1958, 1824–28, 678, 1191, 1953.

23. *Downfall* 1863–66, 1954, 976, 572–73, 2505. For simpler irony about the Catholic yoking of religion to violence, see 757–59 and 1389–90.

24. *Downfall* 2709–10, 2715–23, 2780. The implied opposition between Robin's gift and Richard's crusading is made clearer in the *Death*, when the evil priest Sir Doncaster attempts to besmirch Robin by portraying Robin's offering in crusader-like terms: "Did he not bring a troop to grace himself, / Like Captives waiting on a conqueror's chair, / And calling of them out, by one and one, / Presented them, like fairings, to the king?" (162–65).

25. *Death* 250–52, 2308.

26. *Death* 930–36, 2080–81, 1967. John's insularism meshes nicely with what the play regards as corrupt Catholic versions of isolationism: when Matilda tries to escape "this woeful world of war" (1789) by entering a nunnery, John is the one who suborns the Abbess and Monk to betray her.

27. *Death* 2953, 2951, 2999–3000. In his final moments Robin requests, "When I am dead, stretch me upon this Bier, / My beads and Primer shall my pillows be" (807–8). Matilda not only enters a nunnery but talks piously about counting her beads (1976–77); she also tries to fend off her enemies with holy water (2529) and a crucifix (2536).

28. Bevington treats the "withdrawal" into the greenwood as a puritan allegory in which "Robin asks only that he be allowed to live in charity with his separated brethren" (*Tudor Drama*, 296). But no one who joins Robin, least of all the Catholic clergymen Tuck, Ely, Doncaster, and the Prior, ever formally renounces the Catholic Church—a minimum requirement, one would think, for puritan separatists.

29. *King John* 2.1.550, 3.1.192.

30. *King John* 3.1.160. For a brief history of John's place in Tudor Protestant polemics, see Elliot, "Shakespeare," 65–69.

31. *King John* 3.1.162–71. Shakespeare's characterization of Pandulph, the only clerical figure in the play, goes a long way toward corroborating John's invective. Pandulph already looks something less than Christian when he responds to John's tirade with a promise of sainthood to whoever assassinates John "by any secret course" (178). He comes to seem still more worldly later on when, after John's victory over his enemies and capture of Arthur, Pandulph first has no words of comfort for Arthur's mother Constance and then coolly anticipates the political advantages that will accrue to the pope by Arthur's foreseeable murder and the Bastard's ransacking of the English church (3.4).

The anti-Catholic thrust of Pandulph's stance on assassination is best witnessed by a Jesuit censor of Shakespeare who struck out these lines from his copy of *King John*; see Frye, *Shakespeare*, 285–87.

32. *King John* 2.1.565–66, 548–49, 562–63.

33. Allen, *Admonition*, 9–10, 26, 24, 23, 48. These are the same reasons highlighted in Sixtus V's *Declaration of the Sentence and Deposition of Elizabeth* (1588), in which Allen seems to have had a hand; see appendix 1 to *The Troublesome Raigne*, ed. Sider, 213–14.

34. *AM* 2.329. Cf. Edward Rishton (1585), who describes the pope as excommu-

nicating Elizabeth "in the same spirit of fortitude in which he formed the Holy League against the Turk, the most cruel enemy of Christ, and with the help of the Catholic king and other states, undertook that most glorious war against him" (Sander and Rishton, *De Origine*, 301). The Armada was in fact partially funded by a crusade tax; Bacon (1592) complained that the pope had granted "many a cruzada" to Philip II "and his predecessors" to fund the holy wars, yet "all have been spent upon the effusion of Christian blood" (*Works*, 8.186). For this issue and for talk of a Crusade against England right from the start of Henry VIII's schism, see Tyerman, *England and the Crusades*, 359–62. On Tasso's *Gerusalemme Liberata* as "suggesting that the reunification [of the church] is indeed a new crusade" (215), see Quint, "Political Allegory."

35. *Troublesome Raigne* x.171–74. Bale in *King Johan* makes the same point with less cost to John: he calls John a Moses whose people "did still in the desert dwell / Till that duke Josue, which was our late king Henry, / Clearly brought us in to the land of milk and honey" (1.1111–13).

36. *King John* 5.7.112–18, 1.1.71.

37. *King John* 2.1.21–30. Austria in the *Troublesome Raigne* has no speech corresponding to this one.

38. *King John* 2.1.4, 72–75; 3.1.142. For evidence that Shakespeare's audience was in a position to recognize the scapegoating impulse in Austria's speech, see Anthony Marten's *Exhortation* (1588). Writing immediately after the Armada victory, Marten defends the English against the sort of charges that Austria makes: even though the English live on an island and therefore have "less cause than any other, to fear the Infidels, being so far remote from us, yet have we been ever as ready, as any other of the mightiest, and richest kingdoms, to travel over sea and land, to spend our lives, lands, and goods, to resist the fury and invasion of the Turks." Why then have the pope and the Spanish king attacked England? Is this, Marten asks, "the reward that we receive for so great desert?" (B2v). Marten's shining example of England's Christian service is, not coincidentally, Richard I.

39. *King John* 3.1.253–54.

40. *King John* 2.1.378–80. In the *Troublesome Raigne*, the Bastard makes no analogy to Jerusalem (ii.302–8).

41. E.g., "nothing hastened their destruction so greatly as their own doggedness and intestive hatred" (Morwyng, *Compendious History*, ‡6v); "though the Jews at the siege of Jerusalem, were pressed by their enemies without the walls, and punished with such a mortality within, that the carcasses of the dead did dung the ground, yet they never went to the wall, till they grew to be factious" (*TN* 1.75–76). A sermon of John Jewel's (1583) applies the topic of Jerusalem's ruinous dissension to England, which Jewel says "could never yet be conquered by any enemy, but only at such time as the people were at variance within themselves" (*Certain Sermons*, 2.1028; cf. 1094–95).

42. *AM* 4.18.

43. *King John* 5.2.25–29, 103–4, 33–39. The Salisbury of *The Troublesome Raigne* makes no comparable speech.

44. Purchas, *Hakluytus Posthumus or Purchas His Pilgrimes*, 1.177; *King John* 5.2.71–72. Purchas goes on to pray "that this Mystical Babylon, which now by usurpation challengeth to be Mistress and Mother of the Church, arriving at that prophesied irrecoverable downfall, Catholic-Roman (universal-particular) may no

more be heard, but true Catholicism recovering her venerable and primary Antiquity, may without distracted faction, in free and unanimous consent, extend her Demesnes of Universality as far as the Earth hath Men, and the light of her truth may shine together with the Sun-beams, round about the habitable world" (*Purchas His Pilgrimes*, 177–78). Christopher Ockland in *The Fountaine and Welspring of All Variance, Sedition, and Deadly Hate* (1589) similarly attacks Rome's supposed centrality to Christendom by arguing that if "Hierusalem [could be] forsaken, much more Rome": "*Hierusalem* and mount *Sion* had these words spoken of her that follow. *Psalm 132*. For the Lord hath chosen *Sion* to be an habitation to himself. This shall be my rest for ever. Here will I dwell, for I have delight therein. Yet *Hierusalem* 40. years after that Christ hath suffered, was sacked (to pretermit in silence, what was done afore to it by the *Assyrians* & their king) The Temple with the city walls and houses was taken, razed, wasted, and consumed, that one stone was not left upon another by *Titus* and *Vespacian*" (20). For a typical comparison of "Romish" to Jewish exclusivity, both of which are said to be based on "the law of the flesh," see Foxe, *A Sermon Preached at the Christening of a Certaine Jew*, C1v–C3v.

45. See, e.g., Tyndale, *Obedience*, 338–39; and *AM* 2.334, 337.

46. *2 Henry IV* 4.5.209–12; *1 Henry IV* 1.2.126; Jewel, *Apologie*, 81; *1 Henry IV* 2.1.61–62.

47. *2 Henry IV* 4.5.236–38. The only reference to the pope in *1 Henry IV* similarly flattens out the world to England's east: in a comic version of the standard Protestant conflation of pope and Turk, Falstaff mentions the "deeds in arms" of "Turk Gregory" (5.3.45).

48. *2 Henry IV* 4.5.235. The chronicle sources for *King John* place Arthur's prison in Tours; the *Troublesome Raigne* locates it in England. Unlike the *Troublesome Raigne*, however, *King John* has the escaping Arthur don a "ship-boy's semblance" (4.3.4), which stresses the analogy between the walled prison and the English isle.

49. *King John* 5.7.64, 4.3.142, 144–45.

50. *King John* 4.3.137, 143 (my emphasis). This difference in Arthur between his little body and noble spirit figures in his first speech, when he welcomes Austria "with a powerless hand, / But with a heart full of unstained love" (2.1.15–16). Neither passage has an equivalent in *The Troublesome Raigne*, which portrays Arthur as a teenager, not a child.

51. *King John* 5.7.57–58. Barbara Traister notes that *King John* is reductive even in regard to the history plays that preceded it: "Its cast of named characters is considerably smaller than those of the earlier plays. It has no fully staged battle scenes, despite the ongoing war between France and England. . . . The panoply and ceremony that marked the first tetralogy have largely vanished" ("The King's One Body," 91).

52. *King John* 5.2.135–36. "The most christian reformation of this church of England, which is to other nations a most worthy spectacle, do they very turkishly deride & mock" (Bale, *Expostulation*, A3r). After recounting the internal divisions of English Protestantism in his *Treatyse of Christian Peregrination* (c. 1597), Gregory Martin adds that he will not even bother to discuss the factionalism among European Protestants: "I have only declared how great diversity and disagreeing there is among your Protestants at home within one little Island" (n.p.). Similarly, William Rainolds lists instances of religious dissension "all appearing manifestly in the practice and behavior of one little Island, and in the compass of a few years," which proves

to him that "such as once divide themselves from the Church, fall from error to error without stay" (*Refutation*, 24). Cf. Bristow, *Brief Treatise*, 119r–v.

53. Foxe, *Christ*, T2r–T3v.

54. *King John* 5.7.116–17. William of Malmesbury quoted in Hay, *Europe*, 31–32.

55. *Henry V* 1.2.269, 226–27, 274, 5.2.353, 206–9.

56. *Henry V* epi.5, 9, 12, 13.

57. The phrase is Sigurd Burckhardt's, from his reading of *King John* in *Shakespearean Meanings*, 141. Although Burckhardt argues that the disintegration of Christendom in the play leads to "that purely instinctual and limited affirmation of community which we call nationalism," he does not consider nationalism an entirely satisfactory alternative to Christendom: "Men no longer united by a common faith in a universal order must hold to what ties remain to them; and in the absence of higher claims to one's loyalty those of the blood are valid. But they are not enough" (141–42). The ascendancy of Burckhardt's skeptical interpretation of the play is readily apparent in a collection of essays on *King John* edited by Deborah Curren-Aquino (*King John: New Perspectives*). For the view that the play leaves its audience in a state of moral uncertainty, see the essays by Hamel, Rackin, Traister, and Champion. For the view that a nationalist realpolitik fills the moral vacuum left by the play, see the essays by Robinson, Vaughan, Kehler, Candido, and Manheim. The major shift in *King John* criticism since Burckhardt has been one of emphasis: now the demise of any "supervening authority" (Burckhardt, *Shakespearean Meanings*, 121) in the world of the play is discussed in terms of the play's strong women rather than its weak men. See Rackin's essay and her *Stages of History*, as well as Carole Levin, "I Trust I May Not Trust Thee."

The difference between Burckhardt's reading and my own is that I believe the attribution to Shakespeare of a provisional nationalism actually smooths over the programmatic ambivalence of the histories. If nationalism in *King John* can finally unite the English, then why do civil wars continue to rage in Shakespeare's histories long after *King John?* And if nationalism is only a provisional option for Shakespeare, then why do his histories continue to focus so exclusively on England's fate? The histories require a reading that accounts more fully for both their national and their supranational leanings.

58. *Richard III* 5.5.40–41; *Henry V* epi.6–8; Pilkington, *Works*, 372, 269–70.

59. Cairns and Richards read these tensions in *Henry V* as symptomatic of the imperialist "contradictions which the play denies in its attempt to stage the ideal of a unified English Nation State" (*Writing Ireland*, 11). Although he maintains that Shakespeare is less successful at suppressing contradictions than Cairns and Richards think, Baker similarly argues that Britain "is being put together" in *Henry V* "as we watch, and the incoherences that bedeviled this confederation in practice are not always eliminated from its performance" (*Between Nations*, 23). My view is that Shakespeare intentionally stages the contradictions.

60. *Richard II* 4.1.78, 5.1.24. Although he sees Shakespeare as entirely secular-minded, Empson makes a similar deduction in his reading of *Henry V.* He argues that Shakespeare felt "one needn't pull a long face about not ruling France" because the loss of France freed England to explore the possibilities of a New World empire and, more important, to pursue "the gradual unification of [its] own islands" ("Falstaff," in *Essays on Shakespeare*, 62–63).

61. *Edward I* 2287, stage direction; *Downfall* 9–13, 2219.

62. She begins act 5 by lamenting that Richard must be imprisoned in "Julius Caesar's ill-erected tower" (2)—i.e., the Tower of London. The very presence of this fortress in England, the relic of a western conquest by an earlier offshoot of Troy, helps to undermine Gaunt's notion that England's insular "fortress" has ever kept it safe in the past. When Richard arrives on the scene, the queen refers to him as "the model where old Troy did stand" (11), which suggests that Troy has already begun to move on.

63. Hayes, in *The Principall Navigations*, ed. Richard Hakluyt (1589), in *Voyages*, ed. Quinn, 2.388. Cf. Alexander, *Doomes-day*, 49–50; and Sibbes, *Bruised Reede*, 341–42. For other Renaissance English writers on the westward progress of religion, see Lovejoy, *Religious Enthusiasm*, 17–19; and my *Empire Nowhere*, 256–57. These references must qualify Shuger's hypothesis that the only writer before George Herbert to envisage a *translatio religionis* was the twelfth-century German bishop Otto van Freising (*Habits of Thought*, 107–12).

64. Purchas, *Purchas His Pilgrimes*, 1.174.

65. Cooper, *Blessing*, 34, 40. Cooper applies the Virgilian tag "Et penitus toto devisos orbe Britannos" to his discussion of England's now spiritual distinctness from the Roman world. For the conventionality of Cooper's treating English insularity as an incitement to New World expansionism, see my *Empire Nowhere*, passim.

66. Cushman, *Sermon*, A2v–A3r. Cf. Sibbes, *Fountaine*, 134; and the epistle dedicatory to Thomas Shepard's *The Clear Sun-Shine of the Gospel Breaking Forth Upon the Indians in New-England* (1648). Condemning the "tyranny" of the Spanish toward native Americans, Sibbes reminds his readers that "there is nothing so voluntary as Faith; it must be wrought by persuasion, not by violence" (*Fountaine*, 136).

67. John Cabot, in the service of Henry VII, completed his first successful voyage to the New World in 1497.

68. Ireland is mentioned in five of Shakespeare's Elizabethan histories as an English possession: in *King John*, for instance, it is one of the territories that both Chatillion and Philip demand of John (1.1.11, 2.1.152). But this supposed possession of Ireland helps ruin England's claim to being a "little world" unto itself, free from the hand of war, especially since Ireland in the histories is generally in a state of rebellion. Moreover, the allusion to Essex's Irish wars in *Henry V* (5.prol.29–35) suggests that England's current overseas interests are not eastward, as Henry V's were, but westward.

69. *Henry VIII* 5.4.14–55. For the colonization of North America as a peaceful revival of the Crusades, see, e.g., Lescarbot, *Nova Francia* (translated 1609), 162.

Chapter Four

1. King, *English Reformation Literature*, 275; the clergymen-playwrights named by King are John Bale, Thomas Becon, John Foxe, William Baldwin, Nicholas Udall, and Nicholas Grimald.

2. *AM* 6.57, quoted in *ES* 1.242n.1. For evidence that Elizabeth's government encouraged Protestant propaganda on the stage in 1559–60, see *ES* 1.243–44. Munday, *Blast*, 58–59, 89.

3. Northbrooke, *Treatise*, 62; Munday, *Blast*, 58, 77–78. Records of theatrical performances outside of London substantiate Munday's charge. In the Court of the

Archdeaconry of Essex in 1566, for instance, it was charged that a churchwarden named Bush "did bring into the church certain players the which did play and declare certain things against the ministers" (Hale, *Series*, 149). On the use of churches as theaters during the Middle Ages and the Renaissance, see Wasson, "The English Church as Theatrical Space."

4. Quoted in *ES* 4.304.

5. The preacher John Stockwood (1579) spoke of "the often and vehement outcrying of God his Preachers against" the theaters (*Very Fruiteful Sermon* [1579], 24); cf. Munday, *Blast*, A4v; and Stephen Gosson, *Playes Confuted*, in *Markets*, 149. Paul's Cross seems to have been a popular venue for these protests. See the Paul's Cross sermons by Walsall and White (both 1578), and the two by Stockwood. An antitheatrical Paul's Cross sermon by a preacher named Spark is mentioned in the preface to the *Blast* (A3v).

6. Becon, *Comparison* (1563), 378; Northbrooke, *Treatise*, 145, 67, 146. Chambers underestimates the issue when he suggests that "a touch of professional *amour propre* gave its sting to the conflict" between player and preacher (*ES* 1.256). The historian Christopher Haigh has argued that during the second half of Elizabeth's reign, the apparent inefficacy of Elizabethan preaching became an open scandal: "It was clear to the ministers, as it must surely be to historians, that the preaching-campaign had produced only a small minority of godly Protestants, leaving the rest in ignorance, indifference, or downright antipathy" (Haigh, "Church," 209; cf. 205–14; Haigh, "Anticlericalism," 73–74; and Haigh, "Puritan Evangelism," passim). But he tends, I think, to take clerical griping too literally. For a more balanced account, see Collinson, "Elizabethan Church," passim; and Spufford, "Can We Count." For other Tudor versions besides Northbrooke's of "the hoary complaint that the preacher is not regarded," see Blench, *Preaching*, 124–25, 237–38, 272–73, 309–10, and 324. For uncommon confidence that by 1587 preaching had begun to make such "places of sin" as the theater "more empty than before," see the *Seconde Parte of a Register*, 2.219.

7. See Haigh, "Continuity." Nonconformists joined the attack as well: reflecting on the poor results of established preachers, Henry Barrow (c. 1590) comments that "it is unsound milk that giveth no increase to the body in 30 years' space" (*Writings . . . 1587–1590*, 501).

8. Gifford, *Briefe Discourse*, 26r. The first quotation from Cawdrey, cited by Haigh ("Church," 209), appears in the 1604 edition of Cawdrey's *Short and Fruitfull Treatise, of the Profite and Necessitie of Catechising*, B6v; the second quotation appears in the 1580 edition, A6v. Haigh cites much of the homiletic literature to which I refer. Wright, *A Summons for Sleepers. . . . Hereunto is annexed, A Patterne for Pastors*, 51.

9. I quote the seminal puritan complaint on the subject, the *Admonition to the Parliament* (1572) of John Field and Thomas Wilcox, 22, 11. For a careful accounting of the established clergy by puritan writers, see the "Survey of the Ministry" (1586) in the manuscript *Second Parte of a Register*, 2.88–174. Under the heading of "What duty is performed" by the minister surveyed, the only interest of the surveyors is whether and how often that minister preaches—and the most common entry is "n.-p.," "no preacher."

10. Wright, *Summons*, 46-47. "The preachers of God, mind so much edifying of souls, that they often forget, we have any bodies. And therefore, some do not so

much good with telling the truth, as they do harm with dulling the hearers" (Wilson, *Arte of Rhetorique*, 278).

11. Wilson, *Arte of Rhetorique*, 27. For the Cambridge Platonist Ralph Cudworth (1647), such intemperate spirituality was itself "Carnal and fleshly": "Let us take heed we do not sometimes call that Zeal for God, and his Gospel, which is nothing else, but our own tempestuous and stormy Passion" (*A Sermon Preached Before the honourable House of Commons*, in Patrides, ed., *Cambridge Platonists*, 118–19).

12. For stage references to sleeping at sermons, see, e.g., Nashe, *Summers Last Will* (1592), 337–38; Barry, *Ram Alley* (c. 1607–8), 5.1, ll. 2336–38; Goffe, *The Careless Shepherdess* (c. 1618–29), praeludium, p. 5; Randolph, *The Muses Looking Glass* (1630), 2.4; Nabbes, *Totenham Court* (c. 1633–34), 5.1; Mayne, *City Match*, 1.3.39–40, copying Cartwright, *Ordinary*, 1.1.3–4 (cf. *City Match* 4.2.51–53); and Thomas Jordan, *Fancy's Festivals* (c. 1654–57): "Sleep goes to Sermons oft'ner than to Plays" (C4v).

13. Nothing irritated puritans so much as the sort of accommodative preaching Wilson recommends. Thomas Cartwright (1572) denounces those "profane preachers" who mix "merry tales" in their sermons (*A Second Admonition to the Parliament*, in Frere and Douglas, eds., *Puritan Manifestos*, 109–10), just as the author of *A Dialogue, Concerning the Strife of Our Churche* (1584) attacks the minister who "can occupy a pulpit an hour or two with fine tales and Fables, and pretty jests to make the people laugh" (56; cf. Gifford, *Briefe Discourse*, 48r).

14. Northbrooke, *Treatise*, 66; Munday, *Blast*, 91. Cf., e.g., Stubbes, *Anatomie*, L7v; Rainoldes, *Th'overthrow*, A3v–A4r; Crosse, *Vertues Common-wealth*, Q2r; Lake, *Probe*, 268; Milles, *Abrahams Sute*, D6r; G[reene], *Refutation*, 60; and [Leighton], *Shorte Treatise*, 237–40.

15. Spivack, *Shakespeare*, 59. In her recent *Inwardness and Theater in the English Renaissance* (1995), Katharine Maus offers the most powerful version of Spivack's position to date. "In the theatrical universe of the morality play," she writes, "it is reasonable to imagine the audience as an essentially unanimous group that sees exemplary versions of itself mirrored in the abstract, generalized situations acted before it." But as sixteenth-century drama begins more and more to address "relatively specialized topics" and to depict "unprecedentedly naturalistic characters," its pedagogical impact is in Maus's view progressively weakened: once "each individual's story is different from every other's, then the exhortatory value of other people's experience becomes questionable." By the time of Marlowe, this "particularizing tendency" in Renaissance drama has grown so powerful that it licenses a corresponding individualism in the audience. "Interpretations" of plays now "proliferate uncontrollably, and in place of consensus one is left with myriad perspectives, each one unique, but none authoritative" (*Inwardness*, 88, 69, 89, 88, 103).

One can acknowledge the remarkable differences between Everyman and Doctor Faustus, however, without adopting Maus's view that these figures occupy disparate interpretive universes: individualized characters no more prevent an audience from drawing general and generally accepted conclusions than personifications assure that an audience will do so. In chapter 5 I outline a protheatrical tradition that saw plays as teaching certain protocols of religious behavior and of interpreting religious behavior, but here I will argue that the audience consensus Shakespeare hoped to generate through his plays is logically distinguishable from the question of their meaning (although their meaning could well have facilitated the consensus he had in mind).

16. Wickham, *Early English Stages*, 2.1.19; Montrose, *Purpose*, 30–31; Greenblatt, *Shakespearean Negotiations*, 126–27.

17. I am not the first to read *Henry V* as a sacramental play. See Joel Altman's superb essay, "Vile Participation," which anticipates my argument about *Henry V* in many respects. Other critics have stressed the importance of the sacrament as a model for Renaissance plays generally. In *Creating Elizabethan Tragedy* (1988), C. L. Barber maintains that sacramental thinking shaped the plays of Marlowe and Shakespeare, but since censorship "obviated the possibility of dealing directly and explicitly" with the sacrament, Shakespearean drama is best described as "post-Christian" (120, 122). Huston Diehl's "Observing the Lord's Supper and the Lord Chamberlain's Men" (1991), another fine essay, anticipates my claims about the relation between Protestant theories of the sacrament and Renaissance drama, although it does not discuss the crucial communitarian dimension of the theories or of the drama they influenced.

More recently, Greenblatt in "The Mousetrap" (2000) has equated the "logic" of *Hamlet* with "the logic of Protestant polemics against the Mass" (155), but he resists concluding that this linkage makes the play religious. On the one hand, he argues that *Hamlet* was "written in the shadow" of "eucharistic controversies" (141) and is therefore permeated with a "deep anxiety about the yoking of the divine spirit to corrupting and corruptible matter" (160). On the other hand, he concludes that *Hamlet* gestures away from the gloom of Christian "orthodoxy" toward the "tolerant acceptance" that one finds in Montaigne's "skeptical materialism" (162).

18. *Henry V* 2.3.51, 4.8.123. For a brief, straightforward statement of the Catholic position, see, e.g., Wright, *Treatise*, 38r; for a similar statement of the Protestant position, see, e.g., Becon, *Catechisme*, 249. For perhaps the most extraordinary rendering of the charge that Catholics worship nothing more than "a thin wafer-cake," see Becon, *Displayeng*, 278–79. Puritans such as Anthony Gilby (1581) were distressed that the ostensibly reformed English church continued to use wafer-cakes in communion rather than "the usual bread of many grains," which Gilby supposed was less likely to stir "vain imaginations" in worshippers (*Pleasant Dialogue*, C1r–v; cf. A2v, F7v, and M5r).

The Protestant resonance of Shakespeare's "wafer-cakes" is noted by Taylor, *Henry V*, 144. Shakespeare more fully evokes a Protestant vision of the eucharist when Fluellen forces Pistol to eat a leek and Gower comments to Pistol, "Will you mock at an ancient tradition, begun upon an honorable respect, and worn as a memorable trophy of predeceas'd valor. . . ?" (5.1.70–72). The difference between a violent communion and a spiritual one is, in my view, the burden of the play.

19. Warner, *Albions England* (1602 edition), 238; *Henry V* 1.1.20, 4.prologue.23; Munday, *Blast*, 69.

20. "Play with your fancies, and in them behold" (*Henry V* 3.pr.7); "Work, work your thoughts, and therein see" (3.pr.25). Shakespeare was far from unique in representing his plays as sacramental experiences. Jonson, for instance, often depicted his plays as feasts for his audiences: see, e.g., the prologue to *Epicoene*, the last line of *The Alchemist*, the prologue to *The New Inn*, and the prologue to *The Sad Shepherd*. In the Induction to *The Staple of News*, as I noted in chapter 1, the playwright

himself becomes food and drink: Mirth describes Jonson as "rolling himself up and down like a tun" in the tiring house; "his sweating," Mirth adds, "put me in mind of a good Shroving dish" (61–66). "The Prologue for the Stage" reinforces the implication that Jonson is himself a kind of eucharist when it claims that the true poet can "steer the souls of men" (23). And "The Prologue for the Court" proves to be even clearer on the sacramental implications of the Induction: it offers the *Staple* "as a *Rite*, / To *Scholars*, that can judge, and fair report / The sense they hear, above the vulgar sort / Of Nut-crackers, that only come for sight" (5–8; the logic here matches the Protestant distinction between true inward and false outward participation in the sacramental rite). As I also noted in chapter 1, Jonson apparently intended the three different characterizations of the *Staple*'s edifying power in the Induction and two Prologues to demonstrate his accommodationist flexibility in addressing diverse capacities. But Jonson's bias toward "scholars" and his emphasis on his own part in the sacramental experience of his play weaken the inclusivism that drew him to the sacramental model in the first place.

21. "An Act to Restrain Abuses of Players" (27 May 1606), in *ES* 4.338–39; Frye, *Shakespeare and Christian Doctrine*, 271, 13, 267.

22. *1 Henry VI* 1.1.40–43, 173–77.

23. Pierce, ed., *Marprelate Tracts*, 399; Bevington, *Tudor Drama*, 201; *2 Henry VI* 3.3.24.

24. Bevington, *Tudor Drama*, 202, 201; *2 Henry VI* 2.1.34–36. The prelate of the *Henry VI* plays may even have reminded Shakespeare and his audience of a third bishop of Winchester, Stephen Gardiner, whose "proud and glorious spirit," "stubborn contumacy against the king, and malicious rebellion against God and true religion," had been denounced by Foxe (*AM* 6.24). For Foxe's report of Gardiner's vicious dealings with a Lord Protector and young king of his own, see *AM* 6.24–266. Gardiner appears as Bishop of Winchester in Shakespeare's *Henry VIII*.

In her discussion of *King John*, Virginia M. Vaughan also argues that Shakespeare's "tendency to ignore specific doctrine" allows him to attack "the venality of the established church" in general, "whether Catholic or Protestant," but she differs from me in claiming that what motivates Shakespeare's assault on the church in *King John* is his secularist loyalty to the state ("*King John*," 70).

25. *Richard II* 3.2.27–35.

26. For the case that *2 Henry IV* was censored, see Clare, "*Art Made Tongue-Tied by Authority*," 68–70. *2 Henry IV* 1.1.189–90; *Richard II* 5.6.29; Erasmus, "Sileni Alcibiadis" (1515; revised 1517/8, 1528), in *CW* 34.281; *2 Henry IV* 1.1.192–96, 201–9.

27. *2 Henry IV* 4.1.85–86, 84, 4.2.4–10, 1.3.86–100.

28. *Henry V* 1.1.9–11, 71, 23, 1.2.110, 132–33.

29. *Henry V* 1.2.20, 222, 262, 307, 2.2.189–91, 3.1.33–34, 4.7.87, 4.8.114–16, 4.1.169; Matt. 18:7 (Geneva version). For the Elizabethan theory of the scourge, see Battenhouse, *Marlowe's Tamburlaine*, 13–15 and 108–13; and Prosser, *Hamlet and Revenge*, 202, who quotes Harry on war.

30. *Henry V* 1.2.293, 4.1.127–28. For those members of the audience who had previously witnessed Harry's father advise him to protect his crown by busying "giddy minds / With foreign quarrels" (*2 Henry IV* 4.5.213–14), Harry's selfish motives would of course be all the plainer. I do not mean to argue, however, that the war truly is Harry's cause alone: the second scene of the play shows how Harry's clergy,

his aristocracy, and even his fellow monarchs press him to declare war. I will shortly examine the social bonds that not only lead to war but are supported by it.

31. *Henry V* 2.2.117, 1.2.131–32, 5.2.59-60, 2.prologue.3-4, 4.1.142–43, 2.3.56, 3.2.37–38, 20, 91–92, 111-13, 133, 2.1.101. Fluellen's oath appears in the Quarto, not the Folio; oddly, Evans does not cite it in his list of variants. Taylor, *Henry V,* 128, notes the pun in "sword." Pistol elsewhere adopts the more direct blasphemy of his captains as part of a comic pretension to a higher class: "*Owy, cuppele gorge, permafoy*" (4.4.37).

32. *Henry V* 3.6.45.

33. *Henry V* 1.1.8–9. Shakespeare further emphasizes the close ties between money and religion in the Catholic world of the play when Harry, meditating on his father's murder of Richard II, tells us he has "five hundred poor" "in yearly pay, / Who twice a day their wither'd hands hold up / Toward heaven to pardon blood; and I have built / Two chantries, where the sad and solemn priests / Sing still for Richard's soul" (4.1.298–302). Harry promises to "do" still "more," yet he also adds a Protestant-sounding qualification about the ultimate inefficacy of good works: "Though all that I can do is nothing worth, / Since that my penitence comes after all, / Imploring pardon" (302–5). For an open attack on the Catholic theology of pardon as profiteering, see *King John*, 3.1.162–71.

34. Thomas Becon, *New Catechisme,* 239; cf. 300–301; Becon, *Displayeng,* 281; Ridley, *Works,* 123. In his *Short Treatise of Certayne Thinges Abused in the Popysh Church* (1548), Peter Moone includes the pax in a long list of the "wares" Catholics substituted for "god's word," "with such Popish peltry / Making us to pay, for the holy consecration[:] / Like thieves that were unsatiate, they robbed body & soul" (B1v, A2v, A4r). Incidentally, Moone seems to have led a company of players: see the *Collections of the Malone Society,* 2.3.261 (my thanks to Alan Nelson for this reference).

35. *Displayeng,* 279. The more familiar Protestant complaint is that papists allow communion in "one kind" only—i.e., of the bread and not the wine—but Becon's accusation that the papists exclude the laity altogether is also common. William Fulke (1581) carefully distinguishes between the two views: "the Popish heretics eat and drink all alone often times, not tarrying for other to communicate with them, and always they drink all alone" (*Rejoynder,* 421).

36. *Henry V,* 1.1.79–81; Jewel, *Apologie,* 3.63. Jewel uses the phrase to characterize the papists' sacrilegious corruption of the Lord's Supper into a "private" ceremony. For a good instance of the Protestant attack on the Catholic clergy as church-robbers, see Ridley, *Works,* 398–404.

37. *1 Henry IV,* 2.2.94, 96. During the reign of Henry VIII, the dissolution of the monasteries was justified on similar grounds: royal plunder of the church would be the first step in restoring clerical plunder to the commonwealth. So Edmund Howes explains in the "Historicall Preface" to his edition of Stowe's *Annales* (1615):

> The general plausible project which caused the Parliament [to] consent unto the reformation or alteration of the Monasteries, was that the King's Exchequer should forever be enriched, the kingdom and Nobility strengthened and increased, and the common Subjects acquitted and freed from all former services and Taxes, to wit, that the *Abbots, Monks, Friars,* and *Nuns* being sup-

press'd, that then in their places should be created forty Earls[,] threescore Barons, and three thousand Knights, and forty thousand Soldiers with skillful Captains, and competent maintenance for them all forever out of the ancient Church revenues, so as in so doing the King and his successors should never want of Treasure of their own, nor have cause to be beholding to the common Subject, neither should the people be anymore charged with Loans, Subsidies, and Fifteens. (C5v–C6r)

"Since which time," Howe mordantly adds, "there have been more statute Laws, Subsidies, and Fifteens than in five hundreth years before."

38. *Henry V* 4.prologue.31–34, 3.1.29–30, 4.3.61–63, 4.6.13–19. Fluellen too clothes warfare in the "ceremonies," "cares," "forms," "sobriety," and "modesty" (4.1.72–74) that Harry has helped to lift from the church.

39. *Henry V* 4.6.28, 4.3.39, 4.7.76-78, 74, 4.6.9. In his other history plays, too, Shakespeare loves to underscore the irony of a bloody sacrament. Thus the French general in *1 Henry VI* declares that "Ten thousand French have ta'en the sacrament / To fire their dangerous artillery / Upon no Christian soul but English Talbot" (4.2.28–30); in *Richard III* the Second Murderer reminds Clarence that he "didst receive the sacrament to fight / In quarrel of the house of Lancaster" (1.4.203–4); while in *Richard II* York reports that a dozen conspirators "have ta'en the sacrament, / And interchangeably set down their hands / To kill the King at Oxford" (5.2.97–99). Cf. *King John* 5.2.6 and *Richard II* 4.1.326–30. For Shakespeare's less habitual reference to the sacrament as a pledge of fellowship in opposition to murderous conflict, see *Richard III* 5.5.15–19 and *Richard II* 1.1.135–41.

40. *Henry V* 2.1.90–92, 4.1.222–23, 5.2.367–68, 353, 206–9. Like *Richard III*, the final play in Shakespeare's first sequence of histories, *Henry V* ends with prayers for Christian amity. To the French monarchy's wish for fellowship between the French and English people, "all" on stage say "amen" (368). Shakespeare notes the failure of this concord only a few lines later, yet his irony seems aimed not at prayers for sacramental unity but rather at faith in the ability of military and political maneuvers to "buy" (5.2.70) such unity—as the church, at the start of the play, had bought its peace with the king, and as Harry hopes that his "five hundred poor . . . in yearly pay" will persuade God "to pardon blood" (4.1.298–300).

41. *Henry V* 1.prologue.13, 10, 9; Pierce, *Marprelate Tracts*, 330. For the purpose of clarity, I have emended the *Riverside*'s "accompt" to "account."

42. Baker, *Theatrum Redivivum*, 138; *Henry V* 1.prologue.3–4, 4.prologue.45–46.

43. *Henry V* 5.2.242–43, 1.1.33, 32, 53–59.

44. *Henry V* 4.1.3–6, 8–12.

45. *Henry V* 4.1.238–40, 101–2, 282–83.

46. *Henry V* 5.2.159–63, 4.1.20–23, 4.3.71, 4.8.106–8.

47. *Henry V* (1.prologue.25). For a reading of the play that treats the analogy between King and Chorus as an equation, see Danson, "*Henry V.*"

48. *Henry V* 1.1.47–48, 38; *2 Henry IV*, 4.2.20–22. Introducing his manuscript life of Elizabeth (1603), John Clapham writes, "The affairs of princes are no fit subject for every private man's pen: their projects and consultations are imparted but to few" ("Certain Observations," 31). But Shakespeare not only undertakes the affairs of his princes as his subject, he also imparts their projects and consultations to many. As the

character Tragedy puts it in Thomas Randolph's *Muses Looking Glass*, "great Kings, and Emperors, / From their close cabinets and Council Tables, / Yield me the fatal matter of my Scene" (10).

The potentiality of the Renaissance English theater to demystify kingship has been powerfully underscored by Franco Moretti in "The Great Eclipse," and by Stephen Orgel in "Making Greatness Familiar." See also Kastan, "Proud Majesty"; and Maus, *Inwardness*, 69. This view has come under vigorous attack by Richard Helgerson, who argues that Shakespeare's history plays increasingly work not to empower the audience but to "efface, alienate, even demonize all signs of commoner participation in the political nation" (*Forms of Nationhood*, 214). Helgerson contrasts Shakespeare's histories with those produced in Philip Henslowe's theater, which Helgerson considers far more populist, in part because the Henslowe histories "lack the elaborate genealogies that are such a prominent feature in all of Shakespeare's English histories. And they pay almost no attention to the strategies by which power is achieved and maintained" (238). But this unwillingness to probe into the affairs of princes (which Helgerson somewhat exaggerates) is precisely what Moretti and Orgel would associate with a conservative theater. To grasp their point, take a dramatist who contrasts even more sharply with Shakespeare than Henslowe's dramatists do. Not once in Jonson's plays for the public theater does a king appear on the stage, yet for a more exclusive audience Jonson wrote masque after masque celebrating the virtues of the reigning monarch. Shakespeare's history plays may consistently focus upon the personal and political dealings of royalty, yet these plays (in which kings more often than not fare quite badly) were produced in the public theater; for the praise of the reigning monarch, Shakespeare never wrote a single masque.

49. *Henry V* 1.prologue.23, 3 and 4.prologue; Calvin, *Institution*, 4.14.9. Altman makes the same point about the Chorus ("Vile Participation," 19n.50).

50. Bullinger, *Sermons*, 4.313; Anon., *An Apologie of Private Masse*, reprinted in Cooper, *Answere*, 40. Greenblatt argues that in *King Lear* Shakespeare offers "no saving institution" against which the "evacuated rituals" of Catholicism "may be set" (*Shakespearean Negotiations*, 127). But this assessment disregards the setting of the play: where in a pagan Britain hundreds of years before Christ's birth was such a "saving institution" to be found? Greenblatt discounts the Protestant implications of his argument when he finds in the story of Edgar and Edmund the traces of "an allegory in which Catholicism is revealed to be the persecuted legitimate elder brother forced to defend himself by means of theatrical illusion against the cold persecution of his skeptical bastard brother Protestantism" (121). Yet Protestants routinely represented *their* faith as the old one, with Catholicism a later heresy. In Jewel's *Certain Sermons* (1583), for instance, Catholic ceremonies are said to be "base-born" (*Works*, 2.991), like Edmund, while the true "sacraments that Christ left for our most comfort have been miserably mangled and defaced" (994), like Edgar. Following this new set of identifications, one could argue that Edgar's theatrical defense typologically anticipates the better Protestant device of a theater that employs illusion to rescue the truth. This reading is untenable for Greenblatt only because he assumes, with the antitheatricalists, that religion must be "purged of theater" (*Shakespearean Negotiations*, 127) in order to survive.

51. Jewel, *Works*, 3.64. For other references to the theatricality of Catholic sacraments, see Barish, *Antitheatrical Prejudice*, 159–65.

52. *AM* 6.448; *Henry V* 4.prologue.53.

53. *Henry V* 1.prologue.28, 32; Pilkington, *Works*, 84.

54. *Henry V* 5.prologue.17–22, 1. prologue.28–32, 2.prologue.37–39, 4.4.71.

55. *Henry V* 1.2.104–10, 2.4.53–62, 50.

56. *Henry V* 4.prologue.51, 22, 26, 49.

57. Cf. Jewel's account (1565) of the holy communion as an "unbloody sacrifice" in his *Replie Unto M. Hardinges Answer* (*Works*, 2.734–35): e.g., "Our christian sacrifices in the gospel, because they are mere spiritual, and proceed wholly from the heart, are called unbloody" (734).

58. *Henry V* 1.prologue.5-8, 32–34. Altman argues just the opposite about the communion inspired by *Henry V*: he maintains that it *joins* "audience to soldiery" ("Vile Participation," 16) rather than differentiates the two. Thus Altman associates the Chorus's repeated characterization of the audience as "gentles" with Harry's promise to his troops that any English soldier who sheds his blood at Agincourt "shall gentle his condition." Yet there is nothing oxymoronic about the Chorus's fusion of gentleness with pardon, whereas Harry's fusion of gentleness with bloodshed strikes the same jarring note as the references to the "gentle" rebel York do in 2 *Henry IV*. Altman, I think, mistakes the scapegoating mode of communion represented *in* the play with the unbloody mode of communion represented *by* the play.

59. *Dialogue* 61. Championing the contentiousness of the godly preacher, Gifford asks, "Will ye charge Christ and his Gospel, because as he sayeth, he came not to send peace, but a sword, to set the father against the son?" (*Countrie Divinitie*, 47v). Cf. Bate, *Portraiture*, 15–17. Reginald Scot (1584?) complained to church officials in Kent of some puritan ministers who "stick not to affirm that the note of a good preacher is to make debate, according to Christ's Matt. 10" (*Second Parte*, 1.233; cf. 238; cited in Collinson, *Religion*, 108). For conflicts generated by or focused upon activist Protestant preachers in Renaissance England, see Haigh, "Church," 214–17.

60. The strongest evidence in the play against viewing Shakespeare as a pacifist is his famous comparison of Harry to Essex in the final prologue, when the Chorus asks the audience to imagine the citizens of London flocking to "their conqu'ring Caesar,"

As by a lower but by loving likelihood,
Were now the general of our gracious Empress,
As in good time he may, from Ireland coming,
Bringing rebellion broached on his sword,
How many would the peaceful city quit
To welcome him!
(5.prologue.28–34)

Most critics read this passage as praise of Essex, although it states only that London's citizens *would* welcome Essex, not that they *should* welcome him. What's more, the passage suggests the same demystifying account of warfare that runs through the rest of the play, with the difference that London appears "peaceful" here in contrast to an Irish rather than a French scapegoat. I do not want to deny, however, that the passage, and the play as a whole, may *sound* like celebrations of militarism.

61. Coverdale, *Fruitfull Lessons* (1593), 411; Coverdale in his final clauses is echoing Heb. 10:24–25. The character Philologus in Nathaniel Woodes's play *The Con-*

flict of Conscience (c. 1570–81) similarly gives the Protestant account of the eucharist a slant tailored to the theater: "And as we the sooner believe that thing true, / For the trial whereof more witnesses we find, / So by the means of the Sacrament many grew / Believing creatures, where before they were blind" (1207–10).

For an impressive account of Shakespeare's theater as a model of radical political democracy, see Arnold, *Third Citizen.*

62. Barrow, *Writings . . . 1587–1590,* 529; "Certain Wicked Sects and Opinions," in Greenwood, *Writings . . . 1587–1590,* 296. Cf. Ainsworth in his *Counterpoyson* (1608): "It seemeth you count nothing *preaching* but that which is in the pulpit; nothing *the word of God,* but that which cometh out of your Minister's lips" (26).

63. Sanderson, *Works,* 1.312–13, 316–17. Thus conformists argued that church sacraments did not require homiletic accompaniment: in his authorized exposition of the Thirty-Nine Articles, *The English Creede* (1585–87), Thomas Rogers cites as an "error" the belief that "the sacrament is not a sacrament if it be not joined to the word of God preached" (*Catholic Doctrine,* 270–71).

64. Tyndale, *Exposicion,* 91. John Bradford (1562) more cautiously maintains that to pardon "such as offend us is *as* a sacrament," "for as certain as we are that we pardon them that offend us, so certain should we be that thou dost pardon us, whereof the forgiving our trespassers is, as it were, a sacrament unto us" (*Godlie Meditations,* 133; the first quotation, with my emphasis, is from a marginal note added to the 1567 edition).

65. *Henry V* 3.ch.34–35. While English reformers typically defined the sacraments as signs that "do exhibit and give the thing that they signify indeed" (Hooper, *Briefe and Clear Confession,* 45), they were also typically vague about how the sacraments "give" grace. Many Protestants regarded this vagueness as a matter of principle: thus Bradford declared that Christ's real spiritual presence is such "as reason knoweth not and the world cannot learn, nor any that looketh in this matter with other eyes, or heareth with other ears, than with the ears and eyes of the Spirit and of faith" ("Sermon," 96–97; see Dugmore, *Mass,* especially 202–47; and my epilogue, below). Other English Protestants expressed more definite thoughts on the matter, but the theory that I am attributing to Shakespeare, in which the sacraments convey the real presence of Christ by promoting a community of worshippers, was a minority opinion. John Frith's *Boke . . . Concerninge the Sacramente* (1533), the first "full exposition of the Lord's Supper from a Reforming point of view" written by an Englishman (Wright, *Works of John Frith,* 58), argues against any equation of Christ's body with the fellowship of communicants. Commenting on Paul's assertions in 1 Cor. 11 that "we, though we be many, are yet one bread and one body, inasmuch as we are partakers of one bread," Frith warns his readers, "Now may you not take Paul that he in this place should directly expound Christ's mind: And that the very exposition of Christ's words when he said, This is my body, should be that it was the fellowship of his body, (as some say, which seeking the key in this place of Paul, lock themselves so fast in, that they can find no way out)" (*Works,* 429). Nevertheless, Frith goes on to claim that the eucharistic "bread, and the eating of it in the place and fellowship where it is received, is more than common bread," because the bread is thereby tied to a congregational profession of faith (432).

Among English reformers, the gift of real presence was more often associated with the peculiarly *dramatic* nature of sacramental representation. To illustrate his claim that the sight of the sacrament "doth more efficaciously move than the bare words might do" (444), Frith cited the example of the Jews who "would not believe" the "words" of Jeremiah (Jer. 27) when he foretold their conquest and enslavement by Nebuchadnezzar: "And therefore he made a chain of fetters of wood, and put them about his neck, and prophesied again," "which thing did more vehemently work in them than the bare words could do" (444). In his *Apology*, Jewel asserted that the Lord's Supper places Christ's sacrifice "as it were, before our eyes" (*Works*, 3.62); similarly, Perkins (d. 1602) maintained that the sacraments "represent the mercies of God before our eyes" "because we are dull to conceive and remember them" otherwise (*Workes*, 1.7). These conventional Protestant sentiments demonstrate the error of thinking that the English church categorically privileged hearing over seeing.

66. Parsons, *Three Conversions*, 3.459; Verstegan to Parsons (1593), in *Letters*, 196; *Henry V* 2.1.11–12 and 3.6.78; *AM* 7.346; Parsons, *Three Conversions*, 3.117.

67. Hutchinson, *Works*, 243–44; cf. Dering, *Preparation*, D6r–D7r.

68. Cooper, *Answere*, 65–66. Parsons (1580) says the same of the mass: "the frequenting of this Sacrament, is the chiefest means to come to all grace, zeal, feeling, and life in spiritual matters" (*Brief Discourse*, 50r). For a powerful exposition of this sacrament-based ecclesiology in the English church, especially as Richard Hooker understood it, see Lake, *Anglicans and Puritans*.

69. *Henry V* 1.prologue.11–14, 2.prologue.16–17, 2.2.8, 1.prologue.16, 19–20 (my emphasis). Shakespeare's commitment to a semiotics of disparity makes him in some respects less indulgent toward the flesh, however, than were conformists such as Hooker (1597), who argued that a "sumptuous" place of worship "serveth as a sensible help to stir up devotion" (*Works*, 2.56–61).

Chapter Five

1. Spenser, *Works*, 8.115–20; Field and Wilcox, *Admonition*, 22. As Renwick notes in his edition of the *Complaints* (236–37), the *Admonition* also caricatures a minister who is in a hurry to witness or perhaps act in an "interlude" (B4v).

2. Scott, *Interpreter*, 12–13; Spenser, *Mother Hubberds Tale*, ll. 385–91.

3. Walsall, *Sermon*, E1v, E3r, E5v; Bolton, *Discourse*, 72–74; Stubbes, *Anatomie*, M1r.

4. Stubbes, *Anatomie*, L7v, L5v, L8r–M1r; Bellarmino, *De Controversiis*, vol. 1 (1590), 1.9.col.34, as cited in Anthony Raspa's edition of Donne's *Pseudo-Martyr*, 273. In the *Pseudo-Martyr* (1610), Donne translates Bellarmino's "semichristianus" as "Half-Christian" (12).

5. Randolph, *Muses' Looking Glass*, 23, 14, and 5. On the greater power of performance over "cold precepts" in animating virtue, see the famous protheatrical speech of the actor Paris in Massinger's *Roman Actor* (1626), 1.3.68–94.

6. *Looking Glass* 63, 3, 16; *ES* 4.321. In act 5 of the *Looking Glass*, Randolph does finally turn from the vices to the virtues, but he gives a speaking part only to "the mother of the Virtues," Mediocrity (86); the virtues themselves have a dance and then exit the stage without saying a word.

7. *Looking Glass* 4, 9–10.

8. *Looking Glass* 1, 38, 2–3. As William Whitaker, at that time perhaps the most admired apologist for the English church, declares in his *Disputatio de Sacra Scriptura* (1588), "it is absurd to dream of any public tribunal of the Holy Spirit; yea, the scriptures themselves plainly teach the contrary, that the testimony of the Holy Spirit is

only private, internal, and secret [privatum, internum, & arcanum]" (*Disputation*, 346; *Disputatio*, 254). If agnosticism about inwardness is thus not the "radical" Protestant development that Katharine Maus claims it to be, neither is its "theatrical analogue" wholly "secular" (*Inwardness*, 103), as I hope to show.

9. *Looking Glass* 15–16, 91–92.

10. R. C., "To Mr. Alexander Goughe," in Ford's *The Queen*, A3r; cited in Myers, *Representation*, 113.

11. Here I am quoting William Warner on the "guiles" of the puritans: "Their Art is feigning good they want, and hiding bad they have" (*Albions England* [1602], 238).

12. Francis Bacon, "Certain Observations Made Upon a Libel" (MS c. 1593; first published in the *Resuscitatio* [1657]), in *Works*, 8.178, 181. For official statements of the Queen's regard for the consciences of her subjects, see, e.g., Neale, *Elizabeth I*, 191–92; and Walsham, *Church Papists*, 11–12. Bunny, *Treatise*, 28. Admittedly, I am bending Elizabethan usage to call this a posture of "toleration," because Elizabethans generally applied the term to a full-scale allowance of another religion. Cf., e.g., Bacon: "there are two extremities in state concerning the causes of faith and religion; that is to say, the permission of the exercises of more religions than one, which is a dangerous indulgence and toleration; the other is the entering and sifting into men's consciences when no overt scandal is given, which is a rigorous and strainable inquisition; and I avouch the proceedings towards the pretended Catholics to have been a mean between these two extremities" ("Certain Observations," 164). For a magisterial sifting of the evidence on English theories of toleration, see W. K. Jordan's *Development of Religious Toleration in England*, which cites most of the sources on toleration I discuss.

13. Hooker, *Works*, 2.354 (my emphasis); Dent, *Plaine Mans Path-way*, 125. Jesuits such as Robert Parsons (1580) were equally appalled by the thought of conformist English Catholics, whom Parsons relentlessly attacked as dissemblers: "there is no enemy of the Catholic religion in the world, whether he be Gentile, Turk, Jew, or heretic, but that he must both think, and speak the worse of the said religion, seeing the professors of the same, are content for worldly policy to dissemble it, and leaving their own Churches, to present themselves to the Churches of their open and professed enemies" (*Brief Discourse*, 14v). On the discourse of church-papistry, see Walsham, *Church Papists*.

14. Sutton, *Summons*, 243. In his *A Key of Knowledge* (1617), Bernard argued that church-papists were paradoxically more dangerous than recusants because the self-betrayal of conformity had "revengefully enraged" them against church and state. Furthermore, church-papists could turn conformity itself into a weapon against zealous ministers:

> It is incredible, what a world of wrong and mischief is wrought upon the truth which we profess, and true professors thereof, by politic conformable Papists, upon the woeful advantage of certain Minister's inconformity. If such a fellow spy out a conscionable painful Minister, and find him obnoxious to the rigor of the law, but in the least point, . . . O then he plies the advantage with such malice and bitterness, by informations, aggravations, exasperations, fawning concurrence with Ecclesiastical Courts, until he have procured the putting out of that burning and shining lamp . . . and God knows, all this is done, not

for preservation of peace, as he publicly pretends; but for promotion of popery, which he secretly intends.(B3v–B4v)

15. Henry Barrow, "Four Causes of Separation" (MS c. 1587), in *Writings* . . .
1587–1590, 54; Francis Johnson to Lord Burghley, 8 January 1594, in Greenwood
and Barrow, *Writings . . . 1591–1593*, 452.

16. Aglionby is quoted in Hartley, ed., *Proceedings*, 1.240. Although Aglionby's
position did not carry the day in the 1571 Parliament, Elizabeth ultimately supported it; see Neale, *Elizabeth I*, 212–16. For Hooker, see *Works*, 2.354. Cf. John
Selden's later and more radical formulation of the same concept: "No man living can
tell whether I am fit to receive the Sacrament, for though I were fit the day before
when he examined me, at least appeared so to him, yet how can he tell what sin I may
have committed that night or the next morning, or what Impious Atheistical
thoughts I may have about me when I am approaching to the very Table?" (*Table-talk*
[published 1689], 149).

17. Bernard, *Christian Advertisements*, 185; Hooker, *Works*, 2.355, 354; Chillingworth, *Religion of Protestants*, 388; cf. the references in Dickens, *Reformation Studies*,
434–35.

18. Rom. 13.1; 1 Cor. 14.40; Downame, *Treatise*, 84–85; *The Examinations of
Henry Barrowe, John Grenewood, and John Penrie* (c. 1593–96), in Barrow, *Writings* . . .
1587–1590, 93–94. For a fine introduction to adiaphorism in England, see Verkamp,
Indifferent Mean. See also Coolidge, *Pauline Renaissance*, 23–54.

19. [Bancroft], "Certain Slanderous Speeches," 153, 109. John Bridges (1587)
went so far as to insist that conformists "dote not" on the currently prescribed ceremonies of the church, "but could well enough be content, so that by order and law
they were removed, and some other as comely and decent ceremonies, by her
Majesty's authority, and by our whole Church's consent, were orderly ordained in
their places" (*Defence*, 800; cited in Lake, *Anglicans and Puritans?*, 106).

20. Wither, *Britain's Remembrancer*, 265v. Taylor the Water Poet (1640) neatly
sums up this position in defending the practice of signing with the cross after baptism: " 'tis a decent and indifferent thing, / And from it doth no superstition spring, /
Yet not so indifferent any should withstand it; / It must be; for the King and Church
command it" (*Differing Worships*, 17–18).

21. Parker, *Briefe Examination* (1566), ****3v. Cf. Calvin (translated 1561): "it is
the part of a godly man to think, that free power in outward things is therefore
granted him, that he may be the freer to all duties of charity" (*Institution*, 3.19.12).
This Pauline emphasis on the need to temper one's Christian liberty with charity
was also turned against conformists, however. Henry Parker's *Discourse Concerning
Puritans* (1641), for instance, reproved conformists such as Hooker for promoting
"Uniformity in Ceremonies to the disadvantage of unity in hearts" (5):

Hooker that sweet and noble Antagonist of Ecclesiastical *Puritans* says much in
defense of the Church's authority in imposing of Ceremonies, but he says
nothing in defense of the Church's Charity in imposing many, and displeas-
ing Ceremonies. So S. *Paul* might have justified himself, as fitter to be sub-
scribed unto and complied withal than his scrupulous brother, and he might
have justified his case concerning eating such and such meats: but S. *Paul* in
wisdom, and Charity, would do neither. S. *Paul* made not his strength an Ar-

gument to make his brother yield who was weak, but he made his brother's weakness an Argument whereby to prevail and win upon him being strong. (40–41)

22. Bancroft, "Slanderous," 157. Bancroft paraphrases Parker, *Briefe Examination*, ***1v, although he adds the language of "charitable intentions."

23. Targoff anticipates this point when she reads Hamlet's advice that Gertrude should "assume a virtue, if you have it not" as congruent with orthodox Protestant accounts that church conformity can, like "use," "change the stamp of nature" (*Hamlet* 3.4.160–70); see Targoff, "Performance."

24. Bevington, *Tudor Drama and Politics*, 253; Tilney, quoted by Gabrieli and Melchiori in their edition of *Sir Thomas More*, 17. Richard Dutton in *Mastering the Revels* makes the same point about Tilney, but in concluding that Tilney's censorship was therefore "more pragmatic than doctrinaire," he overlooks the religious context for Tilney's leniency (81, 86).

25. Holinshed, *Chronicles* (1587), quoted in Gabrieli and Melchiori, eds., *Sir Thomas More*, 239.

26. *Sir Thomas More* 2.3.99–101. The reference to Paul actually appears in Shakespeare's revised version of 2.3, but since the original version of this scene has not survived, it is unclear whether Shakespeare adds the reference or simply retains it from the original.

27. *Sir Thomas More* 4.1.107–8, 79, 4.3.2–4, 4.2.83, 4.4.151–52, 155.

28. *Sir Thomas More* (2.3.157; my emphasis). When Surrey calls More "the most religious politician" in England (3.1.140), he is speaking more pointedly about More's conformism than modern usage of the terms *religious* and *politic* allows us to appreciate. The puritan Josias Nichols (1602) treats these words as opposites when he castigates a time-server in religion as a "neutral Politician" (*Plea*, Q1v, misnumbered 204). But, as I noted in chapter 1, conformists such as Wither recognized a pious sort of time-server who chose (in Parker's words) to moderate and qualify his liberty, according to charity toward his neighbor, and obedience to his prince:

Yea, wheresoe'er I am, I will suppose
The *Spirit* in that *Church* much better knows
What best that place befitteth, than I do:
And, I will live conformed thereunto,
In ev'ry thing that's merely politic,
And injures not the Doctrines *Catholic*.
(*Britain's Remembrancer*, 266v; misnumbered)

Gabrieli and Melchiori mistakenly assume that an interest in freedom of conscience aligns the play with puritans, nonconformists, and Roman Catholics (*Sir Thomas More*, 16).

29. Hartley, *Proceedings*, 240; *Sir Thomas More* 5.4.103–5.

30. These lines appear in the original version of the scene (3.1.14–15), which is written in the hand of Anthony Munday. In further notes I will try to indicate how Munday's version of *Sir Thomas More* is generally more pointed about conformism than are the revised versions of the play.

31. *Sir Thomas More* 3.1.46–48, 56, 73–74, 241. The revised scene makes Falkner an unrepentant believer in the essential relation between his inward and outward

states: he worries that he has lost his religion with his hair and been transformed into a "Brownist" (247) or a "Sar'cen" (258).

32. *Sir Thomas More* 3.2.143–44, 161–62, 268, 298, 295–96, 300–301, 274.

33. Stubbes in the *Anatomie* accuses players of being "double-dealing ambodexters" and "dissembling *Hypocrites*" (L5v), but the characterization is a commonplace.

34. *Sir Thomas More* 1.2.68, 2.3.184, 3.2.272, 3.1.40–41. More asks his servant to "act like a formal player our grave part" in the original version of the scene (3.1.25; *Sir Thomas More*, 215), where More urges his servant to "act thy part" (29–30), not "my part," as it is in the revised scene (45–46). Gabrieli and Melchiori gloss "formal player" as a "regular, professional actor" (*Sir Thomas More*, 215), but the phrase also suggests that players are people who manipulate forms. When More in the original scene with his servant instructs him to "dress" his "behavior / According to my carriage," and "beware / Thou talk not overmuch, for 'twill betray thee" (16–18), he offers advice about one's proper bearing toward magistrates that any conformist would endorse.

In some respects, the rebels seem more evocative of the professional players who enacted *Sir Thomas More* than More's disguised servant is. When Surrey warns the rebels that in the future they must "shun such lewd assemblies as beget / Unlawful riots, and such traitorous arts" (2.4.164–65), he echoes standard attacks on the public theaters.

35. *Sir Thomas More* 5.2.11–13. More, who is called "the best friend that the poor e'er had" (5.1.43; cf. 2.3.47, 63, and 5.1.12), responds to his downfall with an invariably cheerful contempt for material things, as when (in the original text) he assures his wife that his losses will not harm their children: "Say they be stripped from this poor painted cloth, / This outside of earth, left houseless, bare; / They have minds instructed how to gather more: / There's no man that's ingenuous can be poor" (4.4.41–44). Gabrieli and Melchiori gloss "painted cloth" as not only the rich hangings in More's house but "the world of outward appearances" generally (*Sir Thomas More*, 224); More also seems to mean his corporeal self.

In George Chapman's *Revenge of Bussy D'Ambois* (c. 1610), Clermont similarly commends playing for its power "To make the proudest outside that most swells, / With things without him, and above his worth, / See how small cause he has to be so blown up, / And the most poor man, to be griev'd with poorness, / Both being so easily borne by expert Actors" (1.1.346–50).

36. *Second Part of a Register*, 2.253; Martin Senior, *Just Censure*, in Pierce, ed., *Marprelate Tracts*, 353. Cf. Sir John Davies's epigram "In Mundayum" (c. 1590): "Munday I swear shall be a holiday / If he forswear himself but once a day" (Simpson, "Unprinted Epigrams," 50). *TN* 3.374.

37. Munday seems to have gathered material on More's life from confiscated Catholic manuscripts that would have been made available to him in his capacity as pursuivant; see Gabrieli and Melchiori, in their edition of *Sir Thomas More*, 8. *AM* 5.99. For a good introduction to the unsaintly side of More, see Elton, "Persecution and Toleration."

38. Jacob, *Confession*, E3r–v; cited in Jordan, *Development*, 2.239. Catholic writers had long argued, as Jacob does, for the state's toleration of "private" meetings. The anonymous author of *Leycesters Commonwealth* (1584) maintained, for instance, that the Spanish king allows the Flemish "to live quietly to God and themselves at home

in their own houses, so they perform otherwise their outward obedience and duties to their prince and country. Which only qualification, tolerance, and moderation in our realm (if I be not deceived, with many more than be of my opinion) would content all divisions, factions, and parties among us for their continuance in peace, be they Papists, Puritans, Familians, or of whatsoever nice difference or section besides" (185).

39. See Nicholl, *Reckoning*, especially 171–84. Nicholl does not mention the preacher-playwright Nicholas Grimald, who spied on Catholics during Edward's reign and betrayed Ridley, among other Protestants, during Mary's reign. "It will not sink into my head to think that Grimald would ever play me such a Judas's part," Ridley (1554) wrote from prison. See Merrill, ed., *Life and Poems*, 36–50.

40. *Selimus* 2.326–39. For the "Ralegh" verses, see Nicholl, *Reckoning*, 298–99; the redactors changed the "Gods" of *Selimus* to "God."

41. G[reene], *Refutation*, 63 [misnumbered 55]. Like many moralists of his day, Richard Rawlidge (1628) ranks playhouses with "Ale-houses," "Bawdy-houses," and "Dicing-houses," "of which, which are the most Receptacles of all manner of baseness and lewdness, is hard to be distinguish'd" (*Monster*, 2).

42. C[hettle]., *Kind Harts Dreame*, 44, 11, 42. This defense of the theater was ratified by no less an authority than Burghley, who, after hearing a case of cozenage in Star Chamber in 1596, ordered "those that make the plays to make a comedy hereof, & to act it with these names" (quoted in *ES* 1.267n.4).

43. *Dreame* 39, 44, 39–40. Cf. Nashe's *Pierce Penilesse* (1592) on playgoing as the only alternative to worse vices: "For whereas the afternoon being the idlest time of the day; wherein men that are their own masters . . . do wholly bestow themselves upon pleasure, and that pleasure they divide (how virtuously it skills not) either into gaming, following of harlots, drinking, or seeing a Play: is it not then better (since of four extremes all the world cannot keep them but they will choose one) that they should betake them to the least, which is Plays?" (*TN* 1.212). Chettle acknowledges his indebtedness to *Pierce* in *Dreame*, 44. Cf. Elizabeth Vere, writing to her uncle Robert Cecil about her husband the Earl of Derby in 1599 or 1600: "Being importuned by my Lord to entreat your favor that his man [Robert] Brown, with his company, may not be barred from their accustomed playing, in maintenance whereof they have consumed the better part of their substance, if so vain a matter shall not seem troublesome to you, I could desire that your furtherance might be a mean to uphold them, for that my Lord taking delight in them, it will keep him from more prodigal courses" (quoted in *ES* 2.127).

44. *Sir Thomas More* 1.2.1–2, 81; Munday, *Blast*, 115–16. For references to cutpurses at playhouses, see *ES* 1.264, 283, 304, 317; 2.403, 441, 447, 545–46; 3.376–77, and 387. For references to purse-cutting at sermons, see, e.g., Jonson, *Bartholomew Fair*, 3.5.120–21; and Massinger, *City Madam*, 3.1.57–58. Baker, *Theatrum*, 60; Dekker, *Jests to Make You Merie* (1607), in *Nondramatic Works*, 2.327, 334. Kemp offers this information about playhouse practices as he disavows any "acquaintance" with the two cutpurses who followed him during his famous dance from Norwich to London (*Kemps Nine Daies Wonder* [1600], quoted in *ES* 2.545–46n.3). *Sir Thomas More* 1.2.87–89 (my emphasis), 148, 92.

45. Heywood, *Apology*, A6r–A7r, B1r, C1v; Studley, *Refutation* (1635), 86–87. Laud too described plays as "things indifferent" (*Works*, 6.236).

46. *Answere for the Tyme*, 39–40. Cf. David Calderwood (1621) on the "ministering garments" of established clergymen: "They serve not for comeliness, and gravity, but are rather ridiculous, and stage-like, meeter for fools and comedians, than for ministers" (*Altar,* 216). For the conventional Protestant comparison of Catholic vestments to a player's garments, see Barish, *Antitheatrical Prejudice,* 159–65.

47. Crosse, *Vertues Common-wealth,* P2r. Cf. Gosson (1582): "if the outward use of things indifferent, as meats, be to be tied to the rule of charity, and not to be taken, when they offend the conscience of the weak; how much less ought we to join with idolaters in their plays, which are naught of themselves, & offensive to the godly?" (*Playes Confuted,* B8v). In his *Treatise of Conscience* (written, one assumes, before his death in 1602), William Perkins denied that plays were things indifferent, "for if it be not lawful to name vices, unless it be in the way of dislike, *Eph. 6.3.* much less is it warrantable to gesture and represent vice in the way of recreation and delight" (*Workes,* 1.539).

48. *TN* 1.213. Nashe had been much less tentative about attacking puritans when he had defended poetry in his preface to Greene's *Menaphon* (1589): see *TN* 3.321 and 323.

49. Field, "Letter," 116–17. At the time, Field was a member of the King's Men.

50. See Kaiser, in his edition of *The Puritan,* xl–xlii. All further citations of *The Puritan* refer to this edition.

51. *Puritan* 1.3.49–51, 1.4.101–3, 56–59, 124–32, 1.1.145–46, 2.1.209–14.

52. *Puritan* 1.4.24–25, 3.5.54–55, 1.2.78–82, 4.2.148–49.

53. *Sir Thomas More* 1.2.73–77; *Puritan* 3.5.73–74, 77. Puritans regularly emphasized how contradictory it was for conformists to attack outward piety as hypocrisy. As Parker's *Discourse Concerning Puritans* argued,

> The most ordinary badge of *Puritans* is their most religious and conscionable conversation, than that which is seen in other men's: and why this should make them odious or suspected of hypocrisy amongst honest and charitable men, I could never yet learn. A seeming religious consists in doing actions outwardly good, and the goodness of those actions is apparent to man: but the false hypocritical end of them is only discerned by God: and therefore with what conscience can I condemn that good which is visible, for that evil which is not visible? (58)

54. *Puritan* 1.2.133–34. Pieboard's bon mot anticipates the famous aphorism of the Cambridge Platonist Benjamin Whichcote (d. 1683): "The *Good Nature* of an Heathen is more God-like, than the furious *Zeal* of a Christian" (from *Moral and Religious Aphorisms* [1707], in Patrides, ed., *Cambridge Platonists,* 327–28). But the disparity between Whichcote's heathen and Pieboard's knave also highlights the peculiar inflection of antisectarian discourse in the theater.

55. Hooker, *Works,* 2.351–52; Middleton, *Family of Love,* 3.2.969–71. This claim about puritan stinginess was not entirely unfounded: see, e.g., Lake, "Charitable," 166–67.

56. Like his fellow conformists, however, Hooker did argue against the puritans that the preaching and sacraments of a knavish minister were valid. For Hooker's logic, see, e.g., his discussion of baptism by women in the fifth book of the *Lawes,* chap. 62.

The issue is the subject of article 26 in the *Thirty-Nine Articles*. For evidence that Pieboard was meant to suggest Peele, see Kaiser, ed., "*Puritan,*" xv–xvi and lvi–lxii.

57. *Puritan* 1.4.176–78. Although proceeding in large part from dimwittedness, such candid avowals separate Nicholas from the Pluses, as do his low class and his willingness to help Idle. Pieboard applauds Nicholas for his petty criminality— "Why now thou art a good Knave, worth a hundred Brownists"—to which Nicholas happily replies, "Am I indeed, la? I thank you truly, la" (3.5.299–301).

58. *Puritan* 3.3.11–12. For the association of puritans with serjeants in other Jacobean and Caroline plays, see Myers, *Representation,* 35 and 42. In *The Muses' Looking Glass,* Bird asks why players could not follow the more "thriving" and "honest" vocation of "Bailies, Promoters, Jailors, and Apparitors, / Beadles, and Marshal's men, the needful instruments / Of the Republic" (3).

59. *Puritan* 3.3.97–112, 3.4.71–74. For the identification of the gentleman as a magistrate, see Kaiser, ed., "*Puritan,*" 142.

60. *Puritan* 3.4.75, 16, 84–85, 180–81. The correlation of cozenage with a witty detachment from excrements is already suggested in *Sir Thomas More.* For instance, the day before his execution More passes kidney stones, and his servant asks if he should take More's urine to the doctor. "No, save thy labor," More replies, "we'll cozen him of a fee. / Thou shalt see me take a dram tomorrow morning, / Shall cure the stone I warrant" (5.3.28–30). As More's jailer comments, "In life and death, still merry Sir Thomas More" (21).

61. *Puritan* 1.4.241–42, 3.1.13–14, 1.4.87. The Oxford English Dictionary defines *formalist* as a term of abuse against conformists only, but Richard Brathwait in his *Good Wife* (1618) calls a "coy precisian" a "formalist" (B3r), and when Wither in *Britain's Remembrancer* bemoans the "fained zeal, and affectation" that has "fool'd this formal *Generation*" (241r), he means to criticize both neuters and puritans (246v–247r).

The joke that puritans place "religion in their garments" (Jonson, *Every Man Out of His Humor,* Induction 42) receives perhaps its earliest extensive theatrical treatment in *The Pilgrimage to Parnassus* (c. 1598).

62. Randolph, *Hey for Honesty,* 4.2.

63. *City Match* 2.1.12–14, 2.2.5–14, 1.1.9–20, 1.4.37–64, 3.3.22, 1.4.14, 3.3.31, 4.2.12–14.

64. *City Match* 5.3.33. For a whore as wearing men like clothes, see 2.1.9–10.

65. *City Match* 5.9.50, 99–101, 1.1.14, 5.9.40.

66. Barrow, *Writings . . . 1587–1590,* 65. "A strange doctrine it is," Barrow (1590) elsewhere writes, "to sever the conscience, and the law; the conscience, and the outward action; they may as well here whiles we live sever the body and the soul, which though they are distinct things, yet can they not be here separate" (413).

67. "To the Reader," 3–4, 7–8; "Prologue at Black-friars," 17–18; "Epilogue at White-hall," 15–16; "Prologue to the King and Queen," 15–22.

68. Shirley, *The Sisters,* in *Six New Playes,* 1–3.

69. *City Match* 2.2.30–34, 1.3.40, 1.4.58–61, 4.2.8. Plotwell's last line in the play does refer to his "blest stars" (5.8.114), however. For "metamorphosis" and "transmutation" as a matter of dress, see, e.g., 1.4.21–26, 3.3.74–77, and 3.4.82–83. A running joke in the play is the claim that the doltish Timothy can be improved without

much ado: thus Plotwell assures his sister that "one month of your / Sharp conversation will refine him" (2.4.61–62; cf. 3.2.164–67 and 4.2.25–30).

70. *City Match* 2.2.33–37.

71. Wright, *Five Sermons*, 39, 53. Hausted betrayed the difference between conformist theory and practice: in the midst of one apparently offensive sermon in 1634, he was dragged from the pulpit, "drawn through the street" by a mob that his superior described as "the greatest uproar and concourse of people that ever I saw at any arraignment," and thereafter suspended from preaching. See Mills, *Peter Hausted*, 38–42.

72. Randolph, *Looking Glass*, 2.

73. Mayne, *City Match*, "To the Reader," 11–13; [Anderton?], *Epigrammes*, 77–83. The Protestant Edward Fowler (1670) later denounced Latitudinarians as "people, whose only Religion it is to temporize, & transform themselves into any Shape for their Secular interests; and that judge no Doctrine so Saving, as that which obligeth [them] to so complying and condescending a humor, as to become all things to all men, that so by any means they may gain something" (Fowler, *Principles*, 8–9, cited in Griffin, *Latitudinarianism*, 6). For a conformist attack (1637) on puritans as becoming all things to all men "not with the same intention of the Apostle, to *gain some*, but to *betray all*," see Sydenham, *Sermons*, 271.

74. T. C., "To Mr. Goughe," in Ford, *The Queen*, A4r; the poem is cited in Myers, *Representation*, 113. In the Prologue to *The Ordinary* (c. 1635), Cartwright himself declares that the stage uses "sublimated follies" to "cheat those men / That first did vent them" (15–19). Cf. Henry Ramsay in *Jonsonus Virbius* (1638): "Who now will *plot* to *cozen Vice*, and tell / The *Trick* and *Policy* of *doing well?*" (*HS* 11.472).

75. Mayne, *Sermon*, 33, 32, 43–44. Taking the opposite stance, Bernard in *The Faithfull Shepheard* (1607) blames the lack of "seemly gesture" in some preachers on their past experience as actors: such preachers employ "vain and fantastical motions ridiculously in a Pulpit, which they have used in profane pastimes" (89).

76. Mayne, *Sermon*, 56–57; Hausted, *Rival Friends*, 7. It is interesting to note that Hausted wrote a mock-confessional poem "in amputationem comae suae," "on the cutting of his hair," which begins,

> Away pernicious excrement be gone,
> Thou hast betray'd my reputation
> To the sincere, and perfect, thou alone
> Link'd with that hellhound thy companion
> Good fellowship, hast caused each good man
> For to despair of my conversion.
> But I disclaim you both, and with you, all
> Those ruffian-like behaviors mimical,
> And apish gestures which in times before
> Have been a scandal to the cloth I wore.
> (quoted in Mills, *Peter Hausted*, 14)

Epilogue

1. Jonson, "To the Immortal Memory and Friendship of That Noble Pair, Sir Lucius Cary and Sir H. Morison," 82 (*HS* 8.245); Gomersall, *Tragedie*, A5v.

2. I quote the 1563 edition of the *Acts* as reprinted in Frith, *Work*, 494 and 519–20.

3. I quote from the original edition of the "Articles," appended to Frith's *Boke . . . Concerninge the Sacramente* (1533), in Frith, *Work*, 450–55. Foxe's version (*AM* 5.11–14) is different in many respects.

Verkamp is seriously mistaken when he claims that "few English reformers would seem to have concurred in Tyndale's and Frith's adiaphoristic designation of the doctrine of the Eucharistic presence" (*Indifferent Mean*, 99). For some early supporters, see Dickens, *Reformation Studies*, 431–32; for Hooker's agreement with Frith, see chap. 1, above; for Foxe, see Frith, *Work*, 519–21.

4. The language of Foxe's version is stronger: "here peradventure many would marvel" (*AM* 5.13).

5. Verkamp notes that "none" of the English reformers ever gave "any formal attention" to the question whether the "doctrine of adiaphoristic liberty" was itself adiaphoric (*Indifferent Mean*, 99).

6. By "Almains" Frith meant the Swiss, or "Helvetians," as Foxe has it (*AM* 5.14).

7. In his *Boke . . . Concerninge the Sacramente*, Frith stated that "men cannot be joined into any kind of religion, whether it be true or false, except they be knit in fellowship by some visible tokens or sacraments" (*Work*, 332).

8. Wright discusses Frith's "good humor" in his edition of the *Work*, 25–27. The alepole analogy appears in Frith's book on the sacrament (*Work*, 334).

9. *AM* 5.6; in the 1583 *Acts*, Foxe praises Elizabeth for allowing "such liberty of conscience without danger professed" (1.xxxiv).

10. Mayne, *City Match* 1.4.58, 2.1.24–25, and 2.2.18–24.

11. Frith, *Work*, 541–43; Mayne, *Sermon*, 33–34. Bale (1548) reported that "in the midst of the fire" Frith "showed the eagerness of Stephen on his face" (quoted in Frith, *Work*, 505); Foxe (1563) claimed that "when as the faggots and fire were cast unto him, he willingly embraced the same" (quoted in Frith, *Work*, 523).

12. Gomersall, *Levites Revenge*, A4r; the clergyman-playwright was Barten Holyday. Gomersall adds that Holyday's "divinity" "makes every place where you will vouchsafe to discourse, to be a pulpit." The dedicatory epistle to Gomersall's *Sermons on St Peter* (1634) also defends wit in preaching: according to the epistle, a sermon must consist of "pleasing words, no less than saving words" (A3r).

13. Mayne, commendatory letter (dated 1653) to Richard Whitlock's *Zootomia* (1654), n.p., cited in *JCS* 4.845; Puller, *Moderation*, A6r–A7r. Upon his return to Oxford, Mayne did not take up playwrighting again, but he did continue to champion the idea of theatrical training for clergymen. In 1664 Anthony à Wood groused that Mayne encouraged a "strange degree and strain of impudence" in a group of undergraduate players at Oxford by "commending them for their ingenuity" and assuring them that "he liked well an acting student," even as they were engaging in what Wood called "drunkenness and wantonness" after their performance (*Life and Times*, 2.2).

14. Hamilton, *Shakespeare*, 86; Shakespeare, *Twelfth Night*, 3.2.31–32, 1.5.217–28, 2.3.140–42, 3.2.70–73, and 5.1.365. Maria tricks Malvolio into getting himself imprisoned in the first place by inducing him to believe that he should do "nothing but smile" (3.4.11).

15. Hamilton, *Shakespeare*, 97, 89, 96. More precisely, Hamilton regards the play as a satire against "church officials" as opposed to "church members" (109)—an odd claim when one considers that Malvolio's enemies include the decidedly nonclerical

Sir Toby, Sir Andrew, Feste, and Maria. Cf. Shuger, "Review," 492–93. The demonization of puritans had its lay promoters too, I am arguing.

16. Hamilton, *Shakespeare*, 94 and 100; for Hamilton's view that "ultimately [Shakespeare] shapes his material" into "a critique of the conformist policies which . . . fostered separation from the church," see 107. This partial reading and its singular emphasis on "the machinery of the ecclesiastical court system" (88) aside, Hamilton anticipates my own point about the play: she too believes that Shakespeare wants to stress "what church members have in common" (107).

17. Shakespeare, *Twelfth Night*, 3.4.115–22, 3.1.26–27, 62–63, and 1.5.86–88. Feste himself subscribes to the theory that wit must observe decorum: "Apt, in good faith, very apt" (1.5.26), he replies to a quip of Maria's. "Good" is often a synonym for "apt" in the play, and in 2.3 Shakespeare places this merry "goodness" in tension with, though not exactly in opposition to, "good life" (35–71).

18. *Twelfth Night*, 3.1.1–10. Olivia and Sebastian are married at "the chantry by"—that is, nearby (4.3.24). For a different account of how the play "approximates an Anglican perspective," see Hunt, "Religion."

19. Greenblatt, *Shakespearean Negotiations*, 94, 125–27; *Hamlet in Purgatory*, 3, 256–57. In the *Hamlet* book, Greenblatt seems less committed than in *Shakespearean Negotiations* to the idea that "Shakespeare was participating in a secularization process." He maintains that the "palpable effect" of *Hamlet* "is something like the reverse": "*Hamlet* immeasurably intensifies a sense of the weirdness of the theater, its proximity to certain experiences that had been organized and exploited by religious institutions and rituals" (253). But it is not clear how this sense of enchantment counts for Greenblatt as nonsecular.

20. *Twelfth Night* 1.5.56 and 3.4.1–5. Ian Green notes that "the English authorities were all in favor of catechizing in school and home"; see his *Christian's ABC*, 170–229.

21. *Henry V* 1.1.10 and 80.

22. Bloom, *Shakespeare*, 716 and xvii.

23. Bloom, *Shakespeare*, 3, 716; Oldisworth, "A Letter to Ben. Jonson. 1629," MS quoted in *HS* 11.396 (information about Oldisworth may be found at *HS* 11.398 and the *DNB* entry for his brother Giles); Herrick, "Prayer," quoted in *HS* 11.415; Sheppard, "The Poet's Invitation to *Ben Jonson's* Ghost to Appear Again," quoted in *HS* 11.503; West, "On Mr. Ben. Johnson.," quoted in *HS* 11.468; George Fortescue, "To the Immortalitie of My Learned Friend, M. Jonson," quoted in *HS* 11.446; Holyday as quoted in *JCS* 4.596; and Jonson, *Timber; HS* 8.583–84. West's and Fortescue's poems appeared in *Jonsonus Virbius*, which offered many other instances of seemingly sacrilegious praise for Jonson: e.g., "Why should not we, learn'd *JONSON*, thee allow / An Altar, at the least?" (*HS* 11.437); "Be thou propitious, *Poetry* shall know, / No *Deity* but *Thee* to whom I'll owe" (443); and finally, the playwright Marmion wonders "Where His Star shines, and what part of the Sky / Holds His compendious Divinity, / There He is fixt, I know it, 'cause from thence, / My self have lately receiv'd influence" (465).

Appendix Two

1. See Carroll, *Fat King*, 168–79; Mowat, "Rogues."

2. Bishop Pilkington writes in 1562 that "in England, after Wycliffe's death, when

persecution arose, . . . some fled into Bohemia and brought the gospel thither, where it continues to this day" (*Works*, 264; cf. 654). Foxe's *Acts and Monuments* has a long section on the history of reformation in Bohemia (3.405–579).

3. One of Autolycus's customers marvels that "you would think a smock were a she-angel, he so chaunts to the sleeve-hand and the work about the square on't" (4.4.208–10). David Kaula rightly describes Autolycus's cozenages as having "'popish' associations" ("Autolycus' Trumpery," 292), but he does not register that Bohemia is where a "popish" superstition is exposed as such.

4. Kaula makes a similar point ("Autolycus' Trumpery," 301–3).

5. Cf., e.g., Lake, *Probe*, 1–2, who adds that "without faith" it is "impossible" for the communicant "to live" either, "because Christ, the only food of life, cannot otherwise be fed on."

6. "Faith" is defined as romantic constancy at 4.4.34 and 460, while in the next scene Perdita is said to possess such beauty that, "would she begin a sect, might quench the zeal / Of all professors else, make proselytes / Of who she but bid follow" (5.1.107–9).

7. Shakespeare repeatedly presents Autolycus as a debased version of a professional player: aside from the fact that his deceits are criminal, he once worked as a puppetmaster (4.3.96–97) and now sells ballads. Yet Autolycus does choose to support the "play" (4.4.655) of Perdita and Florizel's escape as a kind of professional courtesy (4.4.679–83). For a repertory reference to the seeming baseness yet actual gentility of Shakespeare's company, see 4.4.337–39.

Appendix Three

1. Targoff notes a similar relation between poetic stealth and spiritual edification in George Wither's *Preparation to the Psalter* (1619): according to Wither, "there lurks in *Poesy* an enchanting sweetness, that steals into the hearts of men before they be aware" (9; cited in Targoff, *Common Prayer*, 83).

2. Greene, *Notable Discovery*, 39; cf. *TN* 1.257 and Chapman's *Monsieur D'Olive* 4.2.40.

A, C, Mery Talys. [London, 1526?].

Adams, Thomas. *The Gallants Burden.* London, 1612.

Agnew, Jean-Christophe. *Worlds Apart: The Market and the Theater in Anglo-American Thought, 1550–1750.* Cambridge: Cambridge University Press, 1986.

Ainsworth, Henry. *Counterpoyson.* [Amsterdam], 1608.

[Ainsworth, Henry, and Francis Johnson]. *A True Confession of the Faith.* [Amsterdam?], 1596.

Alexander, William, Earl of Stirling. *Doomes-day.* 1614. In *Poetical Works,* ed. L. E. Kastner and H. B. Charlton. 2 vols. Edinburgh and London: William Blackwood & Sons, 1921–29. Vol. 2, 1–379.

Allen, William. *An Admonition to the Nobility and People of England and Ireland.* 1588. New York: Scolar, 1971.

———. *A True, Sincere, and Modest Defense of English Catholics.* 1584. In *The Execution of Justice by William Cecil and A True, Sincere, and Modest Defense of English Catholics by William Allen,* ed. Robert M. Kingdon. Ithaca: Cornell University Press, 1965.

Altman, Joel. "'Vile Participation': The Amplification of Violence in the Theater of *Henry V.*" *Shakespeare Quarterly* 42 (1991): 1–32.

[Ames, Richard?]. *A Search after Wit.* London, 1691.

Ames, William [d. 1633]. *Conscience with the Power and Cases Thereof.* Translation of *De conscientia.* [Leyden and London], 1639.

Anderson, Benedict. *Imagined Communities: Reflections on the Origin and Spread of Nationalism.* 1983; rev. ed., London: Verso, 1991.

[Anderton, James?]. *Epigrammes.* [Rouen, not after 1633].

An Answere for the Tyme. [Rouen?], 1566.

Arnold, Oliver. *The Third Citizen: Shakespeare's Theater, the Early Modern House of Commons, and the Tragedy of Political Representation.* Baltimore: Johns Hopkins University Press, forthcoming.

Auksi, Peter. *Christian Plain Style: The Evolution of a Spiritual Ideal.* Montreal: McGill-Queen's University Press, 1995.

Awdeley, John. *The Cruel Assault of Gods Fort.* London, [c. 1560].

———. *The Fraternitie of Vacabondes.* 1565. In Kinney, ed., *Rogues,* 91–101.

———. *A Godly Ditty or Prayer to be Song unto God for the Preservation of His Church, Our Queene and Realme, Against All Traytours, Rebels, and Papisticall Enemies.* London, [1569?].

———. *The Wonders of England.* London, [1559].

Aydelotte, Frank. *Elizabethan Rogues and Vagabonds.* 1913; rpt., New York: Barnes & Noble, 1967.

Bacon, Francis. *Works.* Ed. James Spedding, Robert Leslie Ellis, and Douglas Denn Heath. 14 vols. 2nd ed. London, 1870–72.

Baker, David J. *Between Nations: Shakespeare, Spenser, Marvell, and the Question of Britain*. Stanford: Stanford University Press, 1997.

Baker, Sir Richard. *Theatrum Redivivum, or the Theatre Vindicated*. Written c. 1635–37, published 1662. New York: Garland, 1973.

Bald, R. C. *John Donne: A Life*. Oxford: Oxford University Press, 1970.

Bale, John. *The Complete Plays of John Bale*. Ed. Peter Happé. 2 vols. Cambridge: D. S. Brewer, 1986.

———. *An Expostulation or Complaynte Agaynste the Blasphemyes of a Franticke Papyst of Hamshyre*. London, [1552?].

———. *The Image of Both Churches*. c. 1545. In *Select Works of John Bale*, ed. Henry Christmas. Cambridge, 1849.

———. *King Johan*. MS c. 1538, rev. c. 1547–60. Ed. Barry B. Adams. San Marino: Huntington Library, 1969.

Bale, John, ed. *The Laboryouse Journey & Serche of Johan Leylande, for Englandes Antiquitees*. London, [1549].

[Bancroft, Richard]. "Certain Slanderous Speeches against the Present Estate of the Church of England." MS c. 1583–85. In *Tracts Ascribed to Richard Bancroft*, ed. Albert Peel. Cambridge: Cambridge University Press, 1953. 22–169.

[Bancroft, Richard]. *A Sermon Preached at Paules Crosse*. London, 1588 [1589].

Barber, C. L. *Creating Elizabethan Tragedy: The Theater of Marlowe and Kyd*. Ed. Richard P. Wheeler. Chicago: University of Chicago Press, 1988.

———. "The Family in Shakespeare's Development: Tragedy and Sacredness." In *Representing Shakespeare: New Psychoanalytic Essays*, ed. Murray M. Schwartz and Coppelia Kahn. Baltimore: Johns Hopkins University Press, 1980. 188–202.

Barber, C. L., and Richard Wheeler. *The Whole Journey: Shakespeare's Powers of Development*. Berkeley: University of California Press, 1986.

Barish, Jonas. *The Antitheatrical Prejudice*. Berkeley: University of California Press, 1981.

———. "War, Civil War, and *Bruderkrieg* in Shakespeare." In *Literature and Nationalism*, ed. Vincent Newey and Ann Thompson. Savage, Md.: Barnes & Noble, 1991. 11–21.

Barrow, Henry. *The Writings of Henry Barrow, 1587–1590*. Ed. Leland H. Carlson. London: George Allen & Unwin, 1962.

———. *The Writings of Henry Barrow, 1590–1591*. Ed. Leland H. Carlson. London: George Allen & Unwin, 1966.

Barry, Lording. *Ram Alley*. 1607–8. Ed. Claude Jones. Louvain: Libraire Universitaire, 1952.

Barton, Anne. *Ben Jonson, Dramatist*. Cambridge: Cambridge University Press, 1984.

Basset, Bernard. *The English Jesuits from Campion to Martindale*. London: Burns & Oates, 1967.

Bastwick, John. *The Answer [The Second Part of the Letany]*. [Leiden], 1637.

Bate, John. *The Portraiture of Hypocrisie*. London, 1589.

Battenhouse, Roy. *Marlowe's Tamburlaine: A Study in Renaissance Moral Philosophy*. Nashville: Vanderbilt University Press, 1941.

———. *Shakespearean Tragedy: Its Art and Its Christian Premises*. Bloomington: Indiana University Press, 1969.

Battenhouse, Roy, ed. *Shakespeare's Christian Dimension: An Anthology of Commentary.* Bloomington: Indiana University Press, 1994.

Baumer, Franklin Le Van. "The Church of England and the Common Corps of Christendom." *Journal of Modern History* 16 (1944): 1–21.

———. "The Conception of Christendom in Renaissance England." *Journal of the History of Ideas* 6 (1944): 131–56.

———. "England, the Turk, and the Common Corps of Christendom." *American Historical Review* 50 (1944): 26–48.

Baxter, Richard. *A Christian Directory.* London, 1673.

Bayly, Lewis. *The Practise of Pietie.* 1st ed., c. 1611. 3rd ed. London, 1613.

Beaumont, Francis, and John Fletcher. *Fifty Comedies and Tragedies.* London, 1679.

Beaumont, Joseph. *Psyche.* London, 1648.

Becon, Thomas. *A Comparison Betwene the Lordes Supper, and the Popes Masse.* 1563. In Becon, *Works,* vol. 3, 351–95.

———. *The Displayeng of the Popishe Masse.* 1563. In Becon, *Works,* vol. 3, 251–86.

———. *An Humble Supplication Unto God.* 1554. In Becon, *Works,* vol. 3, 223–50.

———. *A New Catechisme.* 1564. In Becon, *Works,* vol. 2, 1–410.

———. *Works.* Vol. 1: *Early Works;* vol. 2: *The Catechism;* vol. 3: *Prayers.* Ed. John Ayre. 3 vols. Cambridge, 1844.

Behn, Aphra. *The Works of Aphra Behn.* Ed. Janet M. Todd. 7 vols. Columbus: Ohio State University Press, 1992–96.

Beier, A. L. *Masterless Men: The Vagrancy Problem in England 1560–1640.* London: Methuen, 1985.

Bellarmino, Roberto. *Disputationes de Controversiis Christianae Fidei Adversus Huius Temporis Haereticos.* Vol. 1. Ingolstadt, 1590.

Bentley, G. E. *The Jacobean and Caroline Stage.* 7 vols. Oxford: Clarendon Press, 1941–68.

———. *The Professions of Dramatist and Player in Shakespeare's Time, 1590–1642.* 2 vols. in 1 (*The Profession of Dramatist in Shakespeare's Time* [1971] and *The Profession of Player in Shakespeare's Time* [1984]). Princeton: Princeton University Press, 1986.

Berlin, Normand. *The Base String: The Underworld in Elizabethan Drama.* Rutherford, N.J.: Fairleigh Dickinson University Press, 1968.

Bernard, Richard. *Christian Advertisements and Counsels of Peace.* London, 1608.

———. *The Faithfull Shepheard.* London, 1607.

———. *A Key of Knowledge.* London, 1617.

———. *Two Twinnes.* London, 1613.

Bernard, Richard, trans. *Terence in English.* Cambridge, 1598.

Bevington, David. *Tudor Drama and Politics: A Critical Approach to Topical Meaning.* Cambridge: Harvard University Press, 1968.

Bietenholz, Peter G. *History and Biography in the Work of Erasmus of Rotterdam.* Geneva: Librairie Droz, 1966.

Blackburn, Ruth. *Biblical Drama under the Tudors.* The Hague: Mouton, 1971.

Bland, Tobias. *A Baite for Momus.* London, 1589.

Blench, J. W. *Preaching in England in the Late Fifteenth and Sixteenth Centuries: A Study of English Sermons 1450–c. 1600.* Oxford: Basil Blackwell, 1964.

Bloom, Harold. *Shakespeare: The Invention of the Human.* New York: Riverhead Books, 1998.

———. *The Western Canon: The Books and School of the Ages.* New York: Harcourt Brace, 1994.

Bolton, Robert. *A Discourse About the State of True Happiness.* London, 1611.

———. *Some Generall Directions for a Comfortable Walking with God.* 1625; 5th ed. London, 1638.

Bond, Ronald, ed. *"Certain Sermons or Homilies" (1547) and "A Homily Against Disobedience and Wilful Rebellion" (1570): A Critical Edition.* Toronto: University of Toronto Press, 1987.

The Booke of the Common Prayer, and Administracion of the Sacramentes, and Other Rites and Ceremonies of the Churche After the Use of the Churche of England. 1549. Reprinted in *The First Prayer-book of King Edward VI.* London, 1888.

Boyle, Marjorie O'Rourke. *Rhetoric and Reform: Erasmus' Civil Dispute with Luther.* Cambridge, Mass.: Harvard University Press, 1983.

Bradbrook, Muriel C. *The Rise of the Common Player: A Study of Actor and Society in Shakespeare's England.* Cambridge, Mass.: Harvard University Press, 1962.

Bradford, John. *Godly Meditations.* 1562; London, 1567.

———. *The Writings of John Bradford.* Ed. Aubrey Townsend. 2 vols. Parker Society. Cambridge, 1848–53.

Bradley, Jesse Franklin, and Joseph Quincy Adams, eds. *The Jonson Allusion-Book: A Collection of Allusions to Ben Jonson from 1597 to 1700.* New Haven: Yale University Press, 1922.

[Brathwait, Richard]. *Anniversaries upon his Panarete, Continued. . . . The Second Yeeres Annivers.* London, 1635.

———. *The Good Wife.* London, 1618.

———. *Whimzies: Or, A New Cast of Characters.* London, 1631.

Braunmuller, A. R., and Michael Hattaway, eds. *The Cambridge Companion to English Renaissance Drama.* Cambridge: Cambridge University Press, 1990.

Brereley, John [Lawrence Anderton?]. *The Protestants Apologie for the Roman Church.* [St. Omer], 1608.

Bridges, John. *A Defence of the Government Established in the Churche of England for Ecclesiasticall Matters.* London, 1587.

Bristow, Richard. *A Brief Treatise.* Antwerp, 1574. *English Recusant Literature,* vol. 209.

Brome, Alexander. "Upon the Ingenious Comedies of Mr. Richard Brome." 1653. In *Alexander Brome: Poems,* ed. Roman R. Dubinski. 2 vols. Toronto: University of Toronto Press, 1982. Vol. 1, 380–81.

Brome, Richard. *A Jovial Crew: or, The Merry Beggars.* Acted c. 1641, published 1652. Ed. Ann Haaker. Lincoln: University of Nebraska Press, 1968.

———. *The Weeding of Covent Garden.* Acted c. 1633, published 1659. In *A Critical Edition of "The Weeding of Covent Garden" and "The Sparagus Garden,"* ed. Donald S. McClure. New York: Garland, 1980.

[Broughton, Richard]. *A Booke Intituled: The English Protestants Recantation.* [Douai], 1617.

Browne, Robert. *The True and Short Declaration.* 1584. In *The Writings of Robert Harrison and Robert Browne,* ed. Albert Peel and Leland H. Carlson. London: George Allen & Unwin, 1953.

Brownlow, F. W. "John Shakespeare's Recusancy: New Light on an Old Document." *Shakespeare Quarterly* 40 (1989): 186–91.

Bullinger, Heinrich. *Fiftie Godlie and Learned Sermons.* Trans. H. I. (1577) from *Sermonum decades quinque* (1549–51). In *The Decades of Henry Bullinger,* ed. Thomas Harding. 4 vols. Parker Society. Cambridge, 1849–52.

Bunny, Edmund. *A Treatise Tending to Pacification.* Appended to *A Booke of Christian Exercise,* by R[obert]. P[arsons]. London, 1584.

Burckhardt, Sigurd. *Shakespearean Meanings.* Princeton: Princeton University Press, 1968.

Burton, Robert. *The Anatomy of Melancholy.* 1st ed. Oxford, 1621.

Bury, John. *The Moderate Christian.* London, 1631.

Butler, Martin. "Ecclesiastical Censorship of Early Stuart Drama: The Case of Jonson's *The Magnetic Lady.*" *Modern Philology* 89 (1992): 469–81.

———. *Theatre and Crisis 1632–1642.* Cambridge: Cambridge University Press, 1984.

C., R. *The Times Whistle.* MS c. 1615. Ed. J. M. Cowper. London, 1871.

Cain, William E. "Self and Others in Two Poems by Ben Jonson." *Studies in Philology* 80 (1983): 163–82.

Cairns, David, and Shaun Richards. *Writing Ireland: Colonialism, Nationalism and Culture.* Manchester: Manchester University Press, 1988.

Calderwood, David. *The Altar of Damascus.* [Amsterdam?], 1621.

Calvin, Jean. *A Commentarie Upon S. Paules Epistles to the Corinthians.* Trans. Thomas Tymme from *Pauli Epistolas* (1551). London, 1577.

———. *In Omnes D. Pauli Epistolas.* Geneva, 1551.

———. *The Institution of Christian Religion.* Trans. T[homas]. N[orton]. from *Institutio Christianae Religionis* (1536–59). London, 1561.

Campbell, Lily B. *Divine Poetry and Drama in Sixteenth-Century England.* 1959; rpt., Berkeley: University of California Press, 1961.

Candido, Joseph. "Blots, Stains, and Adulteries: The Impurities in *King John.*" In Curren-Aquino, ed., *King John,* 114–25.

Canne, John. *A Necessitie of Separation from the Church of England, Proved by the Nonconformists Principles.* 1634. Ed. Charles Stovel. London, 1849.

Carroll, William C. *Fat King, Lean Beggar: Representations of Poverty in the Age of Shakespeare.* Ithaca: Cornell University Press, 1996.

Cartwright, Thomas. *A Confutation of the Rhemists Translation.* [Leiden], 1618.

Cartwright, William. *Comedies, Tragi-Comedies, With Other Poems.* London, 1651.

———. *The Plays and Poems of William Cartwright.* Ed. G. Blakemore Evans. Madison: University of Wisconsin Press, 1951.

Casaubon, Meric. *A Treatise Concerning Enthusiasme.* London, 1655 [1654].

Cawdrey, Robert. *A Short and Fruitfull Treatise, of the Profit and Necessitie of Catechising.* 1580; rev. ed., London, 1604.

Chalfant, Fran C. *Ben Jonson's London: A Jacobean Placename Dictionary.* Athens: University of Georgia Press, 1978.

Chamberlain, John. *The Letters of John Chamberlain.* Ed. Norman Egbert McClure. 2 vols. Philadelphia: American Philosophical Society, 1939.

Chambers, E. K. *The Elizabethan Stage.* 4 vols. Oxford: Clarendon Press, 1923.

Champion, Larry S. "'Havoc in the Commonwealth': Perspective, Political Ideology, and Dramatic Strategy in *Sir John Oldcastle* and the English Chronicle Plays." *Medieval and Renaissance Drama in England* 5 (1991): 165–79.

———. "The 'Un-end' of *King John:* Shakespeare's Demystification of Closure." In Curren-Aquino, ed., *King John*, 173–85.

Chapman, George. *The Plays of George Chapman: The Comedies.* Ed. Alan Holaday. Urbana: University of Illinois Press, 1970.

———. *The Plays of George Chapman: The Tragedies.* Ed. Allan Holaday et al. Woodbridge, Suffolk: D. S. Brewer, 1987.

C[hettle]., H[enry]. *Kind Harts Dreame.* 1592. Ed. G. B. Harrison. 1923; rpt., Edinburgh: Edinburgh University Press, 1966.

Chillingworth, William. *The Religion of Protestants.* 1638. In *The Works of William Chillingworth.* Philadelphia, 1840.

Clapham, John. "Certain Observations Concerning the Life and Reign of Queen Elizabeth." MS 1603. In *Elizabeth of England*, ed. Evelyn Plummer Read and Conyers Read. Philadelphia: University of Pennsylvania Press, 1951.

Clare, Janet. *"Art Made Tongue-Tied by Authority": Elizabethan and Jacobean Dramatic Censorship.* Manchester: Manchester University Press, 1990.

Clark, Arthur Melville. *Thomas Heywood: Playwright and Miscellanist.* 1958; rpt., New York: Russell & Russell, 1967.

Clark, Ira. *Professional Playwrights: Massinger, Ford, Shirley, and Brome.* Lexington: University Press of Kentucky, 1992.

Coghill, Nevill. "Comic Form in *Measure for Measure.*" *Shakespeare Survey* 8 (1955): 14–27.

Coleridge, Samuel. *Shakespearean Criticism.* Ed. Thomas M. Raysor. 2 vols. London: Dent, 1960.

Collections of the Malone Society. Vol. 2, pt. 3. Oxford: Oxford University Press, 1931.

Colley, Linda. "Shakespeare and the Limits of National Culture." Hayes Robinson Lecture Series 2. Egham, Surrey: Royal Holloway, University of London, 1999.

Collinson, Patrick. "Ben Jonson's *Bartholomew Fair:* The Theater Constructs Puritanism." In *The Theatrical City: Culture, Theatre and Politics in London, 1576–1649*, ed. David L. Smith, Richard Strier, and David Bevington. Cambridge: Cambridge University Press, 1995. 157–69.

———. *The Birthpangs of Protestant England: Religious and Cultural Change in the Sixteenth and Seventeenth Centuries.* New York: St. Martin's Press, 1988.

———. "The Cohabitation of the Faithful with the Unfaithful." In *From Persecution to Toleration: The Glorious Revolution and Religion in England*, ed. Peter Grell, Jonathan I. Israel, and Nicholas Tyacke. Oxford: Clarendon Press, 1991. 51–76.

———. "Elizabethan and Jacobean Puritanism as Forms of Popular Religious Culture." In *The Culture of English Puritanism, 1560–1700*, ed. Christopher Durston and Jacqueline Eales. New York: St. Martin's Press, 1996. 32–57.

———. "The Elizabethan Church and the New Religion." In Haigh, ed., *Reign*, 169–94.

———. *The Religion of Protestants: The Church in English Society 1559–1625.* Oxford: Clarendon Press, 1982.

C[ollop]., J[ohn]. *Medici Catholicon.* London, 1656 [1655].

Cook, John. *King Charls* [sic] *His Case.* London, 1649.

Coolidge, John. *The Pauline Renaissance in England: Puritanism and the Bible.* Oxford: Clarendon Press, 1970.

Cooper, Thomas. *An Admonition to the People of England.* 1589. Ed. Edward Arber. Birmingham, 1882.

[Cooper, Thomas]. *An Apologie of the Private Masse . . . with an Answere and Confutacion.* 1562. Reprinted as *An Answer in Defence of the Truth.* Ed. William Goode. Cambridge, 1850.

Cooper, Thomas. *The Blessing of Japheth.* London, 1615.

Copley, Anthony. *An Answere to a Letter of a Jesuited Gentleman.* London, [1601].

Corbet, Richard. *The Poems of Richard Corbet.* Ed. J. A. W. Bennett and H. R. Trevor-Roper. Oxford: Clarendon Press, 1955.

Coverdale, Miles. *Fruitfull Lessons.* 1593. In *The Writings and Translations of Miles Coverdale,* ed. George Pearson. Parker Society. Cambridge, 1844. 195–421.

Cowell, John. *The Interpreter.* Cambridge, 1607.

Cox, John D., and David Scott Kastan, eds. *A New History of Early English Drama.* New York: Columbia University Press, 1997.

Cranmer, Thomas. *Miscellaneous Writings and Letters.* Ed. John Edmund Cox. London, 1846.

Crockett, Bryan. *The Play of Paradox: Stage and Sermon in Renaissance England.* Philadelphia: University of Pennsylvania Press, 1995.

Crompton, Richard. *The Mansion of Magnanimitie.* London, 1599.

Crosse, Henry. *Vertues Common-wealth.* London, 1603.

Curren-Aquino, Deborah T., ed. *King John: New Perspectives.* Newark: University of Delaware Press, 1989.

[Cushman, Robert]. *A Sermon Preached at Plimmoth in New-England.* London, 1622.

Danson, Lawrence. "*Henry V*: King, Chorus, and Critics." *Shakespeare Quarterly* 34 (1983): 27–43.

Davenport, Robert. *A New Trick to Cheat the Divell.* Acted c. 1624–39, published 1639. London, 1639.

Davies, Catherine. "'Poor Persecuted Little Flock' or 'Commonwealth of Christians': Edwardian Protestant Conceptions of the Church." In *Protestantism and the National Church,* ed. Peter Lake and Maria Dowling. London: Croom Helm, 1987.

Davies, John, of Hereford. *The Complete Works of John Davies of Hereford.* Ed. Alexander Grosart. 2 vols. [Edinburgh], 1878.

Davies, Norman. *The Isles: A History.* Oxford: Oxford University Press, 1999.

Dawson, Anthony B. "Mistris Hic & Haec: Representations of Moll Frith." *Studies in English Literature, 1500–1900* 33 (1993): 385–404.

Dee, John. *General and Rare Memorials.* [London, 1577].

The Defence of Conny Catching. By Cuthbert Cunny-catcher. 1592. Ed. G. B. Harrison. 1922; rpt., New York: Barnes & Noble, 1966.

Dekker, Thomas. *The Belman of London.* London, 1608.

———. *Dramatic Works.* Ed. Fredson Bowers. 4 vols. Cambridge: Cambridge University Press, 1953–61.

———. *The Guls Horn-Booke.* In *Nondramatic Works,* ed. Grosart, vol. 2, 193–266.

———. *Lanthorne and Candle-light.* 1608. In Kinney, ed., *Rogues,* 213–60.

———. *The Nondramatic Works of Thomas Dekker.* Ed. Alexander Grosart. 5 vols. [London], 1884–86.

———. *The Whore of Babylon.* Acted c. 1606, published 1607. Ed. Marianne Gateson Riely. New York: Garland, 1980.

Dent, Arthur. *The Plaine Mans Path-way to Heaven.* 1601; rev. ed., London, 1603.

———. *The Ruine of Rome.* London, 1603.

[Dering, Edward, d. 1576]. *A Preparation Into the Waye of Lyfe.* Ed. William Hopkinson. London, 1581.

Devereux, E. J. *Renaissance English Translations of Erasmus: A Bibliography to 1700.* Toronto: University of Toronto Press, 1983.

A Dialogue Concerning the Strife of Our Church. London, 1584.

Dickens, A. G. *Reformation Studies.* London: Hambledon, 1982.

Dickens, A. G., and Whitney R. D. Jones. *Erasmus the Reformer.* London: Methuen, 1994.

Diehl, Huston. "Observing the Lord's Supper and the Lord Chamberlain's Men: The Visual Rhetoric of Ritual and Play in Early Modern England." *Renaissance Drama* 22 (1991): 147–74. Revised version in Diehl, *Staging Reform,* chap. 4.

———. *Staging Reform, Reforming the Stage: Protestantism and Popular Theater in Early Modern England.* Ithaca: Cornell University Press, 1997.

Differences in Matters of Religion, Betweene the Easterne and Westerne Churches. London, 1625.

Donne, John. *Letters to Severall Persons of Honour.* 1651. Ed. Charles Edmund Merrill, Jr. New York: Sturgis & Walton, 1910.

———. *Pseudo-Martyr.* 1610. Ed. Anthony Raspa. Montreal: McGill-Queen's University Press, 1993.

———. *The Sermons of John Donne.* 10 vols. Ed. George R. Potter and Evelyn Simpson. Berkeley: University of California Press, 1953–62.

Dorman, Thomas. *A Proufe of Certeyne Articles in Religion, Denied by M. Juell.* Antwerp, 1564.

Dorsch, T. S., ed. *"The Comedy of Errors," by William Shakespeare.* Cambridge: Cambridge University Press, 1988.

Downame, George. *A Treatise Upon John 8.36. Concerning Christian Liberty.* London, 1609.

Drayton, Michael. "The Sacrifice to Apollo." 1619. In *Works,* ed. Hebel, vol. 2, 357–58.

———. *Works.* Ed. J. William Hebel (vols. 1–4); ed. Kathleen Tillotson and Bernard H. Newgate (vol. 5). 5 vols. Oxford: Basil Blackwell, 1961.

Drayton, Michael, Richard Hathway, Anthony Munday, and Robert Wilson. *I Sir John Oldcastle.* Acted 1599, published 1600. In *The Oldcastle Controversy: Sir John Oldcastle, Part 1 and The Famous Victories of Henry V,* ed. Peter Corbin and Douglas Sedge. Manchester: Manchester University Press, 1991.

Duffy, Eamon. "The Godly and the Multitude in Stuart England." *Seventeenth Century* 1 (1986): 31–55.

———. *The Stripping of the Altars: Traditional Religion in England 1400–1580.* New Haven: Yale University Press, 1992.

Dugmore, Clifford William. *The Mass and the English Reformers.* London: Macmillan, 1958.

Dutton, Richard. *Mastering the Revels: The Regulation and Censorship of English Renaissance Drama.* Iowa City: University of Iowa Press, 1991.

Dyke, Daniel [d. 1614]. *Two Treatises.* London, 1616.

Edwards, Philip. *Shakespeare and the Confines of Art.* London: Methuen, 1968.

Elliot, John R. "Shakespeare and the Double Image of King John." *Shakespeare Studies* 1 (1965): 64-84.

Elton, G. R. "Persecution and Toleration in the English Reformation." In *Persecution and Toleration,* ed. W. J. Shiels. Oxford: Basil Blackwell, 1984. 163–88.

Elyot, Thomas. *Dictionary.* 1538. Ed. R. C. Alston. Menston: Scolar Press, 1970.

Empson, William. "Falstaff." Revised version of "Falstaff and Mr. Dover Wilson" (1953). In *Essays on Shakespeare,* ed. David B. Pirie. Cambridge: Cambridge University Press, 1986. 29–78.

Erasmus, Desiderius. *Collected Works.* Ed. Peter G. Bietenholz et al. Toronto: University of Toronto Press, 1974–.

———. *Enchiridion Militis Christianis.* 1504. Trans. William Tyndale[?], 1533. Ed. Anne M. O'Donnell. Oxford: Oxford University Press, 1981.

———. *The First Tome or Volume of the Paraphrase of Erasmus.* Ed. Nicholas Udall, trans. Udall et al. London, 1548.

———. *Opera Omnia.* Ed. Jean Le Clerc. 10 vols. 1703–6. Hildesheim: Georg Olms, 1961–62.

———. *Opus Epistolarum Des. Erasmi Roterdami.* Ed. P. S. Allen et al. 12 vols. Oxford: Clarendon Press, 1906–58.

———. *Paraclesis.* 1516. Trans. William Roy[?] as *An Exhortation to the Diligent Studye of Scripture.* [Antwerp], 1529.

———. *Querela Pacis.* 1517. Trans. Thomas Paynell as *The Complaint of Peace,* 1559. Ed. William James Hirten. New York: Scholars' Facsimiles & Reprints, 1946.

———. *The Second Tome or Volume of the Paraphrase of Erasmus.* Ed. and trans. Miles Coverdale et al. London, 1549.

[Fennor, William?]. *Pasquils Palinodia.* London, 1619.

Field, John, and Thomas Wilcox. *An Admonition to the Parliament.* 1572. In Frere and Douglas, eds. *Puritan Manifestoes,* 1–55.

Field, Nathan. "Feild the Players Letter to Mr. Sutton, Preacher att St. Mary Overs., 1616." In *Illustrations of the Life of Shakespeare Part 1,* ed. James Orchard Halliwell-Phillipps. 1874; rpt., New York: AMS Press, 1973.

[Fish, Simon]. *A Supplicacyon For the Beggers.* c. 1529. In *Four Supplications 1529–1553,* ed. Frederick J. Furnivall and J. Meadows Cowper. London, 1871.

Flecknoe, Richard. *Love's Dominion.* London, 1654.

Fletcher, John. *Women Pleas'd.* Acted c. 1619–23, published 1647. In Fredson Bowers, gen. ed., *Dramatic Works in the Beaumont and Fletcher Canon.* Cambridge: Cambridge University Press, 1966–. Vol. 5, 441–538.

Fletcher, John, [and Philip Massinger?]. *Beggars Bush.* Acted c. 1613–22, published 1647. Ed. John H. Dorenkamp. The Hague: Mouton, 1967.

Foley, Henry, ed. *Records of the English Province of the Society of Jesus.* 7 vols. London, 1877–83.

[Ford, John]. *The Queen, or the Excellency of Her Sex.* London, 1653.

[Fowler, Edward?]. *The Principles and Practices, of Certain Moderate Divines in the Church of England.* London, 1670.

Foxe, John. *The Acts and Monuments.* 1563–83. The copytext is the 1583 *Acts,* very freely edited. Ed. Stephen Cattley and George Townsend. 8 vols. 1837–41, 1843–49; rpt., New York: AMS Press, 1965.

———. *Christus Triumphans.* 1556. In *Two Latin Comedies by John Foxe the Martyrologist: "Titus et Gesippus" and "Christus Triumphans,"* ed. and trans. John Hazel Smith. Ithaca: Cornell University Press, 1973.

———. *A Sermon of Christ Crucified.* London, 1570.

———. *A Sermon Preached at the Christening of a Certaine Jew.* London, 1578.

Frere, Walter Howard, and Charles Edward Douglas, eds. *Puritan Manifestoes: A Study of the Origin of the Puritan Revolt.* 1907; rpt., London: S.P.C.K., 1954.

Friedman, Donald. "John of Gaunt and the Rhetoric of Frustration." *ELH* 43 (1976): 279–99.

Fripp, Edgar I. *Shakespeare Man and Artist.* 2 vols. 1938; rpt., London: Oxford University Press, 1964.

Frith, John. *The Work of John Frith.* Ed. N. T. Wright. Oxford: Sutton Courtenay Press, 1978.

Frye, Roland Mushat. *Shakespeare and Christian Doctrine.* Princeton: Princeton University Press, 1963.

Fulke, William. *Rejoynder.* London, 1581.

Gager, William. *The Complete Works.* Ed. Dana F. Sutton. 4 vols. New York: Garland, 1994.

G[ainsford?]., T[homas?]. *The Rich Cabinet.* London, 1616.

Gardiner, Samuel, ed. *Documents Relating to the Proceedings against William Prynne.* [Westminster], 1877.

Gardiner, Stephen. *Letters.* Ed. J. A. Muller. Cambridge: Cambridge University Press, 1933.

Garter, Thomas. *The Most Virtuous and Godly Susanna.* Written c. 1565, published 1578. Ed. B. Ifor Evans and W. W. Greg. Malone Society. Oxford: Oxford University Press, 1937.

George a Greene, The Pinner of Wakefield. Acted c. 1592, published 1599. Ed. John S. Farmer. [Amersham]: Tudor Facsimile Texts, 1913.

Gibson, Thomas. *A Fruitful Sermon.* London, 1584.

Gifford, George. *A Briefe Discourse of Certaine Points of the Religion, Which Is Among the Common Sort of Christians, Which May Be Termed the Countrie Divinitie.* London, 1581.

———. *Sermons Upon the Whole Booke of the Revelation.* London, 1596.

———. *A Short Treatise Against the Donatists of England, Whome We Call Brownists.* London, 1590.

Gilby, Anthony. *An Answer to the Devellish Detection of S. Gardiner.* [London], 1547.

[Gilby, Anthony]. *A Pleasant Dialogue.* [Middelburg?], 1581.

Gildersleeve, Virginia Crocheron. *Government Regulation of the Elizabethan Drama.* 1908; rpt., New York: Burt Franklin, 1961.

Goffe, Thomas. *Three Excellent Tragedies.* London, 1656.

Gomersall, Robert. *The Levites Revenge.* London, 1628.

———. *Sermons on St Peter.* London, 1634.

———. *The Tragedie of Lodovick Sforza Duke of Millan.* London, [1628].

Gosson, Stephen. *Markets of Bawdrie: The Dramatic Criticism of Stephen Gosson.* Contains *The Schoole of Abuse* (1579), *An Apologie of the Schoole of Abuse* (1579), and *Playes Confuted in Five Actions* (1582). Ed. Arthur F. Kinney. Salzburg: Institut für Englische Sprache und Literatur, Universität Salzburg, 1974.

Green, Ian. *The Christian's ABC: Catechisms and Catechizing in England c. 1530–1740.* Oxford: Clarendon Press, 1996.

G[reene]., I[ohn]. *A Refutation of the Apology for Actors.* 1615. Ed. Richard Perkinson. New York: Scholars' Facsimiles & Reprints, 1941.

Greenblatt, Stephen. *Hamlet in Purgatory.* Princeton: Princeton University Press, 2001.

———. "The Mousetrap." In *Practicing New Historicism,* by Catherine Gallagher and Stephen Greenblatt. Chicago: University of Chicago Press, 2000. 136–62.

———. *Renaissance Self-Fashioning: From More to Shakespeare.* Chicago: University of Chicago Press, 1980.

———. *Shakespearean Negotiations: The Circulation of Social Energy in Renaissance England.* Berkeley: University of California Press, 1988.

Greene, Robert. *A Disputation, Betweene a Hee Conny-catcher, and a Shee Conny-catcher.* 1592. Ed. G. B. Harrison. 1922; rpt., New York: Barnes & Noble, 1966.

———. *A Notable Discovery of Coosnage.* 1591. Ed. G. B. Harrison. 1922; rpt., New York: Barnes & Noble, 1966.

———. *The Repentance of Robert Greene Maister of Artes.* 1592. Ed. G. B. Harrison. 1922; rpt., New York: Barnes & Noble, 1966.

———. *1 Selimus.* Acted c. 1592, published 1594. Ed. W. Bang. Malone Society. [London]: Chiswick Press, [1909].

Greenfeld, Liah. *Nationalism: Five Roads to Modernity.* Cambridge, Mass.: Harvard University Press, 1992.

Greenwood, John. *The Writings of John Greenwood, 1587–1590.* Ed. Leland H. Carlson. London: George Allen & Unwin, 1962.

Greenwood, John, and Henry Barrow. *The Writings of John Greenwood and Henry Barrow 1591–1593.* Ed. Leland H. Carlson. London: George Allen & Unwin, 1970.

Griffin, Martin I. J., Jr. *Latitudinarianism in the Seventeenth-Century Church of England.* Annotated by Richard H. Popkin, ed. Lila Freedman. Leiden: E. J. Brill, 1992.

Grimald, Nicholas. *Christus Redivivus.* Acted c. 1540, published 1543. In Merrill, *Life and Poems,* 55–125.

Gurr, Andrew. *The Shakespearean Stage 1574–1642.* 3rd ed. Cambridge: Cambridge University Press, 1992.

———. *The Shakespearian Playing Companies.* Oxford: Clarendon Press, 1996.

Hacket, John. *Loyola.* Acted 1623. London, 1648.

Hadfield, Andrew. *Literature, Politics and National Identity: Reformation to Renaissance.* Cambridge: Cambridge University Press, 1994.

Haigh, Christopher. "Anticlericalism and the English Reformation." In Haigh, ed., *English Reformation Revised,* 56–74.

———. "The Church of England, the Catholics and the People." In Haigh, ed., *Reign,* 195–219, 282–85.

———. "The Continuity of Catholicism in the English Reformation." In Haigh, ed., *English Reformation Revised,* 176–208.

———. "Puritan Evangelism in the Reign of Elizabeth I." *English Historical Review* 92 (1977): 30–58.

Haigh, Christopher, ed. *The English Reformation Revised.* Cambridge: Cambridge University Press, 1987.

———. *The Reign of Elizabeth I.* London: Macmillan, 1984.

Hale, William, ed. and comp. *A Series of Precedents and Proceedings.* London, 1847.

Hall, Joseph. "An Holy Panegyric." 1613. In *Works*, ed. Philip Wynter. 10 vols. 1863; rpt., New York: AMS Press, 1969. Vol. 5, 91–117.

———. *Mundus alter et idem.* 1605. Trans. John Healey as *The Discovery of a New World*, 1609. Rpt. of 1609 ed., ed. Huntington Brown. Cambridge, Mass.: Harvard University Press, 1937. Trans. from 1605 ed. by John Millar Wands. New Haven: Yale University Press, 1981.

Hall, Kim F. *Things of Darkness: Economies of Race and Gender in Early Modern England.* Ithaca: Cornell University Press, 1995.

Hamel, Guy. "*King John* and *The Troublesome Raigne*: A Reexamination." In Curren-Aquino, ed., *King John*, 41–61.

Hamilton, Donna. *Shakespeare and the Politics of Protestant England.* Lexington: University of Kentucky Press, 1992.

Hanmer, Meredith. *The Jesuites Banner.* London, 1581.

Harding, Thomas. *A Confutation of a Booke Intituled An Apologie of the Church of England.* Antwerp, 1565.

———. *A Rejoindre to M. Jewels Replie.* Louvain, 1567.

Harington, John. *A Tract on the Succession to the Crown.* MS 1602. Ed. Clement R. Markham. London, 1880.

Harman, Thomas. *A Caveat for Common Cursitors.* 1566. In Kinney, ed., *Rogues*, 109–53.

Harsnett, Samuel. *A Declaration of Egregious Popish Impostures.* London, 1603.

Hartley, T. E., ed. *Proceedings in the Parliaments of Elizabeth I.* Vol. 1 (covering 1558–81). Wilmington, Del.: Michael Glazier, 1981.

Harvey, Gabriel. *Fowre Letters and Certeine Sonnets.* 1592. Ed. G. B. Harrison. London: Bodley Head, 1922.

Harvey, Richard. *Philadelphus.* London, 1593.

Hausted, Peter. *The Rival Friends.* 1632. Ed. Laurens J. Mills. Bloomington: Indiana University Press, 1951.

[Hausted, Peter?]. *A Satyre Against Seperatists.* London, 1642.

Hay, Denys. *Europe: The Emergence of an Idea.* 1957; rev. ed., Edinburgh: Edinburgh University Press, 1968.

Hayes, Edward. [Narrative of Sir Humphrey Gilbert's Last Expedition]. In *The Principall Navigations, Voyages and Discoveries of the English Nation*, ed. Richard Hakluyt. 1589. Reprinted in *The Voyages and Colonizing Enterprises of Sir Humphrey Gilbert*, ed. D. B. Quinn. 2 vols. Hakluyt Society. London, 1940. Vol. 2, 385–426.

Hazlitt, William. "On Shakspeare and Milton." In *Lectures on the English Poets.* 1818; 2nd ed., 1819. In *The Collected Works of William Hazlitt*, ed. A. R. Waller and Arnold Glover. 12 vols. London: J. M. Dent, 1902–4. Vol. 5, 44–68.

Hazlitt, William Carew, ed. *The English Drama and Stage under the Tudor and Stuart Princes 1543–1664.* London, 1869.

Heinemann, Margot. "Political Drama." In Braunmuller and Hattaway, *Cambridge Companion*, 161–206.

———. *Puritanism and Theatre: Thomas Middleton and Opposition Drama under the Early Stuarts*. Cambridge: Cambridge University Press, 1980.

Helgerson, Richard. *Forms of Nationhood: The Elizabethan Writing of England*. Chicago: University of Chicago Press, 1992.

Heminges, William. *William Hemminge's Elegy on Randolph's Finger*. MS c. 1632. Ed. G. C. Moore Smith. Oxford: Basil Blackwell, 1923.

Herbert, George. *The Complete English Poems*. Ed. John Tobin. London: Penguin, 1991.

Heyd, Michael. *"Be Sober and Reasonable": The Critique of Enthusiasm in the Seventeenth and Early Eighteenth Centuries*. Leiden: E. J. Brill, 1995.

Heywood, Thomas. *An Apology for Actors*. 1612. Ed. Richard Perkinson. New York: Scholars' Facsimiles & Reprints, 1941.

———. *Gunaikeion: or, Nine Bookes of Various History. Concerning Women*. London, 1624.

———. *Reader, Here You'l Plainly See Judgment Perverted by These Three: A Priest, A Judge, a Patentee*. [London], 1641.

———. *Troia Britanica*. London, 1609.

———. *A Woman Killed With Kindness*. Acted 1603, published 1607. Ed. R. W. Van Fossen. Cambridge, Mass.: Harvard University Press, 1961.

Heywood, Thomas, [et al.?]. *The First and Second Partes of King Edward the Fourth*. Acted c. 1599. 1599; London, 1600.

Hierarchomachia, or The Anti-Bishop. MS c. 1630. Ed. Suzanne Gossett. London: Associated University Presses, 1982.

Hieron, Samuel. *The Preachers Plea*. London, 1604.

Hill, Christopher. *Liberty against the Law: Some Seventeenth-Century Controversies*. New York: Penguin, 1996.

———. "The Ratsbane of Lecturing." In *Society and Puritanism in Pre-revolutionary England*. 2nd ed. New York: Shocken, 1967. 79–123.

———. "William Perkins and the Poor." In *Puritanism and Revolution: Studies in Interpretation of the English Revolution of the Seventeenth Century*. London: Secker & Warburg, 1958. 215–38.

Holden, William P. *Anti-Puritan Satire, 1572–1642*. New Haven: Yale University Press, 1954.

Holinshed, Raphael, et al., eds. *The Chronicles of England, Scotlande, and Irelande*. 1577. "Augmented and continued" by John Hooker et al., 1587. 2 vols. reprinted in 6. London, 1807–8.

Holyday, Barten, trans. *Aulus Persius Flaccus His Satires*. Oxford, 1616.

Honan, Park. *Shakespeare: A Life*. Oxford: Oxford University Press, 1998.

Honigmann, E. A. J. *Shakespeare: The "Lost Years."* 1985; 2nd ed., Manchester: Manchester University Press, 1998.

Honigmann, E. A. J., and Susan Brock, eds. *Playhouse Wills 1558–1642: An Edition of Wills by Shakespeare and His Contemporaries in the London Theatre*. Manchester: Manchester University Press, 1993.

Hooker, Richard. *Of the Lawes of Ecclesiasticall Politie*. Books 1–4, 1594; book 5, 1597; books 6 and 8, 1648; book 7, 1662. In *The Folger Library Edition of the Works of Richard Hooker,* ed. W. Speed Hill. Cambridge, Mass.: Harvard University Press, 1977.

Hooper, John. *A Briefe and Clear Confession of the Christian Faith.* 1581. In *Later Writings of Bishop Hooper,* ed. Charles Nevinson. Parker Society. Cambridge, 1852. 19–63.

———. *Early Writings.* Ed. Samuel Carr. Parker Society. Cambridge, 1843.

Hotson, Leslie. *The Commonwealth and Restoration Stage.* 1928; rpt., New York: Russell & Russell, 1962.

Howes, Edmund. "Historicall Preface." In John Stow and Edmund Howes, *The Annales.* London, 1615.

Hulme, T. E. "Romanticism and Classicism." Written c. 1913–14, published 1924. In *Critical Theory since Plato,* ed. Hazard Adams. New York: Harcourt Brace Jovanovich, 1971. 767–74.

Humphreys, A. R., ed. *"Much Ado about Nothing," by William Shakespeare.* London: Methuen, 1981.

Hunt, Maurice. "The Religion of *Twelfth Night.*" *CLA Journal* 37 (1993): 189–203.

Hutchinson, Lucy. *Memoirs of the Life of Colonel Hutchinson.* MS. c. 1664–71. Ed. James Sutherland. London: Oxford University Press, 1973.

Hutchinson, Roger. *A Faithful Declaration of Christes Holy Supper.* 1560. In *Works,* ed. John Bruce. Parker Society. Cambridge, 1842. 209–88.

Hutton, Ronald. *The Rise and Fall of Merry England: The Ritual Year, 1400–1700.* Oxford: Oxford University Press, 1994.

Ingram, R. W., ed. *Records of the Early English Drama: Coventry.* Toronto: University of Toronto Press, 1981.

Jacob, Henry. *A Confession and Protestation of the Faith of Certain Christians in England.* [Amsterdam, 1616].

Jardine, Lisa. "Much Ado about Shakespeare." *Times* (London). 2 January 1999, 3.

Jewel, John. *An Apologie, or Aunswer in Defence of the Church of England.* 1562. Trans. Lady A[nne] B[acon] from *Apologia Ecclesiae Anglicanae,* 1562. In *Works,* ed. Ayre, vol. 3, 48–112.

———. *Certaine Sermons.* 1583. In *Works,* ed. Ayre, vol. 2, 965–1097.

———. *Replie Unto M. Hardinges Answeare.* 1565. In *Works,* ed. Ayre, vol. 1, 81–552.

———. *A Treatise of the Sacraments.* Appended to *Certaine Sermons.* 1583. In *Works,* ed. Ayre, vol. 2, 1098–1139.

———. *Works.* 4 vols. Ed. John Ayre. Parker Society. Cambridge, 1845–50.

Jonson, Ben. *Ben Jonson.* Ed. C. H. Herford and Percy and Evelyn Simpson. 11 vols. Oxford: Oxford University Press, 1925–52.

Jonsonus Virbius: or, The Memorie of Ben Johnson Revived by the Friends of the Muses. Compiled by Brian Duppa. 1638. In *Ben Jonson,* ed. Herford and Simpson, vol. 11, 428–81.

Jordan, Thomas. *Fancy's Festivals.* 1654–57. London, 1657.

Jordan, W. K. *The Development of Religious Toleration in England.* 4 vols. Cambridge: Harvard University Press, 1932–40.

Judges, A. V. *The Elizabethan Underworld.* 1930; rev. ed., London: Routledge & Kegan Paul, 1965.

Kastan, David Scott. "Proud Majesty Made a Subject: Shakespeare and the Spectacle of Rule." *Shakespeare Quarterly* 37 (1986): 459–75.

Kaula, David. "Autolycus' Trumpery." *Studies in English Literature* 16 (1976): 287–303.

Kay, W. David. "Jonson, Erasmus, and Religious Controversy: *Discoveries*, Lines 1046–1062." *English Language Notes* 17 (1979): 108–12.

Kearney, Hugh. *The British Isles: A History of Four Nations*. Cambridge: Cambridge University Press, 1989.

Keats, John. *The Letters of John Keats*. Ed. Hyder E. Rollins. 2 vols. Cambridge, Mass.: Harvard University Press, 1958.

Kehler, Dorothea. "'So Jest with Heaven': Deity in *King John*." In Curren-Aquino, ed., *King John*, 99–113.

Kelton, Arthur. *A Chronycle with a Genealogie Declaring that the Brittons and Welshemen are Linealiye Dyscended from Brute*. [London, 1547].

Kemp, William. *Kemps Nine Daies Wonder*. London, 1600.

King, John N. *English Reformation Literature: The Tudor Origins of the Protestant Tradition*. Princeton: Princeton University Press, 1982.

King Leir and His Three Daughters. Acted c. 1588–94, published 1605. *"The True Chronicle History of King Leir and His Three Daughters, Gonorill, Ragan, and Cordella," A Critical Edition*. Ed. Donald M. Michie. New York: Garland, 1991.

Kinney, Arthur F., ed. *Rogues, Vagabonds and Sturdy Beggars: A New Gallery of Tudor and Early Stuart Rogue Literature*. Amherst: University of Massachusetts Press, 1990.

A Knack to Know a Knave. Acted 1592, published 1594. Ed. G. R. Proudfoot. Malone Society. Oxford: Oxford University Press, 1964.

Knapp, Jeffrey. *An Empire Nowhere: England, America, and Literature from Utopia to The Tempest*. Berkeley: University of California Press, 1992.

Knight, G. Wilson. *The Wheel of Fire: Essays in Interpretation of Shakespeare's Sombre Tragedies*. London: Oxford University Press, 1930.

Kohn, Hans. "The Genesis of English Nationalism." *Journal of the History of Ideas* 1 (1940): 69–94.

Kronenfeld, Judy. *King Lear and the Naked Truth: Rethinking the Language of Religion and Resistance*. Durham, N.C.: Duke University Press, 1998.

Lake, Osmund. *A Probe Theologicall*. London, 1612.

Lake, Peter. *Anglicans and Puritans? Presbyterianism and English Conformist Thought from Whitgift to Hooker*. London: Allen & Unwin, 1988.

———. "'A Charitable Christian Hatred': The Godly and Their Enemies in the 1630s." In *The Culture of English Puritanism, 1560–1700*, ed. Christopher Durston and Jacqueline Eales. New York: St Martin's Press, 1996. 145–83.

Laud, William. *Works*. Ed. William Scott and James Bliss. 7 vols. Oxford, 1847–60.

The Laughing Mercury. 8–16 September 1652.

Lawrence, D. H. "Why the Novel Matters." Written c. 1925, published 1936. In *Study of Thomas Hardy and Other Essays*, ed. Bruce Steele. Cambridge: Cambridge University Press, 1985. 191–98.

[Leighton, Alexander]. *A Shorte Treatise Against Stage-Playes*. 1625. In *The English Drama and Stage under the Tudor and Stuart Princes 1543–1664*, ed. William Carew Hazlitt. London, 1869.

Lescarbot, Marc. *Nova Francia: Or the Description of That Part of New France, which is One Continent with Virginia*. 1609. Trans. P. Erondelle. London, 1609. Ed. H. P. Biggar. New York: Harper, 1928.

[Leslie, John]. *A Treatise of Treasons*. [Louvain], 1572. *English Recusant Literature*, vol. 254.

L'Estrange, Nicholas. "Merry Passages and Jests." MS c. 1640. In *Anecdotes and Traditions, Illustrative of Early English History and Literature*, ed. William J. Thoms. London, 1839.

Levin, Carole. "'I Trust I May Not Trust Thee': Women's Visions of the World in Shakespeare's *King John*." In *Ambiguous Realities: Women in the Middle Ages and Renaissance*, ed. Carole Levin and Jeanne Watson. Detroit: Wayne State University Press, 1987. 219–34.

Levins, Peter. *Manipulus Vocabulorum. A Dictionarie of English and Latin Words*. 1570. Early English Text Society, vol. 27. London, 1867.

Leycesters Commonwealth. [By Charles Arundell et al.?] Ed. D. C. Peck. Athens, Ohio: Ohio University Press, 1985.

Liber Vagatorum; Der Betler Orden. c. 1509. Ed. with a preface by Martin Luther. 1528. Trans. John Camden Hotten as *The Book of Vagabonds and Beggars*. London, 1860.

Lloyd, David. *Memoires*. London, 1668.

Locrine [The Lamentable Tragedie of Locrine]. Acted c. 1591–95, published 1595. Ed. Jane Lytton Gooch. New York: Garland, 1981.

Lovejoy, David S. *Religious Enthusiasm in the New World: Heresy to Revolution*. Cambridge, Mass.: Harvard University Press, 1985.

Manheim, Michael. "The Four Voices of the Bastard." In Curren-Aquino, ed., *King John*, 126–35.

Manningham, John. *The Diary of John Manningham of the Middle Temple, 1602–1603*. Ed. Robert Parker Sorlien. Hanover, N.H.: University Press of New England, 1976.

Marcus, Leah S. *The Politics of Mirth: Jonson, Herrick, Milton, Marvell, and the Defense of Old Holiday Pastimes*. Chicago: University of Chicago Press, 1986.

Marlowe, Christopher. *Edward II*. Acted c. 1592, published 1594. Ed. W. Moelwyn Merchant. London: A. & C. Black, 1967.

———. *Tamburlaine the Great*. Acted c. 1587, published 1590. Ed. J. S. Cunningham. Manchester: Manchester University Press, 1981.

Marmion, Shackerley. *The Antiquary*. Acted 1634–36. London, 1641.

———. *Hollands Leaguer*. Acted 1631. London, 1632.

Marshall, Peter. *The Catholic Priesthood and the English Reformation*. Oxford: Clarendon Press, 1994.

Marten, Anthony. *An Exhortation, to Stirre up the Mindes of All Her Majesties Faithfull Subjects, to Defend Their Countrey in This Dangerous Time, From the Invasion of Enemies*. London, 1588.

Martin, Gregory. *A Treatise of Schisme*. Douay [London], 1578.

———. *A Treatyse of Christian Peregrination*. [Paris], 1583 [c. 1597]. *English Recusant Literature*, vol. 167.

Massinger, Philip. *The Plays and Poems of Philip Massinger*. Ed. Philip Edwards and Colin Gibson. 5 vols. Oxford: Clarendon Press, 1976.

Maus, Katharine Eisaman. *Inwardness and Theater in the English Renaissance*. Chicago: University of Chicago Press, 1995.

Maxwell, James. Prospectus for "Britaines Union in Love." 1604. London, British
    Library, Royal MS 18A.51, 8v.
Mayne, Jasper. *The City Match*. Acted c. 1637, published 1639. Ed. John Woodruff
    Ward. Ph.D. diss., University of Delaware, 1975.
———. *A Sermon Concerning Unity & Agreement*. [Oxford], 1646.
McDonald, Russ. *The Bedford Companion to Shakespeare*. New York: St. Martin's
    Press, 1996.
McEachern, Claire. *The Poetics of English Nationhood, 1590–1612*. Cambridge: Cam-
    bridge University Press, 1996.
Mercurius Britanicus, no. 12. 9–16 [November, 1643].
Merrill, L. R. *The Life and Poems of Nicholas Grimald*. New Haven: Yale University
    Press, 1925.
Middleton, Thomas. *The Family of Love*. Acted c. 1602–7, published 1608. Ed. Simon
    Shepherd. Nottingham: Nottingham Drama Texts, 1979.
———. *Hengist King of Kent, or The Mayor of Queenborough*. Acted c. 1618, published
    1661. Ed. R. C. Bald. New York: Charles Scribner's Sons, 1938.
———. *A Mad World, My Masters*. Acted c. 1604, published 1608. Ed. Standish Hen-
    ning. Lincoln: University of Nebraska Press, 1965.
———. *The Puritan; or, The Widow of Watling Street*. Acted 1606, published 1607. Ed.
    Donald F. Kaiser. Ph.D. diss., University of Wisconsin, 1966.
Middleton, Thomas, and Thomas Dekker. *The Roaring Girl*. Acted c. 1611, published
    1611. Ed. Paul Mulholland. Manchester: Manchester University Press, 1987.
Middleton, Thomas [and/or Samuel Rowley, John Ford, Thomas Dekker?]. *The
    Spanish Gypsy*. Acted c. 1623, published 1653. Ed. Edgar C. Morris. Boston:
    D. C. Heath, 1908.
Milles, Robert. *Abrahams Sute*. London, 1612.
Mills, Laurens J. *Peter Hausted: Playwright, Poet, and Preacher*. Bloomington: Indiana
    University Press, 1944.
Milton, John. *The Works of John Milton*. Ed. Frank Allen Patterson et al. 18 vols. New
    York: Columbia University Press, 1931–38.
Milward, Peter. *Shakespeare's Religious Background*. Chicago: Loyola University
    Press, 1973.
Minsheu, John. *Guide Into Tongues*. London, 1617.
Montagu, Richard. *Appello Caesarem*. London, 1625.
Montrose, Louis. "The Purpose of Playing: Reflections on a Shakespearean An-
    thropology." *Helios*, n.s. 7 (1980): 51–74.
———. *The Purpose of Playing: Shakespeare and the Cultural Politics of the Elizabethan
    Theatre*. Chicago: University of Chicago Press, 1996.
Moone, Peter. *A Short Treatise of Certayne Thinges Abused in the Popysh Church*.
    [Ipswich, 1548].
More, Henry. *Enthusiasmus Triumphatus*. Cambridge, 1656.
More, Thomas. "Eruditissima Epistola . . . Qua Respondet Indoctis ac Virulentis
    Litteris Monachi." 1520. Trans. and ed. Daniel Kinney as "Letter to a Monk."
    In *The Yale Edition of the Complete Works of St. Thomas More*. New Haven: Yale
    University Press, 1986. Vol. 15, 197–311.
Moretti, Franco. "The Great Eclipse: Tragic Form as the Deconsecration of Sover-
    eignty." 1979. In *Signs Taken for Wonders: Essays in the Sociology of Literary*

Forms, trans. Susan Fischer, David Forgacs, and David Miller. 1983; rev. ed., London: Verso, 1988. 42–82.

Morwyng, Peter, trans. *A Compendious and Moste Marveylous History of the Latter Times of the Jewes Commune Weale*, by Joseph ben Gorion [pseudonym]. 1558; rev. ed., London, 1561.

Moryson, Fynes. *An Itinerary Containing His Ten Yeeres Travell*. 1617. Rpt. in 4 vols. Glasgow: James MacLehose & Sons, 1907.

Mowat, Barbara A. "Rogues, Shepherds, and the Counterfeit Distressed: Texts and Infracontexts of *The Winter's Tale* 4.3." *Shakespeare Studies* 22 (1994): 58–76.

Mulholland, Paul. "The Date of *The Roaring Girl*." *Review of English Studies*, n.s. 28 (1977): 18–31.

Munday, Anthony, and Henry Chettle. *The Death of Robert, Earl of Huntington*. Acted 1598, published 1601. In *The Huntingdon Plays: A Critical Edition of "The Downfall" and "The Death of Robert, Earl of Huntingdon,"* ed. John Carney Meagher. New York: Garland, 1980.

———. *The Downfall of Robert, Earl of Huntington*. Acted 1598, published 1601. In *The Huntingdon Plays: A Critical Edition of "The Downfall" and "The Death of Robert, Earl of Huntingdon,"* ed. John Carney Meagher. New York: Garland, 1980.

Munday, Anthony, et al. *Sir Thomas More: A Play by Anthony Munday and Others, Revised by Henry Chettle, Thomas Dekker, Thomas Heywood, and William Shakespeare*. Ed. Vittorio Gabrieli and Giorgio Melchiori. Manchester: Manchester University Press, 1990.

[Munday, Anthony? and] Salvianus. *A Second and Third Blast of Retrait from Plaies and Theaters*. 1580. Ed. Arthur Freeman. New York: Garland, 1973.

Murray, Robert H. *Erasmus and Luther: Their Attitude to Toleration*. New York: Macmillan, 1920.

Musculus, Wolfgang. *The Temporisour*. Trans. R. P[ownoll]. from a French translation of the Latin. 1555; rpt., Edinburgh, 1584.

Myers, Aaron Michael. *Representation and Misrepresentation of the Puritan in Elizabethan Drama*. Philadelphia: University of Pennsylvania Press, 1931.

Nabbes, Thomas. *Totenham Court*. 1633–34. London, 1638.

Narcissus. MS 1603. Ed. Margaret L. Lee. London, 1893.

Nashe, Thomas. *Works*. Ed. R. B. McKerrow. 5 vols. 1903–10. Ed. F. P. Wilson. Oxford: Basil Blackwell, 1958.

Neale, J. E. *Elizabeth I and Her Parliaments 1559–1581*. 1958; rpt., New York: Norton, 1966.

Nelson, Alan. "George Buc, William Shakespeare, and the Folger *George a Greene*." *Shakespeare Quarterly* 49 (1998): 74–83.

Nicholl, Charles. *A Cup of News: The Life of Thomas Nashe*. London: Routledge & Kegan Paul, 1984.

———. *The Reckoning: The Murder of Christopher Marlowe*. 1992; rpt., London: Picador, 1993.

Nichols, Josias. *The Plea of the Innocent: Wherein is Averred; That the Ministers & People Falslie Termed Puritans, Are Injuriously Slaundered*. [London], 1602.

Nicolas, Harris. *Memoirs of the Life and Times of Sir Christopher Hatton*. London, 1847.

Norden, John. *A Mirror for the Multitude*. London, 1586.

———. *A Progresse of Pietie*. 1596. Reprinted as *A Progress of Piety*. Cambridge, 1847.

[Northampton, Henry Howard, Earl of]. *A Defense of the Ecclesiasticall Regiment in Englande*. London, 1574.

Northbrooke, John. *A Breefe and Pithie Summe of the Christian Faith*. London, 1571; rev. ed., 1582.

———. *The Poore Mans Garden*. London, 1571; rev. ed., 1575 and 1582.

———. *A Treatise Wherein Dicing, Dauncing, Vaine Playes or Enterluds With Other Idle Pastimes etc. Commonly Used on the Sabboth Day, Are Reproved*. [1577?] Ed. Arthur Freeman. New York: Garland, 1974.

[Ockland, Christopher]. *The Fountaine and Welspring of All Variance, Sedition, and Deadly Hate*. London, 1589.

O'Connell, Michael. "The Idolatrous Eye: Iconoclasm, Anti- theatricalism, and the Image of the Elizabethan Theater." *ELH* 52 (1985): 279–310.

Orgel, Stephen. "Making Greatness Familiar." *Genre* 15 (1982): 41–48.

Orgel, Stephen, ed. *Ben Jonson: The Complete Masques*. New Haven: Yale University Press, 1969.

Ormerod, Oliver. *The Picture of a Puritane*. 2nd ed. London, 1605.

Owen, John. *Works*. 16 vols. 1850–53; rpt., Edinburgh: Banner of Truth Trust, 1965.

[Parker, Henry?]. *A Discourse Concerning Puritans*. 2nd ed. London, 1641.

[Parker, Matthew?]. *A Briefe Examination for the Tyme, of a Certaine Declaration*. [London, 1566].

Parker, Patricia. "Anagogic Metaphor: Breaking Down the Wall of Partition." In *Centre and Labyrinth: Essays in Honour of Northrop Frye*, ed. Eleanor Cook et al. Toronto: University of Toronto Press, 1983. 38–58.

———. "Shakespeare and the Bible: *The Comedy of Errors*." *Recherches Sémiotiques/ Semiotic Inquiry* 13 (1993): 47–72.

[Parsons, Robert]. *A Brief Discourse Contayning Certayne Reasons Why Catholiques Refuse to Goe to Church*. Douay [England, by the secret English press], 1580.

[Parsons, Robert]. *An Epistle of the Persecution of Catholikes in England*. Trans. G. T. Douay in Artois [Rouen], 1582.

[Parsons, Robert]. *A Temperate Ward-word, to the Turbulent and Seditious Wach-word of Sir Francis Hastings Knight*. By N. D. [Antwerp], 1599.

[Parsons, Robert]. *A Treatise of Three Conversions of England*. 3 vols. [St. Omer], 1603[–4].

Patrides, C. A., ed. *The Cambridge Platonists*. London: Edward Arnold, 1969.

Patterson, W. B. *King James VI and I and the Reunion of Christendom*. Cambridge: Cambridge University Press, 1997.

Peck, Francis, ed. *Desiderata Curiosa*. London, 1779.

Peele, George. *Life and Works*. Ed. Charles Tyler Prouty et al. 3 vols. New Haven: Yale University Press, 1952–70.

Penry, John. *The Notebook of John Penry 1593*. Ed. Albert Peel. London: Office of the Royal Historical Society, 1944.

Perkins, William. *Workes*. 3 vols. London [and Cambridge], 1612[–13].

Peterson, Richard S. *Imitation and Praise in the Poems of Ben Jonson*. New Haven: Yale University Press, 1981.

Petti, Anthony G., ed. *Recusant Documents from the Ellesmere Manuscripts*. St. Albans: Catholic Record Society, 1968.

Phaer, Thomas. *The Whole xii Bookes of the Aeneidos of Virgill.* Part of 10th book to the end, trans. Thomas Twyne. London, 1573.

Pierce, William, ed. *The Marprelate Tracts: 1588, 1589.* London: James Clarke, 1911.

Pilkington, James. *The Works of James Pilkington.* Ed. James Scholefield. Cambridge, 1842.

Poole, Josua. *The English Parnassus.* London, 1657.

Poole, Kristen. *Radical Religion from Shakespeare to Milton: Figures of Nonconformity in Early Modern England.* Cambridge: Cambridge University Press, 2000.

———. "Saints Alive! Falstaff, Martin Marprelate, and the Staging of Puritanism." *Shakespeare Quarterly* 46 (1995): 47–75.

Pound, John. *Poverty and Vagrancy in Tudor England.* 2nd ed. London: Longman, 1986.

Probst, Neil P., and Robert C. Evans. "Bishop Duppa and Jonson's 'Epick Poem.'" *Notes and Queries* 240 (1995): 361–63.

Prosser, Eleanor. *Hamlet and Revenge.* 1967; 2nd ed., Stanford: Stanford University Press, 1971.

Prynne, William. *Histrio-Mastix.* 1633. Ed. Arthur Freeman. New York: Garland, 1974.

———. *The Perpetuitie of a Regenerate Mans Estate.* London, 1626.

Puller, Timothy. *The Moderation of the Church of England.* London, 1679.

Purchas, Samuel. *Hakluytus Posthumus or Purchas His Pilgrimes.* 4 vols. 1625. Reprinted in 20 vols. Glasgow: MacLehose & Sons, 1905–6.

Quint, David. "Political Allegory in the *Gerusalemme Liberata.*" [1990]. Revised version in *Epic and Empire: Politics and Generic Form from Virgil to Milton.* Princeton: Princeton University Press, 1993. Chap. 5.

Rackin, Phyllis. "Patriarchal History and Female Subversion in *King John.*" In Curren-Aquino, ed., *King John,* 76–90.

———. *Stages of History: Shakespeare's English Chronicles.* Ithaca: Cornell University Press, 1990.

Radford, John. *A Short Treatise Against Adiaphorists, Neuters, and Such as Say They May Be Saved in Any Sect or Religion, and Would Make of Many Divers Sects One.* Appended to *A Directorie.* [English secret press], 1605. *English Recusant Literature,* vol. 19.

Rainoldes, John. *Th'overthrow of Stage-Playes.* 1599. Ed. Arthur Freeman. New York: Garland, 1974.

Rainolds, William. *A Refutation of Sundry Reprehensions.* Paris, 1583. *English Recusant Literature,* vol. 263.

Randall, Dale. *Jonson's Gypsies Unmasked.* Durham, N.C.: Duke University Press, 1975.

Randolph, Thomas. *The Drinking Academy.* MS c. 1625. Ed. Samuel A. Tannenbaum and Hyder E. Rollins. Cambridge, Mass.: Harvard University Press, 1930.

———. *The Muses Looking Glass.* Acted c. 1630. In *Poems with the Muses Looking-Glasse.* Oxford, 1638.

———. *Plutophthalmia Plutogamia. A Pleasant Comedie, Entituled Hey for Honesty, Down with Knavery.* Adaptation of *Plutus,* by Aristophanes. Acted c. 1627. London, 1651.

Rankins, William. *A Mirrour of Monsters.* 1587. Ed. Arthur Freeman. New York: Garland, 1973.

Rawlidge, Richard. *A Monster Late Found Out and Discovered. Or the Scourging of Tiplers.* Amsterdam [London], 1628.

Renwick, W. L., ed. *"Complaints," by Edmund Spenser.* London: Scholartis, 1928.

Ribner, Irving. *The English History Play in the Age of Shakespeare.* Rev. ed. London: Methuen, 1965.

Rid, Samuel. *The Art of Jugling or Legerdemaine.* 1612. In Kinney, *Rogues,* 261–91.

———. *Martin Mark-all, Beadle of Bridewell.* 1610. In Judges, *Elizabethan Underworld,* 383–422.

Ridley, Nicholas. *Works.* Ed. Henry Christmas. Cambridge, 1841.

[Ridpath, George]. *The Stage Condemn'd.* London, 1698.

Riggs, David. *Ben Jonson: A Life.* Cambridge, Mass.: Harvard University Press, 1989.

Roberts, Peter. "Elizabethan Players and Minstrels and the Legislation of 1572 against Retainers and Vagabonds." In *Religion, Culture and Society in Early Modern Britain,* ed. Anthony Fletcher and Peter Roberts. Cambridge: Cambridge University Press, 1994.

Robinson, Hastings, ed. *Zurich Letters.* Cambridge, 1842.

Robinson, John. *A Justification of Separation from the Church of England.* 1610. In *The Works of John Robinson,* ed. Robert Ashton. 3 vols. London, 1851. Vol. 2.

Robinson, Marsha. "The Historiographic Methodology of *King John.*" In Curren-Aquino, ed., *King John,* 29–40.

Rogers, Richard. *Seven Treatises.* London, 1603.

Rogers, Thomas. *The Catholic Doctrine of the Church of England.* Ed. J. J. S. Perowne. Cambridge, 1854.

Rollins, Hyder. "A Contribution to the History of the English Commonwealth Drama." *Studies in Philology* 18 (1921): 267–333.

R[owlands]., S[amuel]. *Greenes Ghost Haunting Conie-catchers.* London, 1602.

Rowley, Samuel. *When You See Me You Know Me.* Acted c. 1604, published 1605. Ed. F. P. Wilson. Malone Society. Oxford: Oxford University Press, 1952.

Rowse, A. L. *William Shakespeare: A Biography.* London: Macmillan, 1963.

S., C. *A Briefe Resolution of a Right Religion.* London, 1590.

Saltonstall, Wye. *Picturae Loquentes.* London, 1631.

Sampson, William. *The Vow Breaker.* Acted c. 1625, published 1636. Ed. Hans Wallrath. Louvain: A. Uystpruyst, 1914.

Sams, Eric. *The Real Shakespeare: Retrieving the Early Years, 1564–1594.* New Haven: Yale University Press, 1995.

Sander, Nicholas. *A Treatise of the Images of Christ.* Louvain, 1567.

Sander, Nicholas, and Edward Rishton. *De Origine ac Progressu Schismatis Anglicani.* 1585. Trans. David Lewis as *Rise and Growth of the Anglican Schism. With Continuation into Elizabeth's Reign by Edward Rishton.* London, 1877.

Sanderson, Robert. *The Works of Robert Sanderson.* Ed. William Jacobson. 6 vols. Oxford, 1854.

Sandys, Edwin [the elder]. *Sermons.* 1585. Ed. John Ayre. Cambridge, 1841.

Sandys, Edwin [the younger]. *Europæ Speculum. Or, A View or Survey of the State of Religion in the Westerne Parts of the World.* Hague, 1629. The text is end-dated

April 9, 1599. It was first published in 1605 in an unauthorized edition as *A Relation of the State of Religion.*

Santayana, George. "The Absence of Religion in Shakespeare." 1896. Revised for *Interpretations of Poetry and Religion* (1900). Ed. William G. Holzberger and Herman J. Saatkamp, Jr. Cambridge: MIT Press, 1989. 91–101.

Sasek, Lawrence A. *The Literary Temper of the English Puritans.* Baton Rouge: Louisiana State University Press, 1961.

Satz, Stanley. "The Friar in Elizabethan Drama." Ph.D. diss., Kent State University, 1972.

Schwyzer, Philip. "Narratives of Nationhood and the Politics of the Past in the Tudor Era." Ph.D. diss., University of California, Berkeley, 2001.

———. "Purity and Danger on the West Bank of the Severn: The Cultural Geography of *A Masque Presented at Ludlow Castle, 1634.*" *Representations* 60 (1997): 22–48.

Sclater, William. *A Brief, and Plain Commentary, With Notes, . . . Upon the Whole Prophecie of Malachy.* London, 1650.

Scott, Cuthbert. *[Two Notable Sermones [the second by Scott]].* London, 1545.

[Scott, Thomas]. *The Interpreter.* [Edinburgh?, 1622].

The Second Parte of a Register, Being a Calendar of Manuscripts under That Title Intended for Publication by the Puritans about 1593. Ed. Albert Peel. 2 vols. Cambridge: Cambridge University Press, 1915.

Selden, John. *Table-talk.* 1689. Ed. Sir Frederick Pollock. London: Quaritch, 1927.

Shakespeare, William. *The Riverside Shakespeare.* 2nd ed. Ed. G. Blakemore Evans et al. Boston: Houghton Mifflin, 1997.

Shapiro, James. *Shakespeare and the Jews.* New York: Columbia University Press, 1996.

Sharpe, J. A. *Crime in Early Modern England 1550–1750.* London: Longman, 1984.

Sheldon, Richard. *A Sermon Preached at Paules Crosse.* London, 1625.

Shepard, Thomas. *The Clear Sun-Shine of the Gospel Breaking Forth Upon the Indians in New-England.* London, 1648.

———. *The Parable of the Ten Virgins.* London, 1660.

Shirley, James. *The Sisters.* 1642. In *Six New Playes.* London, 1653.

Shuger, Debora. *Habits of Thought in the English Renaissance: Religion, Politics, and the Dominant Culture.* Berkeley: University of California Press, 1990.

———. "Hypocrites and Puppets in *Bartholomew Fair.*" *Modern Philology* 82 (1984): 70–73.

———. "Review of *Reading between the Lines* by Annabel Patterson and *Shakespeare and the Politics of Protestant England* by Donna Hamilton." *Shakespeare Quarterly* 44 (1993): 488–93.

———. "Subversive Fathers and Suffering Subjects: Shakespeare and Christianity." In *Religion, Literature, and Politics in Post-Reformation England, 1540–1688,* ed. Donna B. Hamilton and Richard Strier. Cambridge: Cambridge University Press, 1996.

Sibbes, Richard. *The Bruised Reede, and Smoaking Flax.* London, 1630.

———. *The Fountaine Opened.* In *Light From Heaven.* London, 1638.

Sidney, Philip. *The Defence of Poesie.* 1595. In *"Defence of Poesie," "Astrophil and Stella," and Other Writings,* ed. Elizabeth Porges Watson. London: Dent, 1997.

Simpson, Percy. "Unprinted Epigrams of Sir John Davies." *Review of English Studies*, ser. 2, 3 (1952): 49–50.

Sirluck, Ernest. "Shakespeare and Jonson among the Pamphleteers of the First Civil War: Some Unreported Seventeenth-Century Allusions." *Modern Philology* 53 (1955): 88–99.

Sixtus V [and William Allen?]. *A Declaration of the Sentence and Deposition of Elizabeth.* 1588. Reprinted in *Troublesome Raigne*, ed. Sider, 212–19.

Slack, Paul. *Poverty and Policy in Tudor and Stuart England.* London: Longman, 1988.

Smith, Henry. *The Sermons.* London, 1592.

Smuts, Robert Malcolm. *Court Culture and the Origins of a Royalist Tradition in Early Stuart England.* Philadelphia: University of Pennsylvania Press, 1987.

Speed, John. *A Description of the Civill Warres of England.* London, 1600 [1601?].

Spenser, Edmund. *Works: A Variorum Edition.* Ed. Edwin Greenlaw et al. With *A Life of Edmund Spenser*, by Alexander Judson. 9 vols. and index. Baltimore: Johns Hopkins University Press, 1932–57.

Spivack, Bernard. *Shakespeare and the Allegory of Evil.* New York: Columbia University Press, 1958.

Spufford, Margaret. "Can We Count the 'Godly' and the 'Conformable' in the Seventeenth Century?" *Journal of Ecclesiastical History* 36 (1985): 428–38.

Spurr, John. *The Restoration Church of England, 1646–1689.* New Haven: Yale University Press, 1991.

The Stage Acquitted. London, 1699.

Stallybrass, Peter, and Allon White. *Politics and Poetics of Transgression.* London: Methuen, 1986.

The Statutes of the Realm. London, 1810–28.

Stockwood, John. *A Sermon Preached at Paules Crosse.* London, [1578].

———. *A Very Fruiteful Sermon Preached at Paules Crosse.* London, 1579.

Strype, John, ed. *Annals of the Reformation . . . in the Church and State of England.* 1728–35. 6 vols. New York: Burt Franklin, 1966.

Stubbes, Phillip. *An Anatomie of Abuses.* 1583; rev. ed., 1583, 1584, 1595. Ed. Arthur Freeman. New York: Garland, 1973.

———. *The Second Part of the Anatomie of Abuses.* 1583. Ed. Arthur Freeman. New York: Garland, 1973.

Studley, Peter. *A Refutation.* Appended to *The Looking-Glasse of Schisme.* 2nd ed. London, 1635.

Sugden, Edward. *A Topographical Dictionary to the Works of Shakespeare and His Fellow Dramatists.* Manchester: Manchester University Press, 1925.

Sutton, Thomas. *Englands First and Second Summons.* London, 1616.

Sydenham, Humphrey. *Sermons Upon Solemne Occasions.* London, 1637.

Tailor, Robert. *The Hogge Hath Lost His Pearl.* 1613. Ed. D. F. McKenzie. Oxford: Oxford University Press, 1972.

Targoff, Ramie. *Common Prayer: The Language of Public Devotion in Early Modern England.* Chicago: University of Chicago Press, 2001.

———. "The Performance of Prayer: Sincerity and Theatricality in Early Modern England." *Representations* 60 (1997): 49–69.

Tawney, R. H. *The Agrarian Problem in the Sixteenth Century.* London: Longmans, Green, 1912.

Tawney, R. H., and Eileen Power, eds. *Tudor Economic Documents.* 3 vols. London: Longmans, Green, 1924.

Taylor, Gary. "Forms of Opposition: Shakespeare and Middleton." *English Literary Renaissance* 24 (1994): 283–314.

Taylor, Gary, ed. *"Henry V," by William Shakespeare.* Oxford: Oxford University Press, 1982.

Taylor, John. *Differing Worships . . . Or Tom Nash His Ghost, (the old Martin queller).* London, 1640.

———. *The Severall Sieges . . . of Jerusalem.* Appended to *Taylors Urania.* London, 1615 [1616].

Taylor, Thomas. *Japhets First Publique Perswasion into Sems Tents.* Cambridge, 1612.

Thompson, Craig R. "Erasmus and Tudor England." In *Actes du Congrès Erasme, Rotterdam, 27–29 octobre 1969.* Amsterdam: North-Holland Publishing, 1971. 29–68.

The Three Parnassus Plays (1598–1601). The Pilgrimage to Parnassus; 1 The Return From Parnassus (both acted c. 1599/1600); *2 The Return From Parnassus* (acted c. 1601–2); published 1606. Ed. J. B. Leishman. London: Ivor Nicholson & Watson, 1949.

Todd, Margo. *Christian Humanism and the Puritan Social Order.* Cambridge: Cambridge University Press, 1987.

Traister, Barbara H. "The King's One Body: Unceremonial Kingship in *King John.*" In Curren-Aquino, ed., *King John,* 91–98.

Trapp, John. *A Commentary or Exposition upon all the Epistles and the Revelation.* London, 1647.

The Troublesome Raigne of John, King of England. Acted c. 1587–91, published 1591. Ed. John W. Sider. New York: Garland, 1979.

Turner, Celeste. *Anthony Mundy: An Elizabethan Man of Letters.* Berkeley: University of California Press, 1928.

Two Wise Men and All the Rest Fools. Acted c. 1619, published 1619. [Amersham]: Tudor Facsimile Texts, 1913.

Tyerman, Christopher. *England and the Crusades, 1095–1588.* Chicago: University of Chicago Press, 1989.

Tyndale, William. *An Answere Unto Sir Thomas Mores Dialoge.* 1531. In *Works,* ed. Walter, vol. 3, 1–215.

———. *An Exposicion Uppon the V. VI. VII. Chapters of Mathew.* 1533[?]. In *Works,* ed. Walter, vol. 2, 1–132.

———. *The Obedience of a Christen Man.* 1528. In *Works,* ed. Walter, vol. 1, 127–344.

———. *The Practyse of Prelates.* 1530. In *Works,* ed. Walter, vol. 2, 237–344.

———. *Tyndale's New Testament.* Ed. David Daniell. New Haven: Yale University Press, 1989.

———. *Works.* 3 vols. Vol. 1: *Doctrinal Treatises;* vol. 2: *Expositions and Notes;* vol. 3: *An Answer.* Ed. Henry Walter. Parker Society. Cambridge, 1848–50.

Ullman, Walter. "'This Realm of England Is an Empire.'" *Journal of Ecclesiastical History* 30 (1979): 175–203.

Ussher, James. *A Briefe Declaration of the Universalitie of the Church of Christ.* London, 1624.

Vaughan, Virginia M. *"King John:* A Study in Subversion and Containment." In Curren-Aquino, ed., *King John,* 62–75.

Vaughan, William. *The Church Militant.* London, 1640.

———. *The Golden-grove.* 1600; 2nd ed., London, 1608.

Verkamp, Bernard J. *The Indifferent Mean: Adiaphorism in the English Reformation to 1554.* Athens, Ohio, and Detroit: Ohio University Press and Wayne State University Press, 1977.

[Verstegan, Richard]. *A Declaration of the True Causes of the Great Troubles.* [Antwerp], 1592.

———. *The Letters and Despatches of Richard Verstegan (c. 1550–1640).* Ed. Anthony G. Petti. London: R. H. Johns, 1959.

Wager, Lewis. *The Life and Repentaunce of Marie Magdalene.* Acted c. 1550–62, published 1566. In *Reformation Biblical Drama in England,* ed. Paul Whitfield White. New York: Garland, 1992.

Walsal, John. *A Sermon Preached at Pauls Crosse.* London, 1578.

Walsham, Alexandra. *Church Papists: Catholicism, Conformity and Confessional Polemic in Early Modern England.* Woodbridge: Boydell & Brewer, 1993.

———. "'A Glose of Godlines': Philip Stubbes, Elizabethan Grub Street and the Invention of Puritanism." In *Belief and Practice in Reformation England: A Tribute to Patrick Collinson from His Students,* ed. Susan Wabuda and Caroline Litzenberger. Aldershot: Ashgate, 1998. 177–206.

Warner, William. *Albions England.* 4 books. London, 1586. 6 books, 1589; 9 books, 1592; 12 books, 1596; 13 books and "Epitome," 1602; *A Continuance,* books 14–16, 1606.

Wasson, John M. "The English Church as Theatrical Space." In Cox and Kastan, eds., *A New History,* 25–37.

[Webster, John?]. *New and Choise Characters,* by Sir Thomas Overbury. 1615. In *The Overburian Characters,* ed. W. J. Paylor. Oxford: Basil Blackwell, 1936.

Webster, Tom. *Godly Clergy in Early Stuart England: The Caroline Puritan Movement c. 1620–1643.* Cambridge: Cambridge University Press, 1997.

Wells, Stanley. *Shakespeare: A Dramatic Life.* 1994. Revised as *Shakespeare: The Poet and His Plays.* London: Methuen, 1997.

Whitaker, William. *A Disputation on Holy Scripture.* Trans. from *Disputatio de Sacra Scriptura* (1588) and ed. William Fitzgerald. Cambridge, 1849.

White, John. *The Planters Plea.* 1630. Ed. Marshall H. Saville. Rockport, Mass.: Sandy Bay Historical Society and Museum, 1930.

White, Paul Whitfield. *Theatre and Reformation: Protestantism, Patronage, and Playing in Tudor England.* Cambridge: Cambridge University Press, 1993.

———. "Theater and Religious Culture." In Cox and Kastan, eds., *A New History,* 133–52.

W[hite]., T[homas]. *A Sermon Preached at Paules Crosse.* London, 1578.

Whitlock, Richard. *Zootomia.* London, 1654.

Wickham, Glynne. *Early English Stages 1300–1600.* Vol. 2, pt. 1: *1576–1660.* London: Routledge and Kegan Paul, 1963.

Wigand, Johann. *De Neutralibus et Mediis.* Trans. Anon. London, 1562.

W[illet]., A[ndrew]. *Ecclesia Triumphans.* Cambridge, 1603.

Wilson, Thomas. *The Arte of Rhetorique.* 1553; rev. ed., 1560. Ed. Thomas J. Derrick. New York: Garland, 1982.

Wither, George. *Britain's Remembrancer.* [London], 1628.

———. *Campo-Musæ.* London, 1643.

———. *A Preparation to the Psalter.* London, 1619.

Womack, Peter. "Imagining Communities: Theatres and the English Nation in the Sixteenth Century." In *Culture and History 1350–1600: Essays on English Communities, Identities and Writing,* ed. David Aers. Detroit: Wayne State University Press, 1992. 91–145.

Wood, Anthony à. *Athenae Oxoniensis.* 2 vols. London, 1691–92.

———. *The Life and Times of Anthony Wood, Antiquary, of Oxford, 1632–1695, Described by Himself.* Ed. Andrew Clark. 5 vols. Oxford, 1891–1900.

Woodes, Nathaniel. *The Conflict of Conscience.* Written c. 1570–81, published 1581. Malone Society. Oxford: Oxford University Press, 1952.

Wright, Abraham. *Five Sermons, in Five Several Styles; or Wayes of Preaching.* London, 1656.

Wright, Leonard. *A Summons for Sleepers. . . . Hereunto is annexed, A Patterne for Pastors.* London, 1589.

[Wright, Thomas.] *A Treatise . . . of the Reall Presence.* Antwerp [London], 1596.

Yates, Frances. "Queen Elizabeth as Astraea." 1947. In *Astraea: The Imperial Theme in the Sixteenth Century.* London: Routledge & Kegan Paul, 1975. 29–87.

———. *Shakespeare's Last Plays.* 1975. Reprinted as *Majesty and Magic in Shakespeare's Last Plays.* Boulder: Shambhala, 1978.

INDEX

"Acte for the Punishment of Vacabondes," 67–68

Acts and Monuments (Foxe), 169–70, 171

Admonition Controversy, 63

An Admonition to the Nobility and People of England and Ireland (Allen), 97

An Admonition to the Parliament (Field and Wilcox), 141

Adoption, 46, 47

Aglionby, Edward, 146, 150

Ainsworth, Henry, 27

The Alchemist (Jonson), 46

Allen, William, 101; *An Admonition to the Nobility and People of England and Ireland,* 97

All's Well That Ends Well (Shakespeare), 52

Altman, Joel, 132

An Anatomie of Abuses (Stubbes), 142–43

Annals of English Drama (Harbage), 188 n8

Anne (Queen of England), 138

Antimaterialism, 131, 132

Antitheatricalism: broad cultural authority, 10, 11; charge that theater worked against Protestant reforms, 18; condemnation of biblical plays, 39; condemnation of theater's willingness to please, 27; on contaminating effect of plays, 41–42, 154–55; emphasis on commercial objectives of theater people, 39; outrage against competition of players with church, 115–17; portrayal of players as rogues, 16, 155; on pseudo-Christianity of theater, 134, 142–43; on theater as indifferent thing, 157; varying religious views, 14; on vices of theater, 20, 39

Apollo Room, The Devil and St. Dunstan's, 46, 201 n79

An Apology for Actors (Heywood), 156, 157–58, 193 n56

Appello Caesarem (Montagu), 194 n61, 209 n40

Archipropheta (Grimald), 188 n8

Armada, 97, 214 n34, 215 n38

Arnold, Oliver, 226 n61

Aubrey, John, 5, 25

Autolycus, 181–82, 239 n3, 239 n7

Awdeley, John, 66; *The Fraternitie of Vacabondes,* 72–73

Bacon, Francis, 91, 145–46, 213 n21, 229 n12

Bacon, Thomas, 126

Baker, David, 91

Baker, Richard, 129

Bale, John: *The Chief Promises of God Unto Man,* 3, 18; *Comedy Concernynge Thre Lawes, of Nature, Moses, and Christ,* 40; *The Image of Both Churches,* 47

Bancroft, Richard, 63, 148, 158

Baptism, and the English liturgy, 31

Barish, Jonas, 10, 11

Barrow, Henry, 137, 147, 204 n3, 219 n7

Bartholomew Fair (Jonson), 11, 46, 71–72, 77

Barton, Anne, 56, 71

Battenhouse, Roy, 9, 204 n109, 222 n29

Baumer, Franklin, 62

Baxter, Richard, 5–6

Bayly, Lewis: *The Practise of Pietie,* 11; on religious minimalism and fear of religious controversy, 19

Beeston, Christopher, 157

Beggars' Bush (Fletcher), 71

Behn, Aphra: *The Lucky Chance,* 180; *The Roundheads,* 179–80; *The Rover,* 180

The Belman of London (Dekker), 69

The Benefice (Wilde), 25

Benjamin, tribe of, 45, 47

Bentley, G. E., 3, 11, 12, 188 n8, 192 n45

Bernard, Richard: on catechism, 197 n26; *Christian Advertisements and Counsels of Peace,* 31; *The Faithfull Shepheard,* 33, 236 n75; on potential productiveness of conformity, 147; *Terence in English,* 35; *Two Twinnes,* 27, 32, 198 n33

Bevington, David, 50, 121, 122

Biblical drama, 1, 39–40, 188 n5

Blackburn, Ruth: *Biblical Drama under the Tudors,* 188 n5

Blackfriars, 53

Blast (A Second and Third Blast of Retrait from Plaies and Theaters) (Munday [?] and Salvianus), 39, 115, 116, 118, 189 n23

1 Blind Beggar of Bednal Green (Chettle and Day), 179

Bloom, Harold, 176, 177, 187 n2, xii

Bolton, Robert, 43, 142

Bonner, Edmund, 7
The Book of Common Prayer, 17, 31
Braithwait, Richard, 196 n4
A Briefe Declaration of the Universalitie of the Church of Christ (Ussher), 31
A Briefe Discourse of Certaine Points of the Religion, Which Is Among the Common Sort of Christians, Which May Be Termed the Countrie Divinitie (Gifford), 29–30, 31, 32–33, 34, 117
Britannia Triumphans (Davenant), xviii
Brock, Susan, 10
Brome, Alexander, 46, 55
Brome, Richard, 24; *Jovial Crew: or, The Merry Beggars,* 77–78, 211 n60; *The Weeding of Covent Garden,* 29, 45, 211 n57
Brownists, 13, 146, 147
The Bruised Reed, and Smoaking Flax (Sibbes), 23, 51
Buc, George, 3
Bunny, Edmund: *A Treatise Tending to Pacification,* 31
Burckhardt, Sigurd, 217 n57
Burton, Robert, 188 n8
Bury, John: *The Moderate Christian,* 34, 37–38
Butler, Martin, 14, 191 n43

Cairns, David, 91
Calfhill, James, 188 n8
Calvin, John, 35, 132
Carroll, William, 181
Cartwright, Thomas, 207 n22, 220 n13
Cartwright, William: antipuritan satire, 51; as clergyman-playwright, 26, 166, 188 n8; *Comedies, Tragi-Comedies, With Other Poems,* 36; denunciation of religious controversy and factionalism, 45; *The Ordinary,* 3, 166
Catechism, 32, 117, 197 n26
Catholicism: as exclusive, 44, 85; objections to Protestant view of sacraments, 132–33, 138; as theater, 7–8, 119, 148, 175; as thievery, 19, 50, 64, 73, 93, 96, 103, 121, 126–27, 129; view of English schism, 61–62, 63, 65, 74; view of eucharist, 119; violence of in Shakespeare's history plays, 121–24. *See also* English Catholics; Pope
Catiline (Jonson), 45
A Caveat for Common Cursitors (Harman), 66, 67
Cawdrey, Robert, 117
Censorship, 1, 14, 16, 55, 119
Chadwyck-Healey database, 179
Chapman, George, 10
Charles I, Sunday masques, xviii, 5, 6

Chettle, Henry: *Kind-Harts Dreame,* 155, 156; *'Tis No Deceit to Deceive the Deceiver,* 159
Chettle, Henry, and Anthony Munday: *The Death of Robert, Earle of Huntingdon, Afterward Called Robin Hood,* 94–95; *The Downfall of Robert, Earle of Huntingdon, Afterward Called Robin Hood,* 86, 92–95, 109
Chettle, Henry, and John Day: *1 Blind Beggar of Bednal Green,* 179
The Chief Promises of God Unto Man (Bale), 3, 18
Chillingworth, William, 147
Christian Advertisements and Counsels of Peace (Bernard), 31
Christs Tears Over Jerusalem (Nashe), 37–38
Christus Redivivus (Grimald), 18
Christus Triumphans (Foxe), 3
The Chronicles of England, Scotlande, and Irelande (Holinshed), 15
Church-papistry, 229 n13, 229 n14
Cicero, 45
The City Match (Mayne), 3–4, 145, 162–68; cozenage in, 163; prologues and epilogues, 164; on religious value of clothing, 165–66; on subject of martyrdom, 172–73; on wit as sole good, 164
Clergymen: accommodationism, 27, 31–35, 37–38; direct participation in theater, 2–3; preaching, 117–18, 219 n6; Shakespeare's portrayal of, 121–24, 127
Clergymen-dramatists, 3–4, 18–19, 26–27, 36, 188 n8
Closet drama, 3
Colley, Linda, 187 n2
Collinson, Patrick, 6
Comedies, 11; distinction between puritans and merry rogues, 16; on soporific effect of sermons, 118
Comedies, Tragi-Comedies, With Other Poems (Cartwright), 36
Comedy Concernynge Thre Lawes, of Nature, Moses, and Christ (Bale), 40
The Comedy of Errors (Shakespeare), 56
Commentary, or Exposition upon all the Epistles and the Revelation (Trapp), 34
Common Prayer: The Language of Public Devotion in Early Modern England (Targoff), 239 n1
Communion: antitheatricalists' desire to exclude players from, 14; Catholic view of, 119; and the English liturgy, 31; notion of Shakespeare's plays as enacting reformed version of, 17, 18, 227 n65; Protestant view of, 18, 119–20, 132–33, 138, 170, 227 n65

Communitarian principles, 27–28
Condell, Henry, 50
Confession, 54
Conformism, 228 n69; case for regulation of outward practices, 147–48; encouragement of ideological flexibility, 149; formalism, 162, 235 n61; and hypocrisy, 145–47; on impossibility of discovering true state of individual soul, 20, 146, 230 n16
Conformist plays, 11
Cooper, Thomas, 7, 110, 121, 139
Corbet, Richard, 2, 26; "Exhortation," 45
Counter-crusading plays, 11, 86
The Countrie Divinitie (Gifford). *See A Briefe Discourse of Certaine Points of the Religion, Which Is Among the Common Sort of Christians, Which May Be Termed the Countrie Divinitie* (Gifford)
Coverdale, Miles, 136
Cowell, John, 76
Cozenage: in *The City Match*, 163; holy, 36–39, 166–67; poetry as, 183–85; in *The Puritan*, 159–60; in *Sir Thomas More*, 155–56; theater as, 69, 143–44, 154–56, 166–67, 184–85
Cranmer, Thomas, 56, 133
Crockett, Bryan, 9, 191 n36
Crusades, 106; in Elizabethan history plays, 84–85, 86, 88–89, 92, 93; hypocritical commitment to, 103; in standard Protestant account, 85
"Cultural saturation" theory, 8, 9
Cushman, Robert, 110–11

Davenant, William: *Britannia Triumphans*, xviii
Davenport, Robert: *A New Trick to Cheat the Divell*, 45
Davies, John: *Microcosmos*, 88
Davies, Norman, 91
Day, John, and Henry Chettle: *1 Blind Beggar of Bednal Green*, 179
The Death of Robert, Earle of Huntingdon, Afterward Called Robin Hood (Munday and Chettle), 94–95
Dee, John, 87
The Defence of Poesie (Sidney), 183–84
Dekker, Thomas: antipuritan satire, 51; *The Belman of London*, 69; detailing of modus operandi of criminals, 156; disparagement of players, 12; *If It Be Not Good, The Devil Is In It*, 50; *Lanthorne and Candle-light*, 69; representation of vagrancy as a vocation, 69; rogue literature, 68–70; rogue pam-

phlets, 67, 71; on rogues, 66, 73; theater as means of celebrating roguery, 65–66; *The Whore of Babylon*, 50, 70, 80
Dekker, Thomas, and Thomas Middleton: *The Roaring Girl*, 20, 69
Dent, Arthur: *The Plaine Mans Path-way to Heaven*, 146
The Devil and St. Dunstan's Apollo Room, 46, 201 n79
The Devil Is an Ass (Jonson), 45
A Dialogue, Concerning the Strife of Our Churche, 136
Dialogue Betweene a Papist and a Protestant, Applied to the Capacity of the Unlearned (Gifford), 32
Dickens, A. G., 28
Dido (Gager), 3
Diehl, Huston, 9; *Staging Reform, Reforming the Stage: Protestantism and Popular Theater in Early Modern England*, 191 n36
A Discourse Concerning Puritans (Parker), 230 n21, 234 n53
Disputatio de Sacra Scriptura (Whitaker), 228 n8
Donne, John, 44, 50
Dorman, Thomas, 7
Dove, John, 137
Downame, George, 147
The Downfall of Robert, Earle of Huntingdon, Afterward Called Robin Hood (Munday and Chettle), 86, 92–95, 109
Dramatists-clergymen, 3, 18–19, 26–27, 36, 188 n8
Drayton, Michael, 24; "The Sacrifice to Apollo," 46
Drayton, Michael, Richard Hathway, Anthony Munday, and Robert Wilson: *1 Sir John Oldcastle*, 179
The Drinking Academy (Randolph), 23
Drummond, William, 26, 44–45
Duppa, Brian (ed.): *Jonsonus Virbius*, 26

Eastward Ho (Jonson), 38–39
Ecumenicalism, 42–44
Edes, Richard, 188 n8
Edward I (Peele), 80–82, 87–92; Crusades in, 88–89; insular internationalism, 91; rogue solution to English schism, 86; westward future, 109
Edward II (Marlowe), 84
1 Edward IV (Heywood), 70, 179, 204 n117
Edwards, Richard, 188 n8
"Egyptians," 75–76
"Elegy" (Jonson), 47

Elizabeth I: religious toleration, 145–46, 229
n12; Scottish policy, 91
Empathy, view of Shakespeare's, xii
Empson, William, xi
Enchiridion Militis Christianis (Erasmus), 31
English Catholics: equation of separatism with
civil war, 84; on factionalism of English
Protestants, 105, 216 n52; on Protestant
clergy, 7
English Protestants: on Catholic clergy as
vagabonds, 73; on Catholic clergy's plunder
of church, 126–27; on Catholics as "Egyptians," 76; conformism, 19–20, 146–49;
defense of moderate reformation, 42–44;
on deficiencies of nation as signs of spiritual greatness, 61; doctrinal minimalism,
31, 44; ecumenicalism, 42–44; elitism, 120;
fear of Reformation's disruption of community, 66, 67, 85; inclusiveness, 30; radical,
27; religious toleration during Elizabethan
period, 145–46; sectarianism, 63; separatism, denial of charges of, 62; two-tier
conception of Christian doctrine, 31–35;
uncertainty about collective identity as
Christians, 15; view of eucharist, 18, 119–
20, 132–33, 138, 170, 227 n65
Epicoene (Jonson), 7
Erasmus, Desiderius: on accommodationism
of Christianity, 197 n28; charges of vagrancy against, 16; on clerical outreach to
the ignorant, 33; doctrinal minimalism, 15,
44, 142; *Enchiridion Militis Christianis*, 31;
Epistles, 43–44; inclusiveness, 28; influence
on English Protestantism, 28–29; *De Libero
Arbitrio*, 44, 52; on the need for "time-
servers," 34; *Paraclesis*, 31, 197 n28; *Paraphrases*, 28, 34, 35; on Paul's accommodationism, 33, 34–35, 183, 198 n29; *Querela
pacis*, 56; *Ratio Verae Theologiae*, 35; religious
impartiality, 52; on self-aggrandizement of
players, 39; "Sileni Alcibiadis," 123
Eucharist. *See* Communion
Europae Speculum (Sandys), 42
Every Man Out of His Humor (Jonson), 25
"Execration Upon *Vulcan*" (Jonson), 44
"Exhortation" (Corbet), 45
Extraclericalism, 136–37, 138, 139–40, 175

The Faerie Queene (Spenser), 62
A Faithful Declaration of Christes Holy Supper
(Hutchinson), 138
The Faithfull Shepheard (Bernard), 33, 236 n75
The Family of Love (Middleton), 161
Fennor, William, 53

Field, John, and Thomas Wilcox: *Admonition
to the Parliament*, 141
Field, Nathan, 3, 44, 158
Flecknoe, Richard: *Love's Dominion*, 195 n76
Fletcher, John, 3, 179; *Beggars' Bush*, 71
The Floating Island (Strode), 166
Ford, John: *The Queen*, 167
*Forms of Nationhood: The Elizabethan Writing of
England* (Helgerson), 83
Foxe, John, 7, 28, 110, 138; *Acts and Monu-
ments*, 169–70, 171; early praise of English
stage, 115; fear of Turkish invasion, 100; on
Frith's death, 173; *A Sermon of Christ Cruci-
fied*, 105–6; on Thomas More, 153
The Fraternity of Vagabonds (Awdeley), 72–73
Friars, 52–53, 54
Frith, John, 169, 170–72, 173, 227 n65, 237
n5, 237 n11
Frith, Mary, 20, 69
Frye, Roland Mushat: *Shakespeare and Chris-
tian Doctrine*, 120–21

Gager, William, 2–3, 188 n8; *Dido*, 3; *Ulysses
Redux*, 3
Gainsford, Thomas, 13
Gallathea (Lyly), 14
Gardiner, Stephen, 28, 222 n24
Garter, Thomas: *Susanna*, 40
Gayton, Edmund, 49
George a Greene, The Pinner of Wakefield, 3, 70
Gibson, Thomas, 197 n26
Gifford, George: *A Briefe Discourse of Certaine
Points of the Religion, Which Is Among the
Common Sort of Christians, Which May Be
Termed the Countrie Divinitie*, 29–30, 31,
32–33, 34, 117; catechism, 32, 33; *Dialogue
Betweene a Papist and a Protestant, Applied to
the Capacity of the Unlearned*, 32; *Sermons
Upon the Whole Booke of the Revelation*, 46
Gilby, Anthony: criticism of inclusiveness
and accommodationism, 42, 43, 221 n18;
A Pleasant Dialogue, 7; Protestant self-
defense, 62
Goffe, Thomas, 3, 36, 188 n8; *Three Excellent
Tragedies*, 184
The Golden-grove (Vaughan), 61
Gomersall, Robert: *The Tragedie of Lodovick
Sforza Duke of Millan*, 3, 169, 173
Good fellows: equation of with thieves, 64–
65, 206 n11; portrayal of theater people as,
24–25; Prince Hal as, 57; spiritual value of,
26, 27
Gosson, Stephen, 14, 39–40, 42
Green, Ian, 32

Greenblatt, Stephen, 35; *Hamlet in Purgatory*, 238 n19; *Renaissance Self-Fashioning: From More to Shakespeare*, xii; on Romantic characterization of Shakespeare, xii; *Shakespearean Negotiations: The Circulation of Social Energy in Renaissance England*, 7, 8, 225 n50; view of secular theater as substitute for Catholic ritual, 19, 119, 175

Greene, Robert: disparagement of players, 12; dissipations, 23–24; *A Notable Discovery of Coosenage*, 184; *The Repentance of Robert Greene Maister of Artes*, 68–69; rogue literature, 68–69; rogue pamphlets, 70; *Selimus*, 154; on vagabonds, 67

Greene, Robert, and Thomas Lodge: *Looking Glasse for London and England*, 1

Greenwood, John, 76

Grimald, Nicholas: *Archipropheta*, 188 n8; *Christus Redivivus*, 18; as informer, 233 n39

Grindal, Edmund, 40

Gurr, Andrew, 23

Gypsies, 75–76, 211 n53

The Gypsies Metamorphosed (Jonson), 78

Habits of Thought in the English Renaissance: Religion, Politics, and the Dominant Culture (Shuger), 208 n39

Hacket, John: *Loyola*, 188 n11

Hall, Joseph, 61

Hamilton, Donna, 9, 174

Hamlet in Purgatory (Greenblatt), 238 n19

Hamlet (Shakespeare), 56

Harbage, Alfred: *Annals of English Drama*, 188 n8

Harding, Samuel, 3

Harding, Thomas, 65

Harington, John: *Tract on the Succession to the Crown*, 52

Harman, Thomas: campaign against rogues, 68, 78; *A Caveat for Common Cursitors*, 66, 67

Harvey, Gabriel, 23–24

Hathway, Richard, 179

Hausted, Peter, 45, 236 n71, 236 n76; *The Rival Friends*, 166, 168

Hayes, Edward, 110

Hazlitt, William, 49

Heinemann, Margot, 14, 189 n18

Helgerson, Richard: *Forms of Nationhood: The Elizabethan Writing of England*, 83, 193 n57, 210 n45, 224 n48

Heminges, John, 24, 50

Heminges, William, 24–25, 27

Henriad (Shakespeare), 57, 70, 181, 204 n117

1 Henry IV (Shakespeare), 108; portrayal of puritanism, 50; portrayal of roguery, 70, 86; use of term "rogue" in, 179

2 Henry IV (Shakespeare), 108; incorporation of papist carnality into English authorities, 103–4; portrayal of clergy, 122–24; portrayal of puritanism, 50, 51; portrayal of rogues, 86; use of term "rogue" in, 179

Henry V (Shakespeare), 11, 108, 176; charges of popish superstition against: 18; defense of theater's carnality, 134–35; on England's insular constraints, 106–7; extraclericalism, 136–37, 139–40, 175; linking of money and Catholic religion, 126–27, 223 n33; sacramental purpose, 19, 119–20, 132, 135–40, 221 n17; theater as alternative to prelatical church, 128–40; yoking of war with spirituality, 124–28

1 Henry VI (Shakespeare): international war as civil war in, 55–56; portrayal of Catholicism, 50; portrayal of clergy, 121, 123

2 Henry VI (Shakespeare): portrayal of Catholicism, 50; portrayal of clergy, 121–22

Henry VIII, 61, 223 n37

Henry VIII (Shakespeare), 51, 111

Herbert, George: *The Temple*, 184

Herrick, Robert: "His Prayer to Ben Jonson," 177

Heyd, Michael, 202 n85

Heywood, Thomas: *An Apology for Actors*, 156, 157–58, 193 n56; argument that dramatists tailor plays to audiences, 28; puritan sympathies, 193 n52; *Troia Britanica*, 193 n52; *A Woman Killed With Kindness*, 24

Heywood, Thomas [et al., eds.]: *1 Edward IV*, 70, 179, 204 n117

"His Prayer to Ben Jonson" (Herrick), 177

History plays, 11; apologetical approach to, 82–83; counter-crusading plots, 84, 86; as critique of English insularism, 83–84; nationalist interpretation of, 15, 80, 81; portrayal of England's separatism, 16–17. *See also* Shakespeare, William—History plays

Histrio-Mastix (Prynne), 2, 10, 39, 40

Holinshed, Raphael, 193 n58; *The Chronicles of England, Scotlande, and Irelande*, 15

Holy cozenage, 36–39, 166–67

Holyday, Barten, 183, 188 n8, 237 n12

Honigmann, E. A. J., 10, 50

Hooker, Richard, 234 n56; on church's toleration of outward vice, 20; encouragement of conformists to extend charity, 160–61; *Of the Lawes of Ecclesiasticall Politie*, 33–34, 43;

Hooker, Richard (*continued*)
on outward religious conformity, 146, 147;
on puritans, 6, 46; view of eucharist, 170
Hooper, John, 62
Hulme, T. E., xii
A Hundred Mery Talys, 40–41
Hus, Jan, 181
Hutchinson, Lucy, 4
Hutchinson, Roger: *A Faithful Declaration of
Christes Holy Supper*, 138
"Hypocrites and Puppets in *Bartholomew Fair*"
(Shuger), 208 n39

If It Be Not Good, The Devil Is In It (Dekker), 50
The Image of Both Churches (Bale), 47
Ireland, 111, 218 n68

Jacob, Henry, 153
James I, 5, 78, 153, 194 n65
Jardine, Lisa, 187 n2
Jerusalem, fall of, 99–100, 102
Jesuits, 73, 209 n42
Jewel, John, 133, 204 n108, 215 n41
Jews, 75, 76
Johnson, Francis, 146
Jones, Inigo, xviii
Jones, Whitney, 28
Jonson, Ben, 5; accommodationism, 49, 199
n42, 202 n87; accommodationist drama,
54; "adoption" of "sons," 46, 47, 201 n76;
alternating pro- and antitheatricality, 13;
antipuritan satire, 51; belief in godly effect
of stage, 38–39; bricklaying career, 12,
192 n49; denunciation of religious controversy and factionalism, 44–45; depiction
of plays as feasts, 221 n20; dissipations, 24,
25; Erasmianism, 29; imprisonment for authoring *Eastward Ho*, 10; notion of good-
fellowship, 26, 27; notion of "rogue," 179;
notion of "tribe," 12, 45–48, 169, 192 n48;
partisan view of church affairs, 55; on preciseness of puritans, 194 n64; resentment of
charges of profaneness, 25–26; tension between accommodationism and egotism, 49;
use of biblical language to invoke countervision of puritan community, 47; veneration
of by Renaissance writers, 176–77
Jonson, Ben—WORKS: *The Alchemist*, 46;
Bartholomew Fair, 11, 46, 71–72, 77; *Catiline*,
45; *The Devil Is an Ass*, 45; *Eastward Ho*, 38–
39; "Elegy," 47; *Epicoene*, 7; *Every Man Out
of His Humor*, 25; "Execration Upon *Vulcan*", 44; *The Gypsies Metamorphosed*, 78;

"Leges Convivales," 46–47; *The Magnetic
Lady*, 48–49; *Mercury Vindicated*, 45; *The
Staple of News*, 47–48; *Timber: Or, Discover-
ies*, 44; *Volpone, or the Fox*, 25–26
Jonsonus Virbius (Duppa), 26
Josephus, Flavius: *Jewish Wars*, 99
Jovial Crew (Brome), 77–78, 211 n60
Julius Caesar (Shakespeare), 56
Justus, Jonas, 33

Kearney, Hugh, 91
Keats, John, 52
Kemp, William, 156
Killigrew, Henry, 3, 188 n8
King John (Shakespeare), 86–87, 108; Chris-
tian supranationalism, 139; portrayal of
Catholicism, 50, 95–99, 104, 214 n31;
simultaneous criticism and defense of
English schism, 95–102, 104–5, 106
King Lear (Shakespeare), 8, 70, 175
The King of Souls (Shuger), 204 n108
King's Men, 3
Knight, G. Wilson, xi

Lanthorne and Candle-light (Dekker), 69
Laud, William, 5, 10, 21, 43, xviii
The Laughing Mercury, 141
Of the Lawes of Ecclesiasticall Politie (Hooker),
33–34, 43
Lawrence, D. H., xi–xii
"Leges Convivales" (Jonson), 46–47
De Libero Arbitrio (Erasmus), 44, 52
The Life and Repentance of Marie Magdalene
(Wager), 40, 41–42
Locrine [The Lamentable Tragedie of Locrine], 70,
73–76, 79
Lodge, Thomas, and Robert Greene: *A Look-
ing Glasse for London and England*, 1
Love's Dominion (Flecknoe), 195 n76
Loyola (Hacket), 188 n11
The Lucky Chance (Behn), 180
Luther, Martin, 33, 52, 75
Lyly, John: *Gallathea*, 14

Macbeth (Shakespeare), 56
A Mad World, My Masters (Middleton), 1, 4
The Magnetic Lady (Jonson), 48–49
Manifest Destiny, 91
Marcus, Leah: *The Politics of Mirth: Jonson,
Herrick, Milton, Marvell, and the Defense of
Old Holiday Pastimes*, 5
Marie Magdalene (Wager), 41–42
Marlowe, Christopher, 13; correlation of itin-

erancy of players with religious and social itinerancy, 65; death of, 24, 196 n3; *Edward II*, 84; *Tamburlaine*, 70

Marprelate, Martin, 1, 4, 121, 152, 157

Marprelatean Protestants, 137

Marston, John, 3

Martin Mark-all, Beadle of Bridewell (Rid), 209 n43

Martyrdom, 172–73

Massinger, Philip, 179

Mayne, Jasper, 26, 188 n8, 237 n13; on accommodationism, 36–37; antipuritan satire, 51; *The City Match*, 3–4, 38, 145, 162–68, 172–73; as clergyman-playwright, 166; conception of "holy cozenage," 166–67; on Jonson, 37; *A Sermon Concerning Unity & Agreement*, 36–37, 72, 167–68, 173

McEachern, Claire, 9, 193 n57

Measure for Measure (Shakespeare), xi, 176; friars in, 52, 53, 203 n104; puritanism in, 50, 51

"Medicalization" of religious controversy, 48, 202 n85

Meighan, Richard, 184–85

Mercurius Britanicus, 6

Mercury Vindicated (Jonson), 45

The Merry Wives of Windsor (Shakespeare), 179

Microcosmos (Davies), 88

Middleton, Thomas: *The Family of Love*, 161; *A Mad World, My Masters*, 1, 4; *The Puritan*, 145, 158–62, 164

Middleton, Thomas, and Thomas Dekker: *The Roaring Girl*, 20, 69

Middleton, Thomas [and/or Samuel Rowley, John Ford, Thomas Dekker?]: *The Spanish Gypsy*, 71

Milton, John, 2

Miracle plays, 115

A Mirrour of Monsters (Rankins), 39

The Moderate Christian (Bury), 34, 37–38

Montagu, Richard: *Appello Caesarem*, 194 n61, 209 n40

Montrose, Louis, 19; on constraints on protheatrical arguments, 191 n42; *The Purpose of Playing: Shakespeare and the Cultural Politics of the Elizabethan Theater*, 7, 8; view of secular theater as substitute for Catholic ritual, 119

Morality plays, 115

More, Sir Thomas, 16

Mother Hubberds Tale (Spenser), 141, 142

Mowat, Barbara, 181

Much Ado about Nothing (Shakespeare), 52

Munday, Anthony, 14, 179; on commercial objectives of players, 39; informer on religious dissidents, 152–53

Munday, Anthony, and Henry Chettle: *The Death of Robert, Earle of Huntingdon, Afterward Called Robin Hood* (Munday and Chettle), 94–95; *The Downfall of Robert, Earle of Huntingdon, Afterward Called Robin Hood*, 92–95, 109

Munday, Anthony, et al.: *Sir Thomas More*, 149–52

Munday, Anthony [?] and Salvianus: *A Second and Third Blast of Retrait from Plaies and Theaters*, 39, 115, 116, 118, 189 n23

The Muses' Looking Glass (Randolph), 143–44

Nashe, Thomas, 54; *Christs Tears Over Jerusalem*, 37–38; disparagement of players, 12; dissipations, 23–24; on Munday, 153; *Pierce Penilesse*, 157, 233 n43; self-styling as "good fellow," 24; on spiritual virtue of good-fellowship, 27

Nationalism: English ambivalence about, 63–66; and imperialism, 91–92; rogue, 93–94; traditional claims about English, 63, 205 n8

"Negative capability," 52

Neo-Christians, xi

Neutrality, religious, 72, 208 n38, 208 n39, 209 n40

New-historical criticism, 2

A New Tricke to Cheat the Divell (Davenport), 23

New World evangelism, 108–12

Nicholl, Charles: *The Reckoning: The Murder of Christopher Marlowe*, 153–54

Nichols, Josias, 231 n28

Nonconformists, 76–77, 147, 219 n7

Norden, John, 63, 65

Northbrooke, John, 5, 41; conforming puritanism, 192 n51; first printed attack on public theaters, 116, 117, 118; opposition to staging of religion, 39–40

A Notable Discovery of Coosenage (Greene), 184

Oldisworth, Nicholas, 176–77, 196 n9

The Ordinary (Cartwright), 3, 166

Othello (Shakespeare), xii

Pallant, Robert, 196 n4

Paraclesis (Erasmus), 31, 197 n28

Paraphrases (Erasmus), 28, 34, 35

Parker, Henry, 4; *A Discourse Concerning Puritans*, 230 n21, 234 n53

Parker, Patricia, 56
Parsons, Robert, 28, 83–84, 101, 138, 229 n13
Paul, Apostle: accommodationism, xi–xiii, 27, 33, 34–36, 52; use of term "adoption," 47, 201 n82
Peele, George, 161; *Edward I*, 80–82, 86, 87–92, 109
"The Performance of Prayer: Sincerity and Theatricality in Early Modern England" (Targoff), 204 n108, 231 n23
Pericles (Shakespeare), 1
Perkins, Richard, 156–57
Perkins, William, 16
Pierce Penilesse (Nashe), 157, 233 n43
Pilkington, James, 74, 107–8, 110, 133
The Plaine Mans Path-way to Heaven (Dent), 146
Plautus: *Menaechmi*, 56
Play-books, 189 n20
A Pleasant Dialogue (Gilby), 7
Plutophthalmia. A Pleasant Comedie, Entituled Hey for Honesty, Down with Knavery (Randolph), 162, 211 n55
Pocock, J. G. A., 91
Poetry, as cozenage, 183–85
Pole, Reginald, 56
The Politics of Mirth: Jonson, Herrick, Milton, Marvell, and the Defense of Old Holiday Pastimes (Marcus), 5
Poole, Josua, 184
Poole, Kristen, 9; *Radical Religion from Shakespeare to Milton: Figures of Nonconformity in Early Modern England*, 191 n35
Pope, the, 61, 73, 106; displaced from Shakespeare's later histories, 103, 107; in *King John*, 50, 95–99, 104
The Practise of Pietie (Bayly), 11
Preachers, call for reform of, 117–18, 219 n6
Preaching, as performance, 6–7, 220 n13
Printed plays, 189 n20
Protestantism. *See* English Protestants
Protheatricalists: admission that plays were not free of vice, 155; alignment of theater with Erasmianism, 14–15; apologetical tradition, 143–45; attack on puritan clothesmongering, 162–63; attack on puritan hypocrisy, 158–68; distinguishing of theatergoing from taverngoing, 196 n4; hampered by prejudices of opponents, 10–11; idiosyncratic stands, 20; lack of published defenses of plays, 14
Prynne, William, 1, 20; on blasphemy of scripture on stage, 40–41; on corrupting effect of theater, 39; desire to exclude players from communion, 14; *Histrio-Mastix*, 2, 10, 39, 40; on linking of playgoing with religious communitarianism, 15; on supplanting of pulpit by theater, 5; on why puritans were hated, 23
Puller, Timothy, 173
Purchas, Samuel, 102, 110, 215 n44
Puritan, use of term in Renaissance, 188 n15
The Puritan (Middleton), 145, 158–62, 164
Puritans: association of certain church ceremonies with theater, 157; attacks on importance of clothes to, 162–63; closing of theaters, 14, 20, 78, 191 n43; derisive image of, 4, 51, 77; "Judaism of," 45–46, 200 n72; loathing of "civil" Christians, 29–30; preaching as performance, 6–7, 220 n13; usefulness of to theater people, 20
The Purpose of Playing: Shakespeare and the Cultural Politics of the Elizabethan Theater (Montrose), 7, 8

Queen Anne's Men, 158
The Queen (Ford), 167
Querela pacis (Erasmus), 56

Radford, John: *A Short Treatise Against Adiaphorists, Neuters, and Such as Say They May Be Saved in Any Sect or Religion, and Would Make of Many Divers Sects One*, 44
Rainoldes, John, 2–3, 192 n51
Randolph, Thomas, 47; dissipations, 24; *The Drinking Academy*, 23; *The Muses' Looking Glass*, 143–44; *Plutophthalmia. A Pleasant Comedie, Entituled Hey for Honesty, Down with Knavery*, 162, 211 n55
Rankins, William: *A Mirrour of Monsters*, 39
Ratio Verae Theologiae (Erasmus), 35
The Reckoning: The Murder of Christopher Marlowe (Nicholl), 153–54
Reformation: dramatization on stage of anxieties about effect of, 85–86; fear of disruption of community as a result of, 66, 67, 85; magnification of threats of war and invasion for England, 16; Protestant defense of moderate reform, 42–44
Religious dissidents: opposition to plays and conformism, 156; spying on, 152–54
Religious drama, 3. *See also* Biblical drama
Renaissance England: belief in society of vagabonds, 66–68; fears of national disintegration, 63; rise of history play, 80. *See also* English Protestants

Renaissance Self-Fashioning (Greenblatt), xii
Renaissance theater: and accommodationist self-fashioning, 36–39; anti-puritanism, 193 n53; as beneficiary of England's spiritual crisis, 7–8; centrality of religion to, 8–10; characterization as secular, 1, 2; coupling with taverns, 23; depiction as godly, 2; dramatization of anxieties about effect of Reformation, 85–86; exclusion of women from stage, 20; frivolity as vehicle for sectarianism, 174; lowly social status, 14; moderation in portrayal of true religion, 15–16, 172; as platform for religious instruction, 118–19, 142–43, 145, 220 n15; portrayed as cozenage, 69, 143–44, 154–56, 166–67, 184–85; shaping of beliefs of members, 13; spying activities on religious dissidents, 153–54; subject of conformist theories of toleration, 149; theater companies, 12; three popular scenarios of, 11; ties to church through politics, 4–5. *See also* Theater people
Repentance (Greene), 68–69
The Repentance of Robert Greene Maister of Artes (Greene), 68–69
Restoration, 173
Restoration drama, 179
"Review of *Reading between the Lines* by Annabel Patterson and *Shakespeare and Politics of Protestant England* by Donna Hamilton" (Shuger), 262 n15
Ribner, Irving, 80
Richard II (Shakespeare): anxieties about English insularism and divisiveness in, 84–85; nationalistic view of, 81–82, 83; portrayal of clergy, 122, 123; westward future for England, 108, 109, 110
Richard III (Shakespeare), 107
Richards, Shaun, 91
Rid, Samuel: *Martin Mark-all, Beadle of Bridewell*, 209 n43
Ridpath, George, 4, 5, xviii
Ritual, transference of from church to theater, 8, 19, 119, 175
The Rival Friends (Hausted), 166, 168
The Roaring Girl (Dekker and Middleton), 20, 69
Robin Hood, 17, 92, 176, 206 n13. *See also The Death of Robert, Earle of Huntingdon, Afterward Called Robin Hood* (Munday and Chettle); *The Downfall of Robert, Earle of Huntingdon, Afterward Called Robin Hood* (Munday and Chettle)

Robinson, John, 27
Rogers, Richard, 193 n56
Rogue: defined as vagabond, 206 n15; use of term in history plays, 179
Rogue literature, 11, 16, 68–73, 206 n13; comic portrayal of rogue society, 71, 76–77; desire to neutralize religious controversy, 71, 73; rogue society based on principles of communion and charity, 77–78, 86
Rogue nationalism, 93–94
Rogue pamphlets, 67, 70–71, 206 n17
Rogues: claims about social organization of, 15, 66–68; as common enemy of divided nation, 67; fear of, 63, 205 n7, 205 n8; as neutralizers of religious controversy, 71, 73; perception of theater people as, 16, 67–68
Roman Catholics. *See* English Catholics
Romeo and Juliet (Shakespeare), 52, 53
Rosseter, Philip, 10
The Roundheads (Behn), 179–80
The Rover (Behn), 180
Rowley, Samuel: *When You See Me, You Know Me*, 70

Sacraments. *See* Baptism; Communion
"The Sacrifice to Apollo" (Drayton), 46
Sampson, William: *The Vow Breaker*, 46
Sams, Eric, 50
Sanderson, Robert, 45–46, 137, 171
Sandys, Edwin [the Elder], 19, 41, 76
Sandys, Edwin [the Younger]: *Europae Speculum*, 42, 62, 74, 75, 87, 205 n4, 210 n46
Santayana, George, 49–50
Satz, Stanley, 53, 204 n109
Schwyzer, Philip, 91, 210 n50
Scott, Cuthbert, 7
Scott, Thomas, 141–42, 167
A Second and Third Blast of Retrait from Plaies and Theaters (Munday [?] and Salvianus), 39, 115, 116, 118, 189 n23
Sectarianism, 15–16, 63
Selden, John, 72
Selimus (Greene), 154
Sermon Concerning Unity & Agreement (Mayne), 36–37, 72, 167–68
A Sermon of Christ Crucified (Foxe), 105–6
Sermons Upon the Whole Booke of the Revelation (Gifford), 46
Shakespeare: The Poet and His Plays (Wells), 203 n99
Shakespeare, William: antisectarian impression of plays, 51; correlation of itinerancy of players with religious and social errancy,

Shakespeare, William (*continued*)
65; critical view of as secular playwright,
120–21; dissipations, 24; fears regarding
potential divisiveness of religious beliefs,
51; on fellowship of theater, 53–57; friars in
plays, 52–53, 54, 55; as jack-of-all-trades,
12–13; notion of plays as enacting reformed
communion, 17, 18, 227 n65; Pauline characterization of, 187 n2; portrayal of Catholicism, 50, 51; portrayal of international war
as civil war, 55–56, 57; portrayal of puritans,
50, 51; references to liturgy, 203 n94; rejec-
tion of religion of the book, 54; religious af-
filiation of family and friends, 50; reticence
about religion, 50, 203 n98. *See also specific
works*
Shakespeare, William—HISTORY PLAYS:
avoidance of identification of true religion
with England, 111–12; comic countervision
to English civil war, 86; conception of
Christian unity, 87; demystification of royalty, 132, 224 n48; irony of bloody sacrament, 127–28, 224 n39; number of, 87; portrayal of churchmen, 121–28; portrayal of
vagrancy, 70; rogue nationalism, 86, 179–
80; western movement of Christian warfare, 108–12. *See also specific works*
Shakespeare and Christian Doctrine (Frye), 120–
21
Shakespearean Negotiations (Greenblatt), 7, 8,
225 n50
Sharpe, J. A., 66
Sheldon, Richard, 44
Shepard, Thomas, 6
Sheppard, Samuel, 177
Shirley, James, 3; *The Sisters*, 164–65
*A Short Treatise Against Adiaphorists, Neuters,
and Such as Say They May Be Saved in Any
Sect or Religion, and Would Make of Many
Divers Sects One* (Radford), 44
Shuger, Debora, 8, 9; *Habits of Thought in the
English Renaissance: Religion, Politics, and the
Dominant Culture*, 208 n39; "Hypocrites
and Puppets in *Bartholomew Fair*", 208 n39;
The King of Souls, 204 n108; "Review of
Reading between the Lines by Annabel Patter-
son and *Shakespeare and Politics of Protestant
England* by Donna Hamilton," 262 n15;
"Subversive Fathers and Suffering Subjects:
Shakespeare and Christianity," 191 n34
Sibbes, Richard, 27; *The Bruised Reede, and
Smoaking Flax*, 23, 51
Sidney, Philip, 28; *The Defence of Poesie*, 183–84
"Sileni Alcibiadis" (Erasmus), 123

I Sir John Oldcastle (Drayton, Hathway, Munday, and Wilson), 64–65, 69, 70, 179
Sir Thomas More (Munday, et al.), 145, 149–52,
163–64; association of conformity with the-
atricality, 149–52, 154; association of in-
ward goodness with detachment from out-
ward things, 161–62; cozenage in, 155–56;
on martyrdom, 149–52, 172; solicitation of
tolerance for petty theft, 160
Smuts, Robert, 45
The Spanish Gypsy (Middleton [and/or Rowley,
Ford, Dekker?]), 71
Spenser, Edmund: *The Faerie Queene*, 62;
Mother Hubberds Tale, 141, 142
Spilt religion, xii
Spivak, Bernard, 119
St. Paul's Cathedral, xviii
The Stage Acquitted, 21
*Staging Reform, Reforming the Stage: Protes-
tantism and Popular Theater in Early Modern
England* (Diehl), 191 n36
The Staple of News (Jonson), 47–48
Stow, John: *Survey of London*, 11
Strode, William, 166, 188 n8; *The Floating Is-
land*, 166
Stubbes, Phillip, 14; *An Anatomie of Abuses*,
142–43; on contaminating effect religious
material on stage, 1; desire to exclude play-
ers from communion, 14; fear of theater as
rival of church, 53; on pseudo-Christianity
of theater, 142–43; on supplanting of pulpit
by theater, 5
"Subversive Fathers and Suffering Subjects:
Shakespeare and Christianity" (Shuger),
191 n34
Surplice, 157, 162
Survey of London (Stow), 11
Susanna (Garter), 40
Sutton, Thomas, 44, 158

Tamburlaine (Marlowe), 70
The Taming of the Shrew (Shakespeare), 179
Tankerfield, George, 138
Targoff, Ramie, 9; *Common Prayer: The Lan-
guage of Public Devotion in Early Modern
England*, 239 n1; "The Performance of
Prayer: Sincerity and Theatricality in Early
Modern England," 191 n36, 204 n108, 231
n23
Tavern: distinguished from theater, 196 n4;
and good fellowship, 23–25, 30, 53, 57, 138;
Jonson's favorites, 25; as setting for plays, 3,
23, 29; theater as, 23; theater linked to, 4, 5,
23–28, 189 n23, 190 n31; worse vice than

theater, 155, 196 n4. *See also* The Devil and St. Dunstan's Apollo Room

Taylor, Thomas, 41

The Tempest (Shakespeare), 54–55, 176, 204 n111

The Temple (Herbert), 184

Terence in English (Bernard), 35

Theater. *See* Renaissance theater

"Theater and Religious Culture" (White), 8, 9, 10

Theater people: conception of inclusiveness of church, 27; defense of their profession, 11–13; defined, 12; divisiveness among, 12; dramatization of communities of rovers, 16; portrayal of religious hypocrisy, 20, 194 n72; professional camaraderie with friars, 53; regard for charity and fellowship over doctrinal precision, 171; rising status of in permanent theaters, 76, 207 n122; satirization of puritans, 20; self-styling as "good fellows," 24; simplification of antitheatricalism into a puritan pathology, 14; view of as fraternity of rogues, 67–68. *See also* Renaissance theater

Theaters, closure of, 78, 191 n43

Thirty-nine Articles, 31

Three Excellent Tragedies (Goffe), 184

Tilney, Edmund, 149

Timber: Or, Discoveries (Jonson), 44

'Tis No Deceit to Deceive the Deceiver (Chettle), 159

Tract on the Succession to the Crown (Harington), 52

The Tragedie of Lodovick Sforza Duke of Millan (Gomersall), 3

Trapp, John: *Commentary, or Exposition upon all the Epistles and the Revelation*, 34

A Treatise Tending to Pacification (Bunny), 31

Tribe, notion of, 12, 45–48, 192 n48

Tribe of Benjamin, 45, 47

Troia Britanica (Heywood), 193 n52

The Troublesome Raigne of John, King of England, 97, 215 n37, 215 n40, 215 n43, 215 n48, 215 n50

Tudor Drama and Politics (Bevington), 5

Turkish invasion, English fear of, 100

Twelfth Night (Shakespeare), 50, 51, 169, 174–76

Two Gentlemen of Verona (Shakespeare), 52

Two Twinnes (Bernard), 27, 32, 198 n33

Two Wise Men and All the Rest Fools, 28

Tyndale, William, 35, 137–38, 169, xii–xiii

Ulysses Redux (Gager), 3

Urban II, 106, 107

Ussher, James: *A Briefe Declaration of the Universalitie of the Church of Christ*, 31, 43; on catechizing, 32, 35, 55

Vagabonds. *See* Rogues

Vaughan, William: *The Golden-grove*, 61

Verkamp, Bernard, 31

Vestiarian Controversy, 157

Volpone, or the Fox (Jonson), 25–26

The Vow Breaker (Sampson), 46

Wager, Lewis: *The Life and Repentance of Marie Magdalene*, 40, 41–42

Walsall, John, 142

Walsingham, Francis, 43

Webster, John, 66, 78–79

The Weeding of Covent Garden (Brome), 29, 45, 211 n57

Wells, Stanley: *Shakespeare: The Poet and His Plays*, 203 n99

West, Richard, 177

When You See Me, You Know Me (Rowley), 70

Whitaker, William: *Disputatio de Sacra Scriptura*, 228 n8

White, Paul Whitfield, 6; "Theater and Religious Culture," 8, 9, 10

Whitgift, John, 147

Whore of Babylon (Dekker), 50

Wickham, Glynne, 119

Wigand, Johann, 19

Wigginton, Giles, 152–53, 154

Wilcox, Thomas, and John Field: *Admonition to the Parliament*, 141

Wilde, Robert: *The Benefice*, 25

William of Malmesbury, 106

Wilson, Robert, 179

Wilson, Thomas, 117–18

The Winter's Tale (Shakespeare), 181–82

Wither, George, 148, 239 n1

Womack, Peter, 82–83

A Woman Killed With Kindness (Heywood), 24

Wright, Abraham, 166

Wright, Leonard, 117